DISCARD

The Moderate Imagination

The Moderate Imagination
The Political Thought of John Updike and the Decline of New Deal Liberalism

Yoav Fromer

 University Press of Kansas

© 2020 by the University Press of Kansas

All rights reserved

Published by the University Press of Kansas (Lawrence, Kansas 66045), which was organized by the Kansas Board of Regents and is operated and funded by Emporia State University, Fort Hays State University, Kansas State University, Pittsburg State University, the University of Kansas, and Wichita State University.

Library of Congress Cataloging-in-Publication Data

Names: Fromer, Yoav, author.
Title: The moderate imagination : the political thought of John Updike and the decline of New Deal liberalism / Yoav Fromer.
Description: Lawrence : University Press of Kansas, 2020. | Includes bibliographical references and index.
Identifiers: LCCN 2019045398
  ISBN 9780700629527 (cloth)
  ISBN 9780700629534 (epub)
Subjects: LCSH: Updike, John—Political and social views. | Politics and literature—United States—History—20th century.
Classification: LCC PS3571.P4 Z665 2020 | DDC 813/.54—dc23
LC record available at https://lccn.loc.gov/2019045398.

British Library Cataloguing-in-Publication Data is available.

Printed in the United States of America

10 9 8 7 6 5 4 3 2 1

The paper used in this publication is recycled and contains 30 percent postconsumer waste. It is acid free and meets the minimum requirements of the American National Standard for Permanence of Paper for Printed Library Materials Z39.48-1992.

Contents

Acknowledgments   *vii*

Introduction   1

1. The Man in the Middle   18

2. The Liberal Education of John Updike   42

3. *The Poorhouse Fair:* The Liberal State and Its Discontents   69

4. Family Matters: Therapeutic Liberalism, Consumer Capitalism, and the Decline of the Family in *Rabbit, Run*   97

5. Sleeping Together, Bowling Alone: *Couples* and the Decline of Civic Engagement   126

6. Things Don't Mix: *Rabbit Redux* and the Unraveling of Postwar Liberalism   156

Conclusion: Liberalism Redux   190

Notes   *207*

Bibliography   *247*

Index   *271*

Acknowledgments

This book has been a long time coming. But it would not have come to fruition without the assistance, advice, support, and cooperation of countless people. Some of them oversaw its entire lifespan—from its inception as an intuition and then an idea, and maturity into a proposal, dissertation, article, and finally a book. Others have been instrumental in a more limited manner and have contributed to specific aspects of this book. But each and every one of these people have helped shape this book in a distinct manner, and for that I am truly grateful.

Jim Miller, who has believed in and supported this project from its infancy, has been instrumental in helping me find my own voice and getting to where it is I wanted to go—even when I did not really know myself. David Plotke has similarly provided me with intellectual guidance and unceasing encouragement, both academic and personal, that was vital and heartwarming at once and often enabled me to go on. Jim's and David's intellect, direction, and empathy were invaluable. Oz Frankel, Robert Boyers, Inessa Medzhibovskaya, Jack De Bellis, Yaron Ezrahi, and Nancy Fraser provided me with substantial insight and helpful criticism about the manuscript that pushed me to rethink, explore, and discover various paths I had completely overlooked. The members of the John Updike Society—particularly Jim Plath, James Schiff, and Judie Newman—were highly supportive and assisted me with formulating my ideas and organizing the manuscript for publication. The John Updike Society conferences in Reading (2014) and Belgrade (2018) were edifying experiences that taught me many things about Updike and his politics.

At Tel Aviv University, Yossi Shain's unwavering support and faith in me was a constant source of inspiration and comfort. Milette Shamir, Yael Sternhell, Michael Zakim, Noam Maggor, Eli Cook, Hana Wirth-Nesher, Nir Evron, and the American Studies Forum contributed to this work and helped me refine parts of the manuscript. In addition, Michael Kimmage, Eric Miller, Jeffrey Ludwig, Scott Dill, Wilfred McClay, Adam Begley, Joshua Cherniss, and George Blaustein shared their time and knowledge with me and offered much-needed advice. Sam Tanenhaus, who endured the midday rackets of Seventh Avenue for over an hour to discuss his love of Updike, and Leon Wieseltier, who shared a very long taxi ride with me in Israel in order to talk about Updike's place in American intellectual history, both profoundly shaped the way I came to understand Updike's work. I am also grateful to David Updike, Bill Wasserman, Christopher Buckley, Elizabeth Moynihan, Midge Decter, and John Bethell, who were candid and open with me and generously shared their personal memories of Updike.

Without the assistance and advice of countless librarians and archivists, I would not have been able to complete this book. I am particularly indebted to Leslie Morris and her team of wonderful archivists at Houghton Library at Harvard University. Their dedication and organization skills were imperative for successfully navigating the labyrinthine depths of the Updike Papers. Patrick Kerwin of the Manuscripts Division at the Library of Congress was similarly of great help in assisting me search the Daniel P. Moynihan Papers. The staffs at the Manuscripts and Archives Divisions of the New York Public Library and Yale University's Sterling Memorial Library kindly assisted me with unearthing valuable documents. I would also like to thank the Updike family, the John Updike Literary Trust, the Wylie Agency, and Penguin Random House for all their aid in facilitating my research and publications.

I am grateful to the New School for Social Research for the generous research fellowships it awarded me and for its countless travel grants, without which I could not have completed my research. The Jack Miller Center provided me funding and stimulating intellectual support as well. I would like to thank David Congdon and the University Press of Kansas for believing in and supporting this interdisciplinary academic project. This book is a testament to their commitment to nurturing original and unorthodox research and making it accessible to the wider public.

My friends and colleagues Brian Steele and Kevin Nesbitt have spent hours talking with me about this book and reading earlier drafts from it. I am particularly grateful to Robert and Lisa Thomas for their friendship and support. Finally, I could not have done this without the consistent and unbreakable support, encouragement, and love of Adi Ann and my family, without which none of this would really matter.

Grateful acknowledgment is made for permission to reprint excerpts from the following copyrighted works: "Midpoint," "Washington," and

"Apologies to Harvard" from *Collected Poems, 1953–1993* by John Updike, copyright © 1993 by John Updike. Used by permission of Alfred A. Knopf, an imprint of the Knopf Doubleday Publishing Group, a division of Penguin Random House LLC. All rights reserved. "The Christian Roommates" from *Music School* by John Updike, copyright © 1962, 1963, 1964, 1965, 1966 and renewed 1994 by John Updike. Used by permission of Alfred A. Knopf, an imprint of the Knopf Doubleday Publishing Group, a division of Penguin Random House LLC. All rights reserved. "A Soft Spring Night in Shillington," "At War with My Skin," "On Not Being a Dove," and "A Letter to My Grandsons" from *Self-Consciousness* by John Updike, copyright © 1989 by John Updike. Used by permission of Alfred A. Knopf, an imprint of the Knopf Doubleday Publishing Group, a division of Penguin Random House LLC. All rights reserved. Excerpt(s) from *Rabbit Redux* by John Updike, copyright © 1971, copyright renewed 1999 by John Updike. Used by permission of Alfred A. Knopf, an imprint of the Knopf Doubleday Publishing Group, a division of Penguin Random House LLC. All rights reserved. Excerpt(s) from *Rabbit, Run* by John Updike, copyright © 1960, copyright renewed 1988 by John Updike. Used by permission of Alfred A. Knopf, an imprint of the Knopf Doubleday Publishing Group, a division of Penguin Random House LLC. All rights reserved. "Freedom and Equality: Two American Bluebirds," "Introduction to the Easton Press Edition of the Rabbit Novels," and "Accepting the Campion Medal" from *More Matter: Essays and Criticism* by John Updike, copyright © 1999 by John Updike. Used by permission of Alfred A. Knopf, an imprint of the Knopf Doubleday Publishing Group, a division of Penguin Random House LLC. All rights reserved. Excerpt(s) and Introduction to the 1977 Edition from *Poorhouse Fair* by John Updike, copyright © 1958, 1977 and copyright renewed © 1986, 2005 by John Updike. Used by permission of Alfred A. Knopf, an imprint of the Knopf Doubleday Publishing Group, a division of Penguin Random House LLC. All rights reserved. "Literarily Personal," "Fictional Houses," and "Emersonianism" from *Odd Jobs: Essays and Criticism* by John Updike, copyright © 1991 by John Updike. Used by permission of Alfred A. Knopf, an imprint of the Knopf Doubleday Publishing Group, a division of Penguin Random House LLC. All rights reserved. Foreword, Appendix: On One's Own Devices, and "Fish Story" from *Hugging the Shore* by John Updike, copyright © 1983 by John Updike. Used by permission of Alfred A. Knopf, an imprint of the Knopf Doubleday Publishing Group, a division of Penguin Random House LLC. All rights reserved. Excerpt(s) from *Couples* by John Updike, copyright © 1968, copyright renewed 1996 by John Updike. Used by permission of Alfred A. Knopf, an imprint of the Knopf Doubleday Publishing Group, a division of Penguin Random House LLC. All rights reserved. Foreword, copyright © 1966, 1967, 1968, 1969, 1970, 1971, 1972, 1973, 1974, 1975 by John Updike. "What Is Female Sexuality?" from *Mademoiselle* copyright © 1971 by John Updike; "What Is Creativity?" from *Playboy* copyright © 1968 by John Updike; "Bech Meets Me," and "A Raw Something," copyright © 1971 by John Updike; "Why Write?," "One Big Interview," "Young Americans," "London Life," "Non-Fiction," and "Africa: Out of the Glum Continent" from *Picked-Up Pieces* by John Updike, copyright © 1966, 1967, 1968, 1969, 1970, 1971, 1972, 1973, 1974, 1975 by John Updike. Used by permission of Alfred A. Knopf, an imprint of the Knopf Doubleday Publishing Group, a division of Penguin Random House LLC. All rights reserved. Excerpts from John Updike Papers at Harvard by John Updike. Copyright © John Updike, used by permission of The Wylie Agency LLC.

Portions of this manuscript first appeared in "A New Deal, A New Updike: The Decline of New Deal Liberalism in John Updike's *The Poorhouse Fair*," *Journal of American Studies* 51, no. 2 (spring 2017): 385–410, copyright © 2016; "The Liberal Origins of John Updike's Literary Imagination," *Modern Intellectual History* 14, no. 1 (April 2017): 187–216, copyright © 2015, reprinted with permission of Cambridge University Press; and "The 'Inside-Outsider': John Updike as a New York Intellectual—from Shillington, Pennsylvania," *John Updike Review* 4, no. 2 (spring 2016): 29–55. Reprinted with permission.

Introduction

The men dark along the bar murmur among themselves.
They have not been lifted, they are left here.

—John Updike, *Rabbit Redux*

Left behind. If there is one underlining assumption in the wake of the 2016 presidential election that has informed the various explanations for why millions of Americans voted for a candidate as eccentric, unpredictable, and unorthodox as Donald Trump, it would be this: they felt left behind. These disaffected voters, the overwhelming majority of them white, mostly from rural or suburban areas in states like Michigan, Wisconsin, Ohio, and Pennsylvania, supposedly rebelled against the coastal and urban elites mobilized behind Hillary Clinton's campaign and helped elevate Donald Trump to the White House. And it was to them, accordingly, that he attributed his remarkable achievement. "Their victories have not been your victories; their triumphs have not been your triumphs," the president said in his inaugural address. Blaming Washington insiders, elites, and the establishment for the grim reality that saw "millions upon millions of American workers left behind," Trump proudly exclaimed that "the forgotten men and women of our country will be forgotten no longer."[1]

But the question is: Forgotten by whom, left behind by what? The president never actually specified, and did not really have to. There were several potential answers to these questions, and they all led back to the usual suspects: left behind by globalization and free trade, and by the economic degradations and growing inequalities that they engendered; by sweeping demographic changes that have redrawn the racial and ethnic makeup of the country while eroding the cultural capital and social status long associated with whiteness; by a rigid and bureaucratized political system that appears increasingly distant from the left behind's lived experiences, obtuse to their communal needs and indifferent, if not hostile to, their grievances; and by a set of secular and cosmopolitan ideals that has no place, or patience, for the values or beliefs that give meaning to their lives and the institutions that seek to preserve them. Whatever the explanation—political, economic, social, cultural, or racial—they all point, either directly or indirectly, to the policies, platforms, and politicians associated with the Democratic Party and are representative of its primary ideological compass: liberalism.[2]

This prevailing narrative for how Trump was elected offers an appealing story—and one that is mostly true. But it is only part of the story. If anything, blaming liberal policies exclusively for the grievances that created what President Trump called "an American carnage" tends to focus too much on the symptoms and too little on the disease. There is no doubt that transformative political, economic, technological, and cultural forces remade America and intruded on the lives of many. But they had been long in the making; brewing for years, decades even, tectonic shifts that long preceded the 2016 election helped shape, maybe even determine, the election's outcome. And they are accordingly rooted as much in the long decline of American liberalism as they are in the meteoric rise of Donald Trump and his peculiar brand of right-wing populism.

Rethinking Trump's historic victory through the broader prism of liberal decline helps explain why, in the wake of the election, more and more scholars of liberalism and liberal pundits have reoriented their critical focus back onto themselves, engaging in an introspective quest to try and answer that agonizing question: where have we gone wrong? Once the independent variables and contingencies were accounted for—Russian hacking, WikiLeaks, fake news, FBI meddling, Clinton's hubris, and flawed electoral campaign strategy—a set of self-reflective explanations materialized. Mark Lilla's polemic *The Once and Future Liberal* provided the opening salvo by castigating liberals for their misplaced emphasis on identity politics and lamenting that they failed to develop instead an ambitious vision of American unity that could inspire *all* citizens. "The great liberal abdication began during the Reagan years. With the end of the Roosevelt Dispensation and the rise of a unified and ambitious right, American liberals faced a serious challenge: to develop a fresh political vision of the country's shared destiny, adapted to the new realities of American society and chastened by the failures of old approaches," Lilla argued. "Liberals failed to do this. Instead they threw themselves into the movement politics of identity, losing a sense of what we share as citizens and what binds us as a nation."[3] Others pointed to language and to the failure of liberals to understand, let alone employ, it correctly. In her sweeping universal study of the evolution of liberal terminology, Helena Rosenblatt found that "we are muddled about what we mean by liberalism" and suggested "it would be good to know what we are speaking about when we speak about liberalism." George Klosko traced the rhetorical features of American liberalism only to find an irreconcilable gap between words and deeds that prevented the transformation—and realization—of American liberalism in the postwar era. "Division in the language of liberalism is bound up with undeveloped philosophical defense of welfare programs," he claimed. "American political leaders have not cast off the political culture's Lockean assumptions, and so produced the contorted arguments we have seen."[4]

It was political theorist Patrick Deneen who offered what amounts to the most damning indictment of liberalism in his eponymous book *Why Liberalism Failed*. In his eyes, liberalism faltered because it failed to offer citizens "power over those forces that no longer seemed under their control: government, economy, and the dissolution of social norms and unsettled ways of life."

> Today's widespread yearning for a strong leader, one with the will to take back popular control over liberalism's forms of bureaucratized government and globalized economy, comes after decades of liberal dismantling of cultural norms and political habits essential to self-governance. The breakdown of family, community, and religious norms and institutions, especially among those benefiting least from liberalism's advance, has not led liberalism's discontents to seek a restoration of those norms.

Like a Frankenstein monster, Deneen opined, "Liberalism has failed—not because it fell short, but because it was true to itself." In four critical areas—politics, economics, education, and science and technology—he claimed "liberalism has transformed human institutions in the name of expanding liberty and increasing our mastery and control of our fates. And in each case, widespread anger and deepening discontent have arisen from the spreading realization that the vehicles of our liberation have become iron cages of our captivity." What was needed, he suggested, was a communitarian and religious alternative that relied on "the fostering of new and better selves, porously invested in the fate of other selves—through the cultivation of cultures of community, care, self-sacrifice, and small-scale democracy."[5]

To readers, scholars, and fans of American novelist John Updike, such arguments that sought to explain the decline of liberalism should sound very familiar: Updike's literature had, after all, anticipated them more than fifty years earlier. As one of the most prolific and successful American authors in the twentieth century—he published twenty-eight novels, fourteen short story collections, nine poetry volumes, and hundreds of essays that, among other things, earned him two Pulitzer Prize awards for fiction—Updike (1932–2009) has long been held as a gifted writer whose rare sensitivity to the quotidian, combined with an extraordinary talent for realism, enabled him to gracefully chronicle the postwar American experience.[6] But what is still overlooked (or at the very least forgotten) is that Updike was more than a man of letters: he was also an ardent man of ideas—political ideas. And that is why his fiction represents not just a florid literary image of life in postwar America, as is often thought, but an investigation into the liberal ideas, institutions, and political culture that helped define it, some of which to this day continue to resonate.

Updike was an ideal interrogator of New Deal liberalism: growing up in rural Pennsylvania, he was white, devoutly Christian, lower middle class, and yet staunchly liberal. As such, he gave voice to the concerns of a large segment of the population that was becoming increasingly alienated from and disenchanted with the Democratic Party and liberal policies. A self-avowed Roosevelt Democrat who proudly claimed the New Deal as his political inheritance, Updike essentially mapped in his early novels, mostly centered in Pennsylvania, the struggle of white working- and lower middle class Americans trying to hold on to that inheritance in the wake of sweeping political, socioeconomic, technological, and cultural transformations remaking America in the middle of the twentieth century. By identifying those fundamental sources of tension that were gradually emerging from *within* New Deal liberalism as early as the 1950s—and that, in many ways, continue to linger to this day—Updike's fiction not only anticipates postwar liberalism's gradual implosion but also unveils some of the root causes behind it.

This book is not exclusively about Updike and it is certainly not about Trump. Nor is it necessarily a conventional history or theoretical study of postwar liberalism or literature. In a way, it touches on all of these topics while striving to employ elements of each in order to creatively weave together multiple fields of scholarship with the aim of generating a richer and more complex understanding of the postwar experience. By delving further and deeper into the subtleties of the American psyche than the social sciences and historiography have independently been able to, Updike's fiction uniquely serves as a historical barometer that registered changes of affect and emotion among millions of Americans and illuminates their shifting sensibilities and pervasive fears of loss, dispossession, humiliation, and powerlessness that monumental political, socioeconomic, and cultural changes produced. Among these fears that Updike revealed: an unprecedented expansion of the federal government, postindustrialization, the Cold War, and America's global ascendance, secularization, demographic shifts, sexual revolution, and racial and ethnic integration. More than anything, Updike's writings help illustrate the fundamental inability of more and more Americans to grasp, let alone cope with, profound transformations they could neither understand nor control.

The key questions that this book explores are: How did seemingly sacrosanct beliefs about the relationship between individual, state, and society shift so dramatically—and how did the meaning of liberalism shift with them? Why did the permeation of secularism and science into rural America spur a cultural backlash—and was there a way to avoid it? How did the bureaucratization of political decision making (via technocrats and interest groups) affect popular democratic participation? How did the structural shift from a production- to consumption-oriented economy and culture redefine the boundaries between public and private life? And finally, why did liberal elites fail to sufficiently address the subsequent sources of tension and discontent that these transformative changes inevitably engendered?

What We Talk about When We Talk about Liberalism

An important clarification is in order before proceeding to answer the questions mentioned above. What do we talk about when we talk about New Deal liberalism? After all, liberalism—an elusive and ever evolving term—has come to mean many things to many people: an ideology, doctrine, philosophy, culture, temperament, and inclination. It has stretched across the Atlantic to transcend time and space and incorporate an array of intellectual traditions and political persuasions. Recent scholarship has broadened its geographic and historic scope far beyond its Anglo-American origins three centuries ago in the works of John Locke, John Stuart Mill, thinkers of the Scottish Enlightenment, and America's founding fathers to find substantial influences in the Marquis de Condorcet and Benjamin Constant's revolutionary France, Immanuel Kant, and Alexander von Humboldt's Enlightenment Germany, and even as far back as the Greek and Roman polis. For all of the differences between these liberal traditions, what ties them together is a commitment to a basic set of Enlightenment principles that includes individualism, political liberty and self-government, free markets, and some form of social equality, as well as a firm belief in reason and historical progress, pragmatism, cosmopolitanism, tolerance, and pluralism.[7]

While at least some of these universal principles informed the liberal tradition wherever it took root, the central focus of this book is not in philosophical conceptions or theoretical definitions but rather in the historically conditioned postwar American liberal order, which was the product of a particular time and place. The American political sphere has been broad and malleable enough to facilitate parallel, often even competing, liberal currents: from left-wing progressive and populist reformers like John Dewey, Herbert Croly, and William Jennings Bryan, who employed liberalism to advance the cause of social democracy, defend individuals from encroaching market forces and monopolies, and establish an American welfare state at the dawn of the twentieth century, to right-wing antistatists like Friedrich Hayek and Milton Friedman, who re-appropriated the term neoliberalism to mount a reactionary defense of free markets and individual rights against government. Since the 1960s the discourse of liberalism has been complemented by liberal republicanism, a rediscovery of classical traditions dedicated to virtue, solidarity, and civic engagement that supplemented, at times even superseded, individual interests, as well as that of racial liberalism, which raised the mantle of civil rights and sought to incorporate African Americans into the liberal project. The latter would evolve into rights-based liberalism, a broadened term associated with identity politics and the particular needs of various groups consolidated along racial, ethnic, gender, and sexual categories to secure their collective rights and advance their political, socioeconomic, and cultural interests within American society.[8]

These varieties of liberalism all had a profound impact, and there was much overlap between them. Some preceded New Deal liberalism and inspired and shaped it; others sought to reform and improve it; and a few even succeeded in displacing it. But none matched its unprecedented political dominance, intellectual pervasiveness, and overwhelming cultural purchase. Emerging out of the harrowing experiences of the Great Depression and World War II, New Deal liberalism gradually consolidated itself during the 1930s and reigned nearly supreme from 1945 to 1968 across America's political, economic, intellectual, and cultural landscapes. So commanding had it become that in 1950 the renowned literary critic Lionel Trilling observed, and not without some regret, that "liberalism is not only the dominant but even the sole intellectual tradition in America."[9]

But it was much more than that. A political project established by politicians, bureaucrats, and intellectuals through what historian Richard Hofstadter called a "chaos of experimentation," liberalism was sustained by a grassroots, bottom-up political coalition of labor and business leaders, civil society organizations, and various racial, ethnic, and religious groups that transcended any geographic and demographic boundaries and came together under a reformulated liberal banner.[10] Conceptualized by public intellectuals like Trilling, Arthur M. Schlesinger Jr., Reinhold Niebuhr, and Louis Hartz, it was celebrated by cultural agents, writers, actors, and artists who all contributed to what Wendy Wall aptly labeled a "conversation on consensus." Facing ideological competition from fascism on the right and communism on the left, New Deal liberalism sought to ameliorate the two central fault lines of American society—class and race—by appealing to a new national cohesion rooted in compromise, moderation, and consensus: "Denying or minimizing the economic and power imbalances, they stressed the harmony of interests among various groups in America society and sought to shore up the status quo," Wall wrote of the government officials and elites at the time who were promoting the liberal spirit of consensus.[11]

Often conflated or confused with consensus liberalism or liberal anticommunism—both of which are reflective but inaccurate and incomplete definitions—New Deal liberalism (interchangeably called here postwar liberalism) was as much a broad set of ideas, beliefs, norms, and sensibilities as it was a coherent political order. Rooted in the new Democratic Party Franklin Roosevelt created—but shared by many Republicans—it evolved and expanded despite numerous challenges and setbacks during the Truman, Kennedy, and Johnson administrations, and remained pervasive even during the Republican presidencies of Dwight Eisenhower and Richard Nixon. At heart, it was dedicated to a set of new governing principles and ideas that were not necessarily always compatible. Politically, it redefined the relationship between the federal government, the individual, and the states by adopting a new and more active understanding of liberty that reinforced the legalistic definition with a social layer and recognized that without establishing some social equality and material welfare, freedom could be neither pursued nor secured. A direct result was the unprecedented growth of the federal government and its increased intervention in the lives of citizens in ways and areas that had previously seemed unimaginable. In terms of governing, this growth was characterized by centralized technocratic decision making and interest group competition that often came at the expense of direct democratic experience and local political participation.[12]

But it stood for far more than just politics. Although it initially sought to restructure American capitalism, New Deal liberalism's economic vision eventually settled for a modus vivendi with it: markets remained free, but they were regulated; business could apply its own prerogatives in terms of production and capital, and since labor rights were ensured, unions got a seat at the bargaining table; and a basic welfare safety net was established to look after workers. Rather than challenging the fundamentals of American political economy, New Deal liberalism embraced Keynesian fiscal measures and deficit spending as a way to secure adequate consumer demand and enable stable growth. Economic thought was symbiotically fused with a new culture of consumption to formulate what came to be known as a "consumer's republic." Culturally, New Deal liberalism celebrated the melting pot's universality and Judeo-Christian harmony under the banner of what Robert Bellah called a "civil religion."[13] This included a shared reverence for America's founding democratic principles and institutions as a way of distinguishing it from the emerging geopolitical threat abroad and at home: the communist other. Such appeals to cultural cohesion and national unity conveniently allowed liberals to sidestep—and conceal—persistent racial segregation and oppression of African Americans in the South and the structural racism perpetuating their inequality in the urban-industrial North.[14] Intellectually, New Deal liberalism was committed to pragmatism, pluralism, experimentation, secularism, and a cult of science that accordingly elevated the university and public education to cardinal status. Socially, it mostly sought to reassert heteronormative patriarchal relations and undo much of the social gains women had made during the war by keeping them, in the words of one historian, "homeward bound." Finally, New Deal liberalism was dominated by a national security mentality with a globalist outlook that was uncompromisingly anticommunist. Imbibing the beliefs that the postwar era, indeed, inaugurated what Henry Luce famously termed the "American century," New Deal liberals embraced an unequivocal posture of American exceptionalism that justified the construction of an international liberal order abroad as well as at home, yet were all too blasé—often even complicit—when civil liberties were trampled within America and human rights were violated in its name beyond its shores.[15]

Why Updike?

Although John Updike would be aghast at even the thought that his fiction embodied, let alone spoke, for New Deal liberalism, his writing was nevertheless its product. And it came to embody what he, himself, called "a post-liberal socio-economic-cultural harmony I was pleased to be a part of" in the postwar years.[16] Updike's fiction was not about politics per se, but his outlook and sensibilities were, inevitably—even if unknowingly—directly informed by them. "Liberals," Jan Zielonka recently complained, "proved better at finger-pointing than at self-reflection. They spend more time explaining the rise of populism than the fall of liberalism. They refuse to look in the mirror and recognize their own shortcomings."[17] This was certainly not the case for Updike: even while cautiously avoiding political issues, he did not shy away from self-reflection. His literature, at least to a certain extent, does exactly what Zielonka demands of liberals: it looks in the mirror. That is why rethinking the decline of New Deal liberalism through a reconceptualization and recontextualization of Updike's early work offers us a way to formulate new answers to the same old questions regarding the roots of liberalism's decline.

In the process, it helps us do something else: redeem Updike's legacy as not just a talented writer who had a way with words, but a serious one whose words go a long way. Since his death in 2009 at the age of seventy-six, there has been a growing interest in Updike's work. The opening of the John Updike Papers at Houghton Library in Harvard University in 2012 has provided a rich trove of autobiographical information that has already sparked renewed interest in his broader legacy. Scholars like James Schiff, Jack De Bellis, Bob Batchelor, Michial Farmer, and Frederic Svoboda have highlighted his previously overlooked skills as a critic, essayist, and poet (in addition to being a novelist), exploring his wider intellectual breadth and impact on American culture, and arguing that "there is an Updike beyond the Rabbit novels." Historian Michael Szalay has provided a fresh take on the Rabbit series in his literary history of the Democratic Party and revealed a correlation between Rabbit's ideas and the Democratic platform of the 1960s. Above all, Adam Begley's comprehensive biography of Updike, the first of its kind, has contributed more than anything to solidifying Updike's reputation as a first-rate novelist who chronicled the vicissitudes of postwar society. What these recent studies essentially suggest is that Updike's work matters for our understanding of contemporary America and that he must therefore be afforded considerable respect and recognition.[18]

But his work still remains controversial. Although recent scholarship and especially Begley's biography have helped establish Updike's unequivocal literary talents and cultural contribution as a novelist, they did not silence lingering complaints, first voiced by John Aldridge nearly a half century ago, that Updike "has nothing to say." Throughout his life Updike was haunted by this persistent rebuke: Norman Mailer claimed that Updike "doesn't know how to finish," and Gore Vidal agreed, "he describes to no purpose." Even Morris Dickstein, a notable historian sympathetic to Updike's fiction, echoed this verdict in contending that Updike was a member of a generation of novelists preoccupied with "cultivating the self" and "obsessed more with Oedipal struggle than with class struggle, concerned about the limits of civilization rather than the conflicts within civilization." The claim that Updike employed excessive style to compensate for chronic lack of substance and that his fascination with the mundane and provincial (ergo "unimportant" in the eyes of some critics) has drained his work of broad universal appeal led Harold Bloom to call him "a minor writer with a major style." David Foster Wallace, who excoriated Updike for being a narcissist, went further by labeling him "a penis with a thesaurus," adding, "has the son of a bitch ever had one unpublished thought?"[19]

Even after his death, such claims persist. Jeffrey Meyers echoed Wallace's infamous scolding by asserting that "Updike's long career combined the blandness of the tranquillized 1950s with the narcissism of the Me Generation," and concluded, "in the end, for all his cataract of words, Updike not only failed to transcend the superficial and vacuous *New Yorker* values but also came to embody them." The writer James Dellingpole employed Updike's work in his argument *against* the necessity of literary canons by bunching him with "Wagner's *Ring* Cycle, ballet, Kabuki theatre, mime, Samuel Beckett, late Pinter, [and] Nigerian poetry" and suggesting that "if you too are as yet unfamiliar with the great Updike's oeuvre, there's no need to feel bad." The possibility of Updike's waning influence led the *Guardian* to raise the question: "Have we fallen out of love with John Updike?"[20]

I certainly hope not. A careful study of Updike's early fiction paints a very different picture; it reveals an author who actively engaged politics in a subtle way, which invites readers to transcend the realism of plot in search of deeper theoretical and historical meaning.[21] This book is not a political biography of John Updike (though it partially offers one). Rather than present a single-author literary study, it seeks to offer a much broader and far more sweeping historical exploration of postwar America that employs Updike's fiction as a lens into deeper political, socioeconomic, and cultural developments. At heart, it makes two novel and complementary arguments. The first challenges the still enduring view of Updike as an apolitical writer who merely champions an inward escape into the self and contends that he actively engaged politics in new and subtle ways. Having been instilled with a solid liberal arts education at Harvard, Updike did not strive for his work to flee the political, as many have claimed; his work aspires to do the exact opposite: his rich political imagination enabled him to employ an arsenal of political theory and a deep historical and philosophical awareness in his fiction in order to interrogate fundamental questions of power, equality, liberty, individualism, capitalism, religion, bureaucracy, and democracy in postwar America.

The second argument this book advances is that, as an acute political thinker, Updike thoroughly enriches our understanding of New Deal liberalism's decline by unveiling some inherent contradictions that were already present at its creation. Conventional explanations for its decline point to the cataclysmic events of the late 1960s—racial discord and the breakdown of law and order, counterculture, and the Vietnam War, stagflation, postindustrialism, and the decline of the welfare state—as primarily responsible for eroding the public legitimacy of the postwar liberal order alongside the corresponding rise of the New Right. However, Updike's early novels (1958–1971), which mostly *precede* these events, already betray a clear uneasiness with certain liberal ideals and institutions among parts of the white working and middle classes long before many of their members abandoned the Democratic Party, coalesced into the so-called silent majority, and realigned with ascending conservative forces.[22]

What this book posits, instead, is that prevailing explanations for the collapse of New Deal liberalism in the late 1960s and early 1970s are symptomatic of a deeper problem: an inability to harmonize the forces of modernity and tradition. Postwar liberalism, in other words, failed because it was unable to reconcile the traditions upon which it was originally founded with the forces of modernity that it itself had unleashed. And it was this fundamental clash between old and new forms of liberalism—carefully delineated in Updike's fiction—that ultimately shaped the political struggles that defined the era and continue to linger, albeit in a different form, to this very day. In politics, the encroaching welfare state created by the New Deal undermined Jeffersonian notions of self-reliance while its technocratic bureaucracy appropriated local sovereignty, engendered political apathy, and alienated individuals from community life and participatory democracy that have long been the sine qua non of traditional liberal democracy. Consumer capitalism provided neither the fulfillment of traditional free enterprise nor the economic security for which it had replaced it, while science, secularism, and technology could not compensate for the erosion of religious institutions and civil society that they had unintentionally precipitated. Emerging therapeutic notions of creative autonomy and personal fulfillment that increasingly dominated American culture could not assuage the anxieties and alienation emanating from the family breakup and civic decline, to which they directly contributed. Put simply: the competing strains of old and new forms of liberalism that the New Deal held together eventually gave out, causing it to collapse onto itself. Reconsidered in this light, the cataclysmic events of the 1960s appear to be the culmination rather than the spark for postwar liberalism's implosion.

There is a scene in the beginning of *Rabbit Redux* (1971), Updike's most self-conscious political novel, that crystalizes these competing tensions. As they leave their struggling soon-to-be-downsized printing press after another day of arduous manual labor, the chief protagonist Harry "Rabbit" Angstrom and his father enter a local tavern in the industrial city of Brewer, Pennsylvania (modeled after Reading), to get a drink.

Inside, they watch the historic launch of Apollo 11 as it unfolds on live television: "The lifting so slow it seems certain to tip, the swift diminishment into a retreating speck, a jiggling star. The men dark along the bar murmur among themselves. They have not been lifted, they are left here."[23] In a way, this somber passage, which sets the disenchanted tone for the rest of the book, encapsulates the fundamental problem that lies at the heart of the entire postwar liberal project: Rabbit and the "men along the bar" have witnessed its launch but have not really experienced it; they are merely spectators—not participants. Alerting us to a growing sense of detachment and alienation between national success and personal failure, the passage suggests that just as the liberal welfare state conquered space and tamed the New Frontier by landing a man on the moon, as President Kennedy had promised to do at the start of the decade, liberalism failed to replicate such success on Earth, at least for many hardworking Americans like Rabbit. Rather than a celebration of this memorable feat, the novel painfully juxtaposes these scientific, bureaucratic, and technological achievements of modernity with a string of social, economic, political, and personal failures. With the Vietnam War, race riots, and economic decline constantly overshadowing the moon landing in the background, Updike's prescient literary imagination effectively reframes the event—one of American liberalism's marked achievements—as a moment of tragedy rather than triumph.

Methodology and Structure

The political theorist Catherine Zuckert has suggested that "the questions that led political scientists to look to works of art for enlightenment concern the aspects of human life that are most difficult, if not impossible, to study and observe externally or objectively—the attitudes, emotions, and opinions that shape and are shaped by people's circumstances, especially their political circumstances."[24] It is this sobering realization in the limits of what history and political science can teach us that motivates the synthetic and admittedly unorthodox interdisciplinary research method of this book. In recent years more and more scholars from both history and political science have embraced literature to enrich their understandings of American political developments and the circumstances that helped drive them: this has resulted in, among other things, new and profound insight regarding democracy, citizenship, race, rights, equality, the nature of work, and the American presidency.[25]

Rather than embrace any particular theoretical model or disciplinary creed, my engagement with Updike's novels follows an analytical methodology that closely borrows from the his own repertoire. "I think books should have secrets, like people do," the young author noted in a 1968 interview. "I think they should be there as a bonus for the sensitive reader or there as a kind of subliminal quavering."[26] Having embraced the mystery of metaphor and invited his readers to look beyond the veneer of narrative in search of hidden meanings, Updike used his own literary criticism as a guide for doing so. Despite being formally trained in the methods of the New Criticism at Harvard, Updike's prolific career as a literary critic suggests he substituted concerns for structure and formalism for more substantial aspects of plot, biography, and historical context. In the foreword to *Picked-Up Pieces,* the second collection of his literary criticism, Updike presented his own "code" for what he deemed to be the preferable manner for reviewing fiction. His first rule: "try to understand what the author wished to do." And most importantly for the reader: "do not imagine yourself a caretaker of any tradition, an enforcer of any party standards, a warrior in any ideological battle."[27]

I have tried to remain loyal to Updike's own formula. Transcending any parochial disciplinary boundaries, my study proceeds along the dual path of textual analysis and close readings of his work that are augmented by rich primary archival materials assembled from the John Updike Papers and relevant historiography. The interdisciplinary analysis of Updike's fiction is closely contextualized by his corresponding nonfiction writings, interviews, and influential contemporary social and historical thought—both of which Updike often imbibed, reinterpreted, and reflected through his own fiction. Grounding Updike's novels in the intellectual discourses of their era and tracing his ideas to prevailing intellectual currents—not to mention to his previously unknown personal relationships with prominent thinkers like Arthur M. Schlesinger Jr., Daniel P. Moynihan, William Buckley Jr., and Christopher Lasch—helps establish his credentials as a serious social thinker and locate the intellectual inspirations that informed his writings. Given that some chapters borrow from political theory and others from historical or sociological scholarship, while a few rely on empirical data, I hope to demonstrate how an innovative interdisciplinary synthesis that ties the humanities and the social sciences in a transmethodological Gordian knot of sorts can enrich our understanding of the past and shine a new, or at least a different, light upon it. Such a mélange of sources and analytical instruments, I hope to demonstrate, is not only warranted but necessary in order to delve deeper into historical-political transformations unfolding in the literary imagination and locate the latent nuances and shifting sensibilities driving them, which do not always register with more conventional empirical methodological approaches.

Looking back to the 1960s in his memoirs, *Self-Consciousness* (1989), Updike revealed that what particularly distressed him about that turbulent era was how his political identity had been shaken. "I was a liberal. The political position I had wormed into on Artie Hoyer's barber's chair—holding my tongue, but inwardly scorning this frantic Republican hatred of governmental activism—had unfairly gone unfashionable on me."[28] In order to carefully unravel this process and highlight how exactly liberalism, indeed, became "unfashionable" to millions of Americans like Updike, this book shall progress along a series of interwoven chapters that proceed chronologically and thematically. Chapter 1 establishes Updike's political biography and introduces the tenets of postwar liberal thought that he embraced and reflected. Chapter 2 goes back to Updike's college experience and explores his undergraduate years at Harvard in the 1950s. Relying on previously unpublished archival materials in Houghton Library, it connects Updike's liberal education with his literary imagination and suggests that the intellectual sensibilities instilled in him at Harvard would eventually come to shape his fiction.

The following chapters reassess the salient novels from Updike's first two decades of writing (with the occasional discussion of relevant short stories and poems). Chapter 3 explores Updike's overlooked debut novel *The Poorhouse Fair*. It employs the political theory of Isaiah Berlin in order to reveal an insightful and politically astute young novelist who subtly described how competing visions of liberalism—a traditional liberalism dedicated to preserving "negative liberty" on one hand and a state-centered, modern bureaucratic welfare state consumed with promoting "positive liberty" on the other—vie for power and dissolve any supposed ideological consensus as early as the 1950s. Chapter 4 moves from the political toward the economic and cultural realms and offers a fresh take on *Rabbit, Run*, Updike's best-known novel. By employing the influential social thought of Daniel Bell and Philip Rieff, it posits that modernizing economic and cultural forces like consumer capitalism and therapeutic liberalism directly contributed to the decline of the traditional civic institution of the family. It locates Updike's ideas at the nexus of a large body of cultural criticism concerned with "family values" that was to emerge in the years following the novel's release and traces a link between Updike's early prescient concerns and later ones raised by prominent liberal intellectuals—and incidentally Updike's friends—Lasch and Moynihan.

The remaining chapters engage the tumultuous experiences of the 1960s in a variety of new ways. Chapter 5 broadens the conventional reading of Updike's most sensational novel, *Couples*, as a tale about sex in the suburbs by investigating its implications upon American democratic culture. It reevaluates the political scientist Robert Putnam's seminal theory of "bowling alone" regarding the decline of civic engagement since the 1960s and considers new explanations for why this decline might have occurred. By pointing to the privatization of the public sphere, it contends that new cultural sensibilies served to undermine traditional notions of civic virtue and, consequentially, transformed politics into a superficial experience long before then. In doing so, it complicates our understanding of postwar democratic theory by challenging the widely accepted perception of the 1960s as a golden age of civic life. Chapter 6 returns to Updike's most explicit (and explosive) political novel, *Rabbit Redux*, in order to offer an alternative explanation for liberalism's decline. It reinterprets conventional histories of the period that locate the roots of liberal implosion in the Vietnam War, racial strife, culture wars, and shortcomings of the welfare state and postindustrialism as symptom of a deeper problem: an inability to reconcile modernity and tradition. This fundamental clash between old and new forms of liberalism suffusing Updike's early fiction culminates in *Rabbit Redux*, which demonstrates how it ultimately helped shape the various political, socioeconomic, and cultural conflicts that defined the era: postindustrial capitalism provided neither the traditional fulfillment of free enterprise nor the economic security it had promised, secularism and science could not compensate for the erosion of religion, the turn to pluralism and interest groups left the individual citizen as alienated as ever from the democratic process, and classic liberal notions of individual liberty could not adjust to new demands for economic justice and racial and gender equality. The concluding chapter looks back to Updike's legacy and ponders on what his fiction can teach us about the potential and possibilities for rejuvenating liberalism in contemporary America.

One final caveat is in order. I do not assume or suggest that Updike ever directly sought to explain American politics. He did not. Updike was careful to distinguish himself from his contemporaries, who politicized fiction, and ardently avoided infusing his own work with any ideological flavor. None of my conclusions are his. At no point do I aspire, let alone contend, to speak for him. What Updike's fiction does do, however, is shine a unique light on the various forces remaking American society in the latter half of the twentieth century—and the complex reactions to them. No less a figure than historian Arthur M. Schlesinger Jr., perhaps the intellectual voice most identified with New Deal liberalism, realized after reading one of Updike's books that "novelists and playwrights may well get things wrong and are not likely to alter professional verdicts. But the power of their imagination may force historians to look freshly at the frieze and to perceive historical figures not as abstractions but as human beings in all their idiosyncrasy and uniqueness, as human beings above all created by their own choices."[29] This, in a nutshell, is what this book has tried to do.

1 | The Man in the Middle

The thrust of the democratic faith is away from fanaticism; it is toward compromise, persuasion and consent in politics, toward tolerance and diversity in society.
—Arthur M. Schlesinger Jr.

Half-measures are most human; Compromise, Inglorious and gray, placates the Wise. By mechanistic hopes is Mankind vexed; The Book of Life is margin more than text.
—John Updike, "Midpoint"

Between is the only honest place to be.
—Lionel Trilling

I like middles. It is in middles that extremes clash, where ambiguity restlessly rules.
—John Updike

In the spring of 1978 John Updike was invited by William Buckley Jr. to publish his testimony before the House Committee on Select Education in the pages of the *National Review*. Updike, by then a renowned and award-winning novelist, was asked by Congress to share his thoughts about federal funding for the humanities, and he promptly agreed to Buckley's proposal (which was conveyed with a caveat: "but I would not want to do that if you are hostile to its appearing in *National Review*"). Updike did not find it hostile, and the piece was published in May of that year. Since Updike voiced concern with government intervention in cultural endeavors, one realizes why Buckley, one of the godfathers of American conservatism, was so enthusiastic to publish his testimony. "I love my government not least for the extent to which it leaves me alone," Updike told legislators, while recommending that they steer clear of active involvement in the arts, lest a "cultural totalitarianism" emerge.[1]

The appearance of Updike's byline on the pages of what was, and for many readers still is, considered the conservative movement's flagship journal led to a series of letters between Updike and Buckley, the founder and longtime editor of the influential magazine.[2] In September of that year, Buckley invited Updike to lunch in order to offer him a surprising assignment:

> What did I hope for, aside from the pleasure of meeting you? To induce you to write an essay on Whittaker Chambers as *a writer*. . . . What I had hoped—indeed, still hope—is that you would undertake to do a review of Chamber's work (this would require reading three, at most four, books) with the view to salvaging his literary reputation from the wreckage of the Hiss case.

Buckley wrote to Updike that "I think you would find, very quickly, the Remnant, easily altered, if someone of your distinction arrested their attention, to the necessity to rescue from the ordure of the Hiss case, a considerable artist."[3] Updike respectfully declined: "I don't want to seem unwilling to share a lunch with you, but I get to New York rarely, and then overcommitted, and I can't imagine what you could say about Whittaker Chambers that might induce me to add to the considerable heap of books by and about this *bedeviled* [added, handwritten, to the typed letter] man already."[4]

That Buckley would invite Updike not only to publish in the preeminent conservative journal when the New Right was at its zenith but to reassess Whittaker Chambers, the author of the anticommunist memoir *Witness*, who was considered to be the father of postwar American conservatism, seems counterintuitive.[5] Updike was after all a staunch liberal and lifelong Democrat who had voted enthusiastically for Jimmy Carter (he accepted an invitation to a White House dinner hosted by Carter in 1980 and recorded his experience of the event by inscribing "Wow" on the invitation's envelope).[6] In addition, he was a supporter of Democratic congressman Michael J. Harrington, who represented Massachusetts's Sixth District (where Updike resided) between 1969 and 1979 and was considered one of the most liberal voices in Congress.[7] Maybe most ironic about Buckley's surprising assignment was the fact that just a few years before Updike published his thoughts on the humanities in the *National Review*, he was also invited by the New School for Social Research in New York—hardly a conservative bastion—to spend a sabbatical teaching there (although he declined, he did however take part in a special lecture series called New Yorker at the New School in 1990).[8]

Given the ideological polarization and deep political divisions that have plagued American politics since the 1960s, it would be hard to find too many intellectuals who would be comfortable reading the *National Review* in the morning and lecturing at the New School in the evening.⁹ Yet what may appear to us today as somewhat anomalous was for Updike what being a liberal was all about. Where exactly did these liberal sensibilities come from? What did they espouse? And how did they inform Updike's literary imagination? This chapter seeks to establish Updike's liberal credentials by recontextualizing the intellectual climate from which they emerged and sketching the closest thing, so far, to his political biography.

The Postwar Liberal Mindset

Born during the Depression, Updike's political sensibilities were forged in the years following World War II and reflected a reconstituted version of American liberalism. The horrors of totalitarianism and the nuclear threat of annihilation that the dropping of the atom bombs and the dawn of the Cold War bred led many intellectuals to shed their progressive beliefs in the potential perfectibility of man, the redemptive qualities of science, and the utopian possibilities of social engineering—without necessarily abandoning their dedication to core egalitarian principles of the Left. In their place, intellectuals adopted a sobering and realist view of politics that was fed by doses of skepticism, irony, and doubt. As a result, pragmatic inclinations of ambivalence, incrementalism, and deep pluralism overtook the ideological maxims that had previously shaped left-liberal thought.¹⁰ "Most political intellectuals in the two decades after World War II agreed that pluralist democracy, democracy which was characterized by openness, compromise, practical problem solving, and the politics of interests, was the practice as well as the norm in America," Robert B. Fowler concluded in his study of postwar political thought.¹¹

The reformulated liberal mindset that emerged after 1945 sought to cope with the sweeping socioeconomic, political, and cultural changes remaking the country alongside the new existential threats through experimentation and moderation. Instead of embracing radical solutions in the economic sphere that sought the abolition of capitalism or anachronistic laissez-faire panaceas, postwar liberals found in the New Deal and its political culture a satisfying balance that could ameliorate the ills of capitalism without having to replace it. According to Howard Brick, this transformative moment that saw the potential displacement of the economy and shift away from a market society expressed the culmination of an imaginative reorientation toward social liberalism that many intellectuals had begun experiencing as early as the 1910s with the emergence of what he dubbed the "postcapitalist vision." This new vision essentially represented "a fusion of liberal and social democratic dispositions—a new social liberalism—that dwelled on the left side of the mainstream reform politics." However, unlike radicalist proposals, it took a more cautious and gradual approach toward change that "could support both 'utopian' and 'ideological' dispositions, looking forward to an imagined future different from the present, while vesting confidence in what currently prevailed as the means of getting there."[12]

Given the fear of mass politics that had degenerated into totalitarianism abroad, postwar liberals placed great faith in the pluralist political model. The New Deal's commensurate reliance on bureaucratic expertise and interest group competition—as opposed to class competition—was considered the ideal manner to keep government, business, and the public all in check and preserve the principles of constitutional democracy necessary for winning the Cold War. "The very absence of any absolute justifications in the modern world was a common ground on which American thinkers sought to justify what values they had and obviously this was never truer than with their endorsement of pluralism. It was the acceptance in principle of the idea that there were no answers," Fowler explained.[13] Since ideologies provided readymade solutions, they were deemed obsolete and dangerous to the rediscovered pragmatism of liberals. "There is today a rough consensus among intellectuals on political issues: the acceptance of a Welfare State; the desirability of decentralized power; a system of mixed economy and of political pluralism," Daniel Bell declared in his aptly titled study of the era—*The End of Ideology*.[14]

No one embodied this new liberal temper better than historian Arthur M. Schlesinger Jr., whose book *The Vital Center* (1949) became a manifesto for many liberals. Conceived as a call to arms, Schlesinger's bestseller called for a coalition dedicated to fighting communism by revitalizing what he perceived to be America's centrist political inheritance:

> So long as society stays free, so long will it continue in its state of tension, breeding contradiction, breeding strife. But we betray ourselves if we accept

contradiction and strife as the total meaning of conflict. For conflict is also the guarantee of freedom; it is the instrument of change; it is, above all, the source of discovery, the source of art, the source of love. . . . The new radicalism derives its power from an acceptance of conflict—an acceptance combined with a determination to create a social framework where conflict issues, not in excessive anxiety, but in creativity. The center is vital; the center must hold.[15]

The way to uphold the vital center and obviate extremism was by perpetual competition between interest groups that would breed mutual accommodation. "The thrust of the democratic faith is away from fanaticism. It is toward compromise, persuasion and consent in politics, toward tolerance and diversity in society; its economic foundation lies in the easily frightened middle class. Its love of variety discourages dogmatism, and its love of skepticism discourages hero worship," he wrote.[16] Although Schlesinger's emphasis on conflict was emblematic of old radical impulses (residues of his previous book on Jacksonian democracy), he adopted a firm anti-ideological stance. "Where Marxism envisioned that struggle as warfare to the apocalyptic death, Schlesinger's versions kept it, through an emphasis on gradualism, pragmatism, and parliamentarianism, as a 'perpetual tension' issuing not in actual warfare or final resolution but in an ongoing balancing and rebalancing of social forces which offered society the best guarantee of freedom, stability, and progress," James Neuchterlein observed.[17]

When the sociologist Robert Nisbet warned in 1953 that "more and more of us have come to feel, with Melville, Hawthorn, and Dostoevsky, that in men's souls lie deep and unpredictable potentialities for evil that no human institutions can control," he was signaling the pivotal shift away from progressive optimism.[18] The rediscovery of man's fallen nature, alongside the recognition of the limits of science and social engineering, helped spark a critical discourse surrounding what Mark Greif called "the age of the crisis of man." It was this imminent sense of crisis that forced many intellectuals to reappraise the project of the Enlightenment and seek a more sobered—and less ambitious—path forward. "The midcentury generations' way of addressing the crisis of man represented a consensus that something specific had gone wrong and must be made right," Greif contended. "Re-enlightenment represented a questioning of what could be left of the Enlightenment without the idea of progress."[19]

This disenchantment fed deep political misgivings that the theologian Reinhold Niebuhr was foremost in highlighting when advocating for what one historian labeled "a non-utopian liberalism."[20] Distinguishing the postwar liberal mindset from that of progressive liberals, Niebuhr warned: "Liberalism has been tempted into an attitude of fatuous optimism. It does not see sin in individual, in society and in nature."[21] By reintroducing human fallibility into the political equation, he demanded of liberals to abandon their optimistic faith in progress, embrace irony as a guiding principle, and formulate a political vision that nurtures the better angels of human nature while keeping vigilance against the devils.[22] "Politics will, to the end of history, be an area where conscience and power meet, where the ethical and coercive factors of human life will interpenetrate and work out their tentative and uneasy compromises," he opined. American liberalism, he insisted, "has little understanding of the fact that politics are morally ambiguous even on the highest level."[23]

Although postwar liberal intellectuals were hardly uniform in their thinking and carried very diverse ideological baggage—many were previously associated with the Popular Front, others with the anti-Stalinist left, while some still remained loyal to populist or progressive causes—what they did share was a newly acquired cautious, at times even tragic, perspective about politics that instilled them with a healthy respect for the limitations of what government could do. Since man was flawed, his political, economic, and cultural ambitions must be circumscribed. This realization led Schlesinger to gravitate toward the center, while it led Trilling to occupy the ambiguous realm of the "in-between" and Niebuhr to advocate for an enlightened Christianity. The newfound awareness of limitations also drove economist John Kenneth Galbraith to distinguish between private and public goods in search of "social balance" and sound the alarm against excessive consumption, and caused Daniel Bell to lament the cultural abandonment of restraint in pursuit of material self-fulfillment.[24] This overwhelming concern with equilibrium and restraint transformed postwar liberalism, in the words of historian Kevin Mattson, into an "intellectual balancing act."[25]

The Literature of Liberalism

Updike's work was a literary reflection of just that balancing act: Reared in the postwar liberal climate, his work was infused with these impulses toward balance and equilibrium. Fiction, he insisted, was "a form of truth seeking"—not pamphleteering. "My view is very primitive. I tend to see everything poised between heaven and hell," he said early on in his career. "I guess I hope to show in fiction that goodness and evil are mixed. My instinct is to show the other side—the 'Yes' and 'No' of circumstances, the comic incongruities of life." He would go on to observe that "to be a person, is to be in a situation of tension, is to be in a dialectical situation. A truly adjusted person is not a person at all—just an animal with clothes on or a statistic. So that it's a happy ending, with this 'but' at the end." Updike further admitted that "There's a yes-but quality about my writing, that evades entirely pleasing anybody. It seems to me that critics get increasingly querulous and impatient for madder music and stronger wine, when what we need is a greater respect for reality, its secrecy, its music."[26]

The "yes-but" quality betrays a certain affinity toward "the middle"—Updike's own version of a literary "vital center"—that served him not simply as a literary tool but as a conceptual approach to reality. "My subject is the American Protestant small-town middle class," he told *Life* magazine in 1966. "I like middles. It is in middles that extremes clash, where ambiguity restlessly rules."[27] It is precisely because Updike intuitively always sought to investigate both sides of an issue and naturally gravitated toward the center that led him to admit during an extended interview with the *Paris Review* in 1968 that "my work is meditation, not pontification" and to insist, "I think of my books not as sermons or directives in a war of ideas but as objects, with different shapes and textures and the mysteriousness of anything that exists."[28] When asked in 1971 about his philosophy, Updike tellingly referred readers to "Midpoint," a lengthy autobiographical poem written in 1968 for his upcoming thirty-seventh birthday. In it he wrote:

> Beware false Gods: the Infallible Man,
> The flawless formula, the Five-Year Plan.
> Abjure bandwagons; be shy of machines,
> Charisma, ends that justify the means,
> And oaths that bind the postulate to kill
> His own self-love and independent Will.
> A Mussolini leads to Hitler; hate
> Apostles of the all-inclusive State.
> Half-measures are most human; Compromise,
> Inglorious and gray, placates the Wise.

> By mechanistic hopes is Mankind vexed;
> The Book of Life is margin more than text.

Updike crafted another poem, titled "Washington," that appeared in the same collection of verse as a strange ode to the nation's capital, with a familiar moderating bent:

> Site, for me, of a secret parliament
> of which both sides agreed to
>   concede
> and left the issue suspended in
>   brandy,
> I think of you longingly, as a
>   Yankee
> longs for Lee, sorry to have won,
> or as Ho Chi Minh mourns for
>   Johnson.[29]

Although critics have misinterpreted Updike's perennial centrism, ambiguity, and unwillingness to provide a satisfying resolution to his plots as evidence that he had nothing of substance to say, a more compelling explanation for these misinterpretations can be found by locating his writing within the context of the prevailing liberal imagination.[30] Updike's predisposition for the balance, synthesis, and deep pluralism that enabled him to simultaneously hold opposing literary ideas is consistent with the same liberal tendency that Lionel Trilling, borrowing from the poet John Keats, famously labeled "negative capability." "This negative capability, this willingness to remain in uncertainties, mysteries, and doubts, is not, as one tendency of modern feeling would suppose, an abdication of intellectual activity," Trilling explained in *The Liberal Imagination* (1949), his seminal study of the relationship between politics and literature. "Quite to the contrary, it is precisely an aspect of their intelligence, of their seeing the full force and complexity of their subject matter."[31] Trilling believed that "proper" novels are endowed with a certain vitality and spirit that generates perpetual tension and constantly invites readers to shift positions, interrogate truths, and approach the text from a variety of lenses, each of which provide new and complex ways of seeing problems—though none that resolve them. After sociologist Richard Sennett complained to Trilling that "you have no position" since "you are always in between," the critic responded, "between, is the only honest place to be."³²

Updike agreed. The great lover of "middles" similarly believed that to refuse to take an immutable position was a legitimate position in and of itself. That is why, like Trilling, he lamented the dearth of conservative ideas circulating in literature at the time. "Not that political conservatives should be barred from the halls of fiction; rather, they should be better represented there, to relieve the present rather shrill unanimity on the left," Updike wrote in the early 1970s. Echoing Trilling's famous call in the opening passages of *The Liberal Imagination* for an emboldened conservatism that could challenge liberalism to make it better, Updike, too, apparently wanted to see new ideas from the Right that would break the intellectual conformity, and complacency, pervasive on the left, and spark intellectual renewal. Whereas public intellectuals like Trilling, Schlesinger, Niebuhr, and Hofstadter employed history, literary criticism, theology, and sociology for the constructive purposes of, in the words of Hofstadter, criticizing liberalism "from within," Updike was merely using a more subtle form to achieve a similar goal. "My fiction about the daily doings of ordinary people has more history in it than history books," he once admitted. "I really believe that you can read novels the way you open a window onto another country. I would even say that nothing allows you to go more deeply into a place than a novel does. . . . That is what I am also trying to do: to say what is changing in the United States—through the imagination."³³

From the onset of his career, Updike insisted he was not a political writer. "Unlike Mailer and Bellow, I don't have much itch to pronounce on great matters, to reform the country, to get elected mayor of New York," he said in 1968. "I find it hard to have opinions. Theologically, I favor Karl Barth; politically, I favor the Democrats. But I treasure a remark John Cage made, that not judgingness but openness and curiosity are our proper business." When asked about his politics a few years later, he insisted on the writer's need to retain some "space" from society: "the American writer has never been much into the political system, has always stood apart." Updike claimed, "I think it was Melville who said that writers are 'ironic points of light.'" Decades later he still reasserted this point: "I do not stand for anything. I write fiction, poetry, and literary criticism that seek to describe the world as it is, with its surprises and its paradoxes. Telling the truth is the main, and perhaps the only, social service a writer can perform."³⁴

Rather than betray a failure of political imagination—as some critics suggested—Updike's perpetual ambiguity fueled a moderate imagination that perfectly reflected postwar liberal sensibilities. Whereas leftist writers like Mailer and Vidal followed in the footsteps of an earlier generation of politically aware novelists (such as Upton Sinclair, Theodore Dreiser, and John Steinbeck) and advocated radical and populist messages that challenged power, denigrated capitalism, and promoted revolutionary ideas, Updike never went down that well-tread ideological path.[35] But likewise, he was never quite comfortable with a blind celebration of the institutions of power or the free market as Herman Wouk, Ayn Rand, and John Dos Passos had done (the latter in his later years).[36] Echoing the disenchanted attitudes of many postwar liberal intellectuals, Updike conceded in a 1971 interview with the *Harvard Crimson* that "There may be something also in the novelist's trade which shades you toward conservatism," and explained: "It is my general sense of human institutions that they are outcroppings of human nature, that human nature is slow to change, that in general when you destroy one set of institutions you get . . . something worse."[37]

He imported these beliefs into his own work. In an essay from that highly politicized period, Updike lamented that "the writer as hero" had been replaced by "the writer as educationist" and complained sardonically "how dare one confess that the absence of a swiftly expressible message is, often, *the* message; that reticence is an important a tool to the writer as expression; that the hasty filling out of a questionnaire is not merely irrelevant but *inimical* to the writer's proper activity . . . that what he makes is ideally as ambiguous and opaque as life itself." What mattered most, he suggested, was to engage the readers and get them to think, ponder, even argue—regardless of what the final outcome of that argument would be. "My books are all meant to be moral debates with the reader," Updike revealed, "and if they seem pointless—I'm speaking hopefully—it's because the reader has not been engaged in the debate."[38]

For all of his qualifications, Updike was proud of his liberal credentials. "By European standards, I don't belong to the extreme left, but by American standards I think I do. Every election I have voted for a Democratic president," he once remarked. Having dubbed himself in his youth "a democratic baby who developed an intense fondness for Harry S. Truman, the most limited man who ever achieved greatness," Updike's dedication to the party of Roosevelt and its institutions was instilled in him through his growing up poor in rural Pennsylvania during the Great Depression.[39] "We were Democrats. My grandfather lived for ninety years, and always voted, and always voted straight Democrat," he recalled. "My parents are closer to me. The events that shaped their views are in my bones. At the time when I was conceived and born, they felt in themselves a whole nation stunned, frightened, despairing. With Roosevelt, hope returned." Since both his father and grandfather worked periodically on Works Progress Association crews around Shillington to make ends meet during the Depression, Updike remained a loyal New Dealer throughout his life and even enthusiastically supported Barack Obama's presidency in 2008.[40]

A New York Intellectual from Shillington

The literary historian David Daiches observed that "the perfect New York intellectual" was "intelligent, curious, humane, well read, interested in ideas, fascinated by other times and places, [and] immensely knowledgeable about European culture."[41] Updike was not Jewish—as many, though not all, of the midcentury New York intellectuals had been—nor did he live in (or love) New York that much. And yet, he met these criteria quite well: his prolific literary criticism covered a huge breadth of material and displayed an unwavering interest, curiosity, and depth of knowledge about a plethora of fields ranging from history, culture, politics, and religion to sports, psychology, and science. Philip Roth captured his colleague's seemingly boundless intellectual horizons when he jokingly complained that Updike "knows so much, about golf, about porn, about kids, about America. I don't know anything about anything.... I'm going to give up writing."[42] It is this quality that distinguished Updike from many of his contemporaries and transformed his fiction into an ideal vehicle for understanding postwar political thought: Not only was Updike not detached from politics and history, as many writers of his generation had been, but he was incredibly insightful and curious of both.[43]

These inclinations led him to gravitate toward the social milieu of New York intellectuals after moving to New York City in the mid-1950s. Ever since Updike was eleven, when his family received a subscription to the *New Yorker* as a Christmas gift from his paternal aunt Mary (who had been the secretary of famed literary critic Edmund Wilson), he was fixated on the magazine and determined to make his way into its pages (first as a cartoonist, then as a writer). In 1955 he realized his dream: not only was he hired to write for the Talk of the Town section, which he continued to do for nearly two years, but he also began a fruitful relationship as a creative writer and critic with the magazine, which, over the next five decades, published hundreds of his short stories, poems, and essays.[44]

Updike's involvement with the *New Yorker* coincided with its transformation from a middlebrow to a highbrow journal of ideas when it began to compete with the *Partisan Review* and *Commentary* by bringing notable thinkers such as Dwight Macdonald, Mary McCarthy, Harold Rosenberg, and Hannah Arendt into its ranks. As conservative pundit Midge Decter put it: "*Partisan Review* was getting to be like a farm team" for the *New Yorker*. That Updike began his lifelong affair with the *New Yorker* just as it was acquiring a vocal political conscience is indicative of his emerging persona as a public intellectual as well. "*New Yorker* contributors assumed the posture of watchdogs of liberty, snapping at those who threatened America's democratic institutions," Mary F. Corey wrote in her study of the magazine. "The *New Yorker* stepped into the ideological vacuum created by the death of the president [Franklin Roosevelt] and the decline of the Left and proved its mettle as a guide through the shifting values of the postwar political world."[45]

Although Updike remained committed to the *New Yorker*, which usually got first dibs on his work for the rest of his career, his careful choices of where else to publish possibly reveal a certain caution toward excessive ideology on any side of the political spectrum. Alongside the *New Yorker*, he mostly published in mainstream journals like *Atlantic Monthly*, *Esquire*, and the *New Republic*. Interestingly enough, he declined solicitations to write for the British journal *Encounter* in 1964 and for *Partisan Review* in 1972 (despite being personally invited to do so by the founding editors of both magazines, Melvin Lasky and William Phillips, respectively). Although no explanation for his decision could be found, it's worth recalling that *Encounter*, cofounded by the so-called godfather of neoconservatism, Irving Kristol, had been covertly funded by the CIA through the Congress for Cultural Freedom during this period, while *Partisan Review* was still notable for its radical voice.[46] One journal Updike tellingly disliked, at least during the heated political climate of the late 1960s and early 1970s, was the *New York Review of Books* (*NYRB*), associated with the New Left at the time. As he told the *Harvard Crimson*,

> I do take people who run the *New York Review of Books* seriously. I find that their contempt for the democratic system is so pervasive and profound as to be death-dealing and menacing, really. It expresses this everywhere, from the drawings up to the feelings that anybody who has power, who actually tries to make decisions involving the whole society, is *ergo* corrupt or insane. You get a kind of Calvinist sense of damnation connected with running the machinery. The machinery is going to be there, in any case—you can't revolutionize social machinery. It's a kind of wariness, a kind of unpleasability; a hopeless miasma arises from those pages.[47]

Getting a couple of bad reviews was apparently not what distanced Updike from the *NYRB* during these years; after all, he would go on to publish in right-wing magazines like the *National Review* and *Commentary*, which had also given him particularly caustic reviews. That Updike, the self-avowed liberal, eventually chose *Commentary* to publish his famous piece "On Not Being a Dove" (1989), in which he explained his controversial stance on the Vietnam War nearly two decades after it ended, is indicative of the broader shifts of the political center and the transformation undergone by American liberalism since the 1960s.[48]

Updike may not have been Jewish, but the *New Yorker* certainly provided him with the ticket into the vibrant world of ideas dominated by New York intellectuals, the famed group of (mostly Jewish) writers, scholars, and critics who wrote for a handful of polemical magazines from the 1930s to the 1960s and redefined American politics and culture.[49] His choice to model Henry Bech, the protagonist of his three-part eponymous short story collection on a middle-aged Jewish novelist from New York who admittedly reflected a composite of Bellow, Mailer, Roth, and Malamud was indicative of just how drawn he had been to the Jewish world of ideas (as several critics observed, Bech became Updike's "alter ego," a "soul mate in disguise").[50]

Although his decision to leave Manhattan in 1957 and relocate his family to coastal Massachusetts may have taken him out of New York, where he never quite felt at ease, it did not remove him from the intellectual orbit of ideas it hosted.[51] Updike's ascendance at the *New Yorker* helped him cultivate personal ties to leading intellectuals, and long after leaving Manhattan he remained a permanent fixture in its vibrant intellectual scene: the *Partisan Review* and *Commentary* regularly reviewed his work; notable critics like Norman Podhoretz, Alfred Kazin, and Cynthia Ozick wrote about him; and he was read, discussed, and admired by influential thinkers such as Macdonald, Lasch, Moynihan, and Schlesinger (whom he befriended while serving as chancellor of the American Academy and Institute of Arts and Letters in the 1980s).[52] McCarthy, a fellow New Yorker writer, was admittedly a fan of his work:

> I've not quite finished *Rabbit, Run*—I must get it back from the person I lent it to and finish it. I thought it was very good, and so stupidly reviewed. I'd read *Poorhouse Fair*, which I thought was really remarkable. Perhaps it suffered from the point-of-view problem, the whole virtuosity of doing it through the eyes of this old man sitting on the verandah of the poorhouse, through his eyes with their refraction, very old eyes, and so on. I think, in a way, this trick prevents him saying a good deal in the book. Nevertheless, it's quite a remarkable book. But anyway, I nearly didn't read *Rabbit, Run* because I thought, Oh my God! from reading those reviews. The reviewers seemed to be under the impression that the hero was a terrible character. It's incredible! No, I think it's the most interesting American novel I've read in quite a long time.[53]

An interesting exchange between the young Updike and the older Macdonald reveals how seriously Updike had taken ideas from the earliest stages of his career. Updike's review of Macdonald's book *Parodies: An Anthology from Chaucer to Beerbohm—and After*, his first book review for the *New Yorker*, published in 1960, caught the attention of the intellectual giant. The essay, full of accolades—"The editor should be praised"; "Macdonald is rather *too* ingenious"—attributes the decline of humor to "a symptom" of the Cold War, and concludes with a strange soliloquy that mourns the waning role of humor as a source of social criticism. "Insofar as 'serious' literature is indeed exclusively serious, then humor, as in the Victorian age, has a duty, in the Parliament of Man, to act as the loyal opposition," Updike wrote. Having been fully integrated into fiction, he felt that humor had become "merely trivial, merely recreational, merely distracting. . . . In the constant humorist there is a detachment and dandyism of the spirit."[54]

Macdonald quickly responded with a two-page typed letter sent to his young colleague to convey appreciation for the review, which he considered to be "certainly the most interesting, to me, that has appeared." After meticulously, and respectfully, recounting some mild points of disagreement with Updike, Macdonald questioned his position on humor and advocated for its importance in contemporary society. "Whatever does this mean that humor is now 'merely . . . recreational . . . distracting'?" he asked. "I don't understand your notion of humor being less needed. . . . What's wrong with the trivial, recreational, distraction? And with detachment and dandyism also?" Note the irony: it is Macdonald, the veteran political writer, who had been an editor of the *Partisan Review* and the founding editor of the magazine *Politics*, who must remind Updike, the novelist, that "one doesn't enjoy humor, or art, because it's important, useful, and concentrating . . . but just because it's pleasurable in and for itself." He continued by remarking, "I'm sure you agree with these truisms. Yet you seem to be saying the opposite," and concluded by commending the recently released *Rabbit, Run* as "an extraordinary performance" and inviting Updike to visit him in his office at the *New Yorker*. After initially replying with a laconic postcard that irritated Macdonald (who later admitted to being "a little miffed" by it), Updike apologized in a lengthy letter with intent to repair Macdonald's opinion of him. It did, and the bond between them was sealed, not simply as colleagues but as fellow intellectuals who believed the worlds of literature and politics were never far apart.[55]

Updike's relationship with Arthur M. Schlesinger Jr. was different. Although he never studied with the famed historian while both were at Harvard in the 1950s, Updike likely encountered his influential ideas through his roommate and friend, Christopher Lasch, a history major who admired Schlesinger's work.[56] Updike and Schlesinger eventually forged an intellectual friendship through their shared affinity for history. In 1974 Schlesinger wrote a favorable review of Updike's only play, *Buchanan Dying* (mostly ignored by critics), that described the last days of President James Buchanan. Written as a tribute to Pennsylvania's sole representative in the White House, it depicted Buchanan as a self-tormented figure obsessing over his fateful days in office and his failure to prevent the Civil War. Although Schlesinger questioned Updike's portrayal of Buchanan as a tragic hero and found his narrative "confused" given the suggestion that conciliation was possible on the question of slavery ("For was not the source of Buchanan's anguish," Schlesinger asked, "his compulsion to see the problems of the South through one eye and the problems of the North through another, his ineradicable relativity in an age of truculent absolutes?"), he still went on to laud Updike's creative use of literature as a means to enrich historical understanding.[57]

After Updike became president of the American Academy and Institute of Arts and Letters (1987–1990), the two formed a cordial relationship. In a set of sporadic correspondences (1991–2002) they shared a mutual admiration for history and commented on each other's work. As editor of the academy's official history, commissioned for its centennial anniversary in 1998, Updike invited Schlesinger to write the chapter about its struggle with modernism (1928–1937), titled "The Infiltration of Modernity." Schlesinger chronicled the failure of conservatives like Robert Underwood Johnson and Henry Adams to prevent the new literary voices of F. Scott Fitzgerald, Eugene O'Neil, Edith Wharton, and Sinclair Lewis (among others) from gaining membership. "The winds of modernism had shaken—and shaken up—the Academy and Institute," Schlesinger wrote. "A diverting chapter in American literary politics had resulted in fatal setbacks to ancient regime." Updike wrote the proceeding chapter, which covered the years 1938–1947, about the outcome of the struggle and subsequent democratization of American culture. "One can build a mansion for art to come and dwell in, only to have it flourish out by the alley," he concluded.[58]

Having worked together on the academy's history, the two men formed a mutual respect and admiration for one another that flourished. Schlesinger commended Updike's second attempt at using fiction to engage the Civil War in *Memories of the Ford Administration* ("I like your perceptive comments on history") and called it a "brilliant and delightful book." Updike, in turn, praised Schlesinger as "the preeminent historian of our friendly institution." In one exchange, Updike responded to a Schlesinger jab at liberalism by noting, "liberal anguish: a great title for a book. Why are liberals so anguished, in their tolerance and, yes, complacency? Only in America."[59] Quite tellingly, Updike's own historical observations impacted the famed historian: Schlesinger credits Updike in his journals with aptly describing the 1960s as that "slum of a decade" and refers to them as "the decade of the murder of hope."[60]

The Art of Criticism

Given that Updike's initial ambition was to become a cartoonist rather than a writer, it's not surprising that he drew political cartoons just as his writing career was launching: between 1958 and 1960 he published over a half dozen cartoons about current events in his local newspaper in

Massachusetts, the *Amesbury Daily News*. In these cartoons, Updike began to directly engage a wide variety of political issues with acerbity and wit that convey a clear interest and depth of knowledge about international affairs and domestic politics. Among other things, he commented upon America's confused policies in the Middle East, submarine warfare with the Soviets, the standoff with China over Taiwan, and rising tensions in West Berlin and the threat of nuclear war, as well as on presidential elections and the quiz show scandal. In a cartoon titled "The Dragon's Mouth" from September 1958, Updike sketched China's topography in the form of a dragon, with Chiang Kai-shek pushing a reluctant President Eisenhower toward the disputed Taiwanese-controlled island of Quemoy (about to be consumed within the dragon's mouth) and telling him: "Just stick your head right in there! C'mon!" In this cartoon, Updike seemed to be warning against the consequences of succumbing to the increasing pressures to intervene in the ongoing Taiwan Strait crisis. In another cartoon from 1960, he turned his attention to domestic affairs and sketched Nixon and Kennedy as toddlers in an effort to question their suitability for the presidency. In the background, Dwight Eisenhower and Lyndon Johnson are portrayed as the responsible adults, with the caption below the presidential candidates reading: "Now how do we get rid of these nursemaids?" Beyond the playful satire, the wide range of issues addressed in Updike's cartoons suggests that timely political questions weighed heavily on his mind.[61]

His political cartooning may have been short-lived, but Updike, like many New York intellectuals, mastered another form: literary and cultural criticism. "A book, in the view of the New York Intellectuals, was a social text, whether it was a novel or a nonfiction account," wrote historian Neil Jumonville.[62] And indeed, Updike's parallel career as a prolific critic suggests that he too took nonfiction writing as seriously as fiction—and was in turn taken seriously by other critics. William H. Pritchard observed that while Updike was an "indefatigable reviewer," his criticism often had an "unwillingness to claim much for itself" and projected a "professedly casual air."[63] Updike certainly reinforced this image by saying that "writing criticism is to writing fiction and poetry as hugging the shore is to sailing in the open sea," choosing for his mammoth collections of essays such cavalier titles as *Picked-Up Pieces* and *Odd Jobs* and scoffing that book reviews were a good way to cover his monthly alimony payments.[64]

But even when sailing close to shore, he had depth. The plethora of book reviews Updike produced throughout the years suggests that he engaged many social and political debates from afar, making use of the outsider perspective of the critic rather than the insider one of the advocate or ideologue. Despite the rather blasé attitude that, at times, Updike exhibited toward the task of literary criticism, he recognized that book reviews "perform a clear and desired social service" and that, given a certain "decline" in literary form, there was an obligation to be "investing fiction with seriousness" through criticism. "An artist mediates between the world and minds," he noted, "a critic merely between minds."[65] Updike was equally adept at carrying out both tasks: many of the book reviews he published during the highly politicized late 1960s and early 1970s, collected in *Picked-Up Pieces*, reflect a concerted effort to employ criticism in the fashion of the New York intellectuals to address ongoing political debates. But there was one important difference with many of the ideological critics at the time: rather than use his own voice to prescribe political solutions, Updike employed the critic's detachment to mask his own attitude toward a variety of contentious matters.

In a review of a 1971 edition of Dostoevsky's *The Adolescent*, Updike questioned the unlikely decision of the translator, Andrew MacAndrew, to reissue one of the Russian novelist's rather obscure works. But the resemblance he found between revolutionary Russia in the late nineteenth century and the revolutionary impulses of contemporary America made the novel seem quite apropos. "Why this novel?" Updike pondered. "Perhaps . . . [MacAndrew] felt it to be especially appropriate to America's present condition of self-doubt and generational estrangement." In order to highlight the similarities he located between his America and Dostoevsky's Russia, Updike went on to quote from the novel at length: "Selfishness displaces the old unifying principle, and the whole system breaks up into a multitude of individuals, each with a full set of civil rights. . . . Whole batches of our best people are tearing themselves away from it and lightheartedly joining the roving packs of the disorderly and the envious." Updike continued: "Sound familiar? Yes, but I doubt that a majority of Americans will embrace Dostoevsky's solution: 'any order as long as it is our native one.'"[66] It is important to recall that Updike's growing concern about social solidarity, and the disintegration of the public sphere in the wake of an inward shift toward self-fulfillment and private consumption echoed the fears of many social critics and scholars at the time (among them Lasch, his old college roommate and lifelong friend) and directly influenced his decision to write the novel *Couples*, published in 1968.[67] Looking back at this turbulent period, he told the *New Edinburgh Review* in 1983: "We had become detached from the national life. Our private lives had become the real concern. There was a monstrous inflation of the private life as against the merged life of the society which struck me and helped me think I should write the book [*Couples*]."[68]

His caustic review of *Dance the Eagle to Sleep* (1970) by Marge Piercy probably betrays more than anything the distaste his postwar liberal sensibilities found in the New Left's ideological literary representations. The review offers a prime example of how Updike's subtle literary criticism served as a vehicle for complex political analysis by merging form and content and using the former to investigate the latter. Calling it "an anti-utopian novel," a "*Lord of the Flies* with girls on the island," Updike lambasted Piercy's cursory engagement with political questions in a novel that he claimed "resorts to a hurried sociological tone, makes people talk like press handouts, and declines to linger upon sensual details."[69] The review offers us a rare glimpse of how Updike's literary criticism consciously transcended stylistic concerns in order to engage their political implications:

> *Dance the Eagle to Sleep* fails as a novel of ideas because "the system" is never allowed to have a cogent, let alone persuasive, spokesman. The policemen are uniformly faceless and brutal, the schoolteachers are all "frustrated, embittered lumps." . . . Anything genial in middle-class life is dismissed as "co-optative softness." Fascinating suggestions pass unchallenged: research scientists have no alternative to participation in nerve-gas projects, Che and Mao will deliver us from toilet training, all people over twenty-five hate all people under twenty-five because television commercials present youthful beauty as an ideal. The actions of the government, as it blitzkriegs the movement into smithereens, pretend to no rationale beyond the author's desire to allegorize the Vietnam war. . . . No mitigating circumstances are allowed in the Piercy condemnation—no historical causality, no suspicion that the system is a self-admittedly imperfect patchwork of changeable human devices, no comparison with other systems, living or dead.[70]

Updike did not defend or endorse "the system" being attacked by Piercy's protagonists, but merely sought to understand it. His main criticism was accordingly rooted in the claim regarding the novel's superficial engagement with complex political ideas, its lack of introspection, and shallow revolutionary dogmas—rather than with the essence of those dogmas. That which was presented as a formal failure possibly masks what Updike may have considered to be a grave political one: behind a literary form that develops only radical characters, voices only their particular ideals, and pays attention only to their radical actions lies an ideological dogmatism that was anathema to Updike's liberal, pluralist, and staunchly anti-ideological sensibility, which prized debate, contradiction, and dialectics above all.

By using formal aspects to help flush out more substantial ones, Updike was able to employ the review to advance a not very implicit critique of the New Left, which at the time was seriously challenging the legitimacy of New Deal liberalism and offering a clear path to replace it.[71] At one point he compared a naïve statement by Marcus, one of the black characters in the novel, who says "We thought guns made us real, but it was people, and we didn't have them," to a similar statement made by Bernardine Dohrn of the Weather Underground, and asserted: "The delusion that better communication would win 'the people' seems shared by the author; her novel leaves us with the impression that the [Weather Underground] movement's only fault was not being strong enough." Updike concluded by questioning the merits of the youthful revolutionaries whose voices Piercy amplifies: "Just as the old novels etched the tragedies of private persons within the gray revolution of industry and technology, new ones may trace the personal liabilities of the anti-Establishment Establishment."[72] It would take another twenty years for Updike to evolve from implicitly attacking the New Left through his criticism to directly airing his grievances with them in his essay "On Not Being a Dove."

Cold Warrior

Given Updike's close ties to liberal intellectuals, it should not be surprising that he was committed to their central cause: anticommunism. Even though he lacked the zeal of such disenchanted ex-leftists like Bell, Niebuhr, and Trilling, Updike had been a good-natured cold warrior at heart: he participated in numerous State Department cultural exchanges and PR delegations that took him for months at a time behind the Iron Curtain and to leftist hotspots in Africa and Latin America (Updike considered this his "small patriotic service, a wearing abroad, at last, my country's colors"). These trips in turn fueled his literary imagination and provided material for his novels *The Coup, Brazil,* and the Bech series. In *Rabbit at Rest* (1990), the final installment of the Rabbit tetralogy, the chief protagonist Harry "Rabbit" Angstrom remarks, "without the Cold War, what's the point of being an American?" and goes on to assert "that all in all this is the happiest fucking country the world has ever seen."[73] Albeit more sobered and self-aware, Updike felt the same way and was deeply shaped by the ideological struggle between superpowers. In addition to participating in myriad cultural affairs during the Cold War, he was involved with Americans for Democratic Action—the foremost liberal anticommunist organization, which counted Schlesinger, Niebuhr, and Galbraith among its founding members. He sat on the advisory board of the Andrei Sakharov Defense Campaign (alongside Schlesinger, Arthur Miller, and Saul Bellow), which was dedicated to securing the release of the famed Soviet dissident and human rights activist. In 1980, Updike was even invited by Midge Decter (by then the wife of *Commentary*'s editor Norman Podhoretz) to join the Committee for the Free World, a think tank founded "in defense of western values." Among its members were prominent neoconservatives like Podhoretz, Bellow, Kristol, Hilton Kramer, and Ambassador Jean Kirkpatrick.[74]

Updike's anticommunism was rooted in somewhat of an old-fashioned, seemingly even naïve, form of patriotism. Emanating from the national "conversation of consensus" that emerged in the postwar era in response to the burgeoning Cold War, it redefined the American experience as exceptional, even messianic.[75] After once hosting a delegation of Soviet authors with Arthur Miller, Updike recalled in his memoirs the playwright telling him, "Jesus, don't they make you glad you're an American?" To which Updike thought: "I was glad, and resented having my native land, with its treasure of natural resources and enlightened institutions and hopeful immigrant peoples, being described as Amerika." Updike's response, somewhat oblivious to the challenges African Americans or women were experiencing at the time, nevertheless reflects a broader sentiment pervasive among postwar liberal intellectuals who refused to denounce their loyalty or rescind their unequivocal support for the United States *despite* its evident flaws. "I'm a product of nearly forty years of Cold War," Updike claimed in a retrospective interview he gave in 1987. "I was one of those people who was brought up to believe, and saw no reason to doubt, that this was the greatest country in the world."[76]

Yet far from being unaware of America's tainted past, Updike's patriotism was tempered by a keen historical awareness of the nation's flaws, as he revealed, indirectly, through a mock interview with his own literary alter-ego Henry Bech:

> Would he [Updike] describe himself, I asked, switching the tape recorder up to fortissimo, as (a) pro-American, (b) a conservative? His turtleish green eyes blinked, recognizing that his shell was being tickled, and that there was no way out but forward. He said he was pro-American in the sense that he was married to America and did not wish a divorce. That the American style and landscape and impetus were, by predetermination, his meat. . . . That, in answer to the second prong of my probe, there were some things he thought worth conserving, such as the electoral college and the Great Lakes; but that by registration he was Democrat and by disposition an apologist for the spirit of anarchy—our animal or divine margin of resistance to the social contract. That, given the need for a contract, he preferred the American Constitution, with its 18th century bow to the pursuit of individual happiness, to any of the totalisms presently running around rabid. That the decisions of any establishment, though properly suspect and frightfully hedged by self-interest and the myopia power brings, must be understood as choices among imperfect alternatives; power participates in the weight and guilt of the world and shrill impotence never has to cash in its chips.[77]

Updike never overlooked the flaws in the system and, as noted in the following chapters, often used his fiction to address the disturbing economic disparities, social conformity, and racism that plagued his native land. But he also believed that, as his most famous protagonist, Harry Angstrom, tells the black revolutionary character Skeeter in *Rabbit Redux*, rejecting the American model for its faults is tantamount to "throwing out the baby with the bathwater." "I think we were founded as a utopia, and that's always in our minds—that we're falling short of being a utopia," Updike opined in a 1990 interview with the British broadcaster Melvyn Bragg.

> It's one of the things that makes American self-criticism so savage and relentless, and I guess it controls the tone of American fiction, to a degree. That is, we're extra hard on ourselves. But it gives a kind of point and a bite to American fiction, also—this feeling that we should be better, that there should be paradise of a kind, and why isn't it? Why is it full of junk? Why is it full of cruelty?[78]

Rereading Updike's patriotic accolades, one can understand why critics on the left accused liberal intellectuals of selling out in the 1950s and 1960s. Even if Updike did not do so knowingly, or willingly, his reverence for America was indeed reflective of this wider postwar embrace by liberals like Schlesinger, Trilling, and Bell, who came to terms with many of the political and economic ideas and institutions that a few years earlier they found anathema. Lamenting what he called "the age of conformity," the literary critic Irving Howe castigated liberal intellectuals for being co-opted—and effectively silenced—by the new consumer-oriented, corporate-dominated political economy. "What has actually been taking place is the absorption of large numbers of intellectuals, previously independent, into the world of government bureaucracy and public committees; into the constantly growing industries of pseudo culture," he claimed. The moment they became "absorbed into the accredited institutions of society," Howe declared, they "cease to function as intellectuals."[79]

But Updike would not have seen it that way. Strangely enough, in 1953 the *Harvard Crimson*, which Updike regularly read as a student (1950–1954), published a review dealing with Howe's critique. In it, R. E. Oldenburg, a classmate from Updike's graduating class, offered an ambivalent verdict on the question of intellectual conformity: "Essential to creative activity is freedom to criticize without fear, the right to love one aspect of America and to loath another." His sobered and nuanced account concedes the danger in "uncritical affirmation of American society," yet commensurately recognizes that such a disposition does not necessarily require its total rejection.[80] Whether or not Updike read the article, it seems like he would have embraced its ambiguous conclusion; one can love America but still disagree with some of what it does.

Conclusion

For Updike, the system may have been flawed—but it still worked. The sociologist Daniel Bell recalled that what united New York intellectuals was that "almost all these individuals come out of themselves."[81] The fact that Updike, like most of the second-generation Jewish immigrants who made up the postwar intellectual community, pulled himself up from his bootstraps, quite literally, was proof in his eyes that there was much to defend, even cherish, in America. He recalled this with great satisfaction in his memoirs:

> By my mid-thirties, through diligence and daring, I had arrived at a lifestyle we might call genteel bohemian: nice old house (broad floorboards, big fireplaces) rather diffidently furnished . . . four dusty but healthy children with Sunday bests at the backs of their closets, two cars, one of them a convertible, and, for dinner, lots of rice casseroles and California wine. To me, this was prosperity. Out of those shadows of debt and financial reversal that had darkened the Shillington house I had emerged into a kind of sunlight.[82]

If the poor Shillington boy could earn generous scholarships to Harvard and then Oxford and achieve fame and fortune as a writer by his own merit and hard work, then, in his eyes at least, there was no reason to doubt the fundamental soundness of the institutions of American society, let alone seek to overthrow them. They could be mended, and therefore should be preserved.

It was the threat to an imperfect system that had fulfilled it promises, at least to him, that fueled Updike's resentment toward the revolutionary politics of the antiwar movement in the 1960s (he carried in his wallet, "like a fortune-cookie slip," a reminder of this in the form of a statement by the Weather Underground that read "We are against everything that's good and decent in honky America. We will loot, burn, and destroy"). As Updike later confided: "Defending the war (or, rather, disputing the attackers of it) was perhaps my way of serving, of showing loyalty to a country that had kept its hackneyed promises—life, liberty, pursuit of happiness—to me."[83] To him. But not necessarily to all Americans. Although the postwar liberal mindset had, unlike previous generations of liberals, made its peace with and even embraced the institutions of political and economic power in pursuit of compromise and consensus, in doing so it unintentionally created moral blind spots to race, gender, and religion that would prove hazardous down the road to the survival of New Deal liberalism.

2 | The Liberal Education of John Updike

The possible Is but a suburb, Harvard, of your city.

—John Updike

In the fall of 1950, John Updike entered Harvard College as a freshman. Eager to study illustration and writing, he gave up a generous scholarship from Cornell for the chance to attend Harvard and contribute to the *Harvard Lampoon* (especially since he was still bent on becoming a cartoonist at that time). His mother, Linda, who was convinced that Harvard would improve his chances of becoming a successful writer, encouraged him to set his sights toward Cambridge.[1] Four years later, in the spring of 1954, Updike's decision seemed to have paid off: he graduated summa cum laude and Phi Beta Kappa, majoring in English, with a Knox fellowship to study drawing at Oxford the following year. Maybe more importantly, Updike produced there a copious collection of verse and prose (including fiction and essays) that were the seeds for what would blossom into a prolific literary career. Harvard also did something else for Updike: It helped make him a self-aware political thinker—and a liberal one at that—who engaged politics in a serious and critical manner through the less-travelled road of literary fiction. If Updike was, indeed, a product of the postwar liberal mindset, it was at Harvard in the early 1950s that these intellectual bonds were forged. Any investigation into his emerging political imagination and the fate of New Deal liberalism must, therefore, begin there.

In many ways Harvard fulfilled the basic pedagogical requirement that any liberal arts education is tasked with: it instilled in Updike new ideas and the ability to think about them in a critical and creative manner. As Jack De Bellis observed, "Harvard was the place where Updike learned how to learn."[2] Updike himself admitted this much in a retrospective essay thirty years after graduating. "I had a lot to learn when I came to Harvard, which was fortunate, since Harvard had a lot to teach," he wrote. "But I loved, strange to say, taking courses."[3] In a 1968 interview he explained the ambivalent feelings he retained toward his alma mater: "My time at Harvard, once I got by the compression bends of the freshman year, was idyllic enough, and as they say, successful; but I felt toward those years, while they were happening, the resentment a caterpillar must feel while his somatic cells are shifting all around to make him a butterfly."[4] Not only had Harvard rigorously trained him in the competencies of English literature and writing, but his experiences there implanted in him new cosmopolitan values and exposed him to an attractive Brahmin culture and its matching set of urbane tastes and sensibilities. In doing so, Harvard permitted the modest and poor—though ambitious and talented—Updike to shed his rural upbringing, which he had long outgrown, and pursue a grander destiny that he and his mother had always felt awaited him.[5] Although at times he found it dull and tiresome, Harvard had proven challenging and enlightening. "Four years was enough Harvard," he would later write. "I still had a lot to learn, but had been given the liberating notion that now I could teach myself."[6]

Recent scholarship has turned the focus back from his career as an established author to Updike's youth and adolescence in search of the forces that initially shaped his writing. Jack De Bellis's study of Updike's precollege years led him to conclude that Updike's high school experience had been "the crucible in which he forged his consciousness" and bred the "world of his creative imagination." In an account of Updike's relationship with his college roommate, the historian Christopher Lasch, Jeffrey Ludwig shined a much needed light on the impact of this unique friendship on their later works. Adam Begley's biography further delves into this underexplored period in Updike's life to better understand its influence on his writing.[7] This chapter offers the first in-depth study of Updike's college years by reconstructing his intellectual christening at Harvard. My purpose is to demonstrate how his liberal education helped him foster a deep form of pluralism with particularly fine-tuned sensibilities for introspection and ambiguity that intuitively sought equilibrium and compromise. Put simply: I wish to suggest that it was at Harvard that Updike discovered the postwar liberal mindset and developed the moderate imagination.

The Atmosphere

By the fall of 1950, when Updike began his freshman semester, Harvard was a very different place than it had been prior to the trials of depression and war. The meritocratic reforms initiated there in the 1930s and boosted by the GI Bill unleashed a "demographic overhaul" that transformed Harvard after World War II by nearly doubling prewar enrollment numbers and enabling someone like Updike, who was in possession of supreme talent though inadequate resources, to attend.[8] "The old Harvard of clubmen, gentleman's C's and acute social stratification was fading away," recalled Arthur M. Schlesinger Jr., who had been both a student and faculty member there during Updike's time. "The invasion of middle westerners, public school graduates and the newer immigrants, I contended, was destroying the homogeneity that had spawned the old-style Harvard man."[9]

Given the postwar equalization of opportunity that was removing relatively entrenched class barriers, it is understandable that the spirit of liberalism was triumphant on campus in those years. In their study of Harvard's postwar political climate, sociologists Seymour Martin Lipset and David Riesman observed that "In general, Harvard students stood out as the most liberal of all on social and political matters" and concluded that Harvard in the 1950s was pervaded by a "pattern of greater liberalism."[10] A series of polls reinforced this conclusion: a majority of students identified as "moderate liberal" and about two-thirds believed that America's two-party system was "satisfactory on the whole and should be essentially retained." So content had Harvard students appeared to be that Chris Niebuhr, the son of Reinhold Niebuhr, who was a student there at the time, tellingly admitted: "In a way, liberalism today is conservative. You talk about conservation of cultural values. I'm for that. But what are the values you want to conserve? Liberal values. The thing is that liberalism has won, and that has a tendency to make us conservative."[11]

This watershed moment, in which a self-assured, postwar liberalism became as interested in conserving its recent accomplishments as it was in advancing new ones, was captured in the tender balancing act of the general education (gen. ed.) reforms. Concerned by an increasingly apathetic, disengaged, and fragmented society that was seemingly driven by careerism and bifurcated along ethnic, socioeconomic, and geographic lines, the Harvard administration under President James Bryant Conant sought to enact a new core curriculum that would establish among students a "coherent national culture" in the wake of World War II. The result was the seminal *Redbook Report* of the Harvard Committee for General Education in a Free Society (1945) that laid out a new curriculum tasked with instilling in students a broader sense of citizenship and responsibility. What the committee ultimately attempted to determine, as one study put it, was "what the war was all about and what curricular legacy it might bequeath to postwar higher education."[12]

The literary historian Kenneth S. Lynn, who experienced these changes firsthand as an undergraduate at Harvard, claimed that sweeping gen. ed. reforms were guided by "cultural concerns" about the fate of an increasingly modernized and secularized American society. In his eyes, they resulted from the understanding "that our involvement in a major world war necessitated a new investigation by educators into the meaning of American democracy."[13] Overshadowing the pedagogical aims of the gen. ed. reforms was a more tacit patriotic-nationalistic realization that if the United States was going to prevail in the Cold War—especially under the mounting geopolitical, economic, and ideological challenges it was facing from communism—future generations of Americans must be equipped with democratic and humanistic values as well as with professional and technical skills.

This helps explain why the reformed gen. ed. curriculum sought to reintroduce religion into the undergraduate program in an effort to instill in students a sense of "shared values." As the historian Eric Miller observed in his biography of Christopher Lasch, Lasch's years at Harvard "coincided with the college's most intensive period of experimentation with a new, liberal arts–driven curriculum" that was pervaded by "the sense that the religious heritage of the West should not be neglected and could actually be appropriated for salutary ends."[14] To some, the gen. ed. reforms appeared so retrograde, even reactionary, that according to Lynn, they "merely echoed ideas and appropriated the imagery of Henry Adams's *Education*."[15]

In truth, the reforms seem far from it. Mostly an amalgam of politically liberal and culturally conservative values, the new curriculum reflected, as the young Niebuhr recognized, what essentially amounted to a conservative institutionalization of liberal ideas. As one key passage from the *Redbook Report* reads:

> It [the overall logic] is evidently to be looked for in the character of American society, a society not wholly of the new world since it came from the old, not wholly given to innovation since it acknowledges certain fixed beliefs, not even wholly a law unto itself since there are principles above the state. This logic must further embody certain intangibles of the American spirit, in particular, perhaps, the ideal of co-operation on the level of action irrespective of agreement on ultimates—which is to say, belief in the worth and meaning of the human spirit, however one may understand it.[16]

The *Redbook* recommendations, as Richard Smith argued in his history of Harvard, essentially represented "a conservative response to radical demands" that sought to satisfy both sides.[17]

The renowned British political philosopher Isaiah Berlin, who taught at Harvard while Updike was there (and whom Updike read as a student), helps shed some light on this particular pluralist bent pervasive in Harvard at the time. In highlighting the difference between democracy and communism, Berlin argued that liberal democrats "desire a necessarily precarious balance between incompatible ideals based on the recognition of the equal or nearly equal validity of human aspirations as such, none of which must be subordinated to any single uncriticisable single principle." Totalitarian ideology, on the other hand, "denies that different ideals of life, not necessarily altogether reconcilable with each other, are equally valid and equally worthy."[18] It is precisely within this pluralist vision Berlin laid forth that we can locate the seeds of Updike's famous "yes-but" quality and the budding liberal pluralism that it reflected: liberal in its uncompromising belief in the autonomous propensities of individuals to formulate their own opinions and make their own choices; pluralist because, in its recognition of the intrinsic value of each individual, it concedes a permanent dissemblance among people that precludes a final reconciliation between competing views or the ability to necessarily reach a resolution on every issue.

As part of the gen. ed. reforms, gradually instituted in the late 1940s and implemented fully in the fall of 1950, just as Updike entered college, incoming students were required to take two yearlong elective courses during their freshman and sophomore years from the new gen. ed. program, which included the humanities, social sciences, and natural sciences. The gen. ed. courses, as the Harvard course catalog explained, "are directed not towards preparations in a particular field or vocation, but towards education for life as a responsible human being and citizen, towards the cultivation of [a] sense of values, and an understanding of the interrelationships among the various fields of learning and the inevitable dependence of any one field upon many others." The underlining goal was clearly established: "the development of clear thinking, and an understanding of the physical and social world in which we live as well as an appreciation of the traditions of western civilization."[19] In order to achieve this, the gen. ed. curriculum attempted to "inculcate a sense of 'shared values' among undergraduates through instruction in the Judeo-Christian tradition," in the words of the writer Alston Chase, a Harvard student in the 1950s who claimed that this, in turn, fueled a fundamental conflict between modernity and tradition:

> The undergraduate curriculum, therefore, was initially designed to be neatly divided into two categories, one general and one specialized, one emphasizing history and values, the other emphasizing the value-free methodologies employed by scholars in the various academic fields. This attempt at balance would give rise to a battle in the long war between humanism and positivism.... By 1950 the Harvard faculty was divided between those who, chastened by their experience in World War II and especially by the bombings of Hiroshima and Nagasaki, saw science and technology as a threat to Western values and even human survival and those—a majority—who saw science as a liberator from superstition and an avenue to progress.[20]

The tension between these forces had become so divisive that Chase strangely implied the gen. ed. curriculum may have even contributed to the antitechnological radicalization of Ted Kaczynski (aka the Unabomber), who incidentally entered Harvard four years after Updike left.[21]

Although the pluralism that suffused the gen. ed. reforms aspired to achieve equilibrium between competing ideas and traditions, different students absorbed the material in different ways. While Updike's roommate (and avowed secularist) Christopher Lasch would complain to his parents about what he deemed a "steady bombardment of religious ideas," Updike felt the opposite, suggesting that religion was not being taken seriously enough.[22] "Practically every course, as my atheistic roommate has bitterly noted, seem[s] to be a course in theology," Updike wrote his parents, "and yet . . . every time a cross, a priest, a cathedral, or the name of God is mentioned, a rash of coughing breaks out."[23] In "The Christian Roommates" (1964), a short story that retains what

Updike would admit to be "all that I seem able to preserve of the Harvard experience," he applied an odd-couple motif to illustrate the tensions between tradition and modernity—and particularly religion and science—that deeply informed his college experience.[24]

The plot revolves around the deteriorating relationship between a pair of freshman roommates at Harvard. The chief protagonist, Orson Ziegler, is an academic overachiever from South Dakota described as a Methodist who gradually becomes "a materialist" and is "disturbingly impressed by Voltaire's indictment of God."[25] Accordingly, we are told that "his future was firm in his mind" and that he had planned it out meticulously: pre-med at Harvard, medical school at Yale, and then a return to his hometown ("where he had his wife already selected") in order to join his father's clinic.[26] Ziegler arrives at Harvard only to be paired with a roommate of quite opposite temperaments. Henry Palamountain (aka Hub) is a self-described "Anglican Christian Platonist strongly influenced by Gandhi" who "consider[s] science a demonic illusion of human *hubris*" and prefers the "excessive introspection" of Hamlet and the metaphysical ruminations of Plato.[27] The rift between the two roommates quickly widens to the point of Ziegler's utter contempt for Hub—the origins of which we are made to clearly understand: "Orson's buzz of unease circled and settled on his roommate, who, it was clear, had thought earnestly about profound matters, matters that Orson, busy as he had been with the practical business of being a good student, had hardly considered."[28] Although at times naïve and stubborn in his zeal, Hub offers a persistent foil to Ziegler's utilitarianism that sets up a dichotomy between diverging outlooks. The supporting character of Kern (who, as a Pennsylvania "farm boy driven by an unnatural sophistication, riddled with nervous ailments," is modeled on Updike himself), sympathetically calls Hub "a saint" and chastises Ziegler for "miss[ing] the point, of what Hub's all about." In doing so, both Updike the writer and Updike the character urge us to reconsider the value behind Hub's unorthodox faith.[29] Early on in the story, Hub tells Ziegler that "people without convictions have no powers of resistance." This becomes a self-fulfilling prophesy in the climactic scene in which Ziegler is repeatedly trounced in an impromptu wrestle with Hub as he too displays no real power of resistance. The story concludes with the narrator recalling that while Hub had become a renegade missionary in Africa, Ziegler's "life has gone much the way he planned it," with one exception. "A kind of scar he carries without pain and without any clear memory of the amputation" has remained with him since college: "He never prays."[30] That Ziegler traded in his faith for science and passions for material success leaves us pondering which of the two uncompromising paths, if any, leads to fulfillment.

What is pertinent about the diverging experiences that such culturally diverse students as Updike and Lasch underwent at Harvard is that both of them still identified as liberals of sorts. Although Updike had already sought to incorporate religious themes into his literary imagination and, prior to arriving at Harvard, in Adam Begley's words, "enjoyed a comfortable, untroubled faith," his letters home demonstrate a staunch liberalism supportive of the Truman administration, and later Adlai Stevenson, and the policies that they espoused. Calling Truman "one of the most important men in the world," Updike attended events for Truman and Stevenson. In one case he and Lasch snuck into a Stevenson rally through a bathroom window, but Lasch was caught by a policeman and made to "crawl right out."[31] Despite Lasch's adherence to the secular humanism of his midwestern progressive upbringing, his dismissal of the same traditional values Updike embraced did not prevent him from sharing his roommate's liberal persuasions while retaining his own growing apprehensions about the path liberalism was treading.[32] That cultural and moral questions had not drawn a wedge in the meaning of postwar liberalism *at that time* is indicative of an important albeit fleeting moment in American political development when cultural disagreements did not obstruct the marriage of conflicted value systems into a coherent and unified political vision. The ability of Updike and Lasch to arrive at the same political endpoint despite starting out from opposite ends—and enduring conflicts along the way—is a reminder of a bygone spirit of compromise that, in our highly polarized contemporary political culture, seems but a chimera.

The Faculty

Given the number of prominent and influential liberal thinkers teaching at Harvard during Updike's undergraduate years, it's not surprising that he absorbed at least some of their intellectual sensibilities. Nearly four decades before he befriended Arthur M. Schlesinger Jr., the famed historian who had just won national acclaim for *The Vital Center* (1949), Schlesinger was among the newly minted celebrities on the faculty at

Harvard when Updike began studying there. Another was the political theorist Louis Hartz, whose best-selling book *The Liberal Tradition in America* (1955), remains to this day one of the most enduring interpretations of American liberalism. Despite being branded a "consensus" historian who had grown complacent with American power, Hartz, like Schlesinger, actually offered a critical introspective account of liberalism that warned against—rather than celebrated—its increasingly inflexible and rigid Lockean devotion. It was this ostensibly blind devotion to their particular and peculiar brand of Lockean liberalism that he feared prevented Americans from understanding other nations: "Can a people that is born equal ever understand peoples elsewhere that have become so?"[33] Schlesinger and Hartz were joined by the economist John Kenneth Galbraith, author of *The Affluent Society* (1958), Isaiah Berlin (who taught at Harvard in 1951 and 1953), and a host of other notable liberal scholars such as V. O. Keys Jr., Talcott Parsons, and Perry Miller. While these influential faculty members disagreed on many things and shied away from any ideological uniformity, they still sounded critical voices *within* liberalism that sought to correct rather than replace what they deemed to be a sound political system ingrained with organic malleability for modification and improvement.[34]

These prominent faculty members may have set the tone on campus, but the handful of teachers who had a direct relationship with Updike were the ones who, in one way or another, seem to have made a lasting impression on him. Among these were Archibald MacLeish, Theodore Morrison, and Harry Levin, who taught English literature and writing in the English Department where Updike majored; Michael Karpovich (Russian literature); Eric Havelock (classics); and Crane Brinton and Gavin Langmuir (social science). It is in Updike's encounter with them and in the way he learned to approach texts that we can begin to trace the emergence of his ambivalent liberal-pluralist bent, which was driven toward integrating—without necessarily resolving—multiple and conflicting ideas. While exploring such influence remains speculative given the difficulty in identifying a tangible connection between any one course and the development of Updike's liberal sensibilities, I focus on the handful of faculty members mentioned above for two reasons. First, they clearly had a lasting impact on Updike during (and after) college. Second, there appears to be a durable link between the ideas and forms to which they introduced Updike and the political imagination that would reveal itself in his fiction.

Many Updike enthusiasts know that Archibald MacLeish denied Updike entrance into his advanced writing course at least twice. But this did not stop Updike, who desperately wanted to study with MacLeish, from attending a poetry appreciation course with him instead, or from maintaining social ties with MacLeish after college.[35] In addition to being a Pulitzer Prize–winning poet, as well as a playwright and journalist, MacLeish had been a loyal New Dealer who filled several key posts in the Roosevelt administration, including librarian of Congress, and who served as assistant secretary of state for public affairs before returning to Harvard in 1949.[36] Influenced by W. B. Yeats, MacLeish believed in the artistic responsibility for "carrying poetry into the public world" and advocated for integrating "the world of emotions" with "the world of events." According to Robert Vanderlan, MacLeish "developed a conception of himself as a public intellectual with crucial responsibilities in the development of a democratic culture" and "believed in the power of ideas and in the responsibility of the people who wielded those ideas to take their ideas into the corridors of power."[37]

MacLeish had developed a critical appreciation of American liberalism. Although he was dubbed "the poet laureate of the New Deal," he sustained a dual role as a dedicated liberal who held power on one hand but was not averse to criticizing it from within on the other—much as Schlesinger, Trilling, Bell, and ultimately Updike himself would eventually do (like MacLeish, Schlesinger would make the full transition into politics by becoming a presidential advisor to President John F. Kennedy).[38] MacLeish's prose demonstrates this ambivalent attitude consistently. For instance, his essay "The Unimagined America" (1943), written as the tide of war was turning, sounds an unexpected warning about the future that stands in stark contrast to the fledgling overconfidence in an impending "American century" that most American intellectuals began expressing.[39] While celebrating the founders' penchant for imagining "a better, a more beautiful, a freer, happier world," he laments the loss of the ability to imagine what had enabled America to prosper in the first place. The major threat to America's future, he feared, was not totalitarianism but the nation's own inability to decide what it stood for. "No one has imagined this America—what its life should be; what life it should lead with its great wealth and the tools in its hands and the men to employ them," he wrote. "But the central question we have never asked. What are they *for*, these plants and products, the statistics? *What are they for in terms of a nation of men*—in Jefferson's terms? [emphasis in the original]" MacLeish was essentially asking Americans to look past the material promises of the New Deal and locate a higher purpose. "Most of us know now that you do not fight a war for the privilege of buying things and then not buying them—for the privilege of becoming the world's most numerous consumers and thereafter the world's most numerous unemployed," he suggested.[40] Liberalism, in other words, cannot simply stand for heightened consumption, technological efficiency, or economic development; material progress must be a means to loftier ends, not an end in itself.

Although his anxiety from America's impending "loss of its own soul" and "moral bankruptcy" intensified in the postwar period with the advent of the Cold War and especially McCarthyism, MacLeish had already begun to diagnose the heart of the problems plaguing the nation in his mind.

> The real question, the question every decent citizen of this country must ask himself in all earnestness of heart and mind and conscience, is the question: what has brought our convictions and beliefs to this low state? What has happened to a tradition of self-reliance, of mutual respect, of confidence in each other, of belief in the people and their capacity to govern themselves, of faith in the institutions through which their self-government operates? What has happened to a tradition which goes back centuries on this continent?[41]

For MacLeish, McCarthyism was a symptom of a deeper malaise; Americans had abandoned their core principles of self-reliance, self-government, social solidarity, and mutual trust. In order to survive as a nation, Americans would need to rediscover these founding principles and experience "a recovery of a sense of purpose." "Purpose is not merely a question of what you mean to do next. Purpose is a question also of *why you mean to do it*. To what end?" What was needed, MacLeish felt, was to reawaken "the belief in man—man as an individual—man as an individual free to think as he pleases and say as thinks—man as an individual answerable only to his conscience and his God—this belief is not easy to articulate in realistic and self-evident terms in an industrialized society, in which men live in universal dependence on each other."[42]

MacLeish's concern from the lack of purpose he sensed in postwar America closely resonates with Matthew Arnold's famous observation a century earlier that "Freedom, like Industry, is a very good horse to ride; [*sic*] but to ride somewhere."[43] This resonation may not be a coincidence.

The considerable influence of the noted Victorian poet, educator, and social critic who similarly sought to locate a sense of purpose for British liberals in the late nineteenth century seems to have been contagious at the time in Harvard's English Department where Updike was majoring; one of MacLeish's most famous poems was, after all, his adaptation of Arnold's "Dover Beach" (1867), aptly titled "'Dover Beach'—a Note to That Poem" (1936).[44]

Another important teacher who left his mark on Updike was Theodore Morrison, who headed the undergraduate writing program. Updike welcomed his criticism (admitting that there is no one "much fairer, or more perceptive," than him) and even gave Morrison the manuscript of his autobiographical novel to review (a rare gesture of faith since Updike eventually decided against publishing it and has restricted access to it in his archives).[45] Tellingly, Morrison also showed keen interest in Arnold and wrote an unorthodox essay (part fact, part fiction) for *Harper's* titled "'Dover Beach' Revisited." In it, he sarcastically questioned attempts by social scientists to analyze the poem with the "scientific analysis" and "objective procedure" that bred a "certainty of result."[46] By surveying various scholarly interpretations of Arnold's poem, Morrison concluded that poetry must submit to pluralism and subjectivity and remain open to multiple readings.

Although the older Updike rarely mentioned Arnold in his prose, the young Updike seems to have greatly admired him. When describing his academic progress in one letter home, Updike complained that he "should get out of [his] system" romantics like Wordsworth, Byron, and Browning when he "should be advancing to the Donne stage of appreciation, and ultimately, to Cowper and Matthew Arnold."[47] This appreciation manifested itself in an analytical paper he wrote for an advanced English course, in which he examined the melancholic impulses in poems by Wordsworth, Byron, Tennyson, and Arnold only to conclude that "Arnold's 'Dover Beach,' the best and most complex of these four poems, is concerned likewise with the ebb of faith. The pivots of Tennyson's meditation—the new vastness, the futile confusion of human effort—combine with Byron's apathy and Wordsworth's historical nostalgia." What makes Arnold's form so compelling, argued Updike, is not just its attention to the decline of religion, but its ability for synthesis and ambivalence in doing so. "Few poems fuse such a sense of immediacy with such weight of universality" as Arnold's, he wrote. "'Dover

Beach' is virtually unique in its elevation of spiritual fatigue to the level of a grand emotion."[48]

Updike's appreciation of Arnold's form is germane for understanding the development of his political sensibilities because of what Arnold symbolized for postwar liberals and the influence his ideas would wield upon them. It was, after all, Lionel Trilling who introduced Arnold's ambivalent brand of liberalism—Trilling called it "liberalism for the future"—to the American public in his doctoral dissertation that would be published as *Matthew Arnold* (1939). This book, as Trilling's biographer Michael Kimmage has noted, became "the foundation of Trilling's career and something of a milestone for his generation" (in turn, it would also provide the stepping stone for his own critique of postwar liberalism a decade later in *The Liberal Imagination*). In Kimmage's words, Trilling had engaged "a singular dilemma ... the dilemma of despair, concentrated [for him] in the figure of Henry Adams and in Matthew Arnold's 'Dover Beach.'"[49]

What Trilling found so attractive about Arnold's liberal temperament was that it too cautioned against the excessive utilitarianism and philistinism of "middleclass liberalism." These qualities, Arnold felt, had contributed to the disintegration of bourgeois society and bred "the emotional situation of the modern man—his insufficiency, his uncertainty, his dilution of spirit," and "a terrible sense of the loneliness of man."[50] For Arnold, such a flawed liberal ethos could only be rescued by looking "beyond machinery" toward culture in order to rediscover "*an inward spiritual activity, having for its characters increased sweetness* (i.e., beauty), *increased light* (i.e., intelligence), *increased life, increased sympathy*" (original italics) that sought "to make the best that has been thought and known in the world current everywhere."[51] That Updike's early fiction primarily dealt with the modern predicament, which he would aptly label "existential desperation" and describe as "the sense that we've gone to the end of the corridor and found it blank," is indicative of how much he might have shared Arnold's concern for some of the corrupting effects of modernity.[52]

Arnold never despaired. Although he looked to culture rather than religion for salvation, he embraced the spirit of compromise and synthesis: When reviewing his response to that ominous "darkling plain," famously described in "Dover Beach" as creeping over Europe, one senses the cautious liberal temperament that would one day suffuse Updike's work. As Trilling noted:

Arnold declared that the modern man was crippled and incomplete. His poetry, on the one hand, is a plangent threnody for a lost wholeness and peace; on the other hand, it is the exploration of two modern intellectual traditions which have failed him and his peers, the traditions of romanticism and rationalism, and, moving back and forth between these two strands, it is an attempt to weave them together into a synthesis. Each alone, he feels, is insufficient, but together they promise much. The effort of reconciliation produces a body of poetry which is philosophical but not systematic; what is declared at one point, is contradicted at another.[53]

Michael Kimmage, who argued that "Matthew Arnold's liberalism was very much an amalgam of conservative and progressive tendencies," found in that very amalgam the link that tied him to Trilling and made him such a potent inspiration for postwar liberals:

> The pivotal event was the French Revolution, which created the modern spirit even while failing to solve the modern crisis in politics. Arnold's ambivalent relationship to this spirit lent drama to his thought because Arnold fell between the established categories of conservative and progressive. He was never merely for or against the French Revolution; he was, in Trilling's mysterious formulation, a "liberal of the future," and Arnold sought to balance the rationalist liberalism of Jeremy Bentham and John Stuart Mill with a culture that could plausibly replace religion as a source of moral and aesthetic excellence. If it achieved such balance, the liberalism of the future would realize the democratic promise of the French Revolution, without yielding to nihilism or anarchy or to the perils of untamed democracy.[54]

In order to successfully endure the transformations unleashed by modernity, such as democratization, industrialization, social mobility, and secularism—changes not that dissimilar to those that occurred in postwar America—Arnold believed that "openness and flexibility of mind are at such a time the first of virtues" since "perfection will never be reached." Rather than resist these tectonic social shifts, Arnold's criticism sought a balanced approach that could establish "the reconciliation of the two traditions whose warfare had so disturbed his youth—rationalism and faith." What is so apropos about Arnold's—and ultimately Updike's—rich pluralism is that it was equally rooted in the modern and traditional experiences. Arnold, as Trilling aptly concluded,

> welcomed the new democracy but he suspected it. He welcomed rationalism but feared its effects. He was far from being at one with established religion

yet he feared the void which its disappearance would leave.... Arnold's criticism was, in effect, his refusal to move forward until Burke and Voltaire compounded their quarrel, bowed to each other and, taking him by either hand, agreed on the path to follow.[55]

It is fair to speculate that the influence of Arnold and Trilling was transmitted to Updike through his close relationship with Harry Levin. The renowned Shakespeare and modernist scholar, with whom Updike remained in contact after college, was considered by Updike an "excellent" teacher and would later be remembered in endearing terms for providing him "access to the world of modern, living letters."[56] Not only did Levin share MacLeish, Morrison, and Trilling's appreciation for Arnold, but more tellingly, he admired Trilling, who he said "has the courage to be a moralist." According to the literary historian John Rodden, Trilling and Levin "were sometimes paired, given that they were the first Jews to receive tenure in major university English departments." Despite their professional rivalry, Rodden claimed that, "like Trilling, Levin was an early champion of literary modernism whose writing and teaching helped institutionalize a modernist canon in postwar American literary studies."[57]

Levin often related his own work to Trilling. Writing about his literary criticism, for instance, he recalled that "I have considered some of the reasons for this flow and ebb of talent in my essay, 'What Was Modernism?,' and have taken note that Lionel Trilling reached a parallel view by a different route." Conceiving of Trilling as an ally in a hostile landscape of postmodern literary critics, Levin concluded that "perhaps we may need critics with apocalyptic sensibilities, like George Steiner, rather than stodgy old humanistic liberals like Professor Trilling and myself."[58] In a warm review of Trilling's essays published in the *NYRB* in 1955, Levin celebrates Trilling as "not only an accomplished interpreter of the nineteenth century; he is, in his own right, a thoughtful mind of the mid-twentieth [century]," and goes on to defend the import of his literary criticism. "Not that his mood is nostalgia for the past; rather, it is a pathos for the present, an urgent awareness of 'our modern fate' well calculated to impress contemporary readers," Levin wrote in an approving tone, commending Trilling's longing for rediscovering a "lost mystique." "Something can be gained by reevaluation ... of writers whose sense of individuality struggled against the encroachments of conformity."[59]

What Levin passed on to Updike was not simply the ideas of Arnold and Trilling but also their unique approach to reading texts. Levin, Updike would recall, "not only opened my eyes to our supreme classic [canon] but, with their emphasis on dominant metaphor, to a whole new way of reading."[60] This new way was a pluralist approach to fiction that, in the face of the then dominant schools of formalism and New Criticism, resisted the dictates of academic literary criticism. "I was so fiercely caustic as to be labeled a young Turk . . . and guarded my independence so jealously that I withdrew from the *Partisan Review* because of its doctrinaire partisanship in those days and disappointed the editor of the *Kenyon Review* by taking a middle ground between New Criticism and old scholarship," Levin revealed in an autobiographical essay. In a line that could have easily been borrowed from Trilling, he further admitted, "It has always seemed to me that, if it is truth we seek, then every conceivable path to it should be considered viable, and that the seeker should try as many of them as he can, or at least do his best to keep them open."[61] As one of his colleagues aptly observed, Levin's criticism was rooted in traditions of "skeptical pluralism" that "ask the reader not to decipher, but to ponder."[62]

Updike's early criticism consistently demonstrates such skeptical pluralism. Having closely studied John Keats, he was familiar with, and alluded to, the idea of "negative capability" that stood at the base of Trilling's concept of *The Liberal Imagination*.[63] Assigned in an English course with evaluating whether objective criticism can assess the irrational inspiration that often suffuses poetry, Updike delicately navigated between the realm of "the mysterious," where faith, madness, and the unconscious generate poetic inspiration, and the realm of reason, which may impose order upon such inspiration, in search of a middle ground. "The modern metaphor of the catalyst, the embodiment of neutrality, is an attempt to remove the supernatural and moral overtones without denying the mystery," Updike wrote. "Even though the art process is described in terms of experienced material transformed into poetry, the transforming agent is admitted to be 'rather mysterious,' that is, unknown." By fusing the rational-structured formalism identified with the style of Alexander Pope with the rapturous, emotional outbursts associated with romantics like Percy Shelley, Updike proposed a compromise: "Indeed, if one considers Pope as emphasizing one aspect of poetry and Shelley, a different aspect, the two do not clash: they dovetail," he wrote. "There is a broad middle way between the extreme banks of brittle formalism and rhapsodic nonsense. The greatest poets—Aeschylus, Dante, Shakespeare, in a way, Goethe—seem to tread the middle of the road, and are usually neglected in a paper of this sort."[64]

Updike opted to broaden his horizons by taking a course on Tolstoy and Dostoevsky in his senior year with the noted Russian historian Michael Karpovich.[65] What is germane about this experience is the palpable presence of Karpovich's liberal ideals in Updike's budding political imagination. After serving the short-lived liberal government of Alexander Kerensky, Karpovich left Russia before the October Revolution and eventually joined the history faculty at Harvard.[66] Containing what the famed Russia historian Martin Malia called an "integral respect for the human worth of the individual," Karpovich represented a "moderate westernism" in the liberal tradition of Alexander Herzen that gravitated toward "the center" and naturally evolved "towards moderation." Fusing literature with politics, Karpovich was dedicated to "tolerance, open-mindedness, pluralism," and, as Malia noted, "believed in the actions of human will and chance in history as opposed to all determinisms. He held to the autonomy of thought and art with respect to politics, and he equated true civilization with a diversified culture and 'marketplace of ideas.'"[67] Most apposite for Updike's intellectual development is the fact that Karpovich's commitment to the Enlightenment never caused him to abandon his faith. "It should be added that his religion blended harmoniously with his other beliefs. Since his rationalism was of a tentative and Kantian variety, there remained vast realms beyond its reach which only faith could fill; consequently, the conflict of reason and revelation was not a problem which agitated M. M. [Karpovich's nickname]," Malia concluded. For Karpovich, he wrote, "liberalism, precisely because it refuses to be categorical, means sanity, balance, judiciousness—that ability 'to encompass both sides of a question' and to see 'that the truth is somewhere in between.'"[68]

Updike's engagement with the classics may have also helped him cultivate his liberal ideals. Eric Havelock's name appears several times in Updike's letters under a mixed aura of admiration ("a very intelligent and fascinating man") and intimidation ("Professor Havelock grows more frightening") that suggests he too left his mark on the young student (so "fond" had he grown of Havelock that he decided to audit one of his courses "just [to] sit in class for an hour and listen to him talk about philosophy").[69] Updike took a Latin course with Havelock in his freshman year. What is poignant about this experience is that it took place as

Havelock was working on his seminal book, *The Liberal Temper in Greek Politics*, which proposed a novel and controversial theory of liberalism. In it, Havelock challenges traditional conceptions of liberalism rooted in universal presuppositions of natural rights and provides an alternative anthropological understanding of a more fluid liberalism grounded in pragmatic adjustments to shifting contingencies as practiced by the pre-Socratic philosophers Democritus, Protagoras, Antiphon, and Lycophron. For Havelock, modern democracy constituted

> a synthesis of the postulates of the Greek liberals on the one hand, and of Greek idealism on the other. Its organs of political power are so framed as to express as far as possible some conformity with the thesis that a common mind exists, that the common men are best judges of their own political interests, that political wisdom is empirical and pragmatic, and that men are naturally more inclined to co-operate than to fight, and that divergent personal opinions can be negotiated to the point of effective decision. This is the kind of political program which would best represent the liberal temper in Greek politics.[70]

Havelock's notion of liberalism resisted the systematic idealism of Plato's republic or Aristotle's polis and opted instead for a more sobered political reality "in which power-patterns existed pragmatically and temporarily" and political institutions reflected "man-made choices for material and natural ends" in a dynamic historical vision "that remained open at both ends."[71] Liberal politics, he suggested, was dedicated to locating "a common opinion" in the tradition of Madison rather than Rousseau through "the process of debate, negotiation and calculation." "The democratic consensus, however approximate, is therefore a natural and historical condition by which all societies operate and function to greater or less degree," Havelock concluded. "It is in democracies that amity is maximized."[72]

Whatever the influence Havelock may have had on Updike, there is little doubt that Updike was fully introduced to the world of political ideas in the yearlong gen. ed. course Social Science 1: Introduction to the Development of Western Civilization. Taught by the French historian Crane Brinton and the medievalist Charles Holt Taylor, the course's intellectual journey through the Western canon left a deep impression on Updike's precocious mind.[73] Their teaching assistant for the course, Gavin Langmuir (referred to by Updike as "the awesome section man"), had a significant influence upon him as well, and was mentioned repeatedly with great adulation in Updike's letters (Updike even consulted him on his mother's novel about Ponce de Leon).[74]

Brinton and Langmuir seem to have fed Updike a blend of classical and modern political thought and medieval Christian philosophy that would combine to formulate his uniquely tempered liberal imagination. Perusing Updike's reading assignments for the gen. ed. courses reveals a greatest hits list of the Western literary cannon: Socrates, Plato, Aristotle, Marcus Aurelius, Augustine, Aquinas, Thomas More, Vico, Locke, Montesquieu, Rousseau, Kant, Adam Smith, Hegel, Fichte, Marx, Feuerbach, and Mill, among others, supplemented with pioneering secondary studies by Isaiah Berlin, Sidney Hook, and Edmund Wilson.[75]

Among the most impressive analytic works by the young Updike were his studies of Karl Marx. In two substantial papers, "Marx: Man of Mission" and "An Exposition of the Morality in the Communist Manifesto," Updike demonstrated a level of erudition and a precociousness of which even seasoned political theorists would not be ashamed. In the first paper, in which Updike wrote about Marx for his final assignment of the yearlong freshman course, he offered a twenty-three-page analysis (ninety-three footnotes) of the intellectual climate from which Marx emerged in order to assess his historical significance. After surveying the historical development of socialist ideas—from Plato, through the Hebrew Bible and the early modern utopian thought of Thomas More, all the way to French revolutionaries Babeuf, Saint Simone, and Proudhon, and then Hegel—he finally reached Marx. Offering a nuanced and sophisticated analysis of the relationship between Marx and his predecessors, Updike acknowledged continuities without overlooking the historic break that Marx had achieved with his theory of historical materialism. "As a historical theorist Marx asserts his least-challenged claim to genius. And it is here that we find that element most difficult for which to find precedent," Updike wrote. "It was this discovery (coupled with its corollary, the continuous struggle between the economically exploited and exploiting class) that Marx himself claimed to be his only original contribution to the system that came to be called Marxism."[76] Considering Marx along a dual axis as both a product of old ideas and a harbinger of new ones, Updike concluded:

> Our study was one of intellectual climate, and personal originality is somewhat irrelevant. But it cannot be claimed with total accuracy that the thought of the era was converging on him [Marx]. There was a great wealth of opinion

and writing in the half-century after the French Revolution; Marx had to extract from this "immense mass of chaotic material" what seemed valid and important.... Marx was a heir of a great transformation in Europe. The English industrial revolution found definitive expression in the classical school of economists. The French Revolution is remembered by the writings of the philosophes. The intellectual upheaval in Germany manifested itself in the idealistic philosophies of Kant and Hegel. In Marx is found a synthesis of aspects of German idealism, French rationalism, and English political economy.[77]

For Updike, what was strangely impressive about Marx was not his obdurate, some would claim dangerous, monism but his capacity to integrate diverging strains of thought into a new theory.

Updike's objective analysis is further on display in his surprisingly well-balanced and sobered approach to Marx (an impressive feat given that it was written at the height of McCarthyism).[78] Such openness may have very well been the result of the pluralist experiment engineered in Harvard at the time. In his book *Education in a Divided World* (1948), Harvard's president James Bryant Conant laid out his vision for a liberal education. "Studying a philosophy does not mean endorsing it, much less proclaiming it.... We study cancer in order to learn how to defeat it," he wrote. "We must study Soviet philosophy in our universities for exactly the same reason.... If an avowed supporter of the Marx-Lenin-Stalin line can be found, force him into the open and tear his arguments to pieces with counter-arguments."[79] In a way this is what Updike was doing. On one hand, his essay recognized the troubling messianism ingrained into Marx's ideas: "Marxian economics are more like a church than a school, although many have dwelt only in the Sunday school in the basement to emerge dissatisfied and critical. It was built for the Salvation of Men, and within its great (and, upon inspection, finely detailed) walls there is room for the proletariat of the world to gather and hear the voice of their God."[80] But he then went on to unpack the dialectic, distinguish utopian from scientific socialism, and elucidate the labor theory of value without concealing his own approbation. "But his genius cannot be denied, he saw more clearly than anyone the disasters and slumps inevitable to capitalism. His insight into the contradictory dynamism of the industrial society cannot be nullified by the hasty conclusions he drew," Updike asserted. "Others heard the call; The charge was in the air.... But only Marx had the acumen to understand it and the power to fulfil [*sic*] it."[81]

It is in his second engagement with Marx as a sophomore in a course called Humanities 4 that Updike seems to have discovered, long before many Marxists did, the humanist bent that some claim is truly indicative of his work. Asked to evaluate moral qualities of *The Communist Manifesto*, Updike applied what can be labeled a genuinely "liberal" reading of Marx that not only attempted to rescue the individual from the deterministic forces of history but along with it to rescue Marx from many of his critics. In a passionate, though not always successful, attempt to demonstrate Marx's underlining concern for individual freedom, Updike warned against the "dangerous confusion" by those assuming that "Marx extends his message to an economic class rather than to the individuals making up that class" and attributed such confusion to "an inconsistency imposed upon Marx by his task: to inculcate the revolt of the proletariat."[82] By distinguishing between means and ends in such a manner, Updike, who retained a sympathetic attitude throughout the essay, challenged the "mechanistic view of man with which Marx has unjustly been credited" and asserted that "historical determinism must not be hastily extended into the individual moral unit" since "Marx assumed the presence of free will, operating even amidst economic pressures."[83]

Updike's somewhat surprising defense of Marx echoes the broader tenets of Marxist humanism, with its emphasis on self-fulfillment and individual value. By claiming that there is no excuse "for over-looking the basic affirmation of individual worth that is apparent even in the wrathful tone of the Manifesto," Updike effectively anticipated the conventional shibboleths of Marxist humanism that would arrive in America a decade later (following the 1959 English translation of *The Economic and Philosophic Manuscripts*).[84] His emphasis on Marx's concerns for preserving the "human dignity" and "consciousness" of individual members of the proletariat in the face of an increasingly alienating workplace suggests that Updike harbored many of the sympathetic assessments of Marx shared by American proponents of Marxist humanism, such as Erich Fromm and Raya Dunayevskaya.[85] Although Updike ultimately conceded the impracticality of Marx's revolutionary solutions due to a misguided belief in human nature, he nevertheless concluded his essay with a touch of romanticism that gently deflates Marx's ideas, in the spirit of Conant's advice, only after having seriously considered them: "Marxist morality is almost certainly beyond application, yet we find it the noblest of all moralities conceived without reference to a supernatural authority, and somewhat regret that, as Shaw said of Christianity, it has never been tried."[86] As a devout New Dealer who admired the fiercely anticommunist Harry Truman and was defiantly proud of America and its institutions, Updike showed a rare receptiveness in his sobered analysis of Marx's ideas—especially in the early 1950s—to alternative, even conflicting ideas, in a way that nicely symbolized a spirit of liberal pluralism taking root.

Updike's sympathetic analysis of Marx did not prevent him from equally appreciating the value of medieval Christianity. On the contrary, his penchant for drawing inspiration from both past and present and locating a middle ground between them is salient in another pair of essays he wrote for Social Science I about the medieval thought of King Louis IX and Peter Abelard. Asked to evaluate the legacy of Louis IX (1214–1270) and determine "what relevant values" of his remain for "a modern Western culture," Updike found quite a few. In the essay titled "Just Ruler, Pious Saint, Chivalrous Knight," he conveyed "qualified admiration" for the king who, despite his "fierce intolerance," upheld firm convictions—a quality Updike found wanting in postwar America. "Our culture is tolerant. It is not because our nation was founded for tolerance of religious belief, or because our Constitution is based upon equality of human rights," Updike explained. "We cannot be equated with medieval fanaticism because the modern Western mind is too full of doubt to believe in anything strongly enough to impose its half-convictions on others." But just as Updike lamented the loss of American conviction, he also recognized the danger rooted in its excess. "The certainty of God gave Louis and his contemporaries a directness of purpose that the befuddled American lacks, but in the end it was the feudal man who was befuddled. It was he who carried his sword in his hand and Christ on his lips, unaware that he had combined the uncombinable."[87]

The ambivalent attitude with which Updike approaches Louis IX's legacy led him to imply that postwar Americans were conscious enough of their own contradictions to be able to retain Christian virtues alongside secular ones without necessarily succumbing to any of their potential vices. As he wrote:

> Our conclusion, then, is that Christianity was in equal discord with twentieth century America and with the society of King Louis IX. The difference between them is the way the two cultures have reconciled themselves to this antagonism. It is this difference in treatment that makes me inwardly sneer at a blood-stained saint. . . . The method of King Louis and of his people, appar-

ently, was to ignore the conflict. They were underdeveloped enough to hold two antagonistic ideas in their minds at once.[88]

It is precisely because American liberalism was supposedly "developed enough" to balance conflicting ideas *without* succumbing to excess or fanaticism that Updike essentially recommended "application of Christian virtue" in postwar America. The fact that Louis IX personified courage, honor, justness, and wisdom—which Updike considered "modern as well as medieval virtues"—led him to believe that they too have a place in American politics. "The conclusion, then, is this: one cannot call our society mental and the medieval, moral, despite all the surface indications of a basic difference. The biggest distinction one might draw is to call medieval Europe God-conscious and assert that modern western culture is Right-conscious," Updike concluded. "So close are we to the soul of medieval Europe."[89]

In another essay on the medieval French philosopher Peter Abelard (1079–1142), Updike again betrayed his propensities toward synthesis of past and present when he celebrated the scholastic teachings linking reason and faith for which Abelard was condemned. In "The Tragedy of Peter Abelard," Updike admirably pointed to the fallen Abelard's "brilliant mind" and posited that "it was his reasoning, questioning mind that made him dangerous. He rose to heights through rationalism; his rationalism caused his downfall." What initially seemed to draw Updike to Abelard (as to other scholastic thinkers like Dante, Thomas Aquinas, and Jacques Maritain, whose work he would also come to appreciate) is the ability to retain genuine faith without forfeiting rational thought. Abelard, Updike insisted, did not "rebel against religion, but only against blind faith" since he believed that "human reason must now be the guide to faith; faith is the <u>result</u> of reason" (original underline).[90] Herein is another early instance of Updike's inchoate spirit of compromise gradually materializing: past and present, faith and reason, and tradition and modernity do not necessarily have to collide; there is a way to benefit from both.

When reappraising Updike's considerable output of critical analysis over his two yearlong gen. ed. courses, we realize that his ostensibly confounding admiration for both Marx and Abelard is actually quite consistent. The intensive academic encounter with different facets of the Western tradition—classic, medieval, early modern, and Enlightenment—taught him to appreciate differing, at times rival, intellectual persuasions. And rather than wholly embrace scientific progress or retreat to the comforts of Christianity, Updike learned to do both. This liberal sensibility that would suffuse his political imagination is on full display in his final paper for Humanities 4, titled "The Decline of Moral Stability since the *Divine Comedy*," which aptly sums up his engagement with the great books of Western civilization:

> The form and pressure of our age emerge from that of the ages preceding. Modern literature would be unfaithful to its function if it reflected obscurely the facts of our moral condition. Science's quest for objective order has dimmed the reality of those ideals to which man looked to order his life; it has emphasized man's insecure and minor place in the physical cosmos; it has, by the very nature of its inductive method, neither provided an absolute purpose nor pointed out an ultimate direction. It explores reality yet suggests no attitude with which that reality may be viewed. The two extremes, objective and subjective, are "determinism" and "absurdity." Both are futile. Helplessness and aimlessness are equally hopeless conditions. . . . Compromise is suggested. The moral schemes and attitudes we have discussed are all based upon some compromise of logical accuracy, man's nature, or external reality.[91]

In order to reach that compromise, Updike exhibited a rare form of sobriety and moderation that many would probably find hard to conceive. "To respect, to envy, to extol the middle ages is just; to desire a return is as incredible as attempting reversal of time so that we may re-enter the security of a childhood lost to us forever. . . . Our reality is inescapable," Updike concluded. "Even were science to attain this impossible omniscience, it would not infringe upon man's prerogative to fancy himself an individual striving through chaos, a link in a chain of order, an insect on a forest floor, a bit of Buddha, or a disciple of Jesus Christ."[92]

Whereas Brinton's course introduced the young Updike to new ideas, it is worth considering whether Updike learned in that course what to do with them. After all, Brinton first won acclaim with his book *The Anatomy of Revolution* (1938), in which he claimed that the "shift in the allegiance of the intellectuals" was the prerequisite stage for any successful revolution.[93] In the early 1950s Brinton, who, according to one colleague, "had hopes that the understanding of laws of behavior, specifically, revolutionary behavior, could either prevent revolutions or limit them," continued to pursue this theme and investigated the status of American intellectuals.[94] In a speech before the American Philosophical Society in 1955 he evaluated the so-called threat of intellectual conformity and concluded that, despite a growing sense of alienation, there was no revolutionary threat of American intellectuals "deserting" or shifting their allegiance.[95] "The intellectual classes," he said, "judged by their works, seem actually good barometers, or good litmus paper. The test is simple: in a stable healthy society the intellectuals support the existing regime; in an unstable society threatened with revolution they turn against the existing regime." Not only was American (and Western) society "healthy" according to Brinton, but the intellectuals themselves—and he emphasized novelists as central to this category—were fully integrated in, and therefore highly appreciative of, these societies.

> Finally, and especially for America—though I think this is basically true throughout the West—the intellectuals are not really alienated from bankers, businessmen, and politicians in just the way my revolutionary generations were alienated from kings, tsars, nobles, gentry, and prelates. It is not merely that, as I have just noted, the intellectuals in the West have no intense new faith, now that Marxism appears to have run its course. They really share, at bottom, the faith of their fellows. They may resent the Cadillac, but they like the Ford. . . . Many of them, if you catch them unawares, look as though they were enjoying themselves.[96]

Although it's unclear if Updike ever absorbed Brinton's benign assessment of the American intellectual class, over the years, as we have already seen, he would come to personify such behavior in both his material and literary experiences, never really leaving any doubt as to the basic fact that he was, indeed, "enjoying" himself in America—and not ashamed of doing so.[97]

Conclusion

Despite the considerable academic training that Updike received in political thought, philosophy, and history, he was still first and foremost a writer. Accordingly, the bulk of his undergraduate studies were dedicated to studying and writing fiction. What this chapter sought to establish was the manner through which Updike's intensive liberal arts education motivated and enabled him to approach literature with a deeper political understanding emblematic of the liberal-pluralist temperament pervasive among postwar liberals at the time. If there is one constant throughout Updike's college essays, it is that the persistent search for what he called "middling" sought synthesis and compromise rather than resolution in both formal and substantive matters.

What I have reconstructed here is a certain intellectual atmosphere that appears to have helped instill in Updike a set of liberal sensibilities. That influential teachers like Levin, MacLeish, Havelock, and Karpovich were also proponents and scholars, in one way or another, of these sensibilities—while their more notable colleagues like Berlin, Hartz, and Schlesinger were tantamount to being the official spokesmen—hardly seems like a coincidence. Updike's college papers further demonstrate a powerful penchant, even urge, toward pluralism, balance, and moderation that suggests a durable link between the ideas he imported as a student and those he would export as a writer. Updike had always claimed to be a born-and-bred old-school liberal; tracing the intellectual development of that liberalism at Harvard in the 1950s enables us to better understand what exactly he meant by it. Similarly, it shines a different light on his emerging body of fiction that possibly demands of us to approach it in new ways.

The older that Updike became, the more unequivocal his appreciation for his Harvard education appeared. In his poem "Apologies to Harvard," Updike graciously attributed his personal success to his alma mater and observed that "The possible Is but a suburb, Harvard, of your city." His actions would speak even louder than his words. As Jack De Bellis observed, a significant part of Updike's adult life remained centered around Harvard long after his graduation: his only teaching job in 1962 was there; his personal papers are archived at Harvard's Houghton Library; he retained a friendship with Harvard classmates (Lasch) and faculty (Levin, MacLeish, and Schlesinger, who would later befriend him); he remained involved in and maintained correspondences with no less than forty-two various Harvard institutions and organizations; and maybe most tellingly, he moved in 1957 from New York to Massachusetts and lived within one hundred miles of Cambridge for the rest of his life.[98]

For his fiftieth-anniversary college reunion in 2004, Updike recalled that

> fifty years from graduation I can at last appreciate how large a role Harvard has played in my life.... Harvard's education in literary appreciation and analysis has stood me in good practical stead as a book reviewer and a creative writer, as well as lubricated the course of all my reading. Friends and teachers

in my undergraduate years—too many of them now dead—served as touchstones and guiding lights, and there was a certain Cantabrigian style, even down to the then-obligatory costume of tweedy coat and striped tie, that I have retained as a template of the civilized life.

In his final submission for the fifty-fifth-anniversary reunion report, published posthumously by members of his graduating class, he gave a parting salute that leaves little doubt as to the considerable impact Harvard had on him: "Daily I thank my lucky stars for the many blessings life has brought me, not least among them admission to Harvard so remarkably long ago."[99]

3 | *The Poorhouse Fair*
The Liberal State and Its Discontents

> *Liberalism has promoted concentration of democratic authority but deconcentration of democratic power.*
> —Theodore Lowi

> *Governments are coercive and punitive in the last resorts, and American freedom is a relative and not an absolute condition.*
> —John Updike

John Updike's *The Poorhouse Fair* is hardly a typical debut novel. Written in 1958, four years after Updike graduated from Harvard when he was only twenty-six, it portrays a somewhat dystopian 1970s America and revolves around the seemingly *un*extraordinary events of a single day that take place in a state poorhouse for the aged in New Jersey as the "inmates" (Updike's term) host their annual fair. Although the young Updike had admittedly been influenced by what he called the "totalitarian nightmare" of George Orwell's *Nineteen Eighty-Four* and Aldous Huxley's *Brave New World* while devising the unorthodox plot, his parochial, almost banal, Americanized adaptation was not only benign but comical. The novel, as Updike later recalled, did not emerge out of a shared anxiety about the possibility of a totalitarian America but from the realization that such a nightmare "would *not* come to pass, at least in the United States." "As in our mundane reality, it is others that die, while an attenuated silly sort of life bubbles decadently on," Updike noted in a retrospective essay about *The Poorhouse Fair*.[1]

What drives the plot is the central conflict between Stephen Conner, the young technocratic prefect who runs the poorhouse in a regimented fashion, and Hook, its oldest inmate and the resident maverick who resists Conner's administrative reforms. Aided each by a band of supporters (Hook is the unofficial "leader" of the inmates while Conner has his faithful assistant, Buddy), the two characters repeatedly spar. But their constant disagreements, mostly over ostensibly trivial matters such as seating arrangements and a stray cat prowling the grounds belie a much thicker and more significant engagement with fundamental questions of power, liberty, and virtue in postwar America. Among them: When can power be employed? To what extent? By whom? For what? What are the limits of liberty—and when can it be curtailed? And what is the role of virtue and morality, if any, in formulating policy? By raising such questions, *The Poorhouse Fair* essentially offers a critical analysis of postwar liberalism that reveals its fundamental inability to sufficiently negotiate the boundaries of its expanding powers with more traditional local sources of democratic authority as well as its inability to balance the preservation of older cultural values with the satisfactions engendered by new material interests.

Although the novel is situated in an apolitical rural setting, the subtle metaphorical spirit that suffuses *The Poorhouse Fair* opens up new vistas for exploring the momentous political, socioeconomic, and cultural shifts transforming the country in the first half of the twentieth-century. The book was written as many Americans were growing alarmed by the unprecedented expansion of the federal government in the wake of the New Deal, World War II, and the Cold War, and its penetration into aspects of their lives previously immune from state intervention. As such, *The Poorhouse Fair* serves as a barometer that gauges public reactions to, and consequences of, these sweeping changes. By measuring the political temperature of postwar liberalism, *The Poorhouse Fair* helps us understand how it was possible that, at a time when liberalism was outwardly brimming with vitality, it had already begun facing serious challenges from within.

Despite receiving little attention from scholars over the years, the standard interpretations of *The Poorhouse Fair* have primarily revolved around the central axis of conflict engendered by the chief protagonists: Conner and Hook. With each of the two characters representing distinct archetypes for opposing forces that are engaged in a 1950s version of the clash of civilizations, scholars have interpreted *The Poorhouse Fair* as a dialectic collision. George Searles, Donald Greiner, and James Schiff have highlighted the novel's dystopian qualities and described it as a struggle between, among other things, secular humanism and religion, spiritual and corporeal, rational and emotional, and individualism and bureaucracy. Judie Newman has sharpened the novel's social analysis by exploring themes of social engineering, conformity, and authoritarianism.[2] What scholars have overlooked, and left unexplored so far, is that many of the abstract ideals that suffuse the novel are grounded in a very real historical-political setting—that of postwar American politics. And as a result, the most important clash manifested in the novel might very well be between rival liberal ideologies.

Since *The Poorhouse Fair* offers us an ideal portal into Updike's fecund albeit unexplored political imagination, it serves as the ideal starting point from which to trace the evolution of his political thought. This chapter reevaluates Updike's debut novel in order to demonstrate two things. First, in his earliest foray into the world of letters, he already proved to be a serious thinker who actively pursued political themes in his fiction in subtle and complex ways. And second, in *The Poorhouse Fair* he used his fine-tuned political instincts to explore competing liberal visions of state power: traditionally minimalist versus modern expansionist. By doing this, I claim that Updike illuminated a fateful bifurcation that was quietly rattling the foundations of American liberalism long before the storms of the 1960s ever began to gather winds. The Vietnam War, racial backlash, counterculture, an exhausted welfare state, and postindustrial decline: Updike's first novel suggests that long before these external shocks materialized, internal philosophical discord among liberals overshadowed the illusion of consensus and laid the groundwork for its eventual implosion.

Statism and Its Discontents

In the character of Stephen Conner, the poorhouse prefect, Updike very consciously constructed an embodiment of the modern American welfare state—or what he himself called "a soulless welfare state."[3] As the archetypal bureaucrat, his character has been crafted meticulously to personify everything the sociologist Max Weber both admired and feared in modernity: he is rational and efficient, cold, calculating, and dull. He draws the legitimacy for his authority from legal-rational grounds—he had been appointed by the federal government—and his office is covered with the state-issued credentials to prove it. His power to command and coerce is rooted in his control over resources (food and medical care) and in his monopoly over the legitimate means of violence in the poorhouse that is literally maintained through the presence of the only firearm on the grounds, located in his office closet (tellingly, the only time it is used is to kill a cat we are specifically told has "flaunted his authority").[4]

Conner is obsessed with order and results, and spends his time compiling balance sheets and longevity reports. "Everything Conner did, he did for a reason; his actions were glass," the narrator observes. Early on, when Conner begins to ponder Hook's animosity toward him, he suggests, "there must be a rational cause that has set him against me." His thought is so rationalized that when he talks to Amy Mortis, an older inmate, about heaven, "He wondered if, technically, she was a dwarf. He wondered what the technical definition of a Dwarf was." That Conner flees into scientific ruminations during a spiritual conversation is telling: the first thing we are told about him is that he "thought of no one as God. . . . He had lost all sense of omen. . . . The theatre of his deeds was filled with people he would never meet—the administrators, the report-readers—and beyond these black blank heads hung the white walls of the universe, the listless, permissive mother for whom Conner felt not a shred of awe."[5] Although he is described as "devout in the service of humanity," much like the doctor in *The Karamazov Brothers,* Conner too appears as a great lover of humanity who cannot stand human beings. In constructing Conner in such a way, Updike precisely embodied Weber's description of modern bureaucrats as "specialists without spirit, sensualists without heart; this nullity imagines that it has attained a level of civilization never before achieved."[6]

Conner projects a distinct architecture of power. The poorhouse grounds that serve as the domain of his control are surrounded by a daunting wall. His office that oversees the entire complex is located in an isolated cupola on the fourth floor of the poorhouse and "was approached by four flights of narrowing stairs, troublesome for these old people. . . . The altitude of the office assured that it would seldom be visited." Although Mendelssohn, his beloved predecessor, chose the office for its discreet exit (he was a drunk), Conner likes it for the access to power that it affords him. Panoptic, legible, and superior—the perspective Conner maintains from his towering office is that of an administration rather than an administrator: "from this height the people in the crowd appeared to bumble like brainless insects, bumping into one another, taking random hurried courses across the grass."[7] In reading this, one cannot help recall the scene in Orson Welles's movie *The Third Man* (1949) in which the villain, Harry Lime (played by Welles), an American criminal in postwar Europe who sells diluted medicine on the black market, stands atop a Ferris wheel overlooking Vienna and justifies his deadly actions in a Kafkaesque manner. "Look down there, would you really feel any pity if one of those dots stopped moving forever?" Lime asks. "Nobody thinks in terms of human beings, governments don't, why should we?" Lime and Conner share a rare quality: "seeing" in terms of a government that is *unable* to distinguish between individual and collective.[8] In crafting the architecture of the poorhouse this way, Updike was consciously aware of the relationship between space and power. As he observed in a retrospective essay:

> Architecture confines and defines us. Our human world speaks to us, most massively, in its buildings, and a fiction writer cannot make his characters move until he has some imaginative grasp of their environment. Nearly thirty years later I can still feel the thrill of power with which, in my first novel, *The Poorhouse Fair*, I set characters roaming the corridors of an immense imaginary mansion which I had based upon an institutional building, for the poor and homeless, that had stood at the end of our street in Pennsylvania.[9]

That Conner is constructed to "see" like an administrative state is emblematic of the creative manner in which Updike translated the analytical qualities of social science into fiction. What is remarkable about his depiction of Conner's poorhouse is how accurately it meets the criteria for the modern forms of governing that shaped the New Deal's state-centered liberalism—a criteria meticulously outlined in James C. Scott's seminal study of state power, *Seeing Like a State* (Updike would later give a speech aptly titled "How Does the State Imagine?" that distinguished between individual and bureaucratic forms of imagination).[10] Although most of Scott's case studies pertain to authoritarian regimes, "the granddaddy" of all high-modernist experiments, in Scott's words, was after all the New Deal's Tennessee Valley Authority.[11]

For Scott, there are four distinct features that define the modern state. The first is "the administrative ordering of nature and society" pursued through "the state's attempt to make a society legible, to arrange the population in ways that simplified the classic state functions."[12] This quest for standardization and legibility is exactly what *The Poorhouse Fair* opens with: Conner has put nametags on all the poorhouse chairs so as to regulate where each resident may sit. Just as Conner oversees the inmates' actions from his broad cupola windows, everything he does is aimed at "admini-stration" (as Hook mockingly pronounces it): he has standardized the health services to operate with the efficiency of a factory line; leisure has been regulated, food service is supervised, and even the tables for the fair have been arranged along strict geometric lines.

The second feature that Scott identifies in a state's power is "the self-confidence about scientific and technical progress" that expresses "the mastery of nature (including human nature), and, above all, the rational design of social order commensurate with the scientific understanding of natural laws." Accordingly, Conner's actions are all empirically based and couched in scientific terms: he refutes religion with theories of paleontology, defends his atheism by citing psychological experiments, believes that meteorology will soon be able to control the weather, and anticipates the day when modern medicine will cure the world of all its ills. At one point, he goes so far as to remark, "Everything, potentially, is a science, is it not?" For Scott, overwhelming faith in science must be coupled with aesthetic sensibility since "the carriers of high modernism tended to see rational order in remarkably visual aesthetic terms. For them, an efficient, rationally organized city, village, or farm was a city that looked regimented and orderly in a geometrical sense."[13] It is no coincidence then that Conner is also an aesthete: beyond the fact that he "liked things clean," we are told that "The sculptor has his rock and the saint the silence of his Lord, but a man like Conner who has vowed to bring order and beauty out of human substance has no third factor." This penchant leads Hook to sardonically tell him "Had you and your kind arranged the stars, you would have set them geo-metrically [*sic*]."[14]

The third distinguishing feature of Scott's modern state is its authoritarian willingness and ability "to use the full weight of its coercive power" toward centralization.[15] Conner uses his coercive power—or threat thereof—to reorganize the poorhouse and enforce order: his sidekick Buddy is instructed to kill a stray cat that had been smuggled into the grounds (since it threatened what was deemed to be the public health); similarly, he physically removes Hook's cigar from his mouth after he had been "forbidden" from smoking. That Conner's rigid mode of administration is constantly contrasted with the more lax, personable—but dangerously incompetent—regime of his predecessor, Mendelssohn (who, in a Weberian sense, enjoyed a "charismatic" source of legitimacy rather than a rational-legalistic one) is a reminder that the successful reordering of the poorhouse—people were living longer and feeling better—was only possible through the centralization of power.

Scott's final criterion for the high-modernist state is also the only one interestingly absent from Updike's poorhouse: "a prostrate civil society that lacks the capacity to resist."[16] *The Poorhouse Fair* early on establishes a subtle democratic tone that tempers its authoritarian bent. Conner himself suggests this when, in response to Amy's complaints of feeling powerless, he proclaims: "That's just the way I want no one to feel. I'm an agent of the National Internal Welfare Department and own nothing here. If it is anyone's property it is yours. Yours and the American people's." Not only does he justify his actions in democratic terms, but he does so in capitalist ones as well. "Part of my policy has been, within the limits of the appropriations, to give the residents here some sense of ownership," Conner tells an inmate who inquired about the assigned seating. "It strengthens, is my belief, rather than weakens a communal fabric to have running through it strands of private ownership." Indeed, the inmates clearly still have some say in how they are to be governed: They threaten to "write [their] grievances to the government in Washington" and in a climactic scene later on they redeem some form of agency when they symbolically rebel by stoning Conner with the same stones he had made them clear from the broken poorhouse wall (the narrator accordingly observes after this incident that they "had shown there were rights.")[17] These acts serve as an explicit reminder that, for all his power, Conner does not rule the poorhouse as an autocrat. And it helps us realize why Updike called the novel "a deliberate anti–*Nineteen Eighty-Four*."[18] Ira Katznelson has claimed that the New Deal sustained "complicated and sometimes unprincipled relationships between democracy and dictatorships."[19] By outlining the similarities and differences between his fictional poorhouse and Orwell's dystopian Oceania, Updike effectively constructed Conner's poorhouse to appear interchangeably democratic *and* authoritarian, possibly reflecting the contradictory new liberal tradition taking root.

Updike's unusual decision to interrogate American society through the metaphorical prism of the federal poorhouse is apposite since the poorhouse symbolizes the quintessential task with which the state-centered liberalism that emerged out of the New Deal was primarily concerned: public welfare.[20] As William Leuchtenburg argued in his history of the New Deal:

> For the first time for many Americans, the federal government became an institution that was directly experienced. More than state and local governments, it came to be *the* government, an agency directly concerned with their

welfare. It was the source of their relief payments; it taxed them directly for old age pensions; it even gave their children hot lunches in school. As the role of the state changed from that of neutral arbiter to a "powerful promoter of society's welfare," people felt an interest in affairs in Washington they had never had before.[21]

Conner's poorhouse closely resembles the New Deal state: everything he does—sending inmates to the infirmary, forbidding them from drinking alcohol, and persuasively urging them to stay out of the sun—is indicative of his attempts to actively promote what he believes to be their welfare. In this regard, the explicit designation of Conner's poorhouse as maintaining sole responsibility for the inmates' sustenance and welfare ("these people, having yielded all authority, looked beyond themselves for everything," the narrator observes) reflects upon the distinct trend towards statism that, as David Plotke has argued, was the central hallmark of the New Deal state.[22] Furthermore, the motif of adolescence—the inmates are constantly referred to as children—illuminates an inverted reality in which the elderly have reverted back to dependency. That Updike chose to populate the poorhouse with mostly blue-collar artisans, farmers, and laborers, is symbolic of the traumatic shift in the lives of many Americans who, in the wake the Great Depression, had been relegated to an unfamiliar state of government dependency.[23]

Just as Conner's poorhouse resembles the American welfare state, it is Conner himself who all too often resembles its loyal servants. Dedicated to pragmatic solutions, scientific management, secular humanism, and bureaucratic organization, Conner is a caricature of the managerial class of administrators who implemented the New Deal. "The Reformers of the thirties abandoned—or claimed they had abandoned—the old Emersonian hope of reforming man and sought only to change institutions," Leuchtenburg explained. "The liberal activists grasped only a part of the truth; they retreated from concepts like 'tragedy,' 'sin,' 'God,' often had small patience with the force of tradition, and showed little understanding of what moved men to seek meaning outside of political experience."[24]

Conner personifies these qualities: he is an avowed atheist who believes in an abstract goodness of men; like Rousseau, he fears that the corrupt institutions—like the broken poorhouse managed by his predecessor—have led them astray ("Man was good," he thinks to himself. "There was destination"). He has no familial longings or sexual desires and fails to register any experiences outside of work. Accordingly, the past in his eyes weighs heavily upon the present, and he considers tradition an impediment to progress that must be discarded ("When would they all die and let the human day dawn?" he wonders). As an Apollonian at heart, he has no awareness of the tragic and can barely stand, let alone understand, any Dionysian impulses for emotional or spiritual fulfillment. Ironically, this mechanical embrace of life has left him aloof from, and unappreciative of, the imminent death present all around him. When he asks Hook, in a heated exchange over his methods, "Is it the wish to eliminate pain that strikes you as amusing?" Hook responds, "Indeed not, but it is an error now to believe that the absence of evil will follow from the elimination of pain."[25] Unconcerned with the tragic implications of the human condition, Conner, like many New Dealers, set out to solve material scarcity without paying attention to the spiritual or emotional vacuum left behind.

While Conner represents a new stage in the development of American liberalism, he also demonstrates a novel understanding of liberty that underscores it. The concept of "positive liberty," as Isaiah Berlin coined it, is concerned with answering the basic question, "what, or who, is the source of control or interference that can determine someone to do, or be, this rather than that?"[26] Updike's *The Poorhouse Fair* answers this question clearly: it is the state personified by Conner that claims the right and power to do so in place of the individual. What is used to justify such intervention, explains Berlin, is the pursuit of liberty in a "positive" sense that actively seeks to obtain a certain self-mastery. Rooted in the Enlightenment's quest to liberate man from his "self-imposed immaturity," "positive liberty" strives toward transcendence and is accordingly dedicated to actively promoting the *freedom* to become that which one potentially could be. Although Berlin was not necessarily opposed to pursuing "positive liberty," he was worried about its potential for self-corruption. "The real self may be conceived as something wider than the individual . . . as a social whole of which the individual is an element or aspect," he wrote. The problem with this conception of liberty, Berlin feared, is "that we recognize that it is possible, and at times, justifiable, to coerce men in the name of some goal (let us say, justice or public health) which they would, if they were more enlightened, themselves pursue, but do not, because they are blind, or ignorant or corrupt. . . . I am then claiming that I know what they truly need better than they know it themselves."[27]

Although Updike never studied with Berlin when he taught at Harvard, he did read him as a student and was familiar with his ideas.[28] It is therefore quite understandable that Conner is committed to promoting individual liberty in the "positive" sense. This is how Updike's narrator describes him: "The limits of being a poorhouse prefect chafed a man dedicated to a dynamic vision: that of Man living healthy and unafraid beneath blank skies, 'integrated,' as the accepted phrase had it, 'with his fulfilled possibilities.'" Conner even admits that "Poverty isn't a positive thing; it's a lack. The scientific state adds; it takes nothing away." What essentially justifies his actions is the liberation of man in the "positive" sense—by making him healthy and productive—so as to enable him to fulfill his destiny of self-mastery. This is accordingly his "conception of heaven":

> I see it placed on this earth. There will be no disease. There will be no oppression, political or economic, because the administration of power will be in the hands of those who have no hunger for power, but who are, rather, dedicated to the cause of all humanity. There will be ample leisure for recreation. . . . Money too may have vanished. The state will receive what is made and give what is needed. Imagine this continent—the great cities things of beauty; squalor gone; the rivers conserved; the beauty of the landscape, conserved. . . . Each man will know himself—without delusions, without muddle, and within the limits of that self-knowledge will construct a sane and useful life. Work and love: parks: orchards. Understand me. The factors which for ages have warped the mind of man and stunted his body will be destroyed; man will grow like a tree in the open. There will be no waste. No pain and above all no *waste*. And this heaven *will* come to *this* earth, and come soon.[29]

A concentrated mélange of Plato, Condorcet, Marx, and Le Corbusier, Conner's idealized America reads like a lost passage from Edmund Wilson's *To the Finland Station*—a book Updike knew well from college—in the sense that it too combined an array of utopian schemes to remake society.[30] But it is this secular messianism that is meant to give us an explanation for Conner's actions. He is no "tyrant" in the classical sense—despite being called as such; instead, by observing that "his intensions were wholly good" and that his was "a work of love," Updike reminded us that like many well-intentioned albeit misguided administrators before him, Conner has allowed the ends to cloud his judgment of the means. When he confides to Lucas, one of the inmates, "I want to help these men to hold up their heads; to retain to the end the dignity that properly belongs to every member, big or little, of humanity," he is answering that basic question Berlin posed: it is the state's responsibility to employ its power in the private sphere to ensure the physical welfare of citizens indispensable for securing their metaphysical one.[31]

There are several subtle ways in which Conner does this. First, we can locate his penchant for the promotion of "positive liberty" in the way he justifies the enforcement of certain regulations: whether he is commanding Lucas to attend the infirmary, forbidding Hook to smoke, or urging Amy to move her table into the shade, he couches these policies in terms of *the inmates'* own welfare and as the products of what "should" be, in his rational universe, their own free will. This is especially evident in his dialogue with Amy:

> C: Wouldn't you prefer a table underneath the trees? You're in a rather exposed position here.
> A: Well, if I weren't exposed who'd see me?
> C: I meant simply up by the walk, in the shade.
> A: I'm usually situated here.
> C: If you prefer it . . . though of course there's no difference. I only thought you looked a little pale.
> A: What do you expect at my age? You expect too much from us old people, Mr. Conner. . . . You expect us to give up the old ways, and make this place a little copy of the world outside, the way it's going. I don't say you don't mean well, but it won't do. We're too old and too mean; we're too tired. Now if you say to me, you must move your belongings over beneath the tree, I'll do it, because I have no delusions as to whose mercy we're dependent on. . . .
> C: There is no reason . . . unless you want to, why you should stand under the sun for ten hours.
> A: This isn't an all-day sun.
> C: Whether it is or not, let me and one of the men move your table and chair underneath the trees. . . . You have free will. I'm not trying to steal your bonnet from you, or your usual place; I had only your welfare in mind.[32]

In this exchange, as in many others, Conner's stubborn attempts at imposing order are not authoritarian or oppressive as much as they are altruistic and paternal; the new liberal state that he embodies similarly undertook the task to actively promote the welfare of its citizens since it had concluded, as Berlin warned, that it is a better judge than they are of how to do so.

The Virtues of Liberalism

Updike came to regret framing Conner in a one-dimensional manner that, like a straw man, inadvertently served to aggrandize Hook. He even conceded, retrospectively, that "the novel . . . is at its weakest with Conner," who "should have been more." However, this salient literary failure, which somewhat undermines the ideological balance of the plot, ironically helps shed greater light on the political dilemmas it deals with.[33] Whereas Conner, the metaphorical manifestation of New Deal liberalism, is the forward-looking man of tomorrow who employs the institutional tools of government to reorganize society, Hook, his archrival (Conner fears he was "capturing the domain") is emblematic of yesterday's America and its classical liberal tradition that refused to be organized as such. As the oldest resident, the ninety-four-year-old Hook belongs to a vanishing breed whose "day of authority had set" and in whose place a new generation of technocrats like Conner had arisen.[34] In many ways, the chief concern of the novel is to interrogate the implications of this changing of the guard. Updike, who conveyed an empathy toward Hook that he had not bestowed upon Conner, betrayed his social and political concerns when recalling: "I suddenly wished to write a memorial to it, a book about America changing. . . . I was trying to do any number of things some of which I've forgotten. I was trying to say something about what I felt the condition of America was in 1957."[35]

Hook and the old liberal tradition he embodies represent the declining forces at the expense of whom such changes were, in Updike's mind, taking place. Unlike Conner's regimented world governed by statistics, rules, and regulations, Hook is a creature of habits: he is a man of custom rather than law who has a "customary" seat in the poorhouse, regularly smokes four cigars, and exercises daily. His proud stewardship of a customary America from which the centralizing forces of the modern state have been absent is embedded in his name, "Hook," which, as George Searles has observed, links past with present.[36] Like Henry Adams, Hook is a life-long educator who ironically appears uneducated for the modern world: he laments the "busyness" and shoddy workmanship of the mass-produced industrial economy, against which he compares the dexterity and artisanship of old-world craftsmanship ("modern day workmen are not what they were"). When he looks out to the developed lands surrounding the poorhouse, his nostalgic impulses lead him instead to see the urban ravaging of what had once been pristine nature.

Highly attuned to the sensory experiences of life, Hook embraces the ecstatic potentialities invited by his senses and is imbued by an Emersonian reverence for nature. He doggedly defends his freedom to think—for instance to believe in God in the face of Conner's obtrusive atheism—and to do as he chooses with his ailing body (like smoke cigars and sit wherever he wants). In constructing him in such a way, Updike admitted that there is "a philosophical ambition here; an attempt, no less, to present the meaning of being alive, as conveyed by its sensations. Our eager innate life, rebounding from the exterior world, affirms itself, and the quality of affirmation is taken to be extrinsic, immanent, divine."[37]

Given Hook's heightened sensitivities, it is understandable that he retains a palpable religious commitment. Suspicious of Conner's secular humanism, he believes in a strict interpretation of scripture, subscribes to divinely ordained virtues, and practices "unrelenting faith." "Now, it has never been claimed, that the Creator's mind is a book open for all to read," he contends during an argument with Conner over the existence of God. "This I do know, that that part of the uni-verse [sic] which is visible to me, as distinct from that which is related to me, is an unfailing source of consolation. Dumb creatures are more than their skeletons." What is apposite about Hook's faith is that it is not necessarily blind; the conscious distinctions he makes between essence and being, his penchant for rationally based deduction, and the fact that the narrator frequently reminds us that Hook is not only an educator but continues to be an educated man who reads the newspaper every day, all suggest that his faith is also grounded in reason. This is an important distinction: instead of reducing Hook to ignorance or zealotry, Updike complicated his character by advancing through him a scholastic synthesis of faith *and* reason that attempts to reconcile the two elements. When Hook talks about religion, he lays forth a rational skepticism that is specifically posteriori: he points to the immaculate nature of flowers, lobsters, and stars as indisputable products of creation. "It seems implaus-ible [sic]," he tells Conner, who insists creation was an "accident." "I do not quite see how any amount of time can gener-ate [sic] something from nothing."[38] Updike, who had labeled Aquinas's *Summa Theologiae* as the most important book of the last millennia and closely studied—and admired—scholasticism at Harvard, affirmed that *The Poorhouse Fair* had indeed been "sketched along Thomist lines."[39]

Echoing Updike's instinctive Lutheran pessimism toward human nature, Hook's faith seems to stem from practical-political as much as spiritual concerns.[40] This especially leads him to dispute Conner's utopian vision of an advanced society potentially expunged of pain *and* evil:

> C: Pain is evil.
> H: The Roman Empire was very pros-perous [*sic*], and yet evil.
> C: There was a good deal of pain in pagan Rome.
> H: Arti-ficially [*sic*] induced. It need not have been. The Emperor Nero, now, besides arranging exhibitions for the enter-tainment [*sic*] of others, had torments inflicted upon himself to re-lieve [*sic*] his boredom.

Without the internal mechanisms of restraint provided by religion, Hook fears there will be no restraining human inclinations for evil; the only preventive measure therefore was obedience to religious commandments. As Hook explains: "Now Nero murdered his mother as the logical out-come [*sic*] of his philosophy. What surprises me in this day and age is that everyone doesn't do the same. Make no mistake. There is little store of virtue left."[41] That he explicitly defines virtue here as "obedience to the commands of God" suggests he may consider the political merits of religion as a potential bulwark against an increasingly decadent secular and materialist society.

It is telling that alongside his fervent religiosity the only personal information shared about Hook's past, other than the fact that he was a teacher, has to do with his firm political inclinations. As a teacher, Hook mastered two subjects: nineteenth-century American politics and Roman history. Interestingly, both of these symbolize golden ages of the republican tradition that Hook personifies. The fact that Hook is committed mostly to a set of rural, communal, populist, agrarian, and artisanal democratic and religious values—quintessential republican qualities—is fitting because they are also Hook's most distinct features: he is a product of the past rooted in the traditions of a bygone America; he laments the development of urban society that has ravaged the pastoral paradise, often extols the virtues of personal responsibility, faith, and craftsmanship, and is suspicious of science and encroaching bureaucracy.[42]

In his historical analysis of republicanism in America, historian Daniel T. Rodgers observed that "no term was more central to the republican paradigm than 'virtue.'"[43] That Hook is committed to cultivating virtues and couches much of his rhetoric in such language is quite telling of certain republican dispositions that are constitutive of his traditional liberalism. On one hand, Hook, who "speaks with individual life," preaches the merits of self-reliance, and stubbornly refuses to conform to Conner's depersonalizing regulations, retains what one critic called a "Kierkegaardian sense of spiritual individuality."[44] But his uncompromising individualism is coupled with a salient communal, artisanal, and religious spirit. Although difficult to conceptualize theoretically, Hook's hybridized brand of liberalism essentially personifies the unique synthesis of liberal *and* republican values that James Kloppenberg identified as constituting "the virtues of liberalism" in America: concerned with community as much as with individualism, Hook's dual conception of virtue, which he confidently describes as "a solid thing, as firm and workable as wood," is not only framed in moral terms but in a classic republican manner that considers virtue "an austerity of the hunt, a manliness from which comes all life, so that it can be written that the woman takes her life from the man. As the Indian once served the elusive deer he hunted, men once served invisible goals, and grew hard in such service and pursuit, and lent their society an indispensable shadow."[45]

The liberal-republican synthesis that defines Hook's persona is firmly established by the historical context in which Updike consciously placed him. As a devoted man of what was once the progressive Left, it is not surprising that we are told "Hook conceived of himself as a politician": he constantly argues politics with Amy, who admires William McKinley, while he extols Grover Cleveland and offers a remarkably Beardian explanation for the Civil War as a clash of economic interests.[46] His salient populist-progressive affinities help explain why his hero is William Jennings Bryan. "Now, that McKinley was nothing but Mark Hanna's parade uniform," Hook tells Amy. "The man he beat was twenty times his greater, and he did it on the strength of New York and Boston money. Bryan." Later on, when Conner mentions Bryan, Amy emphasizes that "Hookie's always talking him up to me." Given Hook's admiration for Bryan and his perennial advocacy of his beliefs—many of which defined pre–New Deal liberalism—it is impossible to overlook the metaphorical significance and not reimagine the personal confrontation between him and Conner on political grounds as symbolic of competing visions of American liberalism that developed in the wake of the New Deal.[47]

Although Bryan's tarnished historical image has become commensurate with intolerance as the result of his participation in the Scopes "Monkey Trial" (that was made infamous by the film *Inherit the Wind* in 1960, which Updike saw—and tellingly disliked), Updike presented, through Hook, a more sympathetic and complex portrait of the "Great Commoner."[48] (It hardly seems a coincidence that the longest and most profound dialogue in the novel is about creation and eerily mimics the memorable trial scene from *Inherit the Wind*). Historian Michael Kazin has argued that Bryan's ideas symbolize "the romance of Jefferson and Jesus."[49] And indeed, what characterized Bryan—like Hook—was the attempt to navigate the sweeping challenges of modernity with a traditional compass. When Bryan warned, "take sentiment from life and there is nothing left," or declared that "the individualist, while contending that the largest and broadest developments of the individual, and hence of the entire population, is best secured by full and free competition, made fair by law, believes in a spiritual force which acts beyond the sphere of the state," he was advocating a religion that sought a way to preserve meaning in an increasingly meaningless reality.[50] As many historians agree, Bryan, who unsuccessfully ran as the Democratic nominee for president three times (1896, 1900, 1908), was one of the last disciples of Jefferson and his brand of a liberal-republican synthesis that sought to fuse Lockean-liberal ideas of natural rights, limited government, and free markets with classical-republican beliefs of community, social equality, direct democracy, and cultivation of virtues.[51] Walter Lippmann observed that what Bryan and his followers truly opposed "from the bottom of their souls" were the modernizing forces that "upset the old life of the prairies, made new demands on democracy, introduced specialization and science, had destroyed village loyalties, frustrated private ambitions, and created the impersonal relationships of the modern world."[52]

Despite his religious fundamentalism, Bryan's politics were often quite practical: he advocated the expansion of the federal government (and supported tariff reduction, progressive income tax, and antitrust legislation) and believed in the redeeming potential of science to improve people's lives. The key distinction, however, between the old and new forms of liberalism that *The Poorhouse Fair* outlines is that Bryan, unlike Conner, embraced these modernizing mechanisms in order to defend and enhance—not replace or attenuate—individual liberty. By asserting that "the chief duty of governments, in so far as they are coercive, is to restrain those who would interfere with the inalienable rights of the individual," Bryan made the classic liberal argument for expanding government solely in order to restrain other elements—in this case uncontrollable market forces—that were decimating the private sphere and encroaching upon the democratic sovereignty of the people.⁵³ The problem with Conner's "new" liberalism in other words was not the means that it employed but the ends for which it employed them. "The Commoner had no grudge against scientists; in his opinion, they had done much to benefit society. As always, however, he remained on guard against elites of any kind that presumed to act or speak for the people. Too many times he had observed self-appointed leaders dismissing and degrading the wisdom of common citizens," the historian LeRoy Ashby observed. "It was one thing for scientists to apply their new discoveries to technological matters; it was quite another for experts to tread onto the more subjective terrain of values and habits."⁵⁴ Just as Bryan had opposed pretentious claims of science to redefine value, Hook resists Conner's encroachments *only* when they seek to do the same by challenging his faith or dictating what he could do with his mind or body.

Postwar liberalism's inability to delineate means from ends and employ its power to augment rather than undermine individual liberty and democratic sovereignty gradually engendered suspicions among many Americans who felt the federal government, like Conner, was concerned not with securing the public welfare but with dictating it. These concerns, initially voiced by Bryan, eventually exploded in opposition to the New Deal. That is why it is fitting to consider Hook not only as a disciple of Bryan but also an echo of those voices of protest his suspicions helped feed. Despite the authoritarian and anti-Semitic bent that marred the populist movements behind Huey Long and Father Coughlin in the 1930s, as Alan Brinkley averred:

> [They] were not the leaders of irrational, anti-democratic uprisings. . . . Instead, they were manifestations of one of the most powerful impulses of the Great Depression, and of many decades of American life before it: the urge to defend the autonomy of the individual and the independence of the community against encroachments from the modern industrial state. Followers of Long and Coughlin yearned for no shining collective future. They called, rather, for a society in which the individual retained control of his own life and livelihood; in which power resided in visible, accessible institutions; in which wealth was equitably (if not necessarily equally) shared.⁵⁵

Whereas Conner pursues "positive liberty" in order to facilitate transcendence and self-mastery, Hook is more concerned with preserving liberty in its "negative" sense, from external intervention—in this case, Conner's regulations. As Berlin put it, the question with which "negative liberty" was primarily concerned is: "What is the area within which the subject—a person or group of persons—is or should be left to do or be what he is able to do or be, without interference by other persons?"[56] Inspired by the classic liberalism of John Locke and J. S. Mill, Berlin envisioned the boundaries of "negative liberty" as defending the sanctity of the individual sphere from all external forces not directly—and adversely—affected by it. The problem, however, as Berlin conceded, was that "Men are largely interdependent and no man's activity is so completely private as never to obstruct the lives of others in any way."[57]

It is fair to assume that Updike was conscious of these theoretical dilemmas by the fact that he explicitly couched the question of the inmates' liberty in the discourse of rights. One of the first things revealed about Conner at the onset of the book is that he is disturbed by a letter of complaint he received from a resident of the nearby town. When one of the inmates enters Conner's office, we are told "his eyes glancing to the letter; *help not hinder, I myself,* and *rights* leaped from between his fingers." The letter periodically resurfaces to weigh heavily on Conner's mind. Although the initial mention of it hints at its preoccupation with the inmates' rights, the (misspelled) letter's content, once revealed, clearly manifests this concern:

> Stephen Conner—Who do you think you are a Big shot? Yr duty is to help not hinder these old people on there way to there final Reward. I myself have heard bitter complant from these old people when they come into town where I live. . . . The nature of there complants I will disclose latter, and will write the U.S. gov.ment depending. Things have not gone so far these old people have no rights no pale peenynotchin basterd can take away.

The dilemma regarding rights that the continued presence of this symbolic letter in Conner's pocket sustains throughout the novel is sparked when Gregg, a somewhat malevolent and reckless inmate, cries out in a typical spat of rage, "I'll kill the rotten queer. I have rights," after Conner disposed of the diseased cat Gregg had smuggled into the grounds—a remark which leads Hook to respond, "No, now, you don't, if truth, be known." What is telling about this exchange over rights is how Updike set it up: "Hook recognized in the small man's melting eyes signs of madness that created a hazard for them all, and the old disciplinarian showed as he said, 'Why, it was better to put it out of its misery than let it linger.'" Whereas Hook had been resisting Conner's attempts to regulate his mind and body, this confrontation with Gregg is indicative of a deeper understanding that the individual sphere cannot be left unregulated; like Berlin, Updike may have actually implied that the individual is free to pursue his personal welfare as long as it does not clash with that of others—in this case, by endangering other residents' health. That Hook shares Conner's concern with Gregg's "hazardous" behavior and endorses his response suggests that even while protecting individual liberty we must be careful to restrict its boundaries when the collective welfare is at stake.[58]

The boundaries of liberty are further explored through the book's use of persistent metaphors borrowed from nature. Although *The Poorhouse Fair* has often been associated with *Nineteen Eighty-Four*, voices from Orwell's other classic, *Animal Farm*, echo throughout the plot. Not only are the inmates constantly compared to animals and referred to, both individually and collectively, as "ants," "pigs," "sheep," and "cattle," the poorhouse itself is called a "zoo" and a "jungle" (this association of humans with animals is further reinforced by the Darwinian vocabulary that suffuses the climactic debate between Conner and Hook over the origins of creation).

It is the presence of Gregg, more than anything, that serves as a literary instrument for addressing political questions of power and liberty. Not only is he most commonly described as an animal (he moves "nimbly as a monkey on a rubber tire in the old-fashioned zoos"), but he often behaves like one. Verbally and physically abusive, Gregg is described as flying into "confused rage"; he wields a knife, gets drunk on illicit alcohol, and leads the symbolic stoning of Conner. When he smuggles the cat into the poorhouse, he does so, as Hook recognizes, "to torment, no doubt." It is no surprise then that Hook, his supposed friend, feels "distaste" toward him and considers him "a malevolent busy force."[59]

What Gregg's character essentially offers us is a foil against which to reevaluate the necessary limits that a state can—and should—place upon individual liberty. That his actions remind us of the close proximity between nature and human nature is no coincidence given the Puritanic inclinations that Hook possesses and his outspoken belief in the presence of evil. Unlike Hook, Gregg is someone who is endowed with the most abject qualities that make a state necessary in the first place. And Updike seems to have directly suggested this in the paternal responses that Gregg's actions repeatedly evoke from him. For instance, at the onset, when Gregg is enraged by Conner's attempt to regulate the seating and engages in a vile diatribe, we are told that Hook's "disciplinarian instincts" were awoken and as result he recalled his days as a schoolteacher. Later on, after Gregg brings the diseased cat into the poorhouse to spite Conner, Hook again recalls an incident from his teaching days when his students bludgeoned a squirrel to death with hockey sticks. "Superimposing his memory of difficult students on Gregg, he perceived the true motive for his act," the narrator observes. "It was a disturbance of accustomed order." By framing Gregg's actions in primordial and juvenile terms, and having them repeatedly evoke Hook's disciplinarian and paternal instincts, Updike's plot tests the limits of liberty and asks us to evaluate the boundary between freedom and authority.[60]

This central question of when to limit individual freedom is directly addressed in an incident involving Mrs. Lucas's parakeet. The bird, which is caged in her room, is occasionally allowed to fly around the poorhouse corridors. "Poor thing has to have some exercise, you can't ask it to sit there like a stuffed ornament, in my daughter's house it had great freedom. It can't have that freedom here, but it has to have some," Mrs. Lucas explains. "In my daughter's house the cat caught it and took off its tail feathers—that's the final result of all the freedom they gave it." The metaphorical significance of the scene is clear: there is such a thing as too much freedom, and just as the parakeet cannot be released in order to protect it from the cat in Mrs. Lucas's daughter's house, the inmates themselves cannot be liberated from all authority. Even the boundaries of "negative liberty" must therefore be carefully fixed, not necessarily because the inmates may hurt themselves but because dangerous others—like Gregg—may do it to them.[61]

The Trials of Consensus

Instead of a liberal consensus, Updike's *The Poorhouse Fair* parts the curtain only to reveal incipient cracks beneath its surface. While the pragmatic necessities of depression and war had, for an extended period of time, been able to gloss over fundamental disagreements and sustain ostensible political accord among liberals, the book punctures such illusions. Like Schlesinger, Trilling, and Hofstadter, the young Updike had apparently grown concerned with the fate of American political culture. And *The Poorhouse Fair* may have been his way of sounding an oblique alarm, one not too different from that raised by some of the leading critics of liberalism at the time. The increasing powerlessness of the individual—a core motif in the novel—suffuses some of the most salient political debates of the era. Unlike the businessmen, libertarians, and southern agrarianists, who led the onslaught against the New Deal under the pretense that it would pave "the road to serfdom" and was anathema to America's founding principles of self-government, *The Poorhouse Fair* does not reject the state per se but merely questions its limits and explores the consequences of its expansion.[62] Partly channeling, often anticipating, important works like Robert Nisbet's *The Quest for Community* (1953), Arthur Ekirch's *The Decline of American Liberalism* (1955), and Theodore Lowi's *The End of Liberalism* (1969), which focused on the corrupting effects of big government and interest group politics on community cohesion and family, individual liberty and democratic participation, *The Poorhouse Fair* makes similar arguments, albeit in a more subtle and restrained manner.

Lowi's book, which claimed consensus "is finished," may be the most germane to this intraliberal discord if only because Lowi, an esteemed political scientist, was himself a dedicated liberal.[63] Unlike conservatives, he believed that government itself was not the problem. "Instead, the issues will be the still older and almost forgotten ones of what kind of government: what ends of government, what forms of government, what consequences of government—for our time and for the future, as the United States faces the revolution of human relations." Much like how the poorhouse inmates acted under Conner, Lowi was disheartened by the gradual abandonment of genuine, and formal, democratic procedures, and by the subsequent relegation of power and decision making to external experts. For Lowi, what was so disturbing about this reallocation of power shifting upwards was the fact that "it shuts out the public." "Liberalism has promoted concentration of democratic authority but deconcentration of democratic power," he wrote. It's likely that the young author of *The Poorhouse Fair* would have agreed.[64]

Far from ideological uniformity, *The Poorhouse Fair* suggests a tense symbiosis between consensus and conflict. After all, the plot is driven by a certain magnetic force that draws the two protagonists together—and the diverging liberal traditions they represent—as much as it pushes them apart. From the very onset, there is a calculated obfuscation of the relationship between Conner and Hook that undermines any attempts at clear dichotomization. Although the novel begins with Conner's ostensibly authoritarian act of regulating the seating, this is curiously enough to invoke Hook's initial reaction: "a reflex of pride twitched the corners of his mouth; he had always preferred, in the days when certain honors were allowed him, to have his name spelled in full, with the dignity of the middle initial." Rather than protest the action, he conveys "disapproval," not at Conner but at Gregg's attempt at removing the nametags with his knife. This benign reaction gradually develops into a certain sense of camaraderie in the subsequent dialogue between the two when Conner agrees with Hook that it is best to put wounded animals out of their misery rather than let them suffer. After Conner and Hook's initial encounter, the narrator even remarks that Conner "had rather enjoyed the balm of standing by Hook's side." In another clue to their tacit bond, we are told later on that "Conner wondered if Hook, like himself, was not excluded from a certain alliance of affection that existed among these people."[65]

Just as Hook soberly understood Conner's need to maintain order and efficiency (especially in the above-mentioned cases, when it was needed to restrain the behavior of inmates like Gregg or to prevent Lucas or Amy from hurting themselves), Conner too undergoes gradual transformation that ends up driving him closer to Hook. Early on in the novel, Conner finds himself contemplating whether he is a "shepherd" to the inmates or their "captive." The recurring use of the shepherding similes (Conner constantly regards himself as the "shepherd" and the inmates as "sheep") acquires new religious flavor in the wake of the climactic stoning incident. "Stunned and quickly sickened Conner felt as a revelation dropped from a red heaven the word *Unjust*," the narrator explains. It is as significant as it is surprising that his reaction to the stoning is couched in moral-religious terms as it suddenly undermines his entire secular raison d'être, which, from the beginning, was meant to set him apart from Hook. More surprising even is his reaction to the stoning, as conveyed to Buddy:

> B: What are you going to do?
> C: Forgive them.
> B: Forgive them? Just that?
> C: All of that. It's a great deal. I'm quite hurt; I had no idea of that much hate.
> D: But at least you can punish their leader.
> C: I'm their leader.[66]

The fact that Conner, the self-avowed secular humanist, who constantly seeks to rationalize his actions, decides in an uncharacteristic moment of *un*reason to demonstrate the compassionate forgiveness that is the sine qua non of Christianity may be a subtle reminder that he is willing to embrace some of Hook's spiritual ideas just as much as Hook is able to accept some of his rationalist ones.

For all the ambiguities that purposely cloud our judgment regarding the relationship between Hook and Conner, the finale suggests that the urge for reconciliation that perennially resurfaces is left unfulfilled. Although Hook remains the only inmate who does *not* partake in the stoning (he is daydreaming nearby when it occurs) and who condemns Gregg's actions afterward ("he was taken aback, and not in his right mind," Hook says), the final passage of the novel displays their inability—and possibly that of the competing forms of new and old liberalism they embody—to achieve harmony:

> His encounter with Conner had commended to trouble him. The young man had been grievously stricken. The weakness on his face after his henchman had stolen the cigar was troubling to recall; an intimacy had been there Hook must reward with help. . . . He stood motionless, half in moonlight, groping after the fitful shadow of the advice he must impart to Conner, as a bond between them and a testament to endure his dying in the world. What was it?[67]

This apparent "intimacy" between the two could be suggestive of an opportunity for reconciliation. Since Hook shows willingness to accept the pragmatic necessities of administration that are essential for ensuring a more secure life for the inmates while Conner, humbled by the stoning, is able to recognize the spiritual facets that provide life with meaning in the first place, then maybe a pathway for reconciling the competing liberal traditions could be found. But, too much of a novelist and too little a politician, Updike never attempted to surmise how such a reconciliation could actually be achieved; instead, by skillfully portraying the malleability of both characters and their dueling notions of liberalism, he left readers with the responsibility to do so for themselves.

The fact that *The Poorhouse Fair* begins and ends with a question is probably not a coincidence (the opening line reads "What's this?" and the closing line reads "What was it?"). Attempting to delicately balance competing values like liberty and equality and individual and society, Updike intended the novel to raise questions rather than resolve them. In interviews about *The Poorhouse Fair*, he admitted to have imprinted it with his "yes-but" quality that would become, to the chagrin of his critics, a hallmark of his fiction and a reminder to the "negative capability" that suffused it.[68] This is markedly on display throughout *The Poorhouse Fair* through Updike's tendency to convey sympathy for Hook's opinions only to persistently then undermine them in subtle ways. For example, a short while after the inmates fondly reminisce about Conner's predecessor, the narrator casually reminds us that "the window and [fire] escape were Conner's innovation; in Mendelssohn's day they would have burned." Later on, when Hook seems to have bested Conner's atheism in their impassioned debate over creation by vindicating the necessity of faith, it is Buddy who is given the last word, which he uses to reveal how prayer failed his ailing brother, who's grave pain was alleviated only by modern medicine ("It would have been such a little thing for God to do," he laments, "yet it was not done, even that little thing").[69]

Clues to the persistence of this "negative capability" in the plot can also be found in Conner's responses to the inmates' complaints: "Half the county home acres were lying fallow, waste. The outbuildings were crammed with refuse and filth. The west wing was a death trap. When Hook, last autumn, ate that unwashed peach, he would have died if Mendelssohn had still been in charge." By masterfully counterweighing the appeal of both characters—and of the competing ideals they espouse—Updike created a delicate symbiosis that sustains the fictional life in this metaphorical ecosystem he built within the poorhouse walls: Conner giveth life, while Hook giveth that life purpose; for every sensual celebration of life by Hook, we are reminded that without Conner, life would not have been possible in the first place.[70]

The formal quality of the novel, and its almost organic resistance to resolution, is critical to our understanding of *The Poorhouse Fair* exactly because it informs the ideas being conveyed. The lingering aporia with which Updike concludes the novel *is* in other words an apt reflection of the internal divisions and deep pluralism sustaining them that defined the postwar liberal mindset. James Kloppenberg reaffirmed this point by lauding the "permanent suspension" of ideological conflict that remains liberalism's key virtue:

> Historically, the reconciling and balancing of competing values, which seems so elusive in the polarized culture of the United States in the end of the twentieth century, has been another defining feature of the liberal and democratic traditions in America. These traditions have not reflected the false dichotomies of our current debates but instead demonstrate the necessity and even the desirability of holding in suspension, and deliberating about the meaning

and implications of, values that may seem incommensurable in theory but that inspire practices capable of sustaining and enriching our lives. The principles we need are right in front of our eyes in the virtues of liberalism: in the deliberate and delicate balancing of freedom against responsibility, of the desire for individual wealth and security against the importance of social equality, and of genuinely constitutive commitments to religious traditions or other cultural ideals against the awareness of the sometime incompatible values of other Americans.[71]

Much like *The Poorhouse Fair*, Kloppenberg suggests that balancing the fundamental tensions between modern and traditional facets of liberalism—freedom versus collective responsibility, individual versus state, faith versus science—*is* what defines American liberalism in the first place.

Conclusion

In *The Age of Reform,* published three years before *The Poorhouse Fair,* Richard Hofstadter traced the origins of New Deal liberalism back to the populist and progressive movements. Instead of continuity, he located distinct differences between what he considered two competing forces. "Many men who lived through Progressivism and had thought of its characteristic proposals as being in the main line of American traditions, even as being restoratives of those traditions, found in the New Deal an outrageous departure from everything they had known and valued," Hofstadter wrote.[72] What is remarkable about his historical portrayal of these dueling liberal impulses is how closely they align with the ideas embodied by *The Poorhouse Fair*'s chief protagonists. When Hofstadter averred that "The key words of Progressivism were terms like patriotism, citizen, democracy, law, character, conscience, soul, morals, service, duty, shame, disgrace, sin and selfishness—terms redolent of the sturdy Protestant Anglo-Saxon moral," which embraced "the ideal of a life lived close to nature and the soil, the esteem for the primary contacts of country and village life, the cherished image of the independent and self-reliant man," he might as well have been describing Hook.

Conner similarly personifies the new liberalism that had replaced it: New Deal liberals, Hofstadter argued, embraced concepts like "needs, organization, humanitarian, results, technique, institution, realistic, discipline, morale, skill, expert, habits, practical, leadership—a vocabulary revealing a very different constellation of values arising from economic emergency and the imperatives of a bureaucracy." Having traded in the moralism of earlier liberals, Hofstadter contended that New Dealers (like Conner) had been overtaken by "the trend toward management, toward bureaucracy, toward bigness everywhere" and motivated by a "pragmatic spirit and its relentless emphasis upon results."[73]

In many ways *The Poorhouse Fair* captures this epochal transition in the evolution of American liberalism that Hofstadter sensed by depicting the moment when core principles began to bifurcate and take on different meanings for different groups. Whereas liberty has been mostly understood in the "negative" sense until the Progressive and New Deal eras by most liberals, the new bureaucratic forces harnessed by Conner developed an alternative and more "positive" interpretation; the idea of equality, accordingly, also began gravitating from political-legal realms toward more inclusive socioeconomic manifestations; all the while, the traditional Jeffersonian belief in participatory democracy and local community sovereignty was being undermined by an expanding bureaucratic apparatus and its rule of experts.

Hofstadter, who mentored Christopher Lasch at Columbia University during his time there, when he and Updike were still close friends, conceded in his seminal study of modern American liberalism that he was "criticizing largely from within" the liberal camp.[74] What Updike essentially did in *The Poorhouse Fair* was employ the metaphorical lens of fiction to do the same. But whereas Hofstadter the historian had looked to the past, Updike the novelist was more concerned with the future. "The book was written by a young man who saw the time he was living in—the Eisenhower years—as a dry period, certainly a dry period for the established church." Updike explained, "I meant the future it portrays to be less a predictive blueprint than a caricature of contemporary decadence."[75] His warning in the novel's epigraph—"If they do this when the wood is green, what will happen when the wood is dry?" (Luke 23:31)—is not simply a clue to the moral degradation the young novelist was sensing but a reminder of his prescient concerns that the dominant liberal culture of the 1950s had abandoned concern for such morality in the first place.

This would eventually incur great political cost. When we reconsider Hook's defining qualities—individualism, antistatism, self-reliance, virtue, faith, a collective consciousness, and patriotism—we encounter something very familiar: the core principles of the New Right. What may, therefore, be so significant and ironic about the novel is that it reminds us that liberalism once held many of the very ideals that would eventually call into question its own legitimacy.[76] That Barry Goldwater mobilized his "suburban warriors" in the name of liberty and in defense from "state tyranny" in the 1960s, that southern segregationists embraced republican rhetoric and raised the banner of democracy under the guise of "states' rights" to defend racial inequality, or that social conservatives like Phyllis Schlafly, Jerry Falwell, and James Dobson helped awaken and mobilize the religious Right by preaching for a return to family values, community, and faith in the 1970s should not have come as a surprise.[77] Updike had, after all, sounded the alarm over a decade earlier and anticipated the consequential need for liberals to address these concerns. It is fitting that, when George Nash, in his formative study of the conservative intellectual tradition in America, identified antistatism and social conservatism as the twin pillars upon which the New Right rests, he was also addressing the central concerns voiced in Updike's debut novel.[78]

In the years after *The Poorhouse Fair* was published, Updike would return to key concepts of power, liberty, and equality that were explored in the novel and engage them in more explicit ways. In a keynote speech he gave at the Chicago Humanities Festival in 1992 titled "From Freedom to Equality," Updike employed an impressive blend of political theory and history that helps shed some light on what the younger Updike may have been thinking while writing his debut novel. Surveying the perpetual tension between freedom and equality in American history ("the two American bluebirds"), Updike invoked some of Lincoln's and Roosevelt's famous speeches and employed the French philosopher Alexis de Tocqueville's *Democracy in America* to advocate for a greater balance between these two conditions while lamenting that they had fallen short of being fully realized. "America promises equal opportunity, the opportunity, relatively unhobbled by feudal or socialist restraints, to get ahead. But to get ahead means to leave someone else behind," he observed (repeatedly pointing to the grim historical experiences of blacks and women). "Governments are coercive and punitive in the last resort, and American freedom is a relative and not absolute condition," he said. "It is not a chemical that can be distilled into pure form; freedom is a coloring, a shimmer, that softens the coercions and hard necessities of being a human creature, a social animal." Updike even adopted parts of

President Roosevelt's seminal Four Freedoms speech (1941) and used it to distinguish between "passive" freedoms from want and fear and "active" freedoms of speech and religion (essentially inverting what Berlin had labeled "negative" and "positive" liberties).[79] "The concepts of equality and freedom are bound up together . . . but you cannot have, I believe, freedom without equality," Updike concluded. "An American degree of personal freedom can flourish only when the economic thrust is not forcing people apart."[80]

George Searles has called *The Poorhouse Fair* "Updike's thesis statement," but in retrospect it was so much more.[81] Not only does it establish him as a self-aware social thinker with a rich political imagination but it provides us with a rare historical snapshot of a pivotal moment in American political development when the internal contradictions of postwar liberalism began to fester and alternative ideological forces destined to take its place quietly emerged. In doing so, it demonstrates the unique capability of fiction to presciently illuminate nuances often overlooked by more conventional historical analysis and locates the subtle shifts in sensibilities that were soon destined to materialize into more concrete forms of discontent and foment tectonic political transformations. Although critics labeled *The Poorhouse Fair*'s denouement a failure of imagination and complained that Updike left the "conflict unresolved," they overlooked the redeeming value of the ambivalent finale.[82] Having declared "my work is meditation, not pontification" and insisted that "I think of my books not as sermons or directives in a war of ideas but as objects, with different shapes and textures and the mysteriousness of anything that exists," Updike envisioned the role of the novelist in edifying rather than political terms: fiction is meant to help us understand challenges—not to overcome them. In other words, Updike used his debut novel to illuminate some of the mounting problems within the New Deal order, while leaving it to readers to come up with solutions by themselves.[83]

4 | Family Matters
Therapeutic Liberalism, Consumer Capitalism, and the Decline of the Family in *Rabbit, Run*

> *Modern culture is defined by this extraordinary freedom to ransack the world storehouse and to engorge any and every style it comes upon. Such freedom comes from the fact that the axial principle of modern culture is the expression and remaking of the "self" in order to achieve self-realization and self-fulfillment. And in its search, there is a denial of any limits or boundaries to experience. It is a reaching out for all experience; nothing is forbidden, all is to be explored.*
>
> —Daniel Bell

> *Emerson wished to give men courage to be, to follow their own instincts; but these instincts, he neglected to emphasize, can be rapacious. A social fabric, he did not seem quite to realize . . . exists for the protection of its members, as do the laws and inhibitions such a fabric demands.*
>
> —John Updike

The publication of *Rabbit, Run* in 1960 instantly transformed John Updike's career. Having enjoyed rather modest success for his debut novel *The Poorhouse Fair* a year earlier, he became a household name with *Rabbit, Run*. The Rabbit series, which evolved over the next three decades into a tetralogy chronicling the life and times of the chief protagonist, Harry "Rabbit" Angstrom, would eventually earn Updike two Pulitzer Prizes and secure Rabbit a place in the pantheon of American literary heroes alongside Huck Finn, Holden Caulfield, and Jay Gatsby, making him, in the words of James Schiff, an "American icon."[1] A testament to the young novelist's literary talents, *Rabbit, Run* remains Updike's most successful work, critically and commercially, having been printed in more than fifty editions and having sold over 2.5 million copies in dozens of languages all around the world.[2]

The plot, considered somewhat scandalous when first published, revolves around the experiences of Rabbit Angstrom, an ex-high-school basketball star from the sleepy Pennsylvania town of Mt. Judge (a fictional depiction of the author's hometown of Shillington) who might very well represent Updike's alternative life path had he stayed behind in Shillington and not become a successful writer.[3] Having won fame too soon in life, Rabbit finds himself by his mid-twenties plagued by a blend of anxiety, ennui, and disappointment that leads him to abandon his pregnant wife and son in search of the glory days of his youth. He has a meaningless job (demonstrating a kitchen gadget in five-and-dime stores), an unfulfilling marriage (his wife, Janice, is an alcoholic who sits around watching television all day), and a growing list of broken dreams. Feeling suffocated and trapped—by his dead-end job, his unloving family, and the small town in which he has lived all his life—he decides to follow his instincts and do the only thing that, as an ex-athlete, comes natural to him: he runs. The novel recounts his circuitous flight that first takes him from his family to a short road trip westward. After his nerves fail him he turns back and seeks advice from his old high-school basketball coach Marty Tothero. Instead of counseling him, Tothero takes him out to dinner and introduces him to a part-time prostitute named Ruth, whom Rabbit later has an affair with and impregnates. When his wife goes into labor with their daughter Becky, Rabbit leaves Ruth and returns home. The novel culminates with a tragic denouement when Janice, inebriated after Rabbit leaves her yet again, accidentally drowns their baby daughter.

Into this eventful plot situated in 1950s Middle America, Updike has inserted a peculiar and colorful cast of supporting characters. Single and self-conscious about her weight, Ruth has become cynical toward life and is discouraged by the prospects of meeting a decent man and finding genuine love; in Rabbit's company she rediscovers that joie de vivre she thought was lost—and is therefore willing to overlook the fact that he is married. Then there is the enlightened local Episcopalian minister named Jack Eccles: As Rabbit's main interlocutor, and only friend, he attempts to reform his behavior and reunite him with Janice through intensive theological-meets-psychoanalytical sessions held on the golf course. The deep existential conversations between the two generate some of the most important and edifying dialogues of the novel. Rabbit also develops a coquettish relationship with the reverend's wife Lucy, a Freudian enthusiast whom he brashly fondles during his first visit to their household. His ailing high-school coach Tothero plays a minor though critical role by introducing him to Ruth. And an old widow named Mrs. Smith, whose garden Rabbit tends to support himself during his self-imposed exile from his family, plays the role of Tiresias by offering profound—and somewhat prophetic—insight about life and death.

Although all of Updike's early works, including *Rabbit, Run*, are deeply rooted in his autobiographical circumstances growing up in Berks County, Pennsylvania, he has admitted that his novels strive to transcend any parochial individual experience and paint a much larger portrait of lower middle-class life in Middle America.[4] "Harry 'Rabbit' Angstrom was for me a way in—a ticket to the America all around me. What I saw through Rabbit's eyes was more worth telling than what I saw through my own, though the difference was often slight," Updike recalled in 1995, admitting that the tetralogy "became a kind of running report on the state of my hero and his nation, and their ideal reader became a fellow-American."[5] As a "running report" on the state of postwar America, *Rabbit, Run* serves as a prime source of insight into its changing political climate. While the novel was never intended to provide explicit political purchase, it is ironically the depoliticized nature of the novel and its focus on the private sphere of family and personal relationships that makes it so valuable to our understanding of postwar politics. By focusing on the family as the imagined site where broader socioeconomic, cultural, and political forces converge—and clash—Updike effectively demonstrated not only that the personal is, indeed, political, but he also provided a subtle and nuanced critique of postwar affluence and the social coin that New Deal liberalism paid in order to sustain it.

In a retrospective essay about *Rabbit, Run*, written several decades after it was published, Updike claimed that, like him, "Harry regards America proprietorially, and is alert to the changes and deteriorations in it."[6] Among those deteriorations was that of the family—one of the central themes of the novel. In an early interview Updike noted that the backdrop to his early fiction was "the nuclear family breaking up" and explained, "I didn't create this breaking up; it was in the society around me. After all, I'm not responsible for the modern world. I'm just a portrayer of it." A few years later he admitted that "I was trying to make the good Protestant point that we're all involved with our fellow man, and we're all members of families, and so the basic image of [*Rabbit, Run*] is of a man running or leaving or going on the road and disrupting his own family."[7] Updike reaffirmed this motif by recalling that "Jack Kerouac's *On the Road* came out in 1957 and, without reading it, I resented its apparent instruction to cut loose; *Rabbit, Run* was meant to be a realistic demonstration of what happens when a young American family man goes on the road—the people left behind get hurt."[8]

Although the motif of family decline has certainly not been lost on scholars and critics—Morris Dickstein has called the novel "a fable about the frustrating constraints of family life, the deadening spiritual limits of adulthood, maturity and civilization itself"—*Rabbit, Run* illuminates something else that has, so far, been mostly overlooked: the larger structural forces causing this decline.[9] Like with *The Poorhouse Fair*, it, too, locates an emerging clash between competing liberal ideals, but this time the ideas regard cultural and economic affairs rather than political ones. This chapter suggests that *Rabbit, Run* is critical for our understanding of postwar liberalism precisely because it illustrates a causal link between modern cultural and economic changes and the decline of the traditional social institution of the family. The novel essentially demonstrates the manner in which the twin forces of modernity—a new cultural sensibility that prescribed a psychological retreat inward into the self and away from collective responsibility and a new political economy reoriented around the monumental shift from collective production toward individual consumption—had come together as early as the 1950s to erode the bonds of the nuclear family.

Given the near total monopolization and politicization of the family by conservatives for the past forty years, it seems odd to recall that there once was a time when it used to be a paramount liberal concern. Looking at Norman Rockwell's iconic painting, "Freedom from Want," which famously portrays an idealized family preparing to feast on a succulent turkey during a bountiful meal, one cannot help but appreciate its celebration of familial domesticity and material prosperity. It was no coincidence that the image, part of a series of four paintings, was meant to commemorate President Roosevelt's Four Freedoms speech (1941), considered a foundational document for the American welfare state and one with which, as noted in the last chapter, Updike was very familiar.[10] As historian Robert O. Self reminds us,

> the New Deal's "Citizen Worker" and the nuclear family he headed remained a mainstay of conventional liberal thinking and a cornerstone of the Keynesian consensus. . . . From the New Deal to the Great Society, social welfare liberals created a social safety net, supported labor unions, subsidized vast suburban

housing tracts, and created government programs to fight poverty either entirely or in large part to strengthen male-breadwinner nuclear families or to compensate for their temporary instability.[11]

This set of family-oriented policies that Self labeled "breadwinner liberalism" was aimed at strengthening families and ensuring the ability of male workers to support a family through pioneering legislative feats, among them: subsidizing homeownership through the Federal Housing Administration; securing collective bargaining rights, fair wages, and decent benefits to workers through the Wagner Act (1935) and the Fair Labor Standards Act (1938); providing financial aid for impoverished families with dependent children (AFDC); and supporting the aged, disabled, and widowed through Social Security.

But something happened to the family along the way; what exactly caused this dramatic change—some have claimed for the worse—has become one of the central fault lines of American politics for the past half century. "The liberal left lost political purchase on the mythology of family, while the conservative right gained political purchase on a new, ever more absolute family mythology," Self suggested.[12] Two competing partisan narratives emerged to explain why this happened. On the left: an economic narrative that one historian called the "creative destruction of a capitalist economy," which claimed neoliberal reforms, automation, and antilabor policies combined to freeze wages, cut benefits, and undermine job security for men, while inadequate wages, unpaid paternity leave, and lack of public daycare (among others things) disproportionately hurt women, leaving families particularly vulnerable to the ravages of a shrinking economy and skyrocketing inflation. The Right embraced a mostly cultural set of explanations that placed blame on the so-called Culture Wars of the 1960s. In this alternative narrative, the real culprits who undermined America's "family values" were feminists, gay and lesbian rights activists, acts of moral permissiveness, juvenile delinquents, acts of inadequate parenting, and those people calling for sexual liberation. "The key to understanding the political fallout of this pivotal era is not simply that conservatives defeated liberals in the electoral arena, but that cultural explanations triumphed over economic ones in setting the terms of public debate and determining the direction of public policies," historian Matthew Lassiter opined.[13]

Rather than point to an either/or explanation for this fallout, *Rabbit, Run* actually suggests that these two forces converge. Over a decade before the family became politicized and captured the center stage of national political debate, Updike's novel anticipates how both economic and cultural transformations were destabilizing it. In her landmark study of postwar families, Elaine Tyler May argued that the suburban home became "a bastion of safety in an insecure world" by its reliance on two important themes: a newfound material sense of security provided by consumer capitalism and a psychological safety valve—what she termed a "therapeutic approach"—that was "geared to helping people feel better about their place in the world" and "offered private and personal solutions to social problems."[14] Instead of upholding the nuclear family and preserving its stability in unstable times, *Rabbit, Run* suggests that these new economic and cultural forces harnessed by New Deal liberalism ended up, unintentionally, undermining its own historical commitment to it.

The Triumph of the Therapeutic

The great irony of *Rabbit, Run* is that the chief protagonist, who ends up destroying his own family, is, at heart, a family man who has left his home not to escape family life but to re-create a better version of it. After Rabbit's first tryst with Ruth, the part-time prostitute, she remarks with some endearment, "you settle right in, don't you?" In the ensuing scene we are subtly led to understand why exactly he does so. While surveying the window curtains in Ruth's apartment, Rabbit experiences a Proustian moment. "He stands paralyzed by a more beautiful memory: his home, when he was a child, the Sunday papers rattling on the floor, stirred by the afternoon draft, and his mother rattling the dishes in the kitchen; when she is done, she will organize them all, Pop and him and baby Miriam, to go for a walk." Immediately after this flashback, Rabbit suggests to Ruth, "Let's go for a walk"—as if trying to recapture that fleeting moment of family happiness. Eccles, too, notices Rabbit's genuine yearning for family by remarking to his wife that Rabbit "is by nature a domestic creature" and that "Rabbit has a gift for housekeeping."[15]

But if Rabbit is a family man, then what leads him to abandon his family? Critics and scholars have often tried to answer this by suggesting that *Rabbit, Run*, in the spirit of 1950s therapeutic culture and its obsession with psychoanalysis, signals "the inward turn of the postwar novel" and its characters, who have disengaged society in pursuit of self-awareness and personal fulfillment. Matthew Wilson has elaborated the anticonformity theme, arguing that in the tetralogy "Updike transforms Rabbit from the traditional solitary American male character fleeing society to a man integrated into society," while Sanford Pinsker claimed the novel "tests the strength of radical Emersonianism against the power of cultural nets."[16] Morris Dickstein has located this Emersonian rediscovery of what he called "the exigent, imperial self" in a growing obsession for "cultivating the self" that resulted from increasing affluence, leisure, and economic security at the time. Writers in the 1950s, he averred, "were obsessed more with oedipal struggle than with class struggle, concerned about the limits of civilization rather than the conflicts within civilization. Their premises were more Freudian than Marxist."[17]

Rather than merely symbolize selfishness, egotism, or solipsism (all of which it does to an extent), the novel expresses an emergent sensibility behind these themes: what social thinkers at the time called "therapeutic-liberalism." The psychological discovery of the conscious self conjoined with new levels of economic security and consumption habits generated by postwar prosperity had transformed the political culture and changed the ways many came to think, or not think, about politics. This reorientation, facilitated by sweeping institutional changes that resulted from the New Deal and the Cold War's unprecedented bureaucratization of power and professionalization of politics by experts and interest groups, ultimately redefined the boundaries between the private and public spheres in favor of the former. Although therapeutic-liberalism is more a sensibility than a coherent political theory, it is essentially the manifestation of broader socioeconomic and cultural trends toward uninhibited individual fulfillment. The social consequences of this therapeutic shift were disengagement from direct democracy and the sacrifice of active citizenship on the newly constructed alters of personal gratification, material and emotional.[18] Having permeated political culture, political theorists claim the emerging therapeutic sensibility facilitated the rise of what Michael Sandel has called the "procedural republic"—a political system that abandoned "a theory of the common good" and instead opted to secure individual rights and prioritize personal over communal goals. What most mattered in this newly circumscribed social contract dedicated to securing individual rights was regulating the procedure through which Americans realized their *own* ideal of "the good," not determining what "the common good" should be in the first place.[19]

The earliest and most poignant critique of therapeutic liberalism, which in a way was also the first attempt to clearly delineate its contours and define it, was offered in Philip Rieff's *The Triumph of the Therapeutic* (1966). The central problem it engaged was the historical transition from "economic man," represented by the self-interested rational thinker engendered by the Enlightenment, into what Rieff called "psychological man—the latest, and perhaps the supreme, individualist—opposed in depth to earlier modes of self-salvation: through identification with communal purpose." Rieff feared that the abandonment of religious values and the traditional institutions that had upheld them, alongside the inability of the Enlightenment to fill the void that had been created by this process, generated a new therapeutic alternative that sought a post-communal culture where people could "live free from communal purpose." "Men may have gone too far, beyond the old deception of good and evil, to specialize at last, wittingly, in techniques that are to be called, in the present volume, therapeutic," he warned. "What is revolutionary in modern culture refers to releases from inherited doctrines of therapeutic deprivation; from a predicate of renunciatory control . . . our culture has shifted toward a predicate of impulse release." The resulting "aversion to culture," Rieff claimed, decimated corporate identity and liberated individuals from communal bonds.[20]

As a sociologist and cultural critic who had distinguished himself by studying Freud, Rieff was concerned with the social and political implications of a post-Freudian psychology that was increasingly promoting a release from the "cultural net," which for centuries had served to save man from himself. Tellingly, his monumental study mirrors some of the more subtle social critiques unveiled in *Rabbit, Run* and helps elucidate them. The link between the two works is already visible in Rieff's admiration for Matthew Arnold and Karl Barth—both of whom had influenced the young Updike. At Harvard, Arnold's poem "Dover Beach" registered deeply with Updike, due primarily to its elegiac lament for the diminishing value of faith in the modern world.[21] Just as Rieff was concerned with the collapse of moral authority and the ensuing "panic and emptiness" that resulted from the decline of Christianity, Updike too had specifically constructed Rabbit to represent "man in a state of fear and trembling, separated from God, haunted by dread, twisted by the conflicting demands of his animal biology and human intelligence, of the social contract and the inner imperatives." Updike further admitted that "*Rabbit, Run* is a fairly deliberate attempt to examine the human predicament from a theological standpoint."[22]

Given their shared existential angst, it is germane that Rieff, like Updike, drew inspiration from the writings of Swiss theologian Karl Barth, whom he employed to highlight the importance of institutions in the preservation of meaning to individual lives. "To give myself brightness and air I read Karl Barth," Updike once revealed. He repeatedly returned to his theology as a source of inspiration and guidance and he even credited Barth with helping him overcome a spiritual crisis while he was writing *Rabbit, Run*.[23] Rieff, too, built explicitly upon Barth's theology when positing that "the death of a culture begins when its normative institutions fail to communicate ideals in ways that remain inwardly compelling." He went on to argue that "The misery of this culture is acutely stated by the special misery of its normative institutions. Our more general misery is that, having broken with those institutionalized credibilities from which its moral energy derived, new credibilities are not yet operationally effective, and, perhaps, cannot become so in a culture constantly probing its own unwitting part."[24]

Rabbit, Run illuminates this "misery of institutions": church, school, workplace, and family all fail to provide Rabbit the restraint and guidance that could have prevented his moral collapse. The reverend Eccles, himself beset by a crisis of faith, takes personal responsibility for the death of Rabbit's daughter at the end of the novel. In one of the final passages, as Rabbit runs yet again, this time from the pregnant Ruth, "he remembers what once consoled him by seeming to make a hole where he looked through into underlying brightness, and lifts his eyes to the church window. It is, because of church poverty or the late summer nights or just carelessness, unlit, a dark circle in a stone façade."[25] That Tothero, Rabbit's teacher and mentor, is the one who introduces him to the prostitute Ruth is equally indicative of the failure of schools. Third, his inability to find useful work that could provide him with meaning and discipline breeds the frustration that eventually leads him to seek gratification through alternative channels (such as sex). Finally, it is the failure of his parents and family to instill in him a sense of love and security that drives him to seek these in Ruth's bed. What is ultimately portrayed here, as Clinton Burhans aptly observed, is "a civilization losing the powers to civilize."[26]

In such a state, Rieff concluded—much like Max Weber, whom he references on this point—modern man was stuck in a "cage" of his own making. "This culture, which once imagined itself inside a church, feels trapped in something like a zoo of separate cages," he opined. "Modern men are like Rilke's panther, forever looking out from one cage into another" since "modern sense of identity seems outraged by imprisonment in either old church or new cage."[27] Modern therapeutic culture, Rieff suggested, created a new cage—far more oppressive than traditional ones: instead of a "cage" in which humans were sentenced together (family, church, community), each individual has constructed a personal cage in the form of *insatiable* longings for self-realization, instinctual gratification, and heightened consciousness.

It is fitting that the central metaphor used by Updike to explain Rabbit's run revolves around Rieff's very motif. The opening scenes of the novel are rife with caged associations that include arabesque descriptions of the basketball net, fraught with metaphorical meaning. For example: it is only by putting the ball in the net while playing basketball, ironically, that Rabbit himself feels liberated from the cultural and sexual nets that are increasingly confining him. The significance of this motif is established early on the first time Rabbit decides to leave his family: "Rabbit freezes, standing looking at his faint yellow shadow on the white door that leads to the hall, and senses he is in a trap. It seems certain. He goes out." This theme is repeatedly compounded as his flight continues. "He doesn't drive five miles before this road begins to feel like a part of the same trap." A few pages later, as he suffers a meltdown and decides to turn back to Mt. Judge, the sense of entrapment culminates: "The names melt away and he sees the map whole, a net, all those red lines and blue lines and stars, a net he is somewhere caught in." The only way to break out of cultural nets, Rieff suggested, is to rebel: "A social structure shakes with violence and shivers with fears of violence not merely when that structure is callously unjust, but also when its members must stimulate themselves to feverish activity in order to demonstrate how alive they are."[28] Late in the novel, when Rabbit tries to justify his actions to his wife Janice, this is exactly the explanation he provides: "I'm not saying I wasn't wrong, but it felt like I had to [run]. You get the feeling you're in your coffin before they've taken your blood out."[29] By equating his feelings of social entrapment with a form of spiritual death, Rabbit suggests that it is only through the "feverish activity" Rieff so dreaded—impulsive, instinctual, and unrestrained—that he could liberate himself from "cultural nets," recapture his youth, and regain a sense of life.

What most distinguishes psychological man and the therapeutic revolution he represents is, according to Rieff, the colonization by personal feelings of all other modes of experience. "Religious man is born to be saved; psychological man is born to be pleased. The difference was established long ago, when 'I believe,' the cry of the ascetic, lost precedent to 'one feels,' the caveat of the therapeutic," Rieff asserted.[30] This is a meaningful point since it is the supremacy—or tyranny—of feeling that essentially drives *everything* Rabbit does, including the breakup of his family. Already in the opening scene, as Rabbit showcases his basketball skills in a random street game he joins, we are told that "naturals know. It's all in how it feels." The imminence of feeling as the paramount source of human agency repeats itself and is vital for the development of the plot. Rabbit's love for basketball, he admits, is due to the fact that "I get this funny feeling I can do anything" while playing. When Eccles asks him why he left his family, Rabbit explains that he "felt the whole business was fetching and hauling," leading Eccles to respond, "You speak of this feeling of muddle . . . in what way do you think you're exceptional?" When Eccles presses him to look at the consequences of his feelings upon Janice, Rabbit concedes: "I don't know what she feels. I haven't known for years. All I know is what's inside *me*. That's all I have."[31]

In a climactic dialogue between the two, Rabbit confesses his motives: "'Well I don't know all this about theology, but I'll tell you, I *do* feel, I guess, that somewhere behind all this'—he gestures outward at the scenery— . . . 'there's something that wants me to find it.'" Not surprisingly, Eccles, often playing the role of the tragedy's one-man chorus, would later observe that "the boy's [Rabbit's] problem wasn't so much a lack of feeling as an uncontrolled excess of it." So central had this motif become to the novel that Updike chose to conclude it with a reminder of the potency of Rabbit's therapeutic transformation. When he visits Ruth in the final scene to beg her to take him back, he exclaims: "I don't know. I don't know any of these answers. All I know is what feels right. You feel right to me. Sometimes Janice used to. Sometimes nothing does." To which Ruth, who might very well be echoing Updike's verdict on the matter, adamantly responds: "Who cares? That's the thing. Who cares *what* you feel?"[32]

Rabbit's feelings are not only a source of self-justification for deserting his home but they eventually cause the literal destruction of his family by setting in motion the chain of events that lead to the tragic death of Becky. The painful scene in which Rabbit leaves Janice for a second time—thus causing her alcohol-infused depression that results in Becky's accidental drowning—is rooted in Janice's sexual rejection of Rabbit. After she refuses to sleep with him a short time after giving birth, a sexually frustrated Rabbit climbs out of bed and decides to leave. "Why can't you try to imagine how I *feel?* I've just had a baby?" Janice pleads, to which Rabbit responds, "I can. I can but I don't want to, it's not the thing, the thing is how *I* feel. And I feel like getting out." It is this harrowing moment induced directly by Rabbit's inability to contain his feelings that culminates in the death of their daughter. The causal link between his feelings and her death is implied afterward, when the narrator reveals that "For what made him mad at Janice wasn't so much that she was in the right for once and he was wrong and stupid but the closed feeling of it, the feeling of being closed in.... What held him back all day was the feeling that somewhere there was something better for him than listening to babies cry and cheating people in used-car lots and it's this feeling he tries to kill." So destructive had this uninhibited urge "to feel" become that a chastened Rabbit decides in the finale to try and expunge it entirely from within himself.[33]

While Rabbit represents a struggle between psychological and religious man—he still affirms his belief in God and admiration for the church despite his unreligious actions—it is in the Eccles household where the triumph of the therapeutic symbolically takes place. Early in the novel, we witness a telling clash of competing faiths between Eccles and his wife Lucy. Unlike the minister, a reform-minded Episcopalian who has sought to incorporate modern therapeutic sensibilities into his Christian belief, Lucy is "psychological woman" personified. During her first exchange with Rabbit she soundly declares, "I think Freud is like God." This is immediately amplified by the ongoing Oedipal struggles behind her: while she is talking to Rabbit, her daughter enters the marital bed, leading her husband to complain, "Lucy! Joyce is getting into bed with me!" The Freudian motif would continue to define relations in the Eccles household. After Lucy chastises her husband for reading to their daughters frightening bedtime stories, Eccles remarks to Rabbit that "It's her psychology. Children are very sacred in psychology." When Rabbit meets Lucy for a second time, he greets her by asking, "How's Freud?" Lucy's Freudian babble surfaces every time an enamored Rabbit thinks of their conversations (he mumbles to himself "sexual antagonism begins practically at birth" without understanding what it means). Freud's presence in the household is compounded when Eccles recalls the Oedipal struggles between himself and his father and between his father and grandfather. In the final dialogue between Lucy and Rabbit, she castigates his faith, calling Christianity "a very neurotic religion." This leads him to conclude that "when she fetches out her psychology, it seems so foolish to Harry his own feeling of foolishness leaves him."[34]

An important moment in the struggle being played out between religious and psychological man occurs during an inhospitable visit Eccles makes to Fritz Kruppenbach, a grumpy old Lutheran minister who presides over the parish to which the elder Angstroms belong. As he often did in his fiction, Updike used this scene to wage a broader philosophical debate. In response to Eccles's plea for help in reuniting Rabbit and Janice, he is vehemently scolded by Kruppenbach, who Updike consciously modeled after Karl Barth. "I know what they teach you at seminary now: this psychology and that. But I don't agree with it," the old Lutheran says. Expressing distaste with worldly affairs and Barth's strict adherence to faith, revelation, and salvation, he reproaches Eccles: "You think now your job is to be an unpaid doctor, to run around and plug up the holes and make everything smooth. I don't think that. I don't think that's your job." He goes on to rebuke Eccles for his enlightened therapeutic sensibilities, insists that his job is to be "an exemplar of faith" and nothing more, and warns him, "Make no mistake. There is nothing but Christ for us. All the rest, all this decency and busyness, is nothing. It is Devil's work."[35] This powerful dialogue that leaves Eccles perturbed reflects the broader clash between competing forms of Christianity: a modern humanistic faith embodied by the socially active, young Eccles and a dogmatic fundamentalism personified by a disengaged old Kruppenbach.[36]

Despite the scolding that Eccles and his therapeutic sensibilities receive, there is the sense, ironically, that at least in the Eccles's household the novel concludes with the therapeutic sensibility prevailing over the religious one. Following Becky's death, Lucy's initial reaction is to blame her husband, since he had persisted with reuniting Rabbit and Janice. In response to her hurtful remark that "you never should have brought them back together," Eccles agrees: "No, I think you're probably right." His admission is followed by a surprising renunciation of faith: "I don't believe in common sense. . . . If it'll make you happy, I don't believe in anything." To which Lucy replies, "you're being psychopathic." This somber dialogue is apposite if only because it suggests that the reformist theologian who attempts to combine faith and psychology has effectively conceded defeat by renouncing the former in favor of the latter and admitting that his Freudian wife might be right.[37]

Since Updike himself frequently paid tribute to Freud in helping shape his literary imagination, it's no surprise that the Freudian emphasis on culture as repression has long been central to the reception of *Rabbit, Run*.[38] Judie Newman, most notably, interpreted the novel as a Freudian tale that "coheres internally around one major organizing theme: that of the relation between the individual and society, particularly expressed as the instinctual, sensual and libidinous dimensions of the human being in conflict with social constraints," and concluded that "Freud's analysis of society as founded upon repression is important in this connection, though Updike is no naïve Freudian and clearly contests Freud's understanding of religious faith as an illusion."[39] Reinterpreting *Rabbit, Run* as a reflection of therapeutic liberalism helps illuminate the social costs entailed by the evolution of Freudian thought outside of the private sphere. That characters in the novel merely feel, display selfishness, or commit adultery is, after all, not that rare in postwar American fiction (or life); central to this novel, however, is an examination of the consequences of these feelings upon society and its institutions. When Rabbit proclaims that "if you have the guts to be yourself, other people'll pay your price," he echoes Updike's own worries about the potential social effects of the new therapeutic sensibilities.[40] Updike admitted as much when he explained that "My work says, 'Yes. But.' Yes, in *Rabbit, Run* to our inner urgent whispers, but—the social fabric collapses murderously." In an essay on Emerson, Updike further emphasized such social concerns by distancing himself from the great transcendentalist: "Emerson wished to give men courage to be, to follow their own instincts; but these instincts, he neglected to emphasize, can be rapacious. A social fabric, he did not seem quite to realize . . . exists for the protection of its members, as do the laws and inhibitions such a fabric demands."[41]

The Cultural Contradictions of Capitalism

Two years before *Rabbit, Run* was published, the liberal economist John Kenneth Galbraith (who taught at Harvard when Updike was there), sounded the alarm against excessive consumption in his best-selling book *The Affluent Society*. In it, the influential economist turned presidential advisor and diplomat advocated for a "social balance" between consuming private and public goods. "If production creates the wants it seeks to satisfy, or if the wants emerge pari passu with the production, then the urgency of the wants can no longer be used to defend the urgency of the production. Production only fills a void that it has itself created," Galbraith warned. "Just as there must be balance in what a community produces, so there must also be balance in what the community consumes."[42] Historians of postwar America have since come to understand the politics and culture of the era as distinctly shaped by the forces of consumption. Alan Brinkley described it as "a world in which both the idea and the reality of mass consumption were becoming central to American culture and to the American economy" and observed that "In an economy driven by consumer spending, it is not surprising that political thought began to reflect consumer-oriented assumptions as well." Lizabeth Cohen similarly affirmed this in her study of postwar America: "mass consumption had become a central defining engine, not simply of the American economy but of its politics and culture."[43]

Rabbit, Run not only anticipates this transformation but chronicles intimately, at times painfully, its social repercussions.[44] Updike, whose concern for meaningful work even suffused his light verse—"Cherish your work; take profit in the task: Doing's the one reward a Man dare ask"—admitted that a key concern of his early novels was indeed the changing economic conditions marked by the decline of the Protestant work ethic.[45] "My novels are all about the search for useful work. So many people these days have to sell things they don't believe in and have jobs that defy describing," Updike told *Life* magazine in 1966. "A man has to build his life outward from a job he can do."[46] While scholars have focused on the decline of useful work and consumer culture as key themes in *Rabbit, Run*, there is a more complex relationship between the new economic realities and the deteriorating social ones that has yet to be sufficiently explored: an emerging contradiction within postwar capitalism between the deteriorating nature of work and the expanding role of consumption. And it is this contradiction that directly contributes to the breakup of the family in the novel and, possibly, in the postwar society that it seeks to reflect.[47]

In his seminal study *The Cultural Contradictions of Capitalism* (1976), Daniel Bell identified a fundamental conflict at the heart of the New

Deal economic thought that he feared was irreconcilable and potentially self-destructive. "In the early development of capitalism, the unrestrained economic impulse was held in check by Puritan restraint and the Protestant ethic. One worked because of one's obligation to one's calling, or to fulfill the covenant of the community. But the Protestant ethic was undermined not by modernism but by capitalism itself," Bell opined. He went on to say:

> By the 1950s, the pattern of achievement remained, but it had been redefined to emphasize status and taste. The culture was no longer concerned with how to work, and achieve, but with how to spend and enjoy. Despite some continuing use of the language of the Protestant ethic, the fact was that by the 1950s American culture had become primarily hedonistic, concerned with play, fun, display, and pleasure—and, typical of things in America, in a compulsive way. . . . The cult of the Orgasm succeeded the cult of Mammon as the basic passion of American life.[48]

Behind this economic transition toward a Fordist economy, Bell, like Rieff, located a cultural embrace of the therapeutic that not only motivated but justified the individual pursuit of gratification:

> Modern culture is defined by this extraordinary freedom to ransack the world storehouse and to engorge any and every style it comes upon. Such freedom comes from the fact that the axial principle of modern culture is the expression and remaking of the "self" in order to achieve self-realization and self-fulfillment. And in its search, there is a denial of any limits or boundaries to experience. It is a reaching out for all experience; nothing is forbidden, all is to be explored.

The result of this incompatibility between production and consumption generated a disjunction in Bell's mind in which "the 'new capitalism' continued to demand a Protestant ethic in the area of production—that is, in the realm of work—but to stimulate a demand for pleasure and play in the area of consumption."[49]

Updike, who seems to have drawn inspiration from Max Weber (who deeply influenced Bell), clearly imbibed many of the ideas behind the Protestant work ethic himself.[50] Describing his youth, he extolled the legacy of Ben Franklin—who had been Weber's primary archetype—and recalled that "The cautious spirit of Ben Franklin's maxims still lived in the air. A penny saved is a penny earned; willful waste makes woeful want; a fool and his money are soon parted."[51] While reminiscing about his father in-law, Updike noted that "He was born tired. His life smells of financial failure and of the guilt and shame that attaches to such failure in these United States. It was the inspiriting genius of Calvinism to link prosperity and virtue, to take material thriving as a sign of salvation. . . . A failure of economic fortune must be a moral failure." He further admitted that his early fiction was about "the descendants of the puritans, people who have inherited a work ethic" and sought to portray "the fading of the work ethic."[52]

Rabbit's character personifies many of the contradictions Bell suggested were undermining postwar capitalism. Alongside his utter lack of self-restraint and unrelenting pursuit of personal gratification is a solid work ethic that helps illustrate the cultural contradictions that suffuse, and complicate, Rabbit's persona. Just as he seems to be the aspiring family man who never really meets his own expectations about fatherhood, his work ethic similarly falls short of ever realizing its full potential. Already in the opening scene, while playing a pickup basketball game with some kids in an alleyway, Rabbit reminds them of the diminishing value of skill. After making a difficult basket, one of the kids hollers at Rabbit, "Luck," to which he immediately replies, "Skill." Rabbit's respect for vocation is enhanced as soon as he gets home and is immediately transfixed by a television commercial for tootsie rolls. Dilvo Ristoff noted that television plays an "enormous" role in the novel since it "invades Rabbit's home and mind, entertaining, preaching and selling."[53] In this scene, ironically, it also reveals his potent work ethic. "The big Mouseketeer has appeared, Jimmy, a grown man who wears circular black ears. Rabbit watches him attentively; he respects him. He expects to learn something from him helpful in his own line of work." The scene concludes with Jimmy instructing the audience on the virtue of work and individuality:

> Know Thyself, a wise old Greek once said. Know Thyself. Now what does this mean, boys and girls? It means, be what you are. Don't try to be Sally or Johnny or Fred next door; be yourself. God doesn't want a tree to be a waterfall, or a flower to be a stone. God gives to each one of us a special talent. . . . And he gives to each of us the special talents to become these things, provided *we work to develop them*. We must *work,* boys and girls.[54]

As the plot progresses, it appears the more Rabbit indulges his instincts for consuming material and physical pleasures (i.e., food and sex), the more his work ethic commensurately deteriorates. Just before joining Tothero for dinner with Ruth and another prostitute in a watershed moment that ultimately leads him to abandon Janice, he exclaims, "I should have gone to work today." In the following scene in the restaurant, he repeats this self-disapprobation while ravenously consuming food, a prelude to his ravenous sexual appetite for Ruth. This is a germane episode: on one hand, the characters sit in a Chinese restaurant (described as a cheesy, cliché-ridden attempt at packaging "authentic" Asian experience by dressing up "permed hair and rouged, sweet-and-sour American face[d]" girls in cheap kimonos and having Asian American waiters speak with phony Chinese accents) and gorge on large quantities of cakes. When they are done, the waiter is "surprised" to see that "they have eaten them all." All the while they are eating, Tothero cannot stop marveling at the "appetite of the young." But it is also at this very moment of unbridled consumption, meticulously described by Updike, that the import of work resurfaces. After Tothero pontificates about "the sacredness of achievement" as the key to athletic success and extols the acumen of a former player ("he knew his trade"), Rabbit explains to Ruth what he does for a living.[55] "I'm sure he does it well," Tothero interjects. "I'm sure that when the MagiPeel Corporation board sits down at their annual meeting, and ask themselves 'Now who has done the most to further our cause with the American public?' the name of Harry Rabbit Angstrom leads the list."[56] This is not just flattery on Tothero's part but an objective assessment based on his experience coaching Rabbit.

During Eccles's visit to the Angstrom household shortly after the restaurant scene, we learn just how hard of a worker Rabbit had been in his youth. After his father admirably recalls how he "was a neat worker," his mother insists that "people now say how lazy Hassy is, but he's not. He never was. When you'd be proud of his basketball in high school you know, people would say, 'Yes well but he's so tall, it's easy for him.' But they didn't know how he had worked at that. Out back every evening banging the ball way past dark." She then goes on to assert that "when he set his mind to something, there was no stopping him. . . . He wanted to be best at that [basketball] and I honestly believe he was." His work ethic is rediscovered in Mrs. Smith's garden, where Rabbit diligently labors for several months. The Edenic quality of his time in the garden (which he describes as being "sort of like heaven"), stands in marked contrast to his depressive experience demonstrating kitchen gadgets and implies that it is not just Janice from whom Rabbit was running—

but his meaningless job as well: "The simplicity. Getting rid of something by giving it to itself. God Himself folded into the tiny adamant structure, Self-destined to a succession of explosions, the great slow gathering out of water and air and silicon: this is felt without words in the turn of the round hoe-handle in his palms." That an ailing Mrs. Smith suggests in their last encounter that Rabbit has brought her and the garden "back to life" is apposite since the garden did, in turn, rejuvenate Rabbit's long lost work ethic.[57]

It is this interplay between a lack of valuable work on one hand and an excess of seemingly valueless consumption on the other that drives the cultural contradictions of capitalism, which are at least partially responsible for the breakup of Rabbit's family. From the onset, Rabbit displays an ominous angst (ergo his name: Angst-rom = Angst-run?) toward the increasing presence of material consumption.[58] During Rabbit's initial flight, Updike exhaustingly detailed the ads sounding on Rabbit's car radio. Everything from plastic seat covers to garage-door operators, life-insurance providers, and banks are advertised in banal and annoying jingles, suggesting that even if Rabbit runs from his family, he cannot run from consumption.[59] At one point, Rabbit realizes he is staring at "the same weathered billboards for the same products you wondered anybody would ever want to buy." Tellingly, the only moment of solace he finds during his nerve-ridden road trip arrives when he notices that "the music on the radio is soothing now, lyrical and unadvertised." Rabbit's sensitivity to shifting economic conditions is further on display when he repeatedly thinks to himself that "the supermarkets are driving these little stores out of business, make them stay open all night."[60]

The most vivid indicator for just how deeply consumption has permeated American culture is evident in its transition from the material to the physical realms. While watching the tootsie roll commercial in the opening scenes, Rabbit undergoes a physical transformation as a direct result of a materially mediated experience. The commercial "echoes like an echo chamber. Son of a bitch: cute. He's seen it fifty times and this time it turns his stomach. His heart is still throbbing; his throat feels narrow." Imbued with a new sense of inspiration, Rabbit is so impressed he tries to emulate what he sees. "That was good. Rabbit tries it, pinching the mouth together and then the wink, getting the audience out front with you against some enemy behind, Walt Disney or the MagiPeel Peeler Company, admitting it's all a fraud but, what the hell, making it likable. We're all in it together. Fraud makes the world go round. The base of our economy." So powerful has the appeal of this artificial reality of consumption become that Rabbit momentarily chooses, in this rather comical scene, to define himself on its terms.[61]

Having returned home from work after a short detour playing basketball, Rabbit encounters Janice watching television commercials (interestingly, when the news comes on, she switches the television off). Spotting a stained glass of an Old Fashioned near Janice he inquires, "How many of those have you had?" That she is apparently drunk while watching television ads and then asks Rabbit for a cigarette already suggests the sheer variety of consumption possibilities—and an inability to restrain the urge to indulge them. This ominous lack of self-restraint for consuming is firmly established in their ensuing conversation. "He feels frightened," the narrator remarks after Janice mentioned a visit to Kroll's department store. "Rabbit's fright then mixes with his fright now and turns it tender. 'What did you buy?'" Janice then "closes her eye for a moment; he can feel the undertow of liquor sweep over her and is disgusted," leading her to cry out to Rabbit: "Don't run from me." This is a foreboding scene that ties together the various forces of consumption in order to explain, at least partially, why Rabbit runs: the consumption of alcohol is followed by the consumption of goods (she bought a bathing-suit), which are then followed by the consumption of cigarettes, all of which fuel Rabbit's "disgust." It is fitting that at this moment of unbridled consumption Rabbit laments that "the poor kid [their son Nelson] must think he has no home." Equally telling is the fact that the last thing Janice asks Rabbit before he abandons her is to buy her cigarettes. This may not be paltry: when Eccles asks Rabbit why he left his family, he candidly replies: "Because she asked me to buy her a pack of cigarettes."[62]

The colonization of the physical realm by the material realm in the novel is demonstrated in the apparent fusion between sexual and material consumption, which have become so distorted that they nearly conflate into the same experience. We are told, for instance, that at the department store where Janice and Rabbit first worked and became acquainted, "they would meet by the doors, chained to keep customers out" on their way to regular afternoon sessions of lovemaking at a friend's apartment. That they had to flee a store that must be chained to keep the customers out in order to make love already juxtaposes the tension between the material and the physical-sexual realms of consumption. Throughout the novel, Rabbit seems increasingly unable to distinguish between the urge to consume goods and consume sex. While surveying the billboards and listening to the radio ads on his initial flight, he thinks to himself that "He's never been to Wilmington. The du Ponts own it. He wonders what it's like to make it to a du Pont." After recalling a visit to a prostitute while in the army in Texas, Rabbit thinks to himself, that "sweet woman, *she* was money."[63]

Although the commodification of women in the novel has rightfully led critics to lambast Updike for patriarchal, even misogynistic, attitudes, it is as indicative of a changing economic culture as much as it is of skewed and chauvinistic gender perceptions.[64] Rabbit's relationship with Ruth, whom he claims to love, is a financial transaction at heart, for which he paid in advance. More importantly, there is a constant tension between his consumption of sex as a service and her need to work in order to provide it. Updike is explicit about this: just before making love to Rabbit, Ruth thinks to herself that "[it's] just harder work than they [men] probably think, women are always working harder than they think." As Judie Newman observed, "what is play for him [Rabbit], is work for Ruth."[65] Even in the hospital after Janice gives birth to Becky, their ostensibly rekindled love is negotiated through the currency of consumption. "I love you," Janice tells Rabbit, "Do you have a quarter?" The strange and untimely coupling of these two extremely different experiences—emotional and material (in order for Janice to operate the television and watch a show in which "all these women have tragedies they tell about and then get money according to how much applause there is"—is quite apropos to the broader problem being unveiled. When the narrator makes clear that "by the time the M.C. gets done delivering commercials and kidding them about their grandchildren and their girlish hairdos there isn't much room for tragedy left," the implications of this carefully crafted scene begin to emerge: sex, love, family, and now tragedy have all become commodities gladly forfeited by an increasingly superficial public in exchange for a shiny kitchen appliance or cash prize.[66]

The noxious relationship between material and physical consumption is solidified, tragically, in the culminating episode of the novel that does not just break up Rabbit's family but literally destroys it. After Rabbit leaves home yet again, unable to satisfy his sexual urges, a distraught Janice seeks comfort by watching television. "For some reason watching this makes her so nervous that just out of television-watching habit she goes to the kitchen and makes herself a little drink," the narrator remarks. It is the television, in other words, that sparks her drinking. A short while and several drinks later, Janice enters the kitchen. "She discovers herself making lunch, like looking down into a food advertisement in a magazine, bacon stops sizzling in a pan at the end of a huge blue arm." In these final moments before Becky drowns, Updike suggested how the real and ideal have become so inverted by new consuming patterns that even Janice's self-perception of herself and her family has been redefined to fit a magazine ad. Furthermore, the two fateful phone calls she receives from her parents that ultimately pressure her into bathing Becky so as not appear a derelict mother are indicative of the irreconcilable tensions between the decline of work on one hand and the advent of consumption on the other. When her father, who has hired Rabbit as an employee in his car lot, calls to inquire why Rabbit did not come in to work that morning, Janice immediately replies: "Everything's all right Daddy. Harry loves his job." The next phone call, received immediately after, is from her mother: "I just got back from shopping in Brewer and your father's been trying to reach me all morning. He thinks Harry's gone again. Is he?"[67]

Instead of confessing the truth, Janice fabricates a business opportunity and claims Rabbit has gone "to sell a car." The lie appears germane since Rabbit not only avoided going to work that morning, which could have prevented the death of Becky, but he did something even worse: he went window shopping. We are specifically told that Rabbit spent that very day "going in and out of department stores with music piping from the Walls and eating a hot dog at the five and ten and hesitating outside a movie house." Despite "increasing twisting inside that told him something was wrong back home," he chooses to walk along "the doors of movie houses and up and down between counters of perfumed lingerie and tinny jewelry and salted nuts." Even his initial reaction to hearing the tragic news of Becky's death is rooted in the experience of consumption: "He doesn't know what he says to Eccles; all he is conscious of is the stacks of merchandise in jangling packages he can see through the windows of the phone-booth door." When he is offered forgiveness by Janice's father, who magnanimously accepts him back into the family, Rabbit replies, "I promise I'll keep my end of the bargain," though he "stops, stifled by the abject sound of his voice. What made him say bargain?"[68]

Updike probably knew the answer to this question but leaves it for readers to formulate a response. Throughout the novel, he carefully unveiled a consumer-oriented culture that has abandoned the Protestant work ethic and invaded the home, reshaping social relations within the family. Rabbit did not go to work that first day he left Janice, thus breaking up the family; he did not go to work again that second fateful time and wound up destroying it. All the while, he and Janice were too busy consuming goods and services in excess rather than productively working. Even if there were many others reasons for the breakdown of Rabbit's family, the cultural contradictions of capitalism appear to be one of them.

Moynihan, Lasch, *and* Updike

Long before the GOP raised the mantle of family values and enlisted it into the conservative cause, Daniel P. Moynihan and Christopher Lasch sounded the alarm and called on liberals to do something about it. Both considered themselves liberals (though would come to define liberalism in very different terms), both were influential public intellectuals, and both were friends and readers of John Updike. Despite their diverging ideological affinities—Moynihan, the legendary social scientist turned White House advisor, ambassador, and senator, would gravitate to the disgruntled right wing of the Democratic Party, disheartened by its post-1968 transformations, while Lasch, a populist-progressive historian and social critic influenced by the neo-Marxism of the Frankfurt school—they were among the first intellectuals to warn against the breakdown of the family.[69] Repositioning *Rabbit, Run* as a natural addition to their body of social science and history not only highlights Updike's credentials as a serious social thinker but demonstrates the manner in which different varieties of liberal thinkers—Moynihan, Lasch, *and* Updike—essentially pursued three different ways to express a similar warning about family decline.

When Moynihan published his groundbreaking and controversial report that bears his name in 1965 about the national crisis in race relations, he pointed to the previously overlooked "weakness of family structure" as a chief explanation for the increasing plight of African Americans. At the time, he was an assistant secretary of labor in the Johnson administration who enthusiastically participated in the War on Poverty. Moynihan's "The Negro Family: A Case for Action" (i.e., the *Moynihan Report*) combined historical interpretation with economic and sociological data to explain the deteriorating conditions of life for urban blacks. In it, he concluded that the legacy of slavery, endemic discrimination, and structural racism had gradually inverted gender roles within the black family, engendering a "distorted" situation in which men wielded too little power while women had too much of it. This, he claimed problematically, resulted in the inability of black men to obey authority, obtain economic independence, and support a family.[70]

One of the major reasons for what Moynihan infamously called "the tangle of pathology" plaguing black communities was the transforming economy. The inability of young black men to compete in the new postindustrial workplace, which demanded an increasingly skilled and educated labor force, left them disproportionately vulnerable to unemployment and poverty and created "a cycle of deprivation." "As jobs became more and more difficult to find, the stability of the family became more and more difficult to maintain," Moynihan wrote. "Employment in turn reflects educational achievement, which depends in large part on family stability, which reflects employment."[71] Although the report unleashed a firestorm of criticism from African American leaders and liberals within his own party who accused him of paternalism, chauvinism, and blaming the victims, Moynihan would return time and again to the stability of the family during his four-term Senate career and repeatedly advocate on its behalf. The *New York Times* accordingly crowned him "one of the country's most prominent authorities on the family."[72]

It was incidentally during these turbulent years that Updike and Moynihan first became acquainted through mutual friends from Massachusetts and began a long correspondence.[73] Moynihan clearly admired Updike's fiction and in their infrequent letters commended him on his work: "I managed three days off this last weekend and spent them—sparingly, lovingly, with Bech [the protagonist from Updike's collection of short stories]," Moynihan wrote Updike in 1970. "You are a master." After publication of his political novel *Memories of the Ford Administration,* Updike sent Moynihan a copy.[74] Their shared concern for the family became apparent in 1992 when Moynihan, by then a third-term senator from New York, was invited to give the annual Blashfield lecture at the American Academy and Institute of Arts and Letters (over which Updike had presided as president two years prior). Moynihan's speech, titled "The Grey Truth," discussed the urban crisis, with an emphasis on the disintegration of the family, and pondered the limits of social science and public policy in administering solutions to this problem. "If social progress is slow, social regression can be rapid," he warned. In what often sounded like a sobered critique of progressive politics, Moynihan proposed embracing "the grey truth" for framing policy while rejecting both excessive optimism and apocalyptic pessimism. Instead, he offered what he considered a sobered, pragmatic, gradualist approach that recognized the limits of social engineering. "What is a group gathered in the name of Arts and Letters to make of all this?" Moynihan asked his audience in the conclusion to a policy speech rife with literary allusions to Yeats and Melville. "First, surely, that poets have not failed to anticipate."[75] Updike, who was present in the crowd of poets, writers, and scholars, lauded the speech: "What you say is true and shapely."[76]

In their subsequent correspondence, Moynihan responded by attaching a Xeroxed page from Ronald Berman's *America in the Sixties: An Intellectual History*, on which he personally highlighted with marker a passage regarding the *Moynihan Report* where Berman argued that novelists like Ralph Ellison and James Baldwin indeed anticipated the decline of the family long before policymakers. "The novelists were more honest than the politicians—they were in fact alone among Negro professionals . . . in their insistence that the quality of Negro life was tragic"—this was the passage Moynihan emphasized. Whether it was a general nod to the social role of writers that he was making or a personal gesture of appreciation toward Updike, in doing so Moynihan forged a link not only between politics and literature but between his own ideas and those of his novelist friend. In the attached letter he sent Updike along with the Xeroxed excerpt, he lamented that no one heeded the warnings that "families are going to hell" and concluded: "We got no thanks for our efforts, of-course, but that did not change the data, if you follow. I am sure you do."[77] Moynihan's "we" referred to the neoconservatives with whom he was unwittingly associated by this time. It's safe to assume that even if Updike did not strive in any fashion to be included into the swelling ranks of these disenchanted liberals, his encouraging response to the speech and the prescient concern he demonstrated in *Rabbit, Run* for the breakup of the family suggest a camaraderie of spirit between the two increasingly distraught liberals.[78]

Like Moynihan, Christopher Lasch started out on the left and was instilled with a Midwestern populism that initially drew him to the progressive wing of the Democratic Party.[79] Although he would gradually drift from mainstream liberalism further left and embrace a peculiar mélange of neo-Marxism and cultural conservatism that made him sui generis, he too came to recognize the decline of the family early on as a paramount threat. As his biographer Eric Miller observed, "From the preoccupation with 'personal growth' and 'the inner life' to the gendered reference to maturity, Lasch revealed himself to be bound up in an acute and bitter reaction against the ongoing, inexorable drift of Western Civilization away from its older moorings, to which he was more attached than he perhaps understood." Lasch's increasing interest in the family culminated in his work *Haven in a Heartless World: The Family Besieged* (1977), in which he offered a fresh and provocative account for what he labeled "the erosion of family life in contemporary society." It incidentally rested on the two familiar forces so prevalent in *Rabbit, Run*: consumer capitalism and the therapeutic culture that it bred. "Far from being isolated," Lasch opined, the modern family is "well integrated into the surrounding structures; or better, it is invaded by them."[80]

Like in Updike's novel, Lasch contended the driving forces behind family decline were the monumental economic transformations of work and consumption. The unprecedented needs of modern capitalism and the Fordist economy had reorganized the labor process—and expanded government's role—in a harmful manner that demanded "the separation between love and discipline" within the family. Instead of providing children with an "ambivalent attachment" through love *and* discipline, Lasch claimed that parents retained the responsibility only for the former while outsourcing the latter to external experts (i.e., therapists, teachers, social workers) through what he called "socialization of reproduction." In doing so, he argued that parents forfeited the disciplinary obligation and relegated themselves to the role of "friends" who "talk about their feelings" with their children instead of placing firm boundaries upon them. The modern family had become, in effect, "an emotional refuge in a cold and competitive society." This did not happen accidentally: Lasch averred that the therapeutic sensibilities that permeated the household were "the extension and solidification of capitalist control through the agency of management, bureaucracy and professionalization."[81] He argued that "The sanctity of the home is a sham in a world dominated by giant corporations and the apparatus of mass promotion" and contended that "the work ethic, nurtured in the nuclear family, gives way to an ethic of survival and immediate gratification." He argued, "Indifference to the needs of the young has become one of the distinguishing characteristics of a society that lives for the moment, defines consumption of commodities as the highest form of personal satisfaction, and exploits existing resources with criminal disregard of the future."[82] Instead of alleviating the increasing pressures placed by market forces on individuals, the appeal to emotions only made things worse. "The therapeutic program eroded the distinction between private life and the marketplace, turning all forms of play, even sex, into work," Lasch concluded.[83] Citing Freud (like Updike), he insisted that "repression of sexuality, in one form or another, remains the very condition of culture" and warned that "the repudiation of monogamy expresses an accurate understanding of possessive individualism extended to the emotional realm."[84]

At least some parts of Lasch's jeremiad concerning the disintegration of the family should sound familiar by now: consumer capitalism and therapeutic liberalism did, after all, help break up the family in *Rabbit, Run*. While the former supposedly "invaded" the household, the latter was enlisted to cover up the invasion and ameliorate its deleterious effects. Although Lasch would significantly expand his argument concerning the therapeutic forces into a sweeping condemnation of American culture in his next and most famous work, *The Culture of Narcissism* (1979), his analysis of family decline essentially gives theory and substance to the affect and concerns that initially materialized in Updike's literary imagination.[85] Not only does Rabbit explicitly display many traits Lasch would diagnose as narcissistic—solipsism, excessive self-admiration, a rejection of monogamy, and an insatiable urge for sex and sexual experimentation—but his family disintegrates as a result of the forces of capitalism and therapeutic liberalism that Lasch so fiercely condemned.

According to his biographer, Lasch's interest in the breakup of the family can be traced as far back as 1961. Although it is likely coincidental that this was just after the publication of *Rabbit, Run*, given the close relationship that existed during these years between Lasch and his old college roommate, it seems plausible that Updike's literary imagination had, at the very least, helped influence Lasch's social commentary.[86] Lasch once admitted that "I was reading everything he [Updike] wrote" and, accordingly, often displayed an intimate familiarity with, and admiration for, Updike's fiction in their correspondences. In one letter to Updike he anxiously conveyed looking forward to reading more books from him, while quoting admirably from the Rabbit novels in another.[87] As Jeffrey Ludwig posited in his study of their friendship, "Lasch and Updike continually made each other better, as people but especially as writers, at a crucial moment in their formative years. In Lasch's case in particular, the relationship shaped the intellectual path he chose to follow for the rest of his life."[88]

There is no evidence that either Moynihan or Lasch absorbed any dramatic lessons from *Rabbit, Run*, if any existed, or sought to voice the novel's concerns in their own research or policy. But reevaluating their works together—*Rabbit, Run* (1960), the *Moynihan Report* (1965), and *Haven in a Heartless World* (1977)—suggests that there was a powerful intellectual current bridging their differences and motivating the three left-liberal thinkers to explore the fate of the family long before conservatives ever seriously thought to do so. Given the interpersonal ties between them and the fact that Moynihan and Lasch were avid readers of Updike's fiction, it is plausible that ideas evinced in Updike's literary imagination somehow, even if indirectly, permeated their political one. While Lasch slid around the political spectrum of Marxism and the New Left, and Moynihan's cautious liberalism gravitated hesitatingly toward neoconservatism in the following years, Updike stayed put in a disappearing center. Yet in their shared concern for the breakup of the family, an ideological adhesive remains for reconnecting the disconnected strands of liberalism.

Conclusion

In recent years scholars have refocused attention on the family in order to explain the political realignment that has defined American politics since the 1960s. "The sense of a crisis of the American family emerged as a mainstream feature of the decade between Woodstock and Reagan's election, as voices from across the political spectrum expressed deep anxieties about a culture of moral permissiveness, the consequences of the sexual revolution, and the nation's uncertain economic future," Matthew Lassiter has claimed. "The postwar embodiment of the American Dream—a heterosexual nuclear family with a working father and stay-at-home mother living in an upwardly mobile suburban neighborhood—appeared on the verge of collapse during the seventies."[89] This still prevailing narrative sets up a starch dichotomy between the chaotic 1960s and the ostensibly pacific 1950s. But *Rabbit, Run* suggests a more complex thread of continuity behind the fate of the family that was rooted in shifting sensibilities that *preceded,* and might very well have contributed to, the turmoil of the late 1960s.[90]

The sense of crisis surrounding the family did not result merely from the cultural effects of Woodstock, Stonewall, or Haight-Ashbury, or exclusively from the advent of neoliberalism and the demise of the family wage. Rather, it might have also emerged, at least indirectly, from a longer and more complicated process unleashed by New Deal liberalism, which sought the integration of seemingly irreconcilable forces. First, new therapeutic sensibilities replaced old communal and familial ones: the psychological shift inward, which was supposed to shelter and liberate individuals from Cold War anxieties, ended up isolating them; instead of shattering the conformity of traditional communities, the pursuit of self-fulfillment and the inner self destabilized them. Second, new consumption norms displaced old production ones: the postwar liberal economic model attempted to ensure market demand through a new cultural reorientation toward mass consumption. But the liberal model was ultimately unable to balance heightened consumption with a traditional sense of productive value, derived from the deeply ingrained ethos of the Protestant work ethic, in a modernizing (and automatizing) workplace that had little use, let alone respect, for it. Like in the finale of *Rabbit, Run,* when these new therapeutic and economic forces converged on the American home in the 1950s, the nuclear family would be the first to pay the price.

5 | Sleeping Together, Bowling Alone
Couples and the Decline of Civic Engagement

> *If an American should be reduced to occupying himself with his own affairs, at that moment half his existence would be snatched from him; he would feel it as a vast void in his life and would become incredibly unhappy.*
> —Alexis de Tocqueville

> *We had become detached from the national life. Our private lives had become the real concern. There was a monstrous inflation of the private life as against the emerged life of the society.*
> —John Updike

In September 1968, John Updike and his wife Mary packed up their luggage, picked up their four kids, and moved to London for the year. Unsettled by the chaos sweeping America at the time and threatening to tear its social fabric apart, the Updikes boarded the SS *Rotterdam* and temporarily retreated across the Atlantic in search of some solace. They found it, along with something else: a sense of community. "An American in London," Updike declared, "cannot but be impressed and charmed by the city." What particularly impressed him were the inviting "institutions of communal existence"—the parks, libraries, and museums he frequented—and the "civic self-confidence" that these institutions instilled in its dwellers. Enamored by a vital sense of community he encountered on the streets of London, Updike observed that "one walks among strangers without feeling menaced" and concluded "this, surely, is a city, a *civitas,* in the root sense."[1]

On April 26, 1968, a few months before embarking on their overseas trip, a portrait of Updike appeared on the cover of *Time* magazine under the headline "The Adulterous Society." Still riding the success of *Rabbit, Run,* which was published earlier in the decade, Updike published a sensational new novel, *Couples,* which chronicled what he called the "post-pill paradise," where affluent suburban couples engaged in extramarital affairs and led a seemingly carefree hedonistic lifestyle. It made a splash. The initial reviews were mixed: some praised *Couples* as witty social commentary that exposed the moral degeneration lurking "beneath this suburban idyll," while others were appalled by the graphic sexuality and scandalized by the polygamous relationships. According to one unhappy critic, the novel proved "you don't have to be a bad writer to come up with an awful novel."[2] But the salaciousness, thanks in part to the unprecedented media attention it garnered, paid off: *Couples* remained on the *New York Times* best-seller list for months and reportedly earned Updike a million dollars.[3] Any attempt to understand why he might have been so exhilarated by the communal spirit he found in London must begin with the communal spirit that *Couples* suggests had been lost in America.

Updike departed the rural Pennsylvania of his youth nearly a decade earlier and relocated, now with his family, to Ipswich, Massachusetts (after a short two-year stint in Manhattan). *Couples* was his first attempt at transplanting his literary imagination as well and setting his novels in a new environment. The book recounts the lives and experiences of a group of ten upper-middle-class couples in the imaginary town of Tarbox, Massachusetts, an old Puritan settlement located about thirty miles south of Boston that was modeled after his adopted hometown. The couples, who have mostly relocated to the New England town, are representative of the cultural heterogeneity that was remaking the town's traditionally WASP composition: although most of them are white Protestant northeasterners, there are three Catholic couples (only one of them practicing), a pair of Jews, an Asian refugee, a midwesterner, and a southern belle (there are no African Americans in Tarbox—but a fair housing committee is nonetheless organized on their behalf). Among the male characters, nearly all are members of the swelling ranks of white-collar professionals: there are government-employed scientists as well as financiers, a real estate developer, a college professor, a dentist, and an airline pilot (the few women who work are part-time teachers).

The novel depicts the vibrant social life of the group and the countless affairs that develop between its members. They play games on weekends (touch football, doubles tennis, and basketball in the day, and parlor games in the evenings), have frequent dinner parties (no one passes up a martini in Tarbox), and go sailing and skiing on holidays. The couples basically do and share everything together—including their beds (they have become so close that even their last names have been fused; the little-Smiths and Applebys have come to be known as the "Applesmiths" and the Constantines and Saltzes have become the "Saltines"). Historically situated in the fall of 1963, the plot unfolds alongside memorable events such as the civil rights movement, the escalating war in Vietnam (Ngo Dinh Diem is overthrown early on in the novel), and President Kennedy's assassination. Although the external world repeatedly overshadows the plot, it is unsuccessful in ever really disrupting the solipsistic social bubble in which the couples have isolated themselves.

Unlike the Rabbit series, there is no single protagonist in *Couples*. Instead, there are as many subplots as there are characters, at times requiring, as critics pointed out, a chart to keep track of what's going on. The central axis of the novel does, however, sluggishly revolve around the romantic escapades of a building contractor Piet Hanema. Part Jesus, part Don Juan, Piet is a devout churchgoer and masterful carpenter who is haunted by a perpetual fear of death emanating from a fatal car accident that killed his parents. As the most religious figure in the novel, he is also ironically the most unfaithful—he has affairs with three married women in the group. It is Piet's relationship with Foxy Whitman, a young housewife who had recently moved to Tarbox with her husband Ken, an assistant professor of biochemistry, which ultimately unsettles things in their "erotic utopia" and blows the lid off the adulterous society. Unlike the other affairs, Piet and Foxy break the unspoken rules when she gets pregnant and has an illegal abortion. This climactic event, arranged by the dentist Freddy Thorne, provides the coup de grace to the increasingly untenable web of deception and leads to the exposure of their illicit affair by Freddy's wife (with whom Piet has also been sleeping). The result is a chain reaction that dissolves the group and sends the couples back into their own homes and beds. The novel ends with Piet leaving his job, divorcing his wife Angela (the angel), remarrying Foxy (the fox), and, having chosen the earthly over the divine, moving away with her from the town that appears to have become, quite literally, a Tar-box.[4]

In addition to revisiting some of the central themes that suffuse *Rabbit, Run*—the decline of religion and useful work alongside the rise of a therapeutic culture and consumer capitalism—*Couples* provides important, and surprising, insight into one of the most salient features of American democracy: civic engagement. It was Alexis de Tocqueville's visit to a New England township 137 years prior—the exact type of town after which Tarbox was modeled—that led the legendary French philosopher to admirably describe Americans' unique devotion to community and declare that "If an American should be reduced to occupying himself with his own affairs, at that moment half his existence would be snatched from him; he would feel it as a vast void in his life and would become incredibly unhappy."[5] Updike's protagonists are similarly unhappy. And it might very well be that Tocqueville, whose work Updike read and imbibed, helped explain why.[6] Scholars have long noticed that the novel deals with a loss of public virtue: James Schiff opined that "Because the long-established institutions of church, work, and politics have ceased to matter to these individuals, they have turned elsewhere, primarily to one another," while Judie Newman questioned their skewed social ethic, in which "People cooperate just to cooperate, rather than for substantive reasons or goals."[7] These are not just literary conditions, but very real and worrisome political trends that transform *Couples* from a sensational novel about sex in the suburbs into a profound literary analysis of political culture.

As a catalyst of the Tocqueville revival among scholars during the 1990s, the political scientist Robert Putnam's landmark study of the decline of American civic engagement, *Bowling Alone,* stands as a remarkable work of scholarship. Looking back to the period during and about which *Couples* was written, Putnam described it as a golden age of civic life.[8] "In the 1960s, in fact, community groups across America had seemed to stand on the threshold of a new era of expanded involvement," Putnam wrote. The new postwar affluence and the leisure it afforded, combined with the Cold War's ever present existential anxieties, he claimed, tightened communities: "Engagement in community affairs and the sense of shared identity and reciprocity had never been greater in modern America, so the prospects for broad-based civic mobilization to address our national failings seemed bright." At the heart of Putnam's "burgeoning civic vitality" were the rising membership rates in proliferating civic organizations such as Elks, Rotary, PTA, NAACP, town committees, and bowling leagues. Putnam argued that civic-minded groups such as these helped generate the social capital that in turn nurtured norms of reciprocity and trustworthiness among people indispensable for maintaining a healthy democracy. Since the late 1960s, however, things began to change: America's civil society seemed exhausted as membership rates in civic organizations gradually plummeted.[9] Economic transformations that demanded longer work hours, expanding geographies and suburbanization, proliferation of new technologies like television and personal computers, and a generational shift of less civic-minded Americans combined to undermine civic engagement. "For the first two-thirds of the twentieth century a powerful tide bore Americans into ever deeper engagement in the life of their communities, but a few decades ago—silently, without warning—that tide reversed and we were overtaken by a treacherous rip current," Putnam opined. "Without at first noticing, we have been pulled apart from one another and from our communities."[10]

This chapter employs *Couples* in an effort to tell a slightly different story about the fate of postwar civil society. Reevaluating it in the context of Putnam's seminal findings suggests that civic decline was certainly not "without warning," as there were some voices, like Updike's, that *did* anticipate and warn that communities were coming apart at a time when they seemed as vigorous as ever. What *Couples* presciently demonstrates is how the monumental shift in political culture and practice unleashed by New Deal liberalism resulted in a reorientation of political activity from the public to the private spheres and underwrote popular disengagement from participatory democracy. Technocrats, bureaucrats, and interest groups—the new harbingers of liberalism—were elevated instead and gradually replaced an active body politic. In contrast to the politicization of the private sphere that drove women, gay and lesbian rights activists, and evangelical Christians out of the private sphere and into politics during these same years (but for opposite reasons), Updike's *Couples* tells an inverted tale about the privatization of the political sphere that drained the democratic experience of intrinsic value, rendering America a democracy without a demos and its politics without purpose.

Couples is as important methodologically as it is substantively because it refocuses our attention from the quantitative data regarding membership rates in civic groups to the qualitative nature of membership itself. Penetrating into the grey area of shifting sensibilities and structures of affect, where statistical data and ethnography cannot always navigate freely or deeply, it demonstrates the power of fiction to provide much needed historical clarity in these ambiguous zones. Effectively serving as a literary case study of civil society, *Couples* enables us to delve beyond the formidable data quantifying civic engagement and question the substantive degree that engagement entailed in the first place.[11]

Community life in Tarbox is, after all, eerily consistent with the civic utopia that Putnam sketched: the characters attend town meetings, are members of fair housing committees, the PTA, and tennis leagues, and play football and parlor games on a regular basis. But Updike effectively punctures this façade by suggesting that membership itself is hollow at the core and that citizens' commitment to their community is tenuous at best. Instead of producing social capital and creating genuine ties of trust and reciprocity, civic association in Tarbox facilitates superficial interactions. Political issues intrude on the couples' lives but political engagement does not result from it: there are town meetings, but they are procedural and everyone in attendance is merely going through the motions; there is talk of taxes and rights, but only as foreplay to sex; there is acute awareness of the war in Vietnam and of Kennedy's assassination but only as scheduling problems for dinner parties and tennis matches. What *Couples* teaches us, in other words, is that community life in America may have begun to come apart in the 1960s not simply because of tectonic structural changes but due to the fact that the social adhesive may not have been that strong to begin with.

The Privatization of the Public

"There is an awful lot of talk in the book," Updike himself once admitted of *Couples*. Although, for the most part, the talk is meaningless. In many ways, it is this dilution of conversation that signals the impending decline of political community in the novel. The great tragedy of the modern age, as Hannah Arendt has argued, is the collapse of the public sphere. In her seminal work, *The Human Condition,* published nearly a decade before *Couples,* she outlined this process by focusing on the diminution of speech. "Wherever the relevance of speech is at stake, matters become political by definition, for speech is what makes man a political being. If we would follow the advice, so frequently urged upon us, to adjust our cultural attitudes to the present status of scientific achievement, we would in all earnest adopt a way of life in which speech is no longer meaningful," Arendt warned. "Men in the plural, that is, men in so far as they live and move and act in the world, can experience meaningfulness only because they can talk with and make sense to each other and to themselves."[12] For Arendt, the problem was rooted in a disturbance of classical equilibrium between public and private spheres that had enabled humans to "experience meaningfulness" together. As a result of this shift, facilitated by the rise of the social sphere and its decimation of the political, the private sphere absorbed much of what previously belonged in public. "While we have become excellent in the laboring we perform in public, our capacity for action and speech has lost much of its former quality since the rise of the social realm banished these into the sphere of the intimate and the private," she wrote.[13]

Even if Updike never addressed Arendt's work, it is likely that he was familiar with it. Since Arendt published several essays in the *New Yorker*—occasionally in the same issue that featured Updike's work—he undoubtedly came into contact with her ideas.[14] More importantly, what links their imaginations (aside from a deep affinity to Kafka) is their shared appreciation of Aristotle.[15] Having studied him closely at Harvard (Updike wrote a comprehensive essay on Aristotle's *Poetics*) and conceded in his memoirs, echoing Aristotle's famous remark, that men are, indeed, "social creatures," Updike clearly absorbed the Greek philosopher's emphasis on social life and even incorporated his theory of action (that Arendt relies upon in her analysis of the public sphere) into his literary criticism. In a review of Gunter Grass's *The Flounder*, for instance, Updike observed that "the writing is animated and the social concern unimpeachable, but while so many lumpy ingredients are being stirred, what Aristotle called the 'action' is put to sleep in a corner of the kitchen."[16] In her own nod to Aristotle, Arendt attributed the concept of the "good life" to active citizenship and participation in public affairs: "It was 'good' to the extent that by having mastered the necessities of sheer life, but being freed from labor and work, and by overcoming the innate urge of all living creatures for their own survival, it was no longer bound to the biological life process."[17] Since the characters in *Couples* are liberated from such "necessities of life" and are blessed with the affluence and leisure that Aristotle and Arendt found indispensable for productive political life, the novel in a way seeks to interrogate the meaning and consequences of the "good life" in postwar America. Updike suggested as much. "These [characters] are the descendants of the Puritans, people who have inherited a work ethic and who find themselves working really no harder than they must," he recalled in a 1971 interview about *Couples*. "In part, the book is about affluence, which, in releasing at least this class of people from pressing financial anxieties, creates new ones."[18]

The plot carefully explores the deterioration of political life in the modern era that had so concerned Arendt. Updike established the political tone of the novel and emphasized the importance of community in the epigraph. Having borrowed a passage from theologian Paul Tillich's *The Future of Religions,* he noted that "There is a tendency in the average citizen, even if he has a high standing in his profession, to consider the decisions relating to the life of the society to which he belongs as a matter of fate on which he has no influence—like the Roman subjects all over the world in the period of the Roman empire, a mood favorable for the resurgence of religion but unfavorable for the preservation of a living democracy."[19] By directly linking the novel to the historical decline of republican Rome and lamenting the loss of faith in the efficacy of individual political action to shape the course of society—a tendency that facilitated the collapse of the Roman republic—Updike invited us to read the narrative that follows this epigraph in a political light. As if to underline this subtext of the novel, he even described how the contractor Piet Hanema, the central character, rejected Platonic thought, since "Piet was an Aristotelian."[20]

The novel establishes the theme of community from the very beginning. As Piet's wife Angela, an aloof and unrealized character with a flair for psychoanalysis, tells him in the opening scene: "He [Freddy Thorne] thinks we're a circle. A magic circle of heads to keep the night out. He told me he gets frightened if he doesn't see us over a weekend. He thinks we've made a church of each other." To which Piet responds, "That's because he doesn't go to a real church." The suggestion that the couples have sought meaning and fulfillment through social interaction as a means to replace, and compensate for, the loss of religion, repeats itself in the novel.[21] In a ski lodge, just before the little-Smiths and Applebys knowingly swap wives for the first time, the dentist Freddy Thorne, the most contemptible character in the novel—and ironically the most prophetic and insightful one—crudely declares that "People are the only thing people have left since God packed up. By people I mean sex. Fucking. . . . In the western world there are only two comical things: the Christian church and naked women. We don't have Lenin so that's it. Everything else tells us we're dead." Part oracle, part Socratic gadfly, Freddy often serves as an outlet via acerbic wit and sarcasm for the latent criticism that Updike's all-knowing narrator is uncomfortable expressing himself. At the end of this monologue, Freddy reveals the tenuous nature of their "community" when he remarks: "We're a subversive cell. Like in the catacombs. Only they were trying to break out of hedonism. We're trying to break back into it. It's not easy."[22]

The fact that the increasing attachment of the couples to each other is primarily oriented toward hedonistic individual pursuit and is devoid of reciprocal value—their communal life is basically rooted in getting laid—is emphasized in an important observation by the narrator. In a momentary lapse of neutrality early in the novel, the narrator reflects that "Duty and work yielded as ideals to truth and fun. Virtue was no longer sought in temple or market place but in the home—one's own home, and then the homes of one's friends."[23] Channeling Arendt's own concerns, Updike's lament suggests that he too had sensed the degeneration of the public sphere and the increasingly distorted reality in which virtue shed much of its political, religious, and economic purchase and had been relegated to the private sphere.[24]

This privatization of public virtue is suggested in *Couples* by the chronic lack of interest displayed toward all matters of public import. In the first dinner party (among many in the novel), the couples mention the recent accidental sinking of the nuclear submarine USS *Thresher*, in which the entire crew was killed. Although the initial interest sparked by the incident prompts some promising replies regarding American Cold War policy, it quickly becomes fodder for jokes that remove the possibility for serious discussion. After Harold, the Francophile stock broker (a self-avowed Republican) conveys the need for "another Diem" in Southeast Asia, Janet Appleby (with whom he is sleeping) aptly interjects, "That's reactionary shit." To which Roger Guerin, a wealthy Brahmin conservative, responds by telling the newly arrived couple, the Whitmans, "Don't take them too seriously. There's nothing romantic or eccentric about Tarbox." With that remark, the short-lived *Thresher* incident is tabled as a roast of lamb and a bottle of Bordeaux quickly drown out any political talk in the room. The meal however does not proceed without Freddy proposing a toast, "For our gallant boys in the *Thresher*."[25] Much as Roger observed, the party shows that the couples do not take anything too seriously; every time a matter of public import surfaces in conversations, it's quickly drained of significance (usually with wine) and reduced to a punch line. It does not matter that most of the women are proud liberal activists and the financiers self-described conservatives: everyone displays an equally lax and frivolous attitude toward politics.

It is not at all surprising then that politics in the novel is either reduced to a game or is simply, and carefully, avoided every time it comes up. Fittingly, the couples' most serious engagement with political questions usually occurs while playing rounds of Botticelli, a parlor game in which well-known figures are chosen and the player must guess their identity by posing a series of questions (the game is called Botticelli because the namesake Renaissance artist marks the minimal standard of fame that a character must have in order to be chosen for the game). During a round of Botticelli, the couples assign Piet the role of Ho Chi Minh. "Irene suggested Vice-President Johnson. Everyone protested that he was much too dreary. Terry Gallagher came up with Ho Chi Minh and it seemed perfect," the narrator observed. Tellingly, the couples do not know all that much about Johnson or Ho (or for that matter the war in Vietnam). But after a set of questions, some jovial, others laced with sexual innuendo, Piet finally guesses correctly and remarks that "It's treasonous . . . how affectionate your impressions were. This enemy of our democracy, all those flowers and delicate grays." To which Irene responds, "Why hate him? He's what they want," while Terry adds, "I thought that was good of me to remember him being a busboy in Paris." It is at this very moment, when the discussion actually seems to gain steam and the potential to lead to enlightening deliberation about the justification of American military intervention, that, as with the *Thresher* incident, it is suddenly cut short: "Thanks, people, but I must go," Terry proclaims, bringing the conversation about Vietnam to a halt.[26]

The game, and scene, enter their last throes as Foxy is chosen as the final player of the evening. While searching for a historical figure to assign her, the narrator observes that "It did not take them long to decide, June having been so fertile of news: Pope John had died, Quang Duc had immolated himself, Valentina Tereshkova had become the first woman in space, John Profumo had resigned, the Lord's Prayer had been banned in the American Public Schools." The symbolism of the game is quite revealing: politics has retained its relevancy to the couples *only* by functioning as comic relief and a source of recreation; it has become a temporary distraction that they often seek to embrace rather than a serious matter to engage. In one lyrical passage, the narrator implies that their social games have become a refuge from the quotidian personal and political burdens weighing down upon them: "An evening without a game" was, for them, "an evening spent among flickering lamps and cranky children and leftover food and the nagging half-read newspaper with its weary portents and atrocities."[27]

Updike never condemns the couples for their apathy, disparages them for their ethics, or renders judgment on their behavior. On the contrary, the dinner parties, the sexual infidelities, and even the lies are all handled with remarkable interest, tenderness, and solicitude that betray his own sympathy for their (and his?) predicament, and an inquisitive penchant as a writer seeking truth rather than preaching it. Instead of judging, Updike peppered the narrative with sympathetic moments that suggest there are some things, like politics, from which people cannot flee—even if they want to. By imposing external realities onto the plot and refusing to succumb to the characters' compelling attempts at ignoring them, Updike slyly hinted at the inescapability of public issues that strangely conflated with private ones. The result is a mutually reinforcing mechanism for escapism and distraction: just as the characters' private life has colonized the public sphere and reduced politics to pillow talk, the political has become an equally attractive and superficial refuge for those wishing to avoid serious engagement with their personal feelings.

This pattern reoccurs frequently throughout the plot. For instance, this is how Marcia breaks off her affair with Frank: "'I'd adore to see you again. You're the love of my life, unfortunately.' Frank could not escape the impression that she was asking him to get a divorce. Meanwhile, our advisory capacity in Vietnam was beginning to stink and the market was frightened, frightened yet excited by the chance of expanding war. Basically business was uneasy with Kennedy; there was something unconvincing about him." This is how the turbulent relations between the spouse swapping little-Smiths and Applebys are described: "This pattern, of quarrel and reunion, of revulsion and surrender, was repeated three or four times that winter, while airplanes collided in Turkey, and coups transpired in Iraq and Togo, and earthquakes in Libya, and a stampede in the Canary Islands, and in Ecuador a chapel collapsed, killing a hundred twenty girls and nuns." In another scene, Foxy reveals to her mother that she is contemplating divorce from Ken: "Foxy said, 'I'm curious about divorce.' In turning her head to mute this admission she read the banner headline of the newspaper left neatly folded at Ken's empty place: Diem Overthrown. Diem. Dies, diei, diei, diem. 'I wonder sometimes if Ken and I shouldn't get one.'"[28]

These fragmented passages that strangely fuse the couples' romantic dilemmas with external political realities from the headlines are not just an attempt at providing historical context but clearly demonstrate that politics continues to impinge upon their lives despite their best efforts to escape it. By oddly inserting political affairs at quintessential moments of the couples' self-absorption, which intuitively have nothing to do with politics (what does poor Diem have to do with Foxy's divorce?), the novel suggests what a superficial experience politics has become: whether it affords the characters an excuse to avoid dealing with their own emotional problems by looking outside, or alternatively enables them to employ their personal problems to avoid dealing with the grave political challenges brewing outside (i.e., the Cold War, the Vietnam War, and the civil rights movement), it is clear that politics has for the most part lost its substantial value.

A salient indicator of this privatization of political life is the persistent conflation of politics with sex. Although the linkage begins subtly and indirectly by the characters' constant association of Kennedy's foreign policy with jokes about his sexual dalliances (for example: he was "sitting up late arguing ideology" with Madam Nhu or Nina Khrushchev), it would gradually evolve from such paltry banter into a more tangible pattern. When Janet and Harold conduct their affair in a friend's bachelor pad in Boston, they have sex in a bedroom decorated with "collages juxtaposing magazine advertisements and war headlines, deodorized nudes with nacreous armpits and bombed peasants flecked with blood, green stamps and Robert McNamara and enraptured models in striated girdles."[29] Having been relegated to the bedroom, it is apposite that the only manner through which the escalating war in Vietnam actually invades the plot is by providing interior design for sex.

Politics and sex, symbolizing quintessentially opposed public and private experiences, become so conflated in *Couples* that the former evolves into a euphemism for the latter. In order to conceal their affairs from their spouses, Frank and Marcia ironically appeal to their civic spirit; Marcia uses her active membership in the town's fair housing committee as an excuse for seeing Frank in Boston, while he in turn explains his absence to his wife Janet in a similar manner. "He [Frank] told me he was getting a haircut," Janet tells Harold when they begin to suspect the affair between their spouses. "But he didn't want to take Franklin [their son] because he might go to the drugstore and have to talk politics." After verifying the affair, Harold muses that "They've set us up for them to be gone for hours. Haircuts. Fair Housing."[30] That visiting the drugstore to "talk politics" or attending a fair housing committee have become excuses for screwing certainly reflects a marked normative shift in the meaning and import of civic engagement.

During a heated political conversation between Irene, the liberal crusader, and Frank, the conservative banker, what begins as serious political deliberation concludes as an aphrodisiac. The debate is sparked after Frank criticizes the expanding welfare state—"The federal government was never meant to be a big mama every crybaby could run to. Minimal government was the founders' ideal. States' rights. Individual rights"—to which Irene responds, "Frank, suppose you were Mrs. Medgar Evers. Would you want to cry or not?" Having turned their attention to civil rights, Frank says, "Ask any intelligent Negro what the welfare check has done to his race. They hate it. It castrates. I agree with Malcolm X." This informed exchange, which includes competing interpretations of constitutional rights, concludes not with a whimper, but quite literally, a bang: "'Can't we shut them up?' Eddie Constantine asked. 'It's sex for Irene' Carol told him, standing and buttoning her shirt. 'Irene loves arguing with right-wing men. She thinks they have bigger pricks.'" Tellingly, the couples label the adjacent room where the two go to find privacy "the political parlor." When Angela reveals to Piet the latest gossip regarding the disintegration of the Saltz-Constantine friendship, she similarly notes that "Irene would sometimes feel guilty enough to go home, leaving Ben talking with Eddie. They would talk everything—space, computers, public versus private schools, religion. Eddie is so lapsed he begins to scream whenever he thinks at all about the Church." To which Piet adds, "then Carol would lay them both." Angela concludes by noting, "Carol's story is that Irene took a fancy to Eddie and lit out after him the way she lights into everything—Fair Housing, or the nursery school, or conservation. He became a cause."[31]

Since politics in *Couples* often masks sexual relations or ambitions and becomes both a distraction from and an excuse for infidelity, it's germane that the few times someone seems to be pursuing genuine political activities, that character's efficacy and value are questioned. When Janet complains about Marcia exhorting her and her husband Frank to join her in civic activity so she could secretly spend more time with Frank, the narrator notes that "Sail, swim, play tennis, go to meetings. She was even trying to get her interested in the Tarbox Fair Housing Committee, which Irene Saltz and Bernadette Ong were organizing." Janet then cuts in and remarks: "I said to her [Marcia], 'But there isn't a single Negro in the town,' and she said, 'that's the point. We're culturally deprived, our children don't know what a Negro looks like.' . . . There's something basically snotty about this committee. It's all because other towns have one. Like a drum-and-bugle corps." This sardonic attitude toward some of the self-righteous liberal activists in the group is frequently displayed. In another scene it is the narrator who makes it a point to remind us that the "chief accomplishment" of the local education committee, in which Marcia is a loyal member, is "to give the high-school library a subscription to *Ebony*." Taking a jab at liberal smugness and conformity (which Updike often made at the time through his acerbic short stories in the *New Yorker*), Harold, the defiant conservative, proclaims that "The trouble with this *merde*-heap of a country, there's no respectable way to not be a liberal."[32]

There are several moments when Updike's mostly neutral third-person narrator resolutely intrudes upon the plot in order to alert us to the growing insularity of the couples' private lives from the tumult engulfing them. As they sit in the ski lodge, the narrator remarks, "The television set, *unwatched,* excited itself with eleven-o'clock news about UN military action in the Katanga province of the Congo; and was switched off." Similarly, in order to avoid self-examination and escape her unfulfilling life as a housewife and mistress, "Janet had taken to reading the newspaper, as if this smudgy peek into other lives might show her the way out of her own." Later on, we are told that

> Television brought them [the couples] the outer world. The little screen's icy brilliance implied a universe of profound cold beyond the warm encirclement of Tarbox, friends, and family. Mirrors established in New York and Los Angeles observed the uninhabitable surface between them and beamed reports that bathed the children's faces in a poisonous, flickering blue. This poison was their national life. Not since Korea had Piet cared about news. News happened to other people.[33]

A formative moment that motivated Updike to write the novel occurred right after the Kennedy assassination. Rather than suddenly alter the course of the plot, this climactic event merely reinforces the characters' civic disengagement by magnifying its extent. Learning about the assassination in his dental clinic while treating Foxy, both Freddy and Foxy intuitively reacted to the event with concern for how it would affect *their* personal lives. "Freddy seemed distended and titillated by this confirmation of chaos. Escorting Foxy out through the anteroom, he said in the hall, 'This fucks up our party, doesn't it?'" Even Foxy, who initially suggests he call off the soiree, is overcome with anguish—not for Kennedy but for the fact she will not get to see her lover Piet. "A distant husband had died and his death less left an emptiness than revealed one already there," the narrator observes, and goes on to note, "Where grief should have dwelt there was a reflex tenderness, a personal cringing." Given the privatized responses to this public event, it is ironic that Freddy's wife, Georgene, manages to convince the couples to attend the black-tie affair by justifying it on the grounds "that on this terrible day she saw nothing wrong in the couples who knew each other feeling terrible together."[34]

But as the novel makes clear, the opposite occurs. What was initially billed as a solemn wake for the dead president quickly degenerates into a bizarre party and an obscene farce. At the beginning of the party, Bea Guerin approaches Piet for an intimate conversation. "'Oh Piet,' she said, 'isn't it awful, that we're all here, that we couldn't stay away, couldn't stay home and mourn decently?' With lowered lids he fumbled out a concurrence, hungering for the breasts that had risen to such roundness their upper rims made a dimpled angle with Bea's chest-wall. *Why don't you want to fuck me?*" A short while later, an aroused Eddie Constantine reveals to Piet that he was talking to Marcia in the kitchen about "some cruddy thing, air pollution" but was looking down her dress the whole time. When he disappears again a short while later with Irene, we are told that he is "in the kitchen talking about air pollution."[35]

From then on things only get stranger, and racier, begging the question whether sex has become a distraction from their collective mourning or the driving force behind it. First, Freddy confronts Piet about sleeping with his wife and warns him that retribution will be swift and painful. Next, Piet, who has not been with Foxy since she gave birth, spots her in the bathroom. After joining her there, she begins nursing him, until they are suddenly interrupted by Piet's wife, Angela, knocking on the door. After acrobatically escaping through the bathroom window so as to avoid being caught, he literally falls in on Ben and Bea "necking" in the yard. As all of this goes on under her own roof, Georgene complains that "It's too tedious, if people aren't going to have their affairs in private." But she is essentially elucidating what by now is already clear: that the private and public experiences have been fused.[36]

Whether or not Updike was trying to purge his own guilt-ridden feelings from having attended a party on the night of Kennedy's assassination, the twenty-five page scene he meticulously crafted reflects the manner in which the private realm has absorbed the public and prevented the type of public-minded mourning he implied was required.[37] While the characters pursue their sexual escapades, there is still a very solemn, respectful, and compassionate attempt at mourning the president's death: Some of the couples watch the ceremonial transfer of the casket on live television while others recall Kennedy's personal charm. When the couples finally get up to dance, it is not without hesitance. "Do you want to? It seems blasphemous, waltzing on the poor guy's grave," Piet tells Angela. After they commence, he admits, "I feel we're insulting Kennedy." To which she responds, "Not at all. Yesterday, he was just our President way down in Washington, and now he belongs to all of us. He's right here. Don't you feel him?"[38]

Angela's willingness to translate a monumental political event into a personal experience is augmented by the background music that Updike chose for the scene: Doris Day's "Wrap Your Troubles in Dreams." The soothing lyrics, which comically suggest listeners ignore the grey skies and "dream your troubles away," is a fitting choice. Updike's decision to quote the line from the song that reads "Castles may tumble, that's fate after all, life's really funny that way" reminds us of the novel's epigraph, which warns against the dangerous effects on democracy of surrendering personal political agency to the hands of fate (or others). Symbolic of their growing apathy as they are dancing in this ambivalent moment of shared guilt, the couples hear Doris Day belt out "Close Your Eyes. Cuh-lozzz yur eyeszz." As the couples continue to dance, the narrator provides a verdict for the evening. "Piet turned in pain from the window and it seemed that the couples were gliding on the polished top of Kennedy's casket."[39]

The characters' unwillingness to abandon private concerns and embrace any public conscience continues after the party concludes. "The three days of omnipresent mourning had passed for these couples of Tarbox as three tranced holidays each alike in pattern," the narrator says. During this time the men played football and the women watched television while the nation collectively mourned. Not sure how to react, they experienced the televised funeral in a confused manner: "Amid drumrolls, the casket gleamed and was gone. The children came crying, bullied by others. Another drink? It was time to go home, but not yet, not quite yet. It was evening before they packed the children into the cars. The space in the cars as they drove home was stuffy with unasked questions, with the unsayable trouble of a king's murder."[40] The garrulous couples can hardly seem to shut up when it comes to juicy gossip or swapping sexual anecdotes about their *private* lives but in the face of *public* tragedy they have lost their power for speech.

In between the two climactic events of the novel, Foxy's abortion and the subsequent unraveling of her and Piet's affair and exposure of the adulterous society, a town meeting occurs. Although it lasts for only three pages and is prosaically buried between very intense moments, what intuitively appears as a short dramatic respite may very well serve as the denouement for the book's subtle political narrative. If we reconsider *Couples*, as I have suggested, a novel that both reveals the decline of American community and explores the circumstances behind it, then the town meeting reflects the culmination of the couples' gradual civic disengagement and represents the dire political implications of their behavior. In carefully constructing the scene of the town meeting, Updike seems to have engaged the celebratory Tocquevillian mantra regarding American public life only to challenge its verisimilitude. While Tocqueville famously claimed that "To take a hand in the regulation of society and to discuss it is [the] biggest concern and, so to speak, the only pleasure an American knows," Updike's *Couples* reveals the exact opposite: Rather than extol democratic participation, the town meeting is a depressing reminder of just how far it has degenerated.[41]

Early in the novel, Frank Appleby casually jokes that "at the last town meeting the fire chief was voted the most neurotic." By the novel's end what appeared initially as a paltry moment of comic relief now becomes an ominous sign of the meaninglessness of political life in Tarbox. The scene opens with a foreboding line: "Town meeting that spring smelled of whiskey. Piet noticed the odor as soon as he entered the auditorium." Updike's narrator then recalls how over the years the town meetings have changed, not for the better. "At the first meeting Piet had attended, the town employees, a shirtsleeved bloc of ex-athletes who perched in the bleachers apart from their wives, had hooted down the elderly town attorney, Gertrude Tarbox's brother-in-law, until the old man's threadbare voice had torn and the microphone had amplified the whisper of a sob." But this vocal and vibrant democratic deliberation, for which the narrator seems to yearn, has gradually waned. "Now the employees, jacketed, scattered, sat mute and sullen with their wives as year after year another raise was unprotestingly voted them." In an elegiac passage, the narrator laments that, unlike the lively and passionate participants in the past, the current town attorney is an "urbane junior partner" who took the job "as a hobby," while the moderator is "a rabbit-eared associate professor of sociology, a maestro of parliamentary procedure." If meetings back in the day featured rowdy citizens drunk on democracy, it is quite indicative that now the lethargic participants are merely drunk on whiskey.[42]

What has happened to the town meetings in Tarbox is emblematic of what is happening to postwar American democracy: everything is being relegated to procedure. Instead of meaningful deliberation at the town hall, there is bland protocol, and nothing seems to captivate let alone energize public interest anymore, while "only an occasional issue evocative of the town's rural past . . . provoked debate." This is how the narrator disapprovingly describes the proceedings: "New schools and new highways, sewer bonds and zoning by-laws all smoothly slid by, greased by federal grants. Each modernization and restriction presented itself as part of the national necessity, the overarching honor of an imperial nation." In light of the new political procedures in Tarbox that now seem to mechanically regulate themselves and the plummeting public participation, it is no surprise that the town's democratic institutions are restructured. "There was annual talk now of representative town meeting, and the quorum had been halved."[43] That the narrator chooses to remind us at this point that "Among Piet's friends, Harold little-Smith was on the Finance Committee, Frank Appleby was chairman of the committee to negotiate with the Commonwealth for taxpayer-subsidized commuter service, Irene Saltz was chairlady of the Conservation Commission" is apropos: what they have in common, other than their political duties to the town, is that they are all members in an adulterous society. Given the manner in which sex is conflated with politics throughout the novel, it is difficult not to correlate the characters' parallel civic activities and draw a causal link between their inflated private lives and the deflated public institutions they administer.

When the meeting ends, the narrator informs us of what by now we already know: "Politics bored Piet." It is then further revealed that "his family had been Republican under the impression that it was the party of anarchy; they had felt government to be an illusion the governed should not encourage. The world of politics had no more substance for Piet than the film world." Piet's political apathy is pertinent since it serves as a foil to his wife Angela's ostensible political dedication. "At Piet's side, Angela, who had to rush into Cambridge after nursery school every day and then fight the commuter traffic home, was exhausted, and kept nodding and twitching, yet as a loyal liberal insisted on staying to add her drowsy 'Ayes' to the others." The narrator sardonically observes that "The self-righteous efficiency of the meeting, hazed by booze, so irritated Piet, so threatened his instinct for freedom, that he several times left the unanimous crowd to get a drink of water." Despite her adherence to procedure and insistence on taking part in the meeting, Angela appears to care as little as Piet does about politics—or at least the humdrum affairs that qualify as such at the town meeting. "In the car he asked her, 'Are you dead?' 'A little. All those right-of-ways and one-foot strips of land gave me a headache. Why can't they just do it in Town Hall and not torment us?'" This is a pivotal moment in the plot: it is not Angela who is "dead," but rather the democratic process and community in which she insisted on participating (tellingly, it is in the following scene that Piet's affair with Foxy is exposed and dissolves their entire community). When Angela suggests "they just do it in Town Hall and not torment us," she is signaling the broader public disengagement at the time from participatory politics and a corresponding expansion of bureaucratic government.[44]

The depressing scene at the town meeting is so sobering, and prescient, exactly because it reflects certain structural changes quietly transforming the country at the time. In *On Revolution* (1963), which was published the same year *Couples* takes place, Hannah Arendt lamented the disappearance of traditional council systems (like town halls) that had housed the public realm and sustained what had symbolized in her eyes classical American democracy. The centralization of power under the welfare state and the consolidation of representative democracy, she argued, created a dangerous situation inimical to genuine democratic politics. Building on Jefferson's republican model, she declared that "the danger was that all power had been given to the people in their private capacity and that there was no space established for them in their capacity of being citizens." "If the ultimate end of revolution was freedom and the constitution of a public space where freedom could appear . . . then the elementary republics of the wards, the only tangible place where everyone could be free, actually were the end of the great republic," Arendt concluded.[45]

Scholars have highlighted the import of domestic space and geography in shaping the plot of *Couples* and focused on how nearly everything occurs indoors.[46] The scene of the town meeting is apposite precisely because it offers a rare departure from the privatized experiences of the characters and documents the disappearance that Arendt so feared of the remaining public spaces for performing and experiencing citizenship *outside* the private sphere. The town meeting is one of the only substantial scenes in the novel that is removed from the domestic space of the couples' homes (the other is fittingly in the local church). And given the pejorative account of the town meeting that Angela equated to "torment" and the bleak dialogue between Angela and Piet in the car ride home, there is little doubt left that neither of them has any intention of attending future meetings. Arendt warned that republican democracy fades once politics becomes "a burden."[47] That politics have become a burden in Tarbox, however, is exactly what the town meeting illustrates. By illuminating this ominous social condition gradually unfolding in the plot, the scene reveals the ironic manner in which Updike, who deplored the New Left's advocacy of radical participatory democracy, had clearly shared at least some of its longings for a revived public sphere.[48]

The novel concludes with a dramatic outburst when the local congregational church that Piet and Foxy attend burns down in a portentous lightning storm. All that is left standing of the old religious edifice, symbolically, is the tin weathercock that rises above its charred remains. When Piet assesses the damage and gives the minister an estimate for the costs of rebuilding, he is reprimanded. "Christianity isn't dollars and cents," the minister insists. "This church isn't that old stump of a building. The church is people, my friend, people. *Human* beings."[49] This is a fitting ending for the intertwined spiritual and political narratives suffusing the novel: not only has religion been replaced by sex, but the political community that it initially helped forge has by now been dissolved by the privatization—and secularization—of public life.

Religion and community in Updike's eyes were inseparable, and essentially represent two aspects of the same social experience. "My father was a Sunday-school teacher, and a number of his colleagues were also Sunday-school teachers, so the Sunday-school and the church had a kind of familial, communal dimension that was not intimidating, but the opposite," Updike said. "The Christian religion is hardly something that you can do alone." He recalled that it was in the congregational church in Ipswich (prominently featured in *Couples*) where he first got involved in community affairs: it "heightened, really, one's respect for your fellow parishioners, since you saw them trying to debate real issues—money issues, and so on."[50] His admiration for the architecture of

New England churches emanated, accordingly, from the fact that they occupy positions "of the utmost civic centrality."[51]

Couples, he revealed, is "not about sex as such: It's about sex as the emergent religion, as the only thing left."[52] When the Tarbox church burns down in the finale, therefore, the ashes we are left with, in a way, represent American civic life itself.

Friends without Benefits

If American community is coming apart, then it is only fitting that genuine bonds of friendship, a constitutive element of any community, can rarely be found among the residents of Tarbox. This is understandable since Updike initially based the novel on a short story he had written (and shelved) a few years earlier, titled "Couples," that, according to him, "bears the muffled heart of Couples, the theme of friendship—of friendships and their inevitable, never-quite-complete betrayal by, if by nothing else, time." Although the short story was published several years after the novel, Adam Begley claimed that "Couples" was meant to explore "the warmhearted camaraderie of friends in the first blush of their acquaintance."[53] But unlike the short story, which offered a skeletal version of the relatively still innocent Tarbox community in its incipient stages of vice and civic disengagement, the novel exposes the coldness and alienation that evolves out of the "warm camaraderie" Updike first envisioned.

In the *Nicomachean Ethics,* Aristotle established a solid link between friendship and politics and averred that "friendship seems to be the bond of Social Communities, and legislators seem to be more anxious to secure it than Justice even."[54] Aristotle envisioned three versions of friendship. The first two were instrumental and rooted respectively in the utility and pleasure friendship was aimed at achieving: "What is good for themselves; that is to say, not in so far as the friend beloved *is* but in so far as he is useful or pleasurable." Unlike these inferior relationships, dedicated to "a matter of result" (i.e., an expectation for some tangible benefit), it was the third iteration, derived from selflessness and virtue, that constituted what he called "perfect friendship." This somewhat idealized relationship existed among "those who are good and whose similarity consists in their goodness: for these men wish one another's good in similar ways; in so far as they are good; and those are specially friends who wish good to their friends for their sakes."[55] In Aristotle's mind, these genuine reciprocal ties among real friends could instill in people the necessary virtues of democratic citizenship.[56]

Given the explicit Aristotelian subtext of *Couples*—Piet was after all "an Aristotelian"—it is germane though ironic that no genuine friendships are actually forged in a novel that emerged out of Updike's interest in friendship. On the contrary, all relationships in the novel eventually reveal themselves—like the community of which they are constitutive—as utilitarian and self-interested. It is telling that the first infidelity in the novel, between Frank Appleby and Marcia little-Smith, is specifically couched in terms of friendship rather than sex. Right before they commence their affair, Marcia insists she does not want to "sexualize the friendship." "Frank, listen. I've become fixated on you, I know it's absurd, and I'm asking for your help. As a friend," she pleads with him (a few lines *after* their affair begins). A short while later it is ironically Marcia who complains about rumors flying regarding the little-Smiths relationship with the Applebys. "Marcia protested, 'But they must think we do *everything*, which seems to me so sick of them, that *they* can't imagine simple friendship.'" Later on, Janet Appleby, who has begun sleeping with Marcia's husband, now makes the same plea while rebuffing Freddy's sexual advances: "You can't imagine just friendship, can you?" He cannot, but neither can any of the other characters because they do not know what it means anymore; just as the public sphere has been privatized and politics confined to the bedroom, so has friendship lost the intrinsic value that Aristotle idealized and been relegated instead to a personal, utilitarian function. In a letter Foxy sends Piet from the Caribbean at the end of the novel, she has an epiphany regarding friendship: "It is refreshing, after our awful Tarbox friends who talk only about themselves, to talk to people who care about art and the theater . . . and international affairs, if that's what they are. I've forgotten what else 'affair' means."[57]

When Piet decides to attend the dramatic town meeting, it is, specifically, "to see his friends." That no one really talks to him there is not surprising. By the finale Piet realizes something important about them: "The world was more Platonic than he had suspected. He found he missed friends less than friendship." In other words, he discovered the idealized notions of friendship and community preferable to their disappointing earthly manifestations in Tarbox. His decision to move away from the town is indeed facilitated by the simple fact that although he had many acquaintances there, none of them were really his friends. Once Piet and his wife separate, "few of the friends he and Angela shared sought him out."[58] Even Matt, his old army buddy and business partner who initially appeared his best friend, quickly dissolves the friendship along with their business partnership once Piet's financial usefulness wears out. When Piet consents to Matt's offer to buy him out, what appears as the most substantial friendship in the novel is revealed to be nothing less than a business transaction worth $5,000. The irony in Piet's eventual alienation from the couples is that he is the only one in the group who actually sought out and provided genuine friendship: he visited the dying John Ong in the hospital when no else would (even though they all used his private tennis court) and he was the only one who checked up on Ben Saltz after he lost his job and was ostracized from the group. The tenuous nature of friendships in *Couples* reveals what philosopher Mark Vernon called "the dangers of knowing so many people, you really know no one."[59]

It is fitting that even Foxy's abortion, one of the climactic moments of the plot, is grounded in terms of friendship. When Piet humbly swallows his pride to ask Freddy, for whom he has demonstrated nothing but contempt, for aid in arranging an illegal abortion, he justifies it as a gesture of friendship. "Sweet Freddy," a chastened Piet pleads with him, "this lady needs your friendship." To which Freddy responds: "But old Piet, pious Piet, *friend* Piet, you speak of her. What about you and me? Don't *you* need my friendship too?" After Ken learns about the abortion and considers filing criminal charges against Freddy, Piet surprisingly comes to his defense by telling Ken, "he didn't have to do it, he did it out of pity. Out of love, even." When asked for whom he showed pity, Piet responds, "His *friends*." This episode is quite indicative of how distorted their understanding of friendship has become. Freddy's gesture should hardly seem to qualify as an act of friendship: he had arranged the abortion after all in return for a night with Angela (which he gets but cannot consummate) and the satisfaction gained by finally obtaining some leverage over the man who slept with his wife.[60]

The decline of friendship throughout the novel overshadows the broader decline of community in Tarbox. By exploring the nature of the relationships among the close-knit group of couples who have ostensibly established vibrant social networks and deep interpersonal ties, Updike exposed traces of specious solidarity and removed the veneer that masked the self-oriented hedonistic ambitions of individual members of the group. In thus challenging prevailing notions of friendship as early as the 1960s, he anticipated what would reveal itself in later decades as a salient social phenomenon. Ever since Vance Packard's seminal study *A Nation of Strangers* (1972) was published, scholars and social critics have worried about the erosion of friendship and increasing social isolation in America. In recent decades this fear of an eroding social fabric has apparently become worse: exacerbated by sweeping technological changes of social media and the internet, countless studies and polls have warned that more and more Americans are unable to forge genuine friendships and as a result America is becoming a "friendless" society.[61]

The Writer as Citizen

Couples might be dismissed as a sensational novel aimed at merely entertaining, if not for the historical and biographical context in which it was created. Updike adamantly insisted that his plot was fictional, "with only a touch of the Ipswich marshes peeking though."[62] But over time it has become evident that there was more truth weaved into the novel than he would have been comfortable admitting. Although we cannot be sure to what extent the adulterous society truly existed, Adam Begley's biography of Updike situates much of the plot in autobiographical experiences and reveals that both he and his first wife Mary had conducted extramarital affairs while living in Ipswich (and that Updike had slept with quite a few of the married women in their tight-knit group).[63] Even if we do not know exactly what went on in Updike's bedroom, we do know just how active he had been outside of it. The fact that Updike avidly participated in the social and political life of the town and held the duties of citizenship in such high regard suggests that his formative novel describing life in Ipswich cannot be fully appreciated without addressing its political implications. Since civic engagement was such a central part of his life at the time, it is natural that it would play a central part in his fiction.

Looking back fondly on his time in Ipswich, Updike recalled that "There was a surge of belonging—we joined committees and societies, belonged to a recorder group and a poker group, played volleyball and touch football in season, read plays aloud and went Greek-dancing and gave dinner parties and attended clambakes and concerts and costume balls, all within a rather narrow society, so that everything resonated." In one nostalgic flashback, he described the thrill of attending town hall meetings:

> I gave my name, was checked off and admitted, and stood there in the doorway of the gymnasium-auditorium in my city suit, looking in at the brightly illuminated faces of my fellow citizens. They were agitated by some thoroughly local issue on the floor; my wife and the friends we had made were somewhere in this solemn, colorful, warm civic mass, and I felt a rush of wonder that I had come to be part of this, this lively town meeting sequestered within the tall winter night.

Life in Ipswich, Updike wrote, was "eased by the cooperative nature" in which "egoistic dread faded within the shared life," and he observed that "an illusion of eternal comfort reposes in clubbiness."[64] The centrality of public life for Updike was captured by *Life* magazine, which noted in an early profile of the writer that

> short of joining the Benevolent and Protective Order of Elks, in fact, he could scarcely be more enmeshed than he is in the life of the town. He is a member of the rebuilding committee of the burnt-down Congregational Church and of the town Democratic committee, a participant in golf, poker and touch football games, and plays the recorder in a group that meets on alternate Wednesday evenings. He and his wife also give and go to a fair number of parties, which he thinks are by no means the frivolous affairs most people consider them. "Parties are somehow deadly serious" Updike says. "To say no to one is to say no to life."[65]

The importance of community instilled in Updike growing up in Pennsylvania strengthened during his time in Ipswich. He could not help but admire his time in London, if only because it reminded him of home.

> Some of the factors blighting American cities ... do seem to have been absent or mitigated here, and London's long primacy has made possible a kind of civic self-confidence absent or ambiguously ironical in America, except in small towns. I have moved here from a small American town, and find familiar virtues: some things are free, some are cheap ... the institutions of communal existence feel accessible.[66]

His admiration for the "institutions of communal existence" often informed his writing. In a warm review of the Indian writer R. K. Narayan's autobiography, for instance, Updike extolled his work for the solicitude it afforded citizenship. After approvingly quoting a passage in which Narayan recalls that in his hometown "one could not traverse the main artery of Mysore, Sayyaji Rao Road, without stopping every few steps to talk to a friend" and notes that "Mysore is not only reminiscent of an old Greek city in its physical features, but the habits of its citizens are also very Hellenic. Vital issues, including philosophical and political analyses, were examined and settled by people (at least in those days) on the promenades of Mysore." Updike concluded:

> Narayan is one of a vanishing breed—the writer as citizen. His citizenship extends to calling up municipal officials about inadequate street lighting, to "dashing off virulent letters to newspapers about corruption and inefficiency." Such protests do not feel, as with so much American social consciousness, forced—a covert bid for power and self-justification.... What a wealth of material becomes accessible to a writer who can so simply proclaim a sense of community! We have writers willing to be mayor but not many excited to be citizens.... An instinctive, respectful identification with the people of one's locale comes hard now, in the menacing cities or disposable suburbs, yet without it a genuine belief in the significance of humanity, in humane significances, comes not at all.[67]

In an essay he penned several years later about architecture in New England, Updike betrayed a similar appreciation for communal life. "We seek, Americans, to inhale freedom, and the air is here, in these communities of houses built one by one, along roads whose curves were derived from the lay of the land. Predating the merciless grid that seized Manhattan and possessed the vast Midwest, New England towns have each at their center an irregular heart of open grass, vestige of the Puritan common," he wrote. "The idea of land held in common ... has permanently imprinted the maps of these towns, and lengthens the perspectives of those who live in them."[68]

It is precisely because of the import of civic engagement to Updike that *Couples* should be more closely read as a critical account of New Deal liberalism's political culture. As Updike himself admitted a few years after its release, the book "was certainly an attempt, maybe an all too deliberate ambitious attempt, to show how estranged the slightly-above middle class was in the '60s from all the institutions that had traditionally served as some kind of inspiration. Politics to these couples is unreal." Accordingly, the characters he constructed were meant "to open outward: that is, to show nobody is an island. There are no islands, so that strangers are momentary characters—they all come into play and are engaged and disengaged." Fifteen years after the publication of *Couples,* Updike revealed in an interview with the *New Edinburgh Review* that the novel is about

> a moment of the American self-consciousness, about a loss of faith, particularly religious faith. The people in it are scoffers as most people are, but they have lost touch with the political life of the nation. The germ event in my life which prompted *Couples* was that on the night of Kennedy being shot, some friends had scheduled a party and after much agonizing, decided to have it, as in the book. In other words we didn't know what gesture to make, so we made none. We had become detached from the national life. Our private lives had become the real concern. There was a monstrous inflation of the private life as against the merged life of the society which struck me and helped me think I should write the book.

Lest we mistakenly confine this "monstrous inflation of the private life" that motivated him to the eccentricities of New England, Updike insisted all Americans could identify with this worrisome social transformation: "I think the events which took place in Tarbox took place to a greater or lesser degree everywhere else. I have a foolish confidence that my locations will serve as an adequate symbol coast to coast."[69]

Conclusion

In one of the more influential works of American political science, Robert Dahl's study of interest group politics, *Who Governs?* (1961), located a new and supposedly benign trend of political apathy that had suffused postwar America. His case study of local politics in New Haven, Connecticut, found that the new political dynamics were governed not solely by elites but through competition among rival groups that vie for power in a pluralist arena open to a variety of interests: "Competing political parties govern, but they do so with the consent of voters secured by competitive elections," Dahl averred. One result of this new pluralist model, which profoundly shaped New Deal liberalism, was, ultimately, a different type of democracy—arguably less democratic. Although the study claimed that competing elites and community leaders compromised with the public to advance common interests, it also claimed that the elites were the ones who mostly drove politics while the public was often driven out. "In the United States generally one of the central facts of political life is that politics—local, state, national, international—lies for most people at the outer periphery of attention, interest, concern, and activity," Dahl wrote. "At the focus of most men's lives are primary activities involving food, sex, love, family, work, play, shelter, comfort, friendship, social esteem and the like. Activities like these—not politics—are the primary concern of most men and women."[70]

Written just a few years after Dahl's groundbreaking study, *Couples* not only portrays this sense of apathy but sheds light on its unintended consequences. In Tarbox politics still *seems* to matter: it frequently comes up in conversation at dinner parties and parlor games, regularly intrudes upon the thoughts of most characters, and retains a central place, at least symbolically, in their daily experiences in civic committees and town meetings. And yet, the characters are rarely, if ever, able or willing to translate talk into action. In a way, *Couples* captures the transitional moment when participatory democracy began to give way to bureaucratic government and interest groups while direct and personal civic engagement degenerated into social alienation and disengagement.

Relying on the standard tools of social sciences, Dahl, like Putnam, constructed analyses of civic engagement with the help of elaborate empirical research. Only what could be measured, compartmentalized, and quantified—economic indicators, voting patterns, surveys, attendance rates, and demographic shifts, alongside myriad personal interviews—were incorporated into the grand narratives they produced. Through his fiction, Updike inserted an original and more nuanced chapter to this story of civic decline that could never fully register within the social scientific inquiry. After all, if one considers the health of civil society in Tarbox solely through the prism of participation in community life, then it would appear to be a Tocquevillian paradise. It is only with the help of Updike's literary sensitivity and its brutal honesty that the curtains are fully removed and the vacuous civic experiences that qualify as community life in Tarbox revealed. Whereas political scientists have relied upon structural factors to explain patterns of civic engagement, Updike has complemented, and complicated, such explanations by forcing us to look inward and explore the intricate cultural and social shifts that may have generated or facilitated the broader structural forces in the first place; it is not the entrance of the television to the homes, the extension of the workday, or longer commutes that alone undermined communal life—on the contrary, technological, economic, and geographic conditions seem to enrich the couples' interconnectivity in the novel. What dissolves their social adhesiveness is the reprioritization of public and private experiences and the subordination of the former to the latter. The privatization of what was previously deemed public experience, as documented in *Couples,* appears to have become a personal process stemming from new cultural norms and a corresponding shift in sensibilities away from the collective conscience inward toward the individual one.

In his history of American civic life, Michael Schudson has interpreted postwar vicissitudes in civic engagement as matters of form rather than substance and lent a rather comforting verdict: "Citizenship in the United Stated has not disappeared. It has not even declined. It has, inevitably, changed." According to Schudson, the rights revolution of the 1960s redefined citizenship and produced a new form of "personalist politics" that extended the democratic process to previously marginalized groups and helped to "fully empower citizens to speak and participate."[71] But speak about what and participate for which purpose? These more nuanced questions of qualitative, as opposed to quantitative, forms of political participation are crucial to ask if we wish to locate, and address, the deeper problems facing American politics. And they are questions that novels like *Couples* can help us investigate in a surprisingly original fashion.

In the final pages of *Couples,* Foxy sends Piet a letter that touches on a discussion she had with her innkeeper in the Caribbean about the Kennedy assassination—a discussion that seems to distill the underlining dilemma with which the novel asks us to grapple. "Forgive me, I am using my letter to you to argue with Larry in. But it made me sad, that he thought that somebody like us (if K. was) wasn't fit to rule us, which is to say, we aren't fit to rule ourselves, so bring on emperors, demigods, giant robots, what have you."[72] Updike did not assign this assertion to one of the main protagonists but outsourced it to a marginal character we know or care little about (Foxy's innkeeper in the Caribbean). He did so because *Couples* does not intend to render judgment on the changing nature of democratic life as much as it prompts us to do so ourselves. As Robert Detweiler aptly concluded, "One can read *Couples* from many different angles of plotting—not because its author presumes that the reader will bring any such versatility *to* the novel but because the novel itself forces any fair reader to grant the legitimacy of its pluralism."[73] Updike never suggested Americans are not fit to rule themselves. But by delicately sketching the changing contours of the political and private spheres and chronicling the abdication of civil responsibility, his most scandalous novel might very well be his most edifying if only because it forces us to reconsider the fate of American democracy under the changing conditions of liberal modernity.

6 | Things Don't Mix
Rabbit Redux and the Unraveling of Postwar Liberalism

> *Turning and turning in the widening gyre*
> *The falcon cannot hear the falconer;*
> *Things fall apart; the centre cannot hold*
> —W. B. Yeats, "The Second Coming"

> *The freshening sky above Mt. Judge is Becky, the child that died, and the sullen sky to the west, the color of a storm sky but flawed by stars, is Nelson, the child that lives. And he [Rabbit], he is the man in the middle.*
> —John Updike, *Rabbit Redux*

The peaceful ten months John Updike spent in London from the fall of 1968 to the summer of 1969 may have temporarily shielded him from the chaos engulfing American society and helped rejuvenate his civic spirit but they could not inoculate him or his fiction from its grim implications for too long. Upon his return to the United States in June 1969, Updike chose to directly engage the pandemonium tearing America apart in an effort to better understand it.[1] The result was *Rabbit Redux* (1971), the sequel to *Rabbit, Run,* and the first explicitly political novel that Updike ever produced. Rather than shy away from the political or deal with it in a more implicit manner, as Updike's other writings do through metaphor, symbolism, and myth, *Rabbit Redux* is mired in politics. The Vietnam War, the civil rights movement, the counterculture, the New Left, and the collapsing welfare state all invaded Updike's literary imagination—and Rabbit's home—in a way that allows the novel to sit comfortably on the bookshelf alongside contemporary political fiction such as Saul Bellow's *Mr. Sammler's Planet* (1970), Norman Mailer's *The Armies of the Night* (1968), and William Styron's *The Confessions of Nat Turner* (1967).

The narrative opens on the eve of the historic moon landing in July

1969 and ends three months later. Harry "Rabbit" Angstrom, by now a faithful LBJ Democrat who is part of the "silent majority"—a phrase popularized by President Nixon in his famous 1969 speech bearing that name—has reunited with his wife Janice, whom he left at the end of the previous Rabbit novel, that takes place a decade earlier. The two lead an apparently serene middle-class life in a quaint ranch house in Penn Villas, a new suburb near Brewer, Pennsylvania. Rabbit works as a linotype setter at a local printing plant and his wife is employed at her father's car dealership. If there is a spitting image of the postwar American Dream, it would be this. But of course there is not.

The tragic plot commences with a reversal of fortune: it is Janice this time who has an affair and temporarily leaves Rabbit for Charlie Stavros, a coworker and bleeding-heart liberal who is vociferously opposed to the Vietnam War, which Rabbit initially supports. During their three months of separation, Rabbit raises their thirteen-year-old son Nelson while undergoing a host of adventures. First, he meets a nineteen-year-old hippie teenager named Jill, who has run away from her affluent Connecticut home. Having essentially been pimped out to Rabbit at a sleazy tavern by a coworker, the androgynous and insecure Jill moves in with Rabbit and substitutes as both his lover and child (as if taking the place of his deceased daughter). After a short while Jill brings home her black boyfriend Skeeter, a proponent of Black Power and a Vietnam vet with messianic fantasies who moonlights as a drug dealer. This trio enters into a bizarre psychosexual three-way relationship that brings the politics of the 1960s—from which Updike had personally tried to flee by moving to England—right into Rabbit's living room: the Vietnam War, racial strife, postindustrial capitalism, and the counterculture are all afforded central roles in the plot as news reports from the television, unwelcome though seemingly inescapable, constantly spew information about the growing body count in southeast Asia, the urban riots in nearby York, Edward Kennedy's scandalous accident at Chappaquiddick, and the trial of the Chicago Eight.

It is in this charged political atmosphere suffusing the plot that Rabbit, Jill, and Skeeter, borrowing a page out of the New Left's own manual, organize their political reeducation: they hold "seminars" in which they each read passages from Frederick Douglass's slave narrative or William Lloyd Garrison's writings and conduct "teach-ins" to discuss the ills of modern capitalism with the help of Karl Marx and Frantz Fanon.[2] Meanwhile, Rabbit's mother is dying from Parkinson's disease, his printing plant is down-sizing due to technological innovation, and his sister Mim, a high-end prostitute on the West Coast, comes for a visit. The plot culminates when Rabbit's neighbors, enraged by the interracial relationship taking place on their block, burn down his house with Jill still in it. The novel concludes after Rabbit helps Skeeter flee the law (even though he abandoned Jill to die), and reconciles with Janice, thus leading us right back where we started a decade earlier: with Rabbit and Janice trying to hold their family together.

The novel was originally published in a dust jacket that featured red, white, and blue stripes—an allusion to the American flag—that were dull and washed out. Commentators observed that the America on display in the novel seemed also to be fading. Although *Rabbit Redux* was criticized for having an excess of sex and violence, its initial reception was mostly positive, as many critics and scholars alike were impressed with Updike's surprisingly bold and uncharacteristic attempt to engage the political turmoil of the era and reassess the troubling state of America.[3] Marshall Boswell observed that *Rabbit Redux* "was the darkest and most violent novel in Updike's entire oeuvre."[4] This is true, but only because the time the plot was focused on was the darkest and most violent time in Updike's America. He himself admitted that "external circumstances bear nightmarishly upon my skittish pilgrim" and that "The book is very much set in the late sixties and is very much informed by the news of that unhappy time."[5]

But while the novel is rooted in the experiences of the late 1960s, its narrative arc reaches further back and represents the final unraveling of the much broader and more complicated fate of New Deal liberalism. In a way, all the various forces that would gradually undermine postwar liberalism and contribute to its eventual implosion after 1968—a process that culminated in the triumph of conservatism with the election of Ronald Reagan in 1980—are already present in the novel: there is racial backlash, moral disintegration, economic stagnation and postindustrialization, urban decay, a breakdown of law and order, and political alienation and civic disengagement from an increasingly incompetent federal government. When Rabbit's house burns down at the end of the novel—a house in which a white working-class man, a Black Power radical, and a flower-child girl had dwelled together—there is a symbolic correlation with the self-immolation of the political house that Roosevelt had built: the New Deal coalition. Writing about the fateful events of 1968, historian Allen Matusow noted that "Liberals had once promised to manage the economy, solve the race problem, reduce poverty, and keep the peace. These promises not only remained unfulfilled; each of them would be mocked by the traumatic events of this election year. With the threads of the American fabric unraveling the electorate would turn elsewhere for leadership."[6] It is indicative of Updike's prescient political instincts that *Rabbit Redux* contains traces of all these conventional explanations for liberalism's demise.[7]

Still, there is even more to it. The key to reevaluating *Rabbit Redux* in the larger context of this book is that it sheds new light on the latent sources of liberalism's decline located in a longer and more complex internal narrative. These can be found in the powerful description of the moon landing at the novel's start. Rabbit and his father witness the monumental event at a local tavern they frequent after work. "The lifting so slow it seems certain to tip, the swift diminishment into a retreating speck, a jiggling star. The men dark along the bar murmur among themselves. They have not been lifted, they are left here."[8] The passage encapsulates a fundamental problem at the heart of the postwar liberal project. Since the moon landing, in Updike's own words, served as the "central metaphor" of the novel, it is fitting that at its core lies a disillusionment not simply from New Deal liberalism but from the promise for the progress and change that it entailed. The unbridgeable gap between the perception of national success and advancement and the bitter reality of individual failure and disappointment articulated in the passage above demonstrates how America was seemingly marching forward while many ordinary Americans were feeling left behind.

A pivotal scene early on in *Rabbit Redux* crystalizes this increasing dissonance between the emerging two Americas—enjoying the fruits of modernity and quietly seething in its discontents. It begins with Rabbit innocently staring at his newly gadget-equipped kitchen and then questioning his place in this modern, and modernized, environment:

> If he goes empty now he won't last at all, because we get emptier. Rabbit turns from the window and everywhere in his own house sees a slippery disposable gloss. It glints back at him from the synthetic fabric of the living-room sofa and chair, the synthetic artiness of a lamp Janice bought that has a piece of driftwood weighted and wired as its base, the unnatural-looking natural wood of the shelves empty but for a few ashtrays with the sheen of fairgrounds souvenirs; it glints back at him from the steel sink, the kitchen linoleum with its whorls as of madness, oil in water, things don't mix. The window above the

sink is black and as opaque as the orange that paints the asylum windows. He sees mirrored in it his own wet hands. Underwater. He crumples the aluminum beer can he has absentmindedly drained. Its contents feel metallic inside him: corrosive, fattening. Things don't mix.⁹

Although the shiny kitchen is full of new appliances, Rabbit feels as empty as ever. The emerging gap between his material wealth and physical comfort and his spiritual poverty and existential discomfort reveals a salient conflict between form and content and the increasing superficiality that ostensible progress and affluence have bred. Since even nature can now be colonized by technology—the natural wood in Rabbit's house has assumed an unnatural, synthetic quality—modernity has become both inescapable and unbearable.

This metaphorically fraught passage masterfully encapsulates what the notion of "madness and civilization" is all about: Rabbit feels like an inmate, but the asylum is his own well-furnished home.¹⁰ The reason for his despair is clear: the new and the old—the unnatural and the natural—do not mix anymore. This dissonance is representative of a far deeper problem. Pluralist liberal sensibilities long sought to balance these competing forces of traditionalism and modernity. But Updike's early novels repeatedly show that there are certain things from the past and the present that do not mix; not all values can be compromised, not all ideals can coincide, and not all ideas can be synthesized. What *Rabbit Redux* does is essentially use the quotidian domesticity of suburban America to suggest something much more profound: the deep pluralism that defined postwar liberalism—like Arthur M. Schlesinger Jr.'s "vital center"—could not hold. Things were, in the words of W. B. Yeats, whose poem "The Second Coming" was employed by many to voice the tragic liberal sensibilities of the era, quite literally falling apart.¹¹

At the end of the novel, as the dawn's early light reveals the red glare of Rabbit's still smoldering home, he ponders his mortality and thinks to himself, "The freshening sky above Mt. Judge is Becky, the child that died, and the sullen sky to the west, the color of a storm sky but flawed by stars, is Nelson, the child that lives. And he, he is the man in the middle." When Janice proposes they sell what is left of the house, Rabbit remarks, "I thought Brewer [the town] was dying," to which Janice responds, "Only in the middle."¹² And indeed, by the novel's finale, we realize that the center that Updike persistently tried to hold on to—his cherished "middleness"—does not hold because it cannot hold irreconcilable forces.

What this chapter suggests then is that *Rabbit Redux* makes explicit what was implicit in Updike's previous novels: liberalism was unable to reconcile the traditions upon which it was originally founded with the forces of modernity that it had unleashed. At Harvard Updike tried to synthesize science with religion and reconcile values of medieval Christianity with the rational sensibilities of the Enlightenment. In his debut novel *The Poorhouse Fair*, he grounded this conflict in the metaphorical landscape of an old-age home that houses a collision between two competing streams of old and new liberalisms, each equipped with their dueling conceptions of liberty, equality, democracy, and virtue. While his earliest works stubbornly refuse to resolve these tensions and sustain that malleable formula of "negative capability"—what Updike called "yes, but"—which enable the coexistence of competing ideas, *Rabbit, Run* and *Couples* question the efficacy of this penchant for compromise by demonstrating how some things do not always mix. The new forces of consumer capitalism and therapeutic liberalism unleashed in the postwar era undermined the traditional family; changing economic and technological conditions distorted the Protestant work ethic by re-creating a labor experience that provided neither economic security nor creative fulfillment; faith and religious institutions could not sustain the new psychological pursuit of self-awareness and individual self-expression, nor could it compete with the promise of science and technology; and traditional Jeffersonian norms of participatory democracy and civic virtue could not survive the bureaucratization of politics and its centralization of power by technocrats and interest groups. *Rabbit Redux* essentially documents the climactic unraveling of all of these tensions and reflects its outcome. And it does so with a vividness that suggests the seeds of liberal decline had been planted earlier than the 1960s and far deeper in the heart of New Deal liberalism than sometimes realized.

The Economic Unraveling

It is quite fitting that one of the more salient qualities of the postwar liberal mind was irony, for Updike imbued much of his fiction with an ironic twist that negotiated the gap between what his characters wanted and what they eventually got. In no place is this ironic fate more visible than in the economic fortunes of *Rabbit Redux*. Throughout the preceding decade, Updike's novels repeatedly set out conflicting visions of economic development that interrogated their effects and outcomes. *The Poorhouse Fair, Rabbit, Run*, and *Couples* (not to mention his other novels from the 1960s not addressed here, like *Of the Farm* and *The Centaur*) often deal, at least indirectly, with a clash between what sociologists Luc Boltanski and Eve Chiapello have called the "first and second spirits of capitalism." Although it is doubtful Updike ever even heard of, let alone read this theory, Boltanski and Chiapello's reconceptualization of the evolution of capitalism similarly pitted conflicting economic visions against each other. Their "first spirit" is associated with the individual's Protestant work ethic and creative self-fulfillment located in the earliest phases of capitalism. The "second spirit" supposedly replaced the first in the early decades of the twentieth century by essentially sacrificing workers' individual creativity and self-expression on the regimented altar of the assembly line in return for financial security and stability.[13] In *The Poorhouse Fair*, there is no resolution between these two spirits: despite the indubitable material benefits provided by Conner's regimentation—residents lived longer and healthier lives—Hook's stalwart sense of creative autonomy and craftsmanship retains its appeal. In *Rabbit, Run*, the balance between the two spirits of capitalism becomes all the more difficult to maintain as Updike's hero oscillates between them: Rabbit leaves a boring job as a kitchen-gadget salesman, which offers him security without fulfillment, for employment as a gardener that offers the exact opposite. Yet he cannot seem to locate a job that offers both. In *Couples*, the tension between the two forms of capitalism is only heightened as Piet, the gifted carpenter, must reluctantly acquiesce to assembling homogenized and prefabricated ranch houses to make ends meet. Eventually, like all other characters in the novel who seem to have abandoned the need for self-fulfillment by embracing cushy white-collar jobs, Piet also succumbs: he gives up his independent trade for a steady paycheck agreeing to work as a building inspector for the US Army, of all places.

In *Rabbit Redux* things only get worse. The lingering tensions between dueling visions of capitalism suffusing New Deal liberalism were meant to provide either creative fulfillment or financial security. But by now Rabbit is left with neither. These dire consequences, stemming from the rise of postindustrialism during this period, can already be glimpsed in the opening sentence of the novel: "Men emerge pale from the little printing plant at four sharp, ghosts for an instant, blinking, until the outdoor light overcomes the look of constant indoor light clinging to them." When comparing this to the opening of *Rabbit, Run*, in which Rabbit tries to hold on to his glory days in an improvised basketball game, we realize that working as a linotype setter for a decade has not only eroded his sense of accomplishment but has literally drained his humanity. The opening lines of *Rabbit Redux*, rife with pathos and regret, emphasize just how far Rabbit's once shining star has fallen: "The small nose and slightly lifted upper lip that once made the nickname Rabbit fit now seem, along with the thick waist and cautious stoop bred into him by a decade of the linotyper's trade, clues to weakness, a weakness verging on anonymity."[14]

The recurring ghostly metaphor that literally haunts Rabbit when he leaves the plant is indicative of the transformation and possible dehumanization that he has experienced inside it. Rabbit's dire spiritual condition—he has become weak, passive, anonymous, a ghostly image of his once vibrant self—is essentially tied to his economic condition. Whereas Rabbit fled his stultifying job as a salesman at the onset of the previous novel in search of self-realization and the freedom that made him feel alive, this time around he has undergone, to borrow a phrase from Karl Polanyi, a "great transformation" of his own: Reluctantly embracing the hierarchal disciplined workplace of the Fordist economy, he forfeited his autonomous ambitions in exchange for material comfort.[15] "The machine stands tall and warm above him, mothering, muttering, a temperamental thousand-parted survival from the golden age of machinery," Rabbit thinks to himself while at work. The narrator comments,

> But the machine is a baby; its demands, though inflexible, are few, and once these demands are met obedience automatically follows. . . . Do for it, it does for you. And Harry loves the light here. It is cream to his eyes, this even bluish light that nowhere casts a shadow, light so calm and fine you can read glinting letters backwards at a glance. It contrasts to the light in his home.[16]

Although the solace he finds at work is partially a product of the acrimony that overshadows his domesticity as result of Janice's affair and the haunting death of their daughter, Rabbit has become a complacent, even obedient, worker by this point in his life, succumbing to the machine from which he fled only a decade earlier.[17]

During a game of Monopoly with Nelson and Jill, a revealing conversation about the value of work ensues. "Whatever men make . . . what they felt when they made it is there. If it was made to make money, it will smell of money. That's why these houses are so ugly, all the corners they cut are still in them. All the savings. That's why the cathedrals are so lovely; nobles and ladies in velvet and ermine dragged the stones up the ramps," Jill says. "Man is a mechanism for turning things into spirit and turning spirit into things." Rather than simply reveal Jill's naïveté, this important monologue, which almost reads like a passage from Marx's *Alienated Labor* and echoes the concerns about the dehumanizing effects of the Fordist workplace sounded by the New Left at the time, helps to demonstrate Rabbit's economic transformation since *she* has essentially imbibed *his* abandoned autonomous spirit and taken his place.[18] This time around it is Jill, the carefree, confused, and unstable teenager, who has embraced therapeutic liberalism and retreated into herself: she has fled her home and family on a journey of self-discovery; she spends all her time reading about yoga, psychiatry, and Zen; and she "reluctantly goes out, even at night" since the streets "strike her as poisonous." Having come from a wealthy Connecticut family, she has enjoyed all the comforts and privileges that Rabbit never knew and is therefore astonishingly indifferent to material concerns. She is open-minded, experimental, and free—with her money (she is profligate about her Porsche), her body (she sleeps with Rabbit, Skeeter, and possibly Nelson and does drugs), and her mind (she is curious and open to new ideas). Once Rabbit comes home, the conversation turns to the possibility of life on other planets. But when he expresses hope that Jupiter "could support a kind of life," Jill scolds his utilitarian bent: "It's your Puritan fear of waste [that] makes you want that. . . . You think the other planets must be used for something, must be *farmed*. Why?"[19]

The tension between the first and second "spirits of capitalism"—between creative autonomy and financial security—that is apparent in Updike's previous novels effectively dissolves by the end of *Rabbit Redux*, leaving Rabbit with neither of them. The final chapter begins with Rabbit being called into his boss's office and getting laid off. "Nothing stands still. They've decided up top to make Verity an offset plant. . . . It's been in the cards for years," his foreman, Ed Pajasek, reluctantly tells him. When Rabbit asks if he still has a place at Verity, Pajasek, surprised by his confusion, responds: "I thought I made that point. That's part of the technical picture, that's where the economy comes. Offset, you operate all from film, bypass hot metal entirely." Because "everything moves faster nowadays," Pajasek explains, Rabbit will be replaced by a new printing machine due to arrive by the week's end. The company can still "keep a few men on, retrain them to the computer tape," since "we've worked the deal out with the union," but Rabbit, who has neither seniority (like his father) nor benefits from affirmative action (like his black coworker Buchanan), is "far down the list." Pajasek's mumbling explanation and the misunderstanding between him and Rabbit reflects his lack of understanding of the larger forces at play. Since Pajasek is merely "imitating someone higher up," it is evident that not even he really comprehends the titanic economic changes baring down upon them. "You learned the skill and now the bottom's dropping out," he tells Rabbit. In the next scene Rabbit's father adds his own two cents: "I've seen the handwriting on the wall all along, whole new philosophy operating at the top now at Verity, one of the partner's sons came back from business school somewhere full of beans and crap." Asked by his boss what he now intends to do, Rabbit deadpans: "Die I guess would be the convenient thing. From the management point of view."[20] It seems that Rabbit's experience here personifies what Updike said years after the novel was published about another of his protagonists who found himself in a similar situation after losing his job: "He learns one of the brutal facts of life under capitalism. When your time is up, you're gone."[21]

In effect, Updike dramatized in this scene the defining characteristics of what Daniel Bell would label "postindustrial society" in his eponymous book released a few years after *Rabbit Redux* was published. They include the decline of steady blue-collar labor and well-paid manufacturing jobs, the rise of less secure temporary employment in a service economy, the proliferation of labor-saving technologies and automation, the growing importance of technical knowledge and creativity at the expense of manual labor, and the weakening of labor unions and depreciation of traditional forms of craftsmanship.[22] When Rabbit skims the want ads after losing his job, there is no place for someone like him anymore: only accountants, administrators, insurance agents, and programmers need apply.

The transition toward a postindustrial economy that effectively costs Rabbit his job also ravaged the old industrial cities of the Northeast and the Midwest, setting in motion a devastating social epidemic of urban decay. Updike seems to have sensed this impending doom and dramatized it as well as any urban historian: the death of Main Street, the flight of small businesses, boarded-up stores, shuttered factories, defaced billboards, forsaken public spaces, and demographic shifts from downtown to the suburbs. The newer part of the city in the novel, West Brewer, "doesn't have the glorious past like the city does," Rabbit observes. "So it's not so disappointed." Through Rabbit's walking the darkening streets of his childhood, literally and figuratively, Updike forced us to experience the dying city of Brewer through Rabbit's sentimental eyes.[23] The local theater where he went to see family movies now screens porn. Everything is in decay:

> The bus works its way down Weiser and crosses the Running Horse River and begins to drop people instead of taking them on. The city with its tired five and dimes (that used to be a wonderland, the counters as high as his nose and the Big Little Books smelling like Christmas) and its Kroll's Department Store... and its flowerpotted traffic circle where the trolley tracks used to make a clanging star of intersection and then the empty dusty windows where stores have been starved by the suburban shopping malls and the sad narrow places that come and go called Go-Go or Boutique and the funeral parlors with imitation granite faces... and a flower shop where they sell numbers and protection and a variety store next to a pipe-rack clothing retailer next to a corner dive called Jimbo's *Friendly* Lounge, cigarette ends of the city snuffed by the bridge.[24]

Updike contrasted this depressing image of Brewer with a reminder of what it once was. Among the articles for which Rabbit sets type, there is one titled "Local Excavations Unearth Antiquities." By inserting these typed articles into his prose (in different font), Updike ironically applied an innovative modernist technique that illuminates the disjunctions between past and present. "As Brewer renews itself, it discovers more about itself. The large-scale demolition and reconstruction now taking place in the central city continues uncovering numerous artifacts of the 'olden times' which yield interesting insights into our city's past," the article says. "Old faded photographs of Weiser Street show a prosperous-appearing avenue of tasteful, low brick buildings with horse drawn trolley tracks." These dual descriptions of Weiser Street are reminders of how far Rabbit's world has fallen. At one point, Rabbit stumbles upon a film crew shooting a movie that seeks to project Brewer as an emblem of Middle America. But gawking at the crew "makes Rabbit feel dim, dim and guilty, to see how the spotlights carve from the sunlight a yet brighter day, a lurid pastel island of heightened reality around which the rest of us—technicians, policemen, the straggling fascinated lake of spectators including himself—are penumbral ghosts, suppliants ignored."[25]

When Rabbit reconciles with Janice at the end of the novel, he is still unable to reconcile himself with the new economic reality. A decade earlier, he had traded in his entrepreneurial spirit for financial security when he decided to work at the printing plant. The historian Jefferson Cowie described this post–New Deal bargain between labor and management as that in which "workers were harnessed to union pay but longed to run free of the deadening nature of the work itself."[26] In other words, Rabbit had not been happy at the printing plant but was secure. But now he has effectively run out of options: he cannot afford returning to work for self-fulfillment and he cannot go back to working for a steady paycheck since there just are not enough of those jobs around anymore. "You look better since you stopped work. Your color is better. Wouldn't you be happier in an outdoor job?" Janice asks. We know that he would be happier in an outdoor job because we are constantly reminded throughout the novel that Rabbit has not forgotten the heavenly bliss he felt working in Mrs. Smith's garden in *Rabbit, Run*. In a scene that meticulously illustrates Rabbit's satisfaction from installing new storm windows, Updike reminded us of the joys of productive labor that have been lost:

> This work soothes him. You slide up the aluminum screen, putting the summer behind you, and squirt the inside window with the blue spray, give it those blue square swipes to spread it thin, and apply the tighter rubbing to remove film and with it the dirt . . . and go inside and repeat the process, twice: that at last four flawless transparencies permit outdoors to come indoors, other houses to enter yours.[27]

Rabbit himself effectively admits he would prefer to work outdoors when he initially responds to Janice's question by raising the possibility that they buy a farm. Updike, who once even envisioned a sequel to *Rabbit Redux* titled *Rural Rabbit*, had already conveyed interest in exploring this possibility earlier on in the novel when Rabbit asks Pajasek about the fate of a former coworker who had previously been let go. "He bought a farm north of here and raises chickens," Pajasek recalls. "If he's not dead by now." Given the correlation of economic independence (let alone farming) to death, it is no surprise that necessity prevails: Rabbit abandons his longing for self-fulfilling work by conceding that "They don't pay. Only morons work outdoors anymore." In light of his poor prospects of getting a decent job (as suggested by the unwelcoming want ads), it becomes evident that a morose Rabbit, susceptible to self-pity by this point, may not be able to find work anywhere anymore. "He calculates: after two months' pay from Verity he has thirty-seven weeks of welfare and then he can live on Pop's retirement. It is like dying now: they don't let you fall though, they keep you up forever with transfusions, otherwise you'll be an embarrassment to them."[28]

It is remarkable just how emblematic Rabbit's gloomy predicament is of the broader social consequences of the structural shifts toward a global economy that were remaking America—and devastating its working class—during this transformative period of the 1970s that the historian Judith Stein called a "pivotal decade."[29] Although Updike's next Rabbit novel, *Rabbit Is Rich,* would masterfully chronicle the daily hardships of skyrocketing inflation and the energy crisis later in the 1970s, *Rabbit Redux* already senses the seemingly inevitable tragic fate awaiting members of the American working class, to which Rabbit and his father belong: they lost the job security that had essentially been the sine qua non of the New Deal economy since the 1930s; the unions, which had once been the working class's trusted protectors, have either abdicated that responsibility or are just too impotent to effectively intervene on workers' behalf; and the working class's ingrained expectations in social mobility and perpetual prosperity have dissipated. "The hope and possibility marbled throughout the confusion of the early part of the decade began to fade into the despair of the new order emerging in the second half," Cowie wrote of the 1970s. Facing a grim future, he claimed, blue-collar workers like Rabbit were left with three options: escape, find ways of forgetting, or "lacking any civic outlets, bury [their] pains deep inside." Since Rabbit already tried the first option a decade earlier (he ran—but came back), and was unsuccessful with the second (despite smoking pot with Skeeter and Jill, he was unable to numb his pain), he too ended up burying his pain deep inside. That is why the ghostly motifs and his perpetual association with and reference to death in the novel remain so haunting. By the 1970s, stably employed members of the working class were becoming, in Cowie's words, "the last of a dying breed." Lacking the skills or knowledge to compete in the new economy, Rabbit effectively also suffers a social and spiritual death; his mind and body live on but by this point all that remains of them is a ghostly image of his past glorious self.[30]

The Limits of Racial Liberalism

Since the social tumult of the 1960s "bare[d] nightmarishly" upon the plot by Updike's own admission, there is little surprise that in *Rabbit Redux* he was forced to do something he had long avoided: deal directly with the combustible issue of race. Skeeter's character remains one of Updike's first (and only) attempts at seriously engaging the African American perspective and through it the broader African American experience. Critics have pointed to the novel's ambiguity and complained that Skeeter is a caricature born out of a blend of ignorance and racism.[31] Skeeter is certainly an unsympathetic protagonist: angry, violent, vulgar, and sexually abusive to Jill (he beats her), he is a drug dealer and deadbeat who cadges off Rabbit and leaves Jill to die in a fire while saving himself without remorse. But though he superficially represents a gross racial stereotype, he also has a genuinely dissenting voice in the plot with important things to say. By letting him say these things, Updike not only added a vital dimension to the story but helped uncover some of the fundamental moral contradictions at the heart of racial liberalism.

It is during the bizarre "teach-ins" conducted in Rabbit's living room, aimed at "reeducating" him, that Skeeter channels many of the criticisms of white liberal hypocrisy made by prominent (and militant) African American leaders like Malcolm X and the Black Panther Party.[32] He blames the North for "copping out" after the Civil War and abandoning the cause of freedom and equality on the altar of mammon. "What's all this about democracy, let's have here a dollar-cracy. Why'd we ever care, free versus slave? Capital versus labor, that's where it's at, right? This poor cunt of a country's the biggest jampot's ever come along so let's eat it, friend. You screw your black labor and we'll screw our immigrant honky and Mongolian idiot labor and, whoo-hee! Halleluiah, right?" Behind Skeeter's endless harangues, which comprise the book's longest chapter and Updike's cringe-worthy attempt at re-creating his dialect, is a basic lament: America missed its opportunity after the Civil War at racial equality. "You didn't lift us up, we held out our hands, man, we were like faithful dogs waiting for that bone, but you gave us a kick," he says. "It wasn't just us, you sold yourselves out, right? You really had it here, you had it all, and you took that greedy mucky road, man, you made yourself the asshole of the planet. Right? To keep that capitalist thing rolling you let those asshole crackers have their way and now you's all asshole crackers." Skeeter's suggestion that "we [African Americans] are what has been left *out* of the industrial revolution" is not only historically sound—historians have come to agree that economic modernization took national precedent over securing racial equality after Reconstruction and facilitated the rise of Jim Crow in the South—but also draws Rabbit's sympathy and agreement.[33] When Skeeter asks Rabbit, "You believe any of this?" Rabbit earnestly responds, "I believe all of it."[34]

Even though he is often reduced to a racial stereotype, Skeeter educates Rabbit—and us readers—about the inherent link between economic and racial injustice. As such, Skeeter illuminates the overlooked manner in which racial injustice was masked by the seemingly fair and colorblind economic policies of New Deal liberalism that, in the wake of the civil rights movement, afforded equal political rights to blacks while ignoring their economic ones.[35] When Rabbit's neighbors confront him on the street and demand he kick Skeeter out of his home, they frame their request in a peculiar manner. His neighbor, a computer engineer named Mahlon Showalter, says

> We came to you in all politeness. I want to repeat, it's the circumstances of what's going on, not the color of anybody's skin. There's a house vacant abutting me and I told the realtor, I said as plain as I say to you, "Any colored family, with a husband in the house, can get up the equity to buy it at the going market price, let them have it by all means. By all means."

When the other neighbor, a Vietnam veteran named Brumbach, begins to spew miscegenous remarks, Showalter whispers to Rabbit, "He's not that stable. He feels very threatened." Rabbit's response is telling: "'It's nice to meet a liberal,' Rabbit says, and shakes his hand. 'My wife keeps telling me I'm a conservative.'"[36]

This is no mere jab at liberal smugness but an indictment of the postwar liberal order. In this pivotal scene Updike captures the hypocritical manner in which New Deal liberalism employed the traditional language of classical liberal self-reliance, property rights, and privacy to conceal what had really been the product of structural economic racism by the modern New Deal state. The suggestion that "anyone" is welcome to buy the house as long as he or she can generate the equity conveniently overlooks the historically conditioned economic barriers for doing so. Matthew Lassiter has found that "During the Civil Rights showdown of the 1960s and early 1970s, white-collar families that claimed membership in the Silent Majority rallied around a 'color blind' discourse of suburban innocence that depicted residential segregation as the class-based outcome of meritocratic individualism rather than the unconstitutional product of structural racism."[37] It is exactly this specious liberal ethos of "meritocratic individualism" that belies more subtle forms of structural racism, which Rabbit's ostensibly off-the-cuff remark invites us to reconsider (for instance: through federally subsidized mortgage loans and insurance, access to credit, interstate highways, infrastructure, and public housing that were exclusively tailored to whites). By continuing to speak the traditional Lockean language of free markets and individual property rights on one hand—which stood at the heart of Louis Hartz's seminal concept of the liberal tradition—while at the same time using the institutions and resources of the modern welfare state to limit or even restrict their realization among blacks on the other, New Deal liberalism sustained an economic system that was philosophically and morally rife with contradictions.[38] And Updike was well aware of this. "There is a freedom of permission, and a freedom of empowerment," he observed in a 1992 speech in which he uncharacteristically advocated the importance of economic equality for preserving political freedom. "When, say, blacks are permitted to eat at a lunch counter with whites, it is a hollow freedom if they can't afford to pay for the lunch."[39]

The deep confusion pervading liberal attitudes toward race is magnified in Rabbit's own ambivalent relationship with blacks in general and Skeeter in particular. Already in the novel's opening scene, upon heading home from work Rabbit thinks to himself: "The bus has too many Negroes." Although he frequently succumbs to racial stereotypes—he complains blacks are too vocal and lazy, are deadbeat fathers, and are dependent on the state ("stop begging for a free ride")—it's vital to recognize that Updike raises such prejudices only to then discredit them. In one scene Rabbit flees from two black youths he thinks are chasing him in a sketchy part of town; when they catch up with him it is not to get his wallet but rather to return Jill's purse left behind at a bar. In another instance Rabbit's coworker, Buchanan, who has borrowed twenty dollars from him, approaches him at work. Instead of hitting him up for another loan—which is what Rabbit anticipates—Buchanan places two crisp ten dollar bills in his hands and remarks, "Never let it be said no black man pays his debts."[40] Updike did not expunge or defend Rabbit's racism—it is there for all to see, straightforward in its ugly truth—as much as he tried to understand it.

It is Skeeter, with whom Rabbit has developed a love-hate relationship, who clearly exposes the racial contradictions suffusing postwar liberal attitudes. On one hand Rabbit fears (and occasionally even despises) him, while on the other, he is fascinated and drawn to what he has to say. After Jill brings Skeeter into his home, Rabbit indignantly asks her "why are you doing this to me?" Although Rabbit beats him to a pulp in one scene, in another he longs to touch him and nearly engages in a three-way sexual act with him and Jill ("Harry wants to touch him but is afraid he will get a shock"). Despite Rabbit's ambivalent feelings toward and inconsistent treatment of Skeeter, Rabbit is increasingly drawn to Skeeter and even begins emulating his behavior. When Skeeter realizes this and asks him, "You like being a nigger, don't ya?" Rabbit firmly replies, "I do."[41]

Beyond the homoerotic motifs in play, Rabbit's ambivalence toward Skeeter reflects one of the central dialectical qualities driving Rabbit's behavior throughout all four novels: his inability to reconcile reason with instinct. This becomes consequential for reevaluating Rabbit's behavior in the context of modernity and its discontents. In the final dialogue of the book, Janice asks Rabbit if he believes Skeeter's ideas: "I would have liked too, but I'm too rational," he responds.[42] Although he ultimately chooses mind over body, throughout the narrative he vacillates between them. "The history of the black body in north America is fundamentally linked to the history of whiteness, primarily as whiteness is expressed in the form of fear, sadism, hatred, brutality, terror, avoidance, desire, denial, solipsism, madness, policing, politics and the production and projection of white fantasies," George Yancy has argued. For whites, Yancy contented, the black body "is to be feared and yet desired, sought out in forbidden white sexual adventures and fantasies."[43] The symbolic association of blacks with an exotic and seemingly unenlightened state of nature—which is exactly what fascinates Rabbit about Skeeter—is suggestive of the critical race theories that have explained ambivalent white attitudes toward blacks as a result of their own repressed longings to abandon reason and re-embrace primordial instincts by returning to a premodern and sexually permissive forbidden past.[44]

Lost in Space

"In some way I felt the little ranch house to be a space capsule spinning in space," Updike said about Rabbit's house in *Rabbit Redux*. "The whole thing, the whole fantasy of the book . . . is related to the true fantasy of our space invasion."⁴⁵ His decision to situate the plot on the eve of the moon landing essentially asks us to confront the meaning of the historic moment and contemplate its implications. Much like Conner, who longed to realize "heaven on earth" in *The Poorhouse Fair* by unleashing the untapped forces of science upon society, President Kennedy's appeal to Americans to conquer the New Frontier and help launch America, figuratively and literally, into space was rooted in a similar liberal reverence, even faith, in science's redemptive powers. "If this capsule history of our progress teaches us anything," Kennedy declared in his famous speech at Rice University in 1962, during which he promised to go to the moon by the end of the decade, "it is that man, in his quest for knowledge and progress, is determined and cannot be deterred."⁴⁶ But not everyone agreed, if only because not everyone benefited. Rabbit and his coworkers do not share in the glory of the moon landing or the scientific promise that it embodies. Far from echoing a dystopian technophobia or an atavistic agrarian reaction, *Rabbit Redux* reveals mounting trepidations from science's increasing dominance over Americans' lives alongside a resounding disappointment from their unfulfilled expectations.⁴⁷ In doing so it sheds light on a central contradiction of the postwar liberal order and attempts to answer the following question: why is it that at the moment America reached its technological zenith, millions of Americans, like Rabbit, were feeling they had hit rock bottom?⁴⁸

Disenchantment with progress—or at least with its material and technological manifestations—is one of Rabbit's primary sources of grievance. "He lives on Vista Crescent," the narrator declares. "Once there may have been here a vista, a softly sloped valley of red barns and fieldstone farmhouses, but more Penn Villas had been added and now the view from any window is as into a fragmented mirror, of houses like this, telephone wires and television aerials showing where the glass cracked." In addition to the bland image of suburban conformity that has vanquished nature, Rabbit's own home is a mechanized, artificial, and inhumane space in which he feels quite literally like an alien.

> The furniture that frames his life looks Martian in the morning light: an armchair covered in synthetic fabric enlivened by a silver thread, a sofa of airfoam slabs, a low table hacked to imitate an antique cobbler's bench, a piece of driftwood that is a lamp, nothing shaped directly for its purpose, gadgets designed to repel repair, nothing straight from a human hand, furniture Rabbit has lived among but has never known.⁴⁹

Updike constructed a thick atmosphere of disappointment in progress by juxtaposing the abstract and distant achievements in space with the immediate and tangible failures on the ground. "Next day [after the shuttle launch], Friday, the papers and television are full of the colored riots in York, snipers wounding innocent firemen, simple men on the street, what is the world coming to? The Astronauts are nearing the moon's gravitational influence." Neil Armstrong's giant leap for mankind demonstrates this point: at exactly the moment when the television screen flashes "Man is on the moon," Rabbit realizes how disappointing his own life has become: "I know it's happened, but I don't feel anything yet," he says. The third-person narrator, employing an innovative present tense, reaffirms this ironic sense of detachment by bringing together the man on the moon and the man in the middle only to show how far apart they are: "But the spacecraft [of Rabbit's home] is empty. A long empty box in the blackness of Penn Villas, slowly spinning in the void, its border beds half-weeded."[50]

Doubts are similarly raised about the virtues of modern medicine. Given the fact that Rabbit's mother is dying from Parkinson's, many of his conversations with his father, Earl, include the latter raving about the wonders of new drugs and the benefits of Medicare (which has just gone into effect). "This new medicine is a miracle, I must admit, ten more years the only way to kill us'll be to gas us to death, Hitler had the right idea," he says, continuing

> Believe it or not there's some advantages to living so long in this day and age. This Sunday she's going to be sixty-five and come under Medicare. I've been paying in since '66, it's like a ton of anxiety rolled off my chest. There's no medical expense can break us now. They called LBJ every name in the book but believe me he did a lot of good for the little man.[51]

While Rabbit recognizes the indisputable benefits of modern medicine (and especially of the drugs his mother is taking), he still questions the irony of living a longer life for which he is forced to sacrifice some of his humanity in return. "The pain of the world is a crater all these syrups and pills a thousandfold would fail to fill," Rabbit thinks to himself. His mother seems to agree. The new drugs are "working" in stabilizing her condition, "but she's so depressed she lacks the will." When Rabbit's mother reveals the nightmares she has been having since going on the new drugs, the reader is reminded of Francisco Goya's "Los Caprichos" etching in which the Spanish painter warned that "the sleep of reason produces monsters." Her "sleep of reason" produces just that: "Earl and I go to the hospital for tests. All around us are tables the size of our kitchen table. Only instead of set for meals each has a kind of puddle on it, a red puddle mixed up with crumpled bedsheets so they're shaped like. Children's sandcastles," she recalls. "And connected with tubes to machines with like television patterns on them. And then it dawns on me these are each people. And Earl keeps saying, so proud and pleased he's brainless, 'The government is paying for it all. The government is paying for it.' And he shows me the paper you and Mim signed to make me one of—you know, them. Those puddles.'" Rabbit responds in a serious tone: "That's not a dream. That's how it is."[52]

The questionable depiction of science and technology in the novel is all the more important because there is nothing else left anymore to compensate for their disenchanting effects and offset their mechanical prescriptions for living and dying. Whereas in previous novels, Updike struggled to balance, at times even challenge, progress with traditional sources of value, like the deep religiosity of Hook, Piet, and the younger Rabbit of *Rabbit, Run,* this time around there is nothing of the sort. The middle-aged Rabbit has mostly abandoned the palpable religious impulses of his youth and become a passive observer of what seems a spent force. Upon entering his ailing mother's room, he notes dryly that "the bedside table supports an erect little company of pill bottles and a Bible." In the past the bible would have meant something to him, maybe even provoked an emotional response; now it means nothing. Later on Skeeter mocks Rabbit, saying that "God's on their side, right? God's white, right?" only to remind him that "Whitey here got so much science he don't even need to play the numbers, right?"[53] Updike's previous works may question the efficacy and limits of science by offering alternative sources of meaning and value, but *Rabbit Redux* does not even seem to offer that.[54]

When Rabbit first heard the phrase "American Dream" as a child, "he pictured God lying sleeping, the quilt-colored map of the U.S. coming out of his head like a cloud." But early on in *Rabbit Redux,* it already becomes evident that Rabbit has lost his faith: he admits that he only prays on buses and has stopped going to church. Instead of engaging in deep spiritual conversation about God, as he did with the Reverend Eccles in some of *Rabbit, Run*'s most profound and majestic dialogues, he has traded places and become the great skeptic while Jill and Skeeter—representatives of the younger generations of social revolution—are infused with a burning faith of a different sort. Updike emphasized Rabbit's waning beliefs by drawing a contrast to Jill, whose faith is artificially stimulated by narcotics and who only sees God every time she "trips," and to Skeeter, who is described as "religious crazy" and whose messianic delusions lead him to proclaim, "I am the Christ of the new Dark Age." "You're nice not to lose faith," Rabbit tells Jill. "Ought to go to church but he can't get himself up to believe it," the narrator observes. After Rabbit questions the existence of God, this dialogue ensues: "'You know what you are?' Jill asks, her eyes the green of a meadow, her hair a finespun amber tangle dissolving into windowlight; a captured idea is fluttering in her head. 'You are cynical.'" To which Rabbit replies: "Just middle-aged. Ideas used to grab me too. It's not that you get better ideas, the old ones just get tired." Rabbit then admits that if "Somebody came up to me and said, 'I'm God,' I'd say, 'Show me your badge.'"[55] Unlike Rabbit or any of Updike's deeply spiritual protagonists in previous novels who carry the cross, Jill's naïveté and Skeeter's fanaticism show the problems of faith and only serve to undermine its appeal.

In his previous works discussed in earlier chapters, Updike sought to maintain a delicate balance between reason and faith. At Harvard he consistently found ways to synthesize dueling visions of progress and tradition (such as Marxist thought and medieval Christianity) and was clearly enamored by the scholastic attempts to fuse reason and faith. The plot of *The Poorhouse Fair* revolves around this axis and is rooted in the ideological collision between the atheistic Conner and the fundamentalist Hook. In both *Rabbit, Run* and *Couples* is a recurring tension between the head and the heart, as deeply religious protagonists struggle to sustain their faith alongside their longing for self-fulfillment while they are often forced to choose between reason and instinct. This is why some of the most powerful dialogues in Updike's novels are between representatives of these two forces (for instance between the liberal Eccles and the dogmatic Kruppenbach in *Rabbit, Run* and between the spiritual Piet and his secular neighbors who mock his devout faith in *Couples*). Updike testified to his own internal struggle with these forces. "Science has made human beings feel less significant: It has diminished our faith. How could it not?" he said in an interview to *U.S. News & World Report*. "In the conflict between science and religion, I'm very much my father's son. He was a teacher of mathematics and a man of great hardheadedness, in a way, who believed that facts can't be ignored. On the other hand, he was also a churchgoing man of a certain piety. I seem to have inherited both strains, and they somewhat awkwardly co-exist for me."⁵⁶

But in *Rabbit Redux* there is no room for coexistence: science has seemingly prevailed, and not necessarily for the better. That the only voices left defending faith, and a very strange and incoherent one at that, are those of Jill and Skeeter, hardly sympathetic spokespersons for any cause, suggests that even Updike suspected the battle for faith might be lost. After noting that Rabbit lives in "an age of specialization and collusion," Updike's narrator rendered judgment on the irrationality that pervades the age of reason in a moving passage: "The book he [Rabbit] has read aloud torments him with a vision of bottomless squalor, of dead generations, of buried tortures and lost reasons. Rising, working, there is no reason any more, no reason for anything, no reason why not, nothing to breathe but a sour gas bottled in empty churches."⁵⁷

Rabbit's retreat from the church and from religion more broadly reflects the exhaustion of mainline centrist religions at the time. Facilitated by a set of landmark Supreme Court rulings in the early part of the decade (*Engel v. Vitale, Schempp v. Abington School District,* and *Murray v. Curlett*) that forced the retreat of religion from public schools (and life), by the end of the 1960s the sense of religious decline was so palpable that *Time* magazine, always a popular voice for the zeitgeist, famously asked on its cover: "Is God Dead?" Three decades later, political scientists Robert Putnam and David Campbell somewhat answered this question in their study of religion in America since the 1960s:

> Perhaps the most noticeable shift is how Americans have become polarized along religious lines. Americans are increasingly concentrated at opposite ends of the religious spectrum—the highly religious at one pole, and the avowedly secular at the other. The moderate religious middle is shrinking. Contrast today's religious landscape with America in the decades following the Second World War, when moderate—or mainline—religion was booming. In the past there were religious tensions, but they were largely between religions . . . rather than between the religious and irreligious.⁵⁸

Lamenting the unraveling of what he called "the great spiritual consensus" between modern Enlightened and traditional Evangelical currents of Christianity, Garry Wills pointed to the waning influence of liberal Protestantism on the one hand and the growing appeal of Evangelicals on the other as a watershed moment of rupture and discord in American religious history.⁵⁹ Having been held together by the Cold War consensus, which helped moderate and balance them, the tenuous truce between competing visions of modern and traditional sects of Christianity, Wills opined, could not survive the cultural shocks of the 1960s, and abruptly broke part.[60] Rabbit's once vigorous faith suffers the same fate by the end of the novel.

Rabbit Redux never really challenges the merits or efficacy of science in the absolutist (or catastrophic) manner employed by the religious Right since the 1970s to demonize abortions, oppose stem cell research, and reject the teaching of evolution.[61] What it does do is voice a genuine concern for the absence of any counterbalancing beliefs and contemplate the social costs that this might entail. "People were taught that they should adopt a new, scientifically informed ethic of constructive self-realization and self-determination as they freed themselves from the restraints of their parochial origins," historian George Marsden has argued. But having abandoned genuine religious pluralism, he contended, liberal Protestants failed to incorporate traditional moral truths and religious principles (like those shared by Catholics, orthodox Jews, and Bible-belt "old-time religion" folk) into mainstream modernist theology, and this, in turn, facilitated the rise of the religious Right.[62] Since *Rabbit Redux* explicitly paints Rabbit as a faithful liberal still loyal to LBJ, Updike's strategic decision to contrast his spiritual decline with America's scientific triumph is a possible indicator of this widening tear within the liberal order; that which would conquer the stars yet had no interest in reaching the heavens.[63]

Compromised Democracy

Updike's works discussed in the previous chapters are animated by a search for normative social behavior and, either directly or indirectly, an equilibrium between self and society. Whether it's individual vs. state (*The Poorhouse Fair*), individual vs. family (*Rabbit, Run*), or individual vs. community (*Couples*), the recurring tensions between liberal and republican visions of democracy, "negative" and "positive" notions of liberty, and the private and public spheres overshadow Updike's plots in search of synthesis, balance, or at the very least coexistence. But in *Rabbit Redux* this elusive search meets a dead end: the deep pluralism that had informed Updike's work since Harvard and had been the hallmark of postwar liberal thought has come apart. Even worse: it has let America come apart as well. The political theorist Robert B. Fowler argued in the years immediately after *Rabbit Redux*'s publication that pluralism "was primarily a defense of old liberal values by new means and in a realistic framework" and insisted that "it did not challenge the liberal ethic of individualism, nor the norms of tolerance, nor the modern welfare state" since it was above all "intended as a reconciliation of democratic theory."[64] But *Rabbit Redux* implies that not everything can be reconciled; if there is room for *everything* in the pluralist compromise, then someone might end up taking a stand for *nothing*. New mechanisms of modern bureaucratic government in the United States were unable to preserve traditional democratic values and popular will. The postwar modus vivendi between the demos and a technocratic state negotiated by elites was supposed to maintain what Robert Dahl called an "American hybrid" by sustaining diverse political interests.[65] Yet if it bred the Vietnam War, racial strife, and the social ferment tearing America apart in the 1960s—or if at the very least it was unable to prevent them—then Updike forced us to reconsider: maybe the pluralist project was somehow flawed to begin with.

The jaded Rabbit we encounter on the pages of *Rabbit Redux* certainly seems to think so. Like with the economy, society, and culture in the novel, Rabbit senses that something has gone fundamentally wrong with America's politics. After his father-in-law asks to hear his thoughts about the troubling state of the nation while attending a baseball game, Rabbit responds: "'I think,' he says, 'about America, it's still the only place.'" Updike's narrative voice then interjects and completes Rabbit's thought for him:

> But something has gone wrong. The ball game is boring. The spaced dance of the men in white fails to enchant, the code beneath the staccato spurts of distant motion refuses to yield its meaning.... There was a beauty here bigger than the hurtling beauty of basketball, a beauty refined from country pastures, a game of solitariness, of waiting, waiting for the pitcher to complete his gaze toward first base and throw his lightning, a game whose very taste, of spit and dust and grass and sweat and leather and sun, was America.... Rabbit waits for this beauty to rise to him, through the cheers and the rhythm of innings, the traditional national magic, tasting of his youth; but something is wrong. The crowd is sparse, thinning out from a cluster behind the infield to fistfuls of boys sprawling on the green seats sloped up from the outfield. Sparse, loud, hard: only the drunks, the bookies, the cripples, the senile, and

the delinquents come out to the ball park. . . . Rabbit yearns to protect the game from the crowd; the poetry of space and inaction is too fine, too slowly spun for them. And for the players themselves, they seem expert listlessly, each intent on a private dream of making it, making it into the big leagues and the big money, the own-your-own-bowling alley money; they seem specialists like any other, not men playing a game because all men are boys time is trying to outsmart. A gallant pretense has been abandoned, a delicate balance is being crushed.[66]

Although there is nothing explicitly political about this passage, the problem that it engages has deep political connotations. The juxtaposition between the abstract ideal of an America that once was and the tangible sights and sounds of what America has become suggests how far things have deteriorated from Rabbit's perspective. The metaphorical conflation of baseball, America's national pastime, with the nation at large betrays many of the mounting anxieties within postwar liberalism: the crowd is an unfit mob from which the game, like America, must be "protected"; the individual players have abandoned their collective identity as a team and instead opted for pursuing a "private dream" of getting rich; rather than enjoy baseball for its intrinsic joys, the game has been instrumentalized like everything else and the players have turned into "specialists like any other." It is this "delicate balance" between the "the traditional national magic" that baseball once provided and what it has now become in a modern society—artificial, commercial, selfish, technocratic, vulgar, ugly, and boring—that has been crushed.

The novel highlights the problems of pluralist politics in a more explicit manner by virtue of the unique cast of characters Updike consciously chose to voice the competing opinions that were struggling to gain prominence in the public sphere at the time it was published. Despite their generic and often reductive qualities, each of the main characters—with the exception of Rabbit—has clear opinions about politics and is afforded ample opportunity to articulate them. "Like Harry, I try to remain open. Revolt, rebellion, violence, disgust are themselves there for a reason," Updike told the *Harvard Crimson* just after the book had come out. "I try to love both the redneck and the flower child, the anarchist bomb-thrower."[67]

Our first taste as readers of the unique cast of characters is of those voices of disgust. Early on in the novel we are confronted with the old generation, belonging to Rabbit's father and father-in-law, who respectively express the traditional liberal and conservative viewpoints and rehash the old political debates of the New Deal era. On one hand, Rabbit's father, Earl, a loyal FDR Democrat, extols Johnson from the novel's opening scene and proclaims that "Wherever he went wrong, it was his big heart betrayed him. These pretty boys in the sky right now, Nixon'll hog the credit but it was the Democrats put 'em there, it's been the same story ever since I can remember, ever since Wilson—the Republicans don't do a thing for the little man."[68] A working-class liberal who raves against Republican plutocrats and about Medicare, Earl (and his unwavering support of the Democratic Party) is matched only by his antagonism for the new forces within the party he fears are taking his place. "It's these God, damn, blacks, is what it is," his father complains in a typical diatribe. "If I'd of had the atomic bomb and these rich-kid revolutionaries to worry about, I'd no doubt just have put a shotgun to my head and let the world roll on without me."

On the opposite end of the spectrum is Rabbit's father-in-law Fred Springer, who initiates a monologue of his own during an outing to a baseball game. "Sniper fire four nights in a row, Harry. What is the world coming to? We're so defenseless, is what strikes me, we're so defenseless against the violent few. All our institutions have been based on trust," Fred says. "It wasn't Vietnam beat Humphrey, it was law and order in the streets. That's the issue that the common man votes upon. Am I right or wrong, Harry?"[69] He then laments that "Things go bad. Food goes bad, people go bad, maybe a whole country goes bad. The blacks now have more than ever, but it feels like less, maybe. We were all brought up to want things and maybe the world isn't big enough to take all that wanting. I don't know. I don't know anything." Fred mainly points the finger at Democrats and complains that America has become a "police state run by the Kennedys," echoing John Bircher–type conspiracy theories that would seem to place him comfortably among the radical Right that Richard Hofstadter warned against ("That's why you have these wars," Fred suggests, "believe it or not, to bail Democrats out of their crazy economics").[70]

Besides these two figures, who neatly represent the *old* binary opposites on the political spectrum, are the *new* ascending forces tearing the New Deal coalition from within. Updike did not only amplify the rebellious voices of the counterculture and Black Power echoed by Jill and Skeeter—the former with her new-age and free-spirited sensibilities and the latter with his historical rage and militant revolutionary fervor—but also provided substantial space for the opinions of Charlie Stavros, an antiwar liberal activist who is sleeping with Rabbit's wife. Described as a "sly" Greek American car salesman and ladies' man, Stavros is a permanent bachelor who is cool, amicable, and easygoing. He is sensitive, thoughtful, and, due to a bad heart, has a joie de vivre that makes it hard for women to resist him and for Rabbit to dislike him. It is precisely because Updike imbued Janice's lover, of all people, with sympathy and intelligence (unlike Skeeter for instance) that ascribes particular import to his views and endows Stavros with a certain gravitas that compels us to closely listen to what he has to say.

After a coincidental meeting with Rabbit and Janice at a local restaurant early in the novel, Stavros and Rabbit get into a heated debate that establishes the political tensions overshadowing the entire plot. During the ensuing ten-page dialogue, they project the dueling visions within liberalism and suggest just how far apart these visions had grown by the end of the 1960s. The pleasantries turn vitriolic after Stavros scoffs at the flag decal Rabbit defiantly put on his car. "'What's wrong with it?' Rabbit asks. 'It's our flag, isn't it?'" When Stavros casually remarks that "A flag is a flag. It's just a piece of cloth," Rabbit insists that "It's more than just a piece of cloth to me." Stavros responds: "Look. The Mississippi is very broad. The Rocky Mountains really swing. I just can't get too turned-on about cops bopping hippies on the head and the Pentagon playing cowboys and Indians all over the globe. That's what your little sticker means to me. It means screw the blacks and send the CIA into Greece." Rabbit's Cold War sensibilities prevent him from even contemplating this: "If we don't send somebody in the other side sure as hell will, the Greeks can't seem to manage the show by themselves.... I just don't see why we're supposed to walk down the street with our hands tied behind our back and let ourselves be blackjacked by every thug who says he has a revolution going."[71]

Turning to the topic of Vietnam, Rabbit claims: "We'd turn it into another Japan if they'd let us. That's all we want to do, make a happy rich country full of highways and gas stations. Poor old LBJ, Jesus, with tears in his eyes on television, you must have heard him, he just about offered to make North Vietnam the fifty-first fucking state of the Goddam Union if they'd just stop throwing bombs." When Stavros, like a Socratic gadfly, pokes holes in Rabbit's narrative and suggests that it was the US that started throwing bombs, Rabbit angrily responds, "'We've stopped; we stopped like all you liberals were marching for and what did it get us?' He leans forward to pronounce the answer clearly. 'Not Shit.'" After listening to Rabbit's views, Stavros offers his own insight, which is as much a critique of the policy as it is of the institutions in which it was formulated:

> My theory is that it's a mistaken power play. It isn't that we want the rice, we don't want *them* to have it. Or the magnesium. Or the coastline. We've been playing chess with the Russians so long we didn't know we were off the board. White faces don't work in yellow countries any more. Kennedy's advisers who thought they could run the world from the dean's office pushed the buttons and nothing happened.[72]

In contrast to Rabbit's instinctive, visceral, and sometimes stubborn responses, Updike has equipped Stavros with a much more historically informed, calculated, and patient reasoning that clearly distinguishes the rationale behind both arguments. Updike emphasized the distinction when he concluded the scene by noting that "Rabbit is locked into his intuition that to describe any of America's actions as a 'power play' is to miss the point. America is beyond power, it acts as in a dream, as a face of God. Wherever America is, there is freedom, and wherever America is not, madness rules with chains, darkness strangles millions. Beneath her patient bombers, paradise is possible." At the end of their conversation, Rabbit apologizes for his zeal: "I just can't stand to hear the U.S. knocked, I'm sure it's psychological."[73]

This exchange is germane for understanding the dissolution of postwar liberalism not simply because of the irreconcilable positions it reveals *within* the New Deal coalition toward the Vietnam War but due to the fundamental cracks it exposes in the structures and practices through which those positions came about. At the height of the debate between Rabbit and Stavros, Janice turns to her lover and quips, "He's silent majority, but he keeps making noise," then remarks, "See how little and tight his mouth gets when he thinks about politics." To which Rabbit angrily responds: "I don't *think* about politics, that's one of my Goddam precious American rights, not to think about politics."[74] This powerful scene elucidates the elementary challenge that the Vietnam War had posed to New Deal liberalism by revealing that the war essentially forced a complacent old-school liberal like Rabbit to do what the pluralist model never really demanded of him: to take a stand and engage politics directly. In other words, it threatened members of the silent majority with the possibility of having to break their silence. If the elite-driven pluralist mode of governing emanating "from the dean's office," in Stavros' words, that dominated American political life in the postwar decades allowed, even encouraged, Americans like Rabbit to detach themselves from politics, Updike implied in this scene that the result of such detachment may very well have been the war itself. Jill of all people seems to get this. "Your life has no reflective content; it's all instinct, and when your instincts let you down, you have nothing to trust. That's what makes you cynical. Cynicism, it has been said, is tired pragmatism. Pragmatism suited a certain moment here, the frontier moment, it did the work, very wastefully and ruthlessly, but it did it," she tells Rabbit, going on to say

> You've never given yourself the chance to think, except on techniques, basketball and printing, that served a self-exploitative purpose. You carry an old God with you, and an angry old patriotism. . . . That is what we Americans think, its win or lose, all or nothing, kill or die, because we've never created the leisure in which to take thought. But now, you see, we must, because action is no longer enough, action without thought is violence. As we see in Vietnam.[75]

Unlike all other characters in the book, Rabbit is the only one who does not really have a firm opinion about the war or anything else. Flanked by young revolutionaries on the left and old reactionaries on his right, he is desperately stranded on an increasingly unstable middle ground. "Politics are inescapable in this era, and his are, predictably, intuitive. He has a fervent, almost religious belief in America. While the younger Rabbit ignored politics, the older one identifies himself with what he perceives as the beleaguered America of the Vietnam era," Matthew Wilson observed. "In his passive mode, Rabbit is ambivalent; by allowing things to happen, he is creating a 'mess,' so he is *both* revolutionary outsider *and* defender of the status quo."[76] But one cannot be both; things do not mix. And Rabbit, like the postwar liberal mindset he espouses, is eventually torn from within by having to choose.

This perpetual oscillation and inconclusiveness is typical of Rabbit when it comes to talking and thinking about politics. After he fails to answer Fred's tirade at the baseball game about the deteriorating state of the nation, his father-in-law remarks, "Harry, your silence disturbs me. Your silence disturbs me." And indeed it disturbs us all. Time and again Rabbit has tried to preserve a middle ground that is simply not there anymore. In one scene, he voices his support for the Vietnam War ("I'm all for it") by explaining his opposition to the antiwar movement rather than voicing his support for the war itself. "I'm not saying it's pleasant to fight in or be caught in. I just don't like the kids making the criticisms. People say it's a mess so we should get out. If you stayed out of every mess you'd never get into anything." Rabbit then, "feeling himself get rabid," goes on and admits, "I guess I don't much believe in college kids or the Viet Cong. I don't think they have any answers. I think they're minorities trying to bring down everything that halfway works. Halfway isn't all the way but it's better than no way."[77]

The recurring motif of the garden, often employed by Updike to illustrate the clash between modern and traditional values, is particularly useful here for understanding Rabbit's inability to bridge the gap between self and society.[78] In *Rabbit, Run*, the protagonist leaves his family to tend Mrs. Smith's garden: he disengages from society in order to reengage himself. In *Rabbit Redux* he returns to the garden for a very different reason. "Not wanting to go inside with the television set. He pulls weeds in the border beds where that first excited summer of their own house Janice planted bulbs and set in plants and shrubs." Although he is often drawn to watching the news, Rabbit has come to detest television for its endless images of war and violence ("Ought to smash it, poison"). In this scene he literally leaves the news behind in order to tend his own garden. Yet this time around, it offers scant escape: "He weeds until he begins to see himself as a weed."[79]

By allowing Jill and Skeeter to stay in his house, Rabbit convened what one scholar called a "community of outsiders" in his own living room.[80] Despite Rabbit's (and Updike's) animosity toward the New Left, this scene surprisingly suggests that Rabbit nevertheless could be receptive to some of its beliefs. In the *Port Huron Statement* (1962), the founding document of Students for a Democratic Society, the foremost organization of the New Left, activists expressed concern for the deep apathy pervasive in public life and claimed that its degenerative effects created "politics without publics." Instead of the centralized pluralist model, they proposed a return to participatory democracy that was committed to several basic goals:

> that decision-making of basic social consequence be carried on by public groupings; that politics be seen positively, as the art of collectively creating an acceptable pattern of social relations; that politics has the function of bringing people out of isolation and into community, thus being a necessary, though not sufficient, means of finding meaning in personal life; that the

political order should serve to clarify problems in a way instrumental to their solution.[81]

For all of his skepticism Rabbit seems to agree with them. He proudly declares "I like learning stuff. I have an open mind" and subsequently immerses himself in endless discussions with Jill and Skeeter and Stavros about slavery, capitalism, imperialism, and foreign policy while partaking in "teach-ins" on his living room floor. By the end of the novel it seems like the rejuvenated republican spirit of the New Left may have penetrated Rabbit's apathetic bubble. After all, instead of fighting to preserve his "previous American right" *not* to care about politics, Rabbit gradually embraces a new and active social consciousness as the plot develops. But this comes at a cost. As a host of characters warn him, he is now in danger of abandoning his own garden, literally and figuratively. His boss Pajasek scolds him for paying *too much* attention to his family and says, "Kid, schmid. You can't live your life that way. You got to reason outwards from Number One. To you, you're number one, not the kid." A few pages later, the police chief offers him similar advice by urging him to look after himself before others. Finally, it is his sister, Mim, who offers her own diagnosis for Rabbit's ills when she comes to visit. "Why don't you tend your own garden instead of hopping around nibbling at other people's," Mim asks. To which Rabbit answers, "I have no garden." Mim in turn responds: "Because you didn't tend it at all. Everybody else has a life they try to fence in with some rules. You just do what you feel like and then when it blows up or runs down you sit there and pout."[82]

In his memoirs, published nearly two decades after *Rabbit Redux*, Updike revealed that the Vietnam War had been so unsettling exactly because it prevented him from tending his own figurative garden. "What angered me most about Vietnam," he candidly admitted, "it made it impossible to ignore politics, to cultivate serenely my garden of private life and printed artifact." Updike's discontent suggests that what particularly grieved liberals like him was the fact that by unveiling structural flaws in the decision-making process of American liberalism the war made it impossible to plead ignorance and continue disengaging from political life. He went on to stress this point by recalling that

> In politics, ever since the hair-raising shouting matches that flew about my burning ears in Artie Hoyer's barber shop, my instinct had been merely to stay

out of harm's way. . . . One source of my sense of grievance against the peace movement when it came was that I hadn't voted for any of its figures—not for Abbie Hoffman or Father Daniel Berrigan or Reverend William Sloane Coffin or Jonathan Schell or Lilian Hellman or Joan Baez or Jane Fonda or Jerry Rubin or Dr. Spock or Eugene McCarthy. I had voted for Lyndon Johnson, and thus had earned my American right not to make a political decision for another four years.

This nearly pathological trust in the legitimacy of the system that was instilled in him ever since he was a kid led Updike to reluctantly support the Johnson administration even when its actions appeared derelict and dangerous. "If he and his advisers . . . had somehow got us into this mess, they would somehow get us out," Updike believed. "And it was a citizen's plain duty to hold his breath and hope for the best, not parade around spouting pious unction and crocodile tears."[83]

In retrospect even Updike conceded he was wrong. "I think the Vietnam episode and the oil dependency are two things that constitute a pilling in, a kind of a shrinking, a making sure of what you have and not being too ambitious—internationally at least," he said in a 1978 interview with the Japanese magazine *Nami*. "It's, in a way, a pleasanter country to live in than it was ten years ago. I mean, there's much less stress. That was a very difficult time, the late sixties here, as in *Rabbit Redux*. Everybody had to rethink where they were and what things meant. I don't wish to return to that." Updike, like many liberals, did rethink their politics; what the Vietnam War ultimately did was challenge complacent and detached notions of citizenship and force liberals to reconsider the merits of the postwar political arrangement that eroded democratic citizenship and distanced the average citizen from the decision-making process. New Deal liberalism was supposed to employ modern technocratic governing techniques to secure, enhance, and cultivate traditional liberal values like liberty, equality, and social justice. But in the wake of the social upheavals of the 1960s, it became clear that liberalism had failed in doing so. While Rabbit gradually sheds his political detachment, which is evident in the beginning of the novel, and becomes highly engaged by its end, Updike gradually lost his own faith in the prevailing political system. "There are two ways to live happily with a government," Updike said. "To accept or to snub it, to identify with it and rejoice in its policies, or to ignore it as an unworthy brawl that has nothing to do with one's self. I could manage neither."[84]

Conclusion

After Rabbit's house burns down the police ask him whether he was running a commune inside. Lest he be confused as a hippie or a member or the New Left, he defensively blurts out, "No, Jesus; listen. I'm a conservative. I voted for Hubert Humphrey." This seemingly comical response is emblematic of a watershed moment not only in the plot but in the broader evolution of postwar liberalism. By the end of *Rabbit Redux*, as by the end of the 1960s it set out to record, the same Rabbit who had been a dedicated liberal and loyal New Dealer now describes himself as a conservative. What essentially occurred in this transition is that liberalism, as Updike complained in his memoirs, had become "unfashionable" to millions of Americans who long considered themselves liberal. The center of American politics—at least as it is painted in the novel—has clearly moved leftward; by standing still in what once was the political center, Rabbit now finds himself standing with the right. Although he continues to hold on to many of the traditional liberal values of liberty, individualism, self-government, and civic virtue shared by protagonists in Updike's previously published books, like Hook and Piet, by the close of the 1960s it appears there was no place left for any of them—at least as Rabbit understands them—under the reconstituted ideological umbrella provided by the new Democratic party that Eugene McCarthy, George McGovern, and others would reshape in the wake of Humphrey's defeat in the 1968 presidential election. If that umbrella now covered Jill, Skeeter, and Stavros, Rabbit's final conversion to conservatism may suggest that there is simply no room there for more moderate voices such as his. The novel's finale implies that Rabbit does not really abandon liberalism; in his mind, at least, it abandons him.

Rabbit Redux marks a cornerstone in Updike's career of social commentary and political fiction. It reveals in its author an astute political observer who recorded with nuance and acuity some of the most salient problems in postwar American life: the numbing effects of modern bureaucracy on individual freedom; the imperious attitude of scientific management toward religious beliefs; the deleterious effects of therapeutic liberalism and consumer capitalism on the family; the personal costs and disappointments of the postindustrial economic transformation; the privatization of the public sphere; and the subsequent decline of community life and democratic politics.

Rabbit may have embraced the title "conservative" by the novel's end but he has no atavistic longings for the past. In his eyes, as in Updike's, this embrace is more of a corrective mechanism to improve the inevitable march of history than a final destination to march back to. It is no coincidence therefore that history is afforded such a central role in this novel. Instead of rejecting the past, like the younger characters do, or trying to blindly preserve it without addressing fundamental problems of racism, injustice, and inequality, as the older generation of characters seems to prefer, Rabbit wants desperately to negotiate between modernity and tradition in order to preserve what is best and replace what is worst. After all, as attracted as Rabbit becomes to Skeeter's and Jill's revolutionary ideas, he recognizes there are things worth preserving. After reading a fiery passage by William Lloyd Garrison—"If the state cannot survive the anti-slavery agitation, then let the State perish"—Skeeter interprets the passage to mean "More Power to the People, Death to the Fascist Pigs." But Rabbit, echoing Updike's own stubborn liberal sensibilities, quietly disagrees: "To me it means, Throw the baby out with the bath."[85]

Conclusion
Liberalism Redux

If we open a quarrel between the present and the past, we shall be in danger of losing the future. Today our concern must be with that future. For the world is changing. The old era is ending. The old ways will not do.

—John F. Kennedy

There is this interest in the past, but in a way the past is all we have. The present is very thin, it's less than a second wide, and the future doesn't exist.

—John Updike

Whatever the many failings of my work, let it stand as a manifestation of my love for the time in which I was born.

—John Updike

In the aftermath of the 2012 presidential election, the *New York Times Book Review* editor at the time, journalist and author Sam Tanenhaus, suggested readers pick up a copy of *Rabbit Redux*. To better understand the mounting angst and discontent shared by many of those dwelling in the nation's heartland—whom he called "the everyman caught in the tangle of postindustrial America" where "all the moral verities that undergird Rust Belt America seem to be corroding"—he prescribed engaging Updike's prescient imagination.[1] Tanenhaus's sharp analysis was four years ahead of its time. While Barack Obama carried most of the Rust Belt states that year, even if just barely, in 2016 Donald Trump swept the entire region, including John Updike's native state of Pennsylvania. And he did so, at least in some part, thanks to the substantial support he received from the "everyman" that Rabbit Angstrom came to represent: disillusioned, angry, white, working- and middle-class male voters.[2]

Nearly fifty years separate Trump's victory and the publication of Updike's *Rabbit Redux*. During those years the nature of the working class itself broadened and shifted endlessly, even unrecognizably, as have the economic structures that define it.³ The local industrial economy that failed Rabbit has become a relic, having been replaced and displaced by a high-tech, global, service-oriented system that has little use for unskilled labor such as his. Race relations have also dramatically altered: despite the election of the nation's first African American president in 2008, racism has not been eradicated as much as it has changed. In place of the blatant bigotry of George Wallace and the dog whistles of Richard Nixon's "Southern strategy," racial inequality has been fused with economic and social injustice to inform struggles over immigration and jobs, access to economic opportunity, education, and criminal justice reform.⁴ The Cold War that overshadowed Updike's early fiction ended with what appeared at the time to be a resounding American victory, while the United States' global presence has since oscillated between intense foreign economic and military intervention (that, among other things, resulted in two prolonged wars in the Middle East) and its more recent penchant for international withdrawal, even isolation. During these years the political pendulum has swung back and forth repeatedly as the White House and Congress have shifted hands between parties and both the GOP and the Democrats underwent bitter internal struggles and subsequent transformations that molded new ideologies and re-created their political identities and electoral base.⁵

This book does not assume to explain these historic developments nor does it pretend to offer insight into (let alone prescriptions for) ameliorating our contemporary political malaise. What it does do is try to aid in better understanding of where this malaise came from. History is not deterministic; contingencies occur, external forces intervene, choices are made, roads are not taken, electoral outcomes and policy decisions actively shape the life of the nation. Looking to Updike's fiction certainly cannot explain Trump's victory. But it can shed light on some of the basic conditions, set in motion a half century ago, that made it possible. Among the outpouring of journalism and scholarship that has tried to make sense of the 2016 election, a recurring motif appears, one that by now should sound all too familiar. "The moral outrage of rural America is a mixture of fear and anger. The fear is that small-town ways of life are disappearing. The anger is that they are under siege," the sociologist Robert Wuthnow recently wrote. Demoralized and bewildered by decades of tectonic change—mostly not in their favor—millions of Americans found themselves living in disintegrating communities, felt ignored by a condescending government that was unresponsive to their particular needs and plights, and saw little hope if the bleak future proceeded on its present course. "Social expectations, relationships, and obligations that constitute the moral communities they [people in rural America] take for granted and in which they live are year by year being fundamentally fractured," Wuthnow asserted. In his eyes, "the outrage of rural America that surprised so many observers during the 2016 presidential election was there well before, and would have been evident had anyone bothered to look."[6]

John Updike looked. And what he found helps piece together at least part of the puzzle. Would Updike have ever voted for Trump? Slim chance. In 2008, a year before his passing, the old-school liberal who proudly declared that he had voted Democrat all his life, revealed that "I'm so for Obama."[7] But the interesting question is would Rabbit have been? Would Hook or Piet? The list of anxieties, grievances, and disappointments that have emerged from the heartland in recent years are not that new, in their substance rather than form. Many of them surfaced in Updike's fiction: broken families and alienated individuals, deteriorating communities and urban decay, dead-end jobs and chronic financial insecurity, empty churches and overbearing technology, a fragmented body politic and civic disengagement, and growing resentment toward a government perceived to be incompetent and oppressive that did not offer people much of a say in how their own lives were to be governed.

The shifting sensibilities driving these complaints have apparently been latent in rural and working-class communities all along, even at a time of ostensible purpose, unity, and prosperity—a time of "consensus"—when there was supposedly nothing to complain about. They were there in Hook's resistance to Conner's regimentation, in Rabbit's initial flight from his home and work, in the couples' escape from public life in Tarbox into each other's beds, and in Rabbit's inability to comprehend why the American Dream he had considered unshakable was suddenly in danger, like his own home, of going up in flames. After the 2016 election, Congressman Matt Cartwright, who represents Pennsylvania's Eighth District in the northeastern part of the state, said that many "voted for the change candidate, and you do that when you are hurting."[8] The tragic sense of pathos suffusing Updike's early fiction is in some way a budding expression of that hurt.

This book has shown Updike to be a savvy social observer, with an ongoing interest in political, philosophical, and theological concerns and a keen awareness of American history and political thought as well as current events. But it also demonstrates how those instincts have allowed his fiction to locate a broader and more subtle thread tying together the various political, economic, social, and cultural transformations wreaking havoc on the American heartland and alienating many Americans from the once seemingly omnipotent liberal order. The conventional explanations for this break, dating back to the cataclysmic events of the 1960s and early 1970s—the Vietnam War, racial strife, culture wars, the transformation to a postindustrial economy, and the exhaustion of the welfare state—are all vital milestones in the gradual disenchantment with New Deal liberalism. But lest we confuse cause for effect, these can be incorporated into a broader and more complex framework that centers on the engagement with modernity. "The civil rights and antiwar and countercultural and women's and the rest of that decade's movements forced upon us central issues for Western civilization—fundamental questions of value, fundamental divides of culture, fundamental debates about the nature of the good life," Todd Gitlin, a prominent voice of the New Left in the 1960s, once wrote. Chief among these debates was the proper way to transition into modernity and the limits, if any, that should be placed upon it.[9]

The ideas and institutions at the heart of the modern project—the Enlightenment, capitalism, science, secularism, liberal democracy, individualism, bureaucracy, and centralized technocratic government—had been gradually planted in America since the late eighteenth and nineteenth centuries. It was only with the coming of the New Deal that they ultimately took root, fully matured, and established their dominance in almost every facet of public and private life. But many of the forces of modernity that New Deal liberalism embraced and employed could not necessarily be reconciled with some of the fundamental traditions upon which it was built; as Updike observed: "Things don't mix." The resulting irony was that many of the forces that ended up undermining New Deal liberalism—a failed economy, racial strife, unjust war, cultural backlash, political discontent, and powerlessness—were the unintended consequences of contradictory ideas and confused policies born in the liberal mind itself. If liberals could not sufficiently cope with fundamental challenges tearing New Deal liberalism apart by the late 1960s, it's only because they themselves helped create them. The disastrous war in Vietnam was the natural outcrop of liberal anticommunism and the new international liberal order that it had constructed after 1945.[10]

The gradual disabling of the welfare state, the subsequent transition to a postindustrial economy, and the rise of neoliberalism were initially liberal economic responses to liberal policy failures.[11] These, in turn, devastated manufacturing, dealt a death blow to unions, and effectively cut off the path to social mobility for millions of working Americans who had been empowered by the New Deal and grew up in the unprecedented prosperity, which had made the New Deal possible in the first place. New Deal liberalism promised, interchangeably, either economic security or creative autonomy, but ended up providing neither.

The contradictions were not just limited to the economy. Racial liberalism sought to afford African Americans the opportunity to realize self-evident truths of liberty and equality enshrined in the Constitution and that lay at the heart of the liberal tradition but was unable—and often unwilling—to make the necessary material and political sacrifices to ensure them. Mounting disappointments from broken promises that liberals had made toward fulfilling racial equality and social justice, especially after President Johnson's ambitious War on Poverty and promise to build a Great Society, fueled the outrage and contributed to the sense of hopelessness and misery that sparked urban rioting across American cities later in the decade. As concluded in the *Kerner Commission Report*, which investigated the urban riots in Newark and Detroit in the summer of 1967: "Frustrated hopes are the residue of the unfulfilled expectations aroused by the great judicial and legislative victories of the Civil Rights Movement and the dramatic struggle for equal rights in the South." Racial liberalism tried to amend the historical wrongs of past generations and resolve the race problem with a host of brave new policies; but deeply rooted structural inequalities and racial biases planted in the heart of New Deal liberalism—as they were in the heart of America—prevented that transformation from reaching its successful completion.[12]

America's emerging civil religion, a product of the Cold War's demand for national solidarity, could not really compensate for the overall waning of genuine religious life.[13] The cult of science and technology catapulted the United States into space and cemented American economic and military supremacy in the Cold War but left little room for alternative sources of meaning and faith in the traditional religious institutions that only decades earlier, in the progressive era, had been the engines of liberal reform.[14] The ascendance of a national consumer culture was supposed to propagate perpetual demand and ensure economic growth, yet ended up undermining families, fragmenting communities, and eroding the values that had long held them together at the core of liberalism's social vision. Its therapeutic culture of self-realization further served to drive people apart and undermined civic engagement and public life. Finally, the centralized bureaucratic welfare state that arose to deal with the new challenges of governing a modern industrialized society tried to expand the definition of liberty from a passive ("negative") experience to an active ("positive") one. In the process of forging this new relationship between state and citizen, it all too often substituted centralized planning for citizenship. Unable to reconcile new technocratic structures and practices of governing with traditional Jeffersonian participatory democracy, which informed earlier liberal visions of government, New Deal liberalism's distant, detached, at times even imperious mode of governing sought to mobilize power to aid the people but ended up unintentionally removing people from any real access to power.[15]

"If we open a quarrel between the present and the past, we shall be in danger of losing the future," President Kennedy, paraphrasing Winston Churchill, warned in his famous acceptance speech at the Democratic National Convention in 1960, where he introduced his vision for the New Frontier. "Today our concern must be with that future. For the world is changing. The old era is ending. The old ways will not do."[16] Given the existential challenges of the Cold War, this statement certainly seemed true at the time. But in retrospect, the progressive march of history that New Deal liberalism was so bent on advancing might have proceeded too far too fast. If, indeed, "the old ways will not do," then Updike's work raises the question: what is left of the past—of its ways, norms, traditions, and institutions? And do these remnants even have a place in the New Frontier, which New Deal liberalism sought to conquer, and in the new—and "great"—society it wished to create?

Updike seems to have understood both the promise and pitfalls of modernity and approached this dilemma with his characteristic ambivalence. In a review of modernist African fiction in the early 1970s, he declared that "the otherworldly faiths have faded, and the earthly paradises—of Marxism, of industrial capitalism—have been debunked by partially coming true. Modernity's birthday party is over."[17] Over, but not forgotten: Updike realized that the past was inherently tied to the present and that it, therefore, needed to offer a guiding light for moving *forward* into the future. "Decline—in manners, craft, landscape, and communal vitality—is not, I hope, unduly harped upon," he wrote in the foreword to his award-winning collection of essays *Hugging the Shore*. "At all times, an old world is collapsing and a new world arising; we have better eyes for the collapse than the rise, for the old one is the world we know."[18] Instead of harping upon the past as conservatives have done, or speeding into the future with progressives, Updike's work is rooted in the present and reflects that unique blend of cautious optimism and sobered pragmatism in which the postwar liberal sensibility had been grounded. "Whatever the many failings of my work," a precocious Updike once wrote home from college, "let it stand as a manifestation of my love for the time in which I was born."[19]

Despite being branded a conservative and a reactionary by some left-wing critics, Updike revealed a much more nuanced perspective about the nature of historical change in his own thoughts.[20] "There is this interest in the past, but in a way the past is all we have. The present is very thin, it's less than a second wide, and the future doesn't exist," he noted in a 1969 interview with the British journalist Eric Rhode. "I wonder if twentieth-century man's problem isn't one of encouragement, the sense that we've gone to the end of the corridor and found it blank." And yet, rather than flee modernity as some reactionaries chose to do and revel in a beatified past, Updike presented a much more sober account of the American condition. "All these investigations of our origins and terrible flaws, the built-in problems of the way things work in America is a little like scouring the plumbing in your own home. It's hard for some of us to get down in the cellar. That doesn't mean it shouldn't be done."[21] A few years later, in a radio interview with Elinor Stout, he emphasized the danger of succumbing to an illusory sense of a bygone golden age. "I just think it's a fact (my nostalgia aside) that we feel lost. Our cities are uglier than they need to be, our lives are harsher than they need to be, and we all, to some extent, are a kind of captive to an America that never was."[22] Although in Updike's eyes the present is not all it should be, the past is no substitute. Make America great again? Updike's portrait of the postwar years suggests it was not that great to begin with. What he sought to do in *Rabbit Redux*, as in much of his early fiction, was liberate Americans from a self-imposed (and misguided) historical captivity by alerting them to the ambivalent appeal of history and exposing its blemishes as well as its beauties. If Rabbit, like the millions of Americans he came to personify, felt lost, it is in no small part due to an inability to surrender his yearning for a simpler world—one, that Updike reminded us, cannot really be re-created because it never actually existed.

In recent years, and certainly following the publication of Adam Begley's biography of Updike in 2014, it seems that more and more scholars and critics have begun to reassess his work in fresh and exciting ways. "Updike strikes me as the kind of writer who is going to be rediscovered, and who is going to keep being rediscovered," William Deresiewicz wrote in the *New Republic*.[23] A careful and nuanced interaction with his texts, as this book has tried to do, alongside a contextualization of broader historical trends and social thought framing Updike's novels at the time of their writing, has hopefully contributed to this fledgling rediscovery of his importance to American intellectual life. Many books from Updike's impressive oeuvre with significant political insight were left out of this study, and should be further explored and developed. *The Coup* reveals the blend of folly, naïveté, and arrogance behind much of America's Cold War foreign policy. *Rabbit Is Rich* masterfully documents the malaise of the 1970s and helps illustrate when and why the fear of America's decline, so palpable to this day, began to emerge. *Rabbit at Rest* chronicles the waning stages of the Cold War and the ideological depletion left in its wake.[24] And *Terrorist,* one of Updike's last novels, deals with the new ethnic, religious, and political challenges and conflicts that the September 11th terrorist attacks unleashed.

This book has exclusively focused on the fate of New Deal liberalism. And by 1972, that fate was sealed. Its residuals would struggle and straddle for another two decades under the shadows of George McGovern, Jimmy Carter, and Walter Mondale's reconstituted Democratic Party, but it had become a spent force: Its goals seemed no longer viable, its policy prescriptions no longer practical, its cultural purchase no longer attractive, and its spirit no longer vital. Elements of New Deal liberalism persevered and were revived under Bill Clinton's and Barack Obama's two-term presidencies. However, the hegemonic, self-confident, and unrivaled liberal order of the postwar years that Lionel Trilling was so uneasy about never really survived the tumults of the 1960s.

Updike insisted that the last thing his fiction was ever meant to do was preach, prescribe, or promote any particular ideology or idea. But that does not mean there are not certain historical lessons to be drawn from a close engagement with it. Three important conclusions with contemporary relevance to our current political climate emerge from this literary exploration of New Deal liberalism that are worth addressing. First, there is much more that unites American liberals than separates them. Second, much of what consists today as conservatism's core values were once an integral part of the liberal creed. Third, there are limits to the politics of compromise: not everyone fits into the pluralist model that postwar liberals so enthusiastically espoused because not everything can be compromised.

Liberals usually interpret the transformative period of 1968 to 1972 as the changing of the guard between the older, postwar establishment associated with the Johnson-Humphrey wing of the Democratic Party and the younger generation of New Left disciples identified with Eugene McCarthy, George McGovern, and Walter Mondale's presidential campaigns.[25] To a certain extent, this ideological fault line dividing left-liberalism created in those acrimonious years continues to define liberal politics and, as the bitter-primaries struggle between Hillary Clinton and Bernie Sanders during the 2016 election suggests, still haunts the Democratic Party. But Updike's work raises the possibility that on many core issues the differences are mostly in style rather than substance and in degree not principle. This is not to suggest that there are not serious disagreements—like over regulation of markets and access to public goods like healthcare and education and foreign policy—yet it is a reminder that, as the historian Doug Rossinow concluded, "Leftist radicalism and liberal reform do retain a common ancestry embodied in the Enlightenment tenets of a universal human destiny, a universal human nature, and the prospect of social transformation which, even if wrenching, will create a better world."[26]

Much of Updike's personal animosity toward the New Left was rooted in the critical reaction by the press and many of his literary peers to his tepid support of the Vietnam War (which was really a refusal to condemn America) in the 1967 collection of essays *Authors Take Sides on Vietnam*; although he admitted to feeling "uncomfortable" about the war, he nevertheless stated: "I am for our intervention if it does some good."[27] This painful episode that unleashed a maelstrom of criticism engendered a sense of wariness and caution that might explain why Updike avoided hereon political debates from a critical distance and would wait until his memoirs two decades after the war to respond to his critics.

The protest movement, which had begun in the solemn Fiftyish pronouncements of the *Port Huron Statement* and the orderly civil-rights strategies, by the time of the '67 Washington march and the '68 convention had become a Yippieish carnival of mischievous voodoo and street theatre and, finally, a nightmare of anarchy, of window-smashing and cop-bopping and drug-tripping and shouting down. The shouting-down part of it, the totalitarian intolerance and savagery epitomized by the Weathermen, but to some extent adopted by student radicals everywhere, amazed and alarmed me. Authority to these young people was Amerika, a bloodstained bugaboo to be crushed at any cost.

In a retrospective essay a few years later about *Rabbit Redux*, Updike revealed what most bothered him about the antiwar movement and the New Left:

> Unlike such estimable elders as Vonnegut, Vidal and Mailer, I have little reformist tendency and instinct for social criticism. Perhaps the Lutheran creed of my boyhood imbued me with some of Luther's conservatism; perhaps growing up Democrat under Franklin Delano Roosevelt inclined me to be unduly patriotic. In any case, the rhetoric of social protest and revolt which roiled the Sixties alarmed and, even, disoriented me. The call for civil rights, racial equality, sexual equality, freer sex, and peace in Vietnam were in themselves commendable and non-threatening; it was the savagery, between 1965 and 1973, of the domestic attack upon the good faith and common sense of our government, especially of that would-be-Roosevelt Lyndon B. Johnson, that astonished me.[28]

Notice that what seems to have riled Updike was not the actual goals of the protest movements—which he tellingly finds "commendable"—but rather their form, temperament, and magnitude.

Disentangling New Deal liberalism from the broader American Left is no easy task; the two are tied at the hip and have mutually reinforced each other repeatedly in a complementary and often symbiotic fashion. Radicals, populists, progressives, the Popular Front, fellow travelers, social Democrats, and even the New Left: they all left substantive imprints on postwar liberalism in policy, in persuasion, in personnel, and especially in politics.[29] It should not be surprising, therefore, that comparing the core values listed in the opening of the *Port Huron Statement*, the New Left's founding manifesto, with the concerns and aspirations manifested in Updike's fiction from the same period, reveals significant overlap. The urge for "finding a meaning in life that is personally authentic" and to realize a new kind of authenticity and independence in which "the object is not to have one's way so much as it is to have a way that is one's own" would have certainly seemed worthy, even admirable, to Hook, Piet, and especially Rabbit. Similarly, the search for genuine human relationships and social bonds that "overcome the idolatrous worship of things by man" and that "go beyond the partial and fragmentary bonds of function" would not seem strange or unfavorable to Updike's protagonists; on the contrary, these were the primary motivations behind his protagonists' actions. In addition, the demand for "a democracy of individual participation," in which "the individual share[s] in those social decisions [determines] the quality and direction of his life," and the demand for fulfilling jobs that "involve incentives worthier than money or survival" are central themes that have suffused Updike's early fiction.[30] He may have been disturbed with the absolutist nature of the New Left's demands and disgusted by the means they chose to pursue them. But like many New Deal liberals, it seems Updike shared their concerns about the political, social, economic, and cultural directions America was heading in even more than he would have probably cared to admit.

Accusations of alleged solipsism in Updike's novels and of an ostensibly skewed perspective as a "privileged white male" could potentially drive him (and his fiction) far from the contemporary liberal sphere, increasingly dominated by identity politics and its overwhelming concern with issues of race, gender, and sexuality. But placing such narrow confines on Updike seems to derive from a rather reductive analysis of his fiction. The individual experiences of his characters and their perpetual search for self-consciousness—which was tellingly also the central motif and title of Updike's memoirs—suggested men *and* women of different classes and ethnicities were deeply rooted in a concrete social milieu. His was a love of self (rather than of *himself*) and of community, two hallmarks of the New Left. "I loved Shillington not as one loves Capri or New York, because they are special, but as one loves one's own body and consciousness, because they are synonymous with being," Updike wrote of the small town in Pennsylvania where he grew up. "If there was a meaning to existence, I was closest to it here." In his memoirs he would go on to describe what he called "incessant sociability" (possibly a clue to a Kantian devotion to an "unsocial sociability") that saw a recurring search to balance his dedication to the self with social responsibility. "Egoistic dread faded within the shared life," he admitted. "One's life is thoroughly witnessed and therefore not wasted."[31] Any narcissistic trends that appear to crystallize through his protagonists' flights from society are accordingly *always* counterweighed, reassessed—and eventually rejected in favor of a compromise between self and society. What Updike's critics have overlooked is that every time Rabbit runs—from his wife, family, or community—he always comes back.

Unlike with the New Left, New Deal liberalism has much less in common with the New Right. But the second lesson we can draw from Updike's work is that they used to have a lot more in common. By failing to sufficiently address cultural concerns shared by many Americans and incorporate traditional norms, customs, and institutions into its modernizing project as early as the 1950s, postwar liberalism essentially created the space for discontent through which the New Right could emerge and gradually ascend to preeminence at its expense. Antistatism, creative autonomy at work (in contemporary terms: entrepreneurship), community, family, faith, and individual freedom: Updike's protagonists, who all valued these very ideals, remind us that long before these ideals were monopolized by conservatives and enlisted into the GOP platform, they were core tenets of the postwar liberal mindset. Updike's college roommate, Christopher Lasch, who himself had partially undergone a similar conversion toward cultural conservatism, seems to have clearly understood this. In one of Lasch's final works, *The True and Only Heaven* (1991), he berated liberals for ignoring the traditional values that many Americans continued to embrace and for exclusively focusing on progress. "Their attack on 'Middle America' which eventually gave rise to a counterattack against liberalism—the main ingredient in the rise of the new right—has blinded them [liberals] to the positive features of petty-bourgeois culture: its moral realism, its understanding that everything has its price, its respect for limits, its skepticism about progress," Lasch wrote. "Whatever can be said against them . . . [they] are unlikely to mistake the Promised Land of progress for the true and only heaven."[32]

By refusing to address deep concerns prevalent among many Americans regarding the consequences of political, economic, social, and cultural modernity, liberalism essentially pushed these concerns into an opposing camp in which they did not necessarily (or exclusively) belong. While many Americans may actually benefit from and prefer liberal economic policies, contemporary liberalism's inhospitable—at times even imperious—attitude on social and cultural matters might have helped drive them away. Re-creating the space within the liberal umbrella for family values—that, as the writings of Updike, Moynihan, and Lasch remind us was not too long ago a liberal concern; small business owners and entrepreneurs (as opposed to corporate capitalism); a greater role for local government and direct democratic action (especially on community-sensitive issues like education and healthcare); and organized religion and patriotism (as opposed to nationalism) at home and abroad, would therefore not be a departure but a return to the principles of postwar liberalism. I am not proposing that liberals accept the teaching of creationism or heed calls to limit abortion or same-sex marriage. What I am suggesting is that even the opposing sides of highly contentious debates must be dignified with some consideration for the complexity and sensitivity that they demand if moderate voters are to be lured back from the conservative camp into which they, like Rabbit, mostly perceive themselves as having been pushed.

Third, and at risk of sounding contradictory, a final lesson that emerges from Updike's novels concerns the limits of compromise. "A revolutionary politics or economics makes no sense to contemporary America," the literary critic Richard Chase declared in 1958. "What does make sense is the liberal virtues: moderation, compromise, countervailing forces, the vital center, the mixed economy."[33] Unfortunately, it was exactly this compromising sensibility, rooted at the heart of New Deal liberalism, that is gradually delegitimized, even challenged, in Updike's early fiction, so much so that by the time *Rabbit Redux* was published, the penchant for compromise, moderation, and nuance that shaped the postwar liberal mind had become unsustainable. When he was writing *Buchanan Dying* (1974), his unorthodox play about President James Buchanan (his only serious attempt at drama), Updike was very much thinking about contemporary America and Lyndon Johnson in particular. "The questions raised in the crisis years 1965–1973 find echo in the pre–Civil War crisis, when a peaceable, compromising, legalistic President presided over a widening split no compromise or legalisms could bridge," Updike lamented in the foreword to the play.[34]

But his sympathetic attempts to redeem Johnson's legacy by reimagining and romanticizing Buchanan's heroic yet unsuccessful bid to "mediate between opposing extremes" and reach compromise on the eve of the Civil War revealed a fundamental flaw in his moderate sensibilities. Yes, Buchanan did represent "perfect ambiguity" and was a "lover of the middle way," as Updike admirably noted, but the middle way is not always the right way.[35] Some issues *cannot* be compromised; and when the passivity of the middle way is complicit in immoral, unjust ,and possibly destructive actions it becomes part of the problem, not the solution. As Martin Luther King Jr. reminded his own liberal sympathizers in his famous letter from Birmingham City Jail, grave injustices like racial segregation and the Vietnam War demanded something that postwar liberalism, with its deep inclinations for ambiguity and complexity, was not equipped to do: take an unequivocal moral stand. King's assertion that "justice too long delayed is justice denied" was not only inconvenient to the moderate temperament of postwar liberals but seemed anathema to it.[36]

This suggests that in order for the postwar pluralist project to have functioned effectively, and fairly, an important condition should have first been in place. The moderation, ambivalence, and compromise that suffused New Deal liberalism were contingent upon the durability of America's constitutional foundations; for them to have actually worked, therefore, foundational questions of liberty, equality, and justice should have first been resolved. Tocqueville may have been the first to recognize the prevailing notion of an American consensus when he observed about Americans that "daily they change, alter and renew things of secondary importance, but they are very careful not to touch fundamentals."[37] The challenges of racial strife and an unjust war in the 1960s were so unsettling exactly because they revealed that fundamental questions so many Americans took for granted as having been resolved had really yet to be settled.[38] The postwar liberal mindset could only have succeeded and persevered if the founding principles upon which it rested were constitutionally solid; since they proved tenuous—the entire project fell apart once confronted by the moral challenges of the Vietnam War and the civil rights movement.

As Updike's moderate imagination suggests: he, too, came to understand this. His increasingly sobered nonfiction writings after the 1960s betray that characteristic impulse toward introspection, reassessment, and self-correction that provided liberalism its unique malleability and penchant for regeneration. The conscious decision to title his novel about the period *Rabbit Redux* ("redux" is derived from the Latin word that means "to bring back") was meant to signal "a return to health" and is indicative of an underlining optimism. Despite his intuitive conservatism, even Rabbit undergoes a gradual evolution throughout the novel that suggests he, like liberalism, learns from his mistakes ("I like learning stuff. I have an open mind," he admits). The same Rabbit who, at the onset of *Rabbit Redux* employs racial epithets, harbors racist stereotypes, and complains there are "too many negroes on the bus" ends up passionately consuming Frederick Douglass's slave narrative and aiding and abetting a Black Power fugitive. "Rabbit tries to learn. Reading aloud the words of Frederick Douglass, he becomes black, and in a fashion seeks solidarity with Skeeter," Updike recalled. "Rabbit's reluctant crossing of the color line represents a tortured form of progress."[39]

The same can be said about the evolution of his views on the Vietnam War. Whereas at the beginning of the novel, Rabbit advocates for the war and attacks the antiwar movement, by the end he has begun to reconsider his position. Asking Skeeter, who served in Vietnam for a year, whether the war was, indeed, "wrong," the latter discharges another of his endless tirades. Calling the Vietnam War "lib-er-al-ism's very wang," Skeeter insists that the war was the natural outcome of the liberal mindset. "What is lib-er-alism? Bringin' joy to the world, right? Puttin' enough sugar on dog-eat-dog so it tastes good all over, right?" At the end of a very long response, Rabbit, out of genuine agreement (but possibly also to silence Skeeter), conveys agreement. "'Right,' Rabbit says, '*Right.*'" When he and his father come across an antiwar vigil later on in the novel that prompts the latter to castigate the protesters, it is Rabbit who surprisingly comes to their defense. "Pop, all they're saying is they want the killing to stop," he says, causing his dad to reproach him: "They've got you too, have they?"[40]

Rather than condemning postwar liberalism, Updike's personal introspective journey reveals one of its most powerful and enduring legacies: reinvention. His candid self-reflections about this tortuous period later in his life suggest that, like his Pennsylvania alter-ego Rabbit Angstrom, he too eventually came to reassess his ways. "America has created a dreamland and, with tragic results, the dreamland has become all there is," he said in one late interview. Having rethought his positions about the war, Updike revealed in a 1990 interview with Melvyn Bragg that "the America of the seventies was really a better place for having gone through the sixties." Asked about the Rabbit novels, he admitted that

> The books are all about his [Rabbit] education, and he's a somewhat slow learner, you may think. Vietnam was a considerable shock for middle-of-the-

road Americans who had known nothing but victories in wars, who had no reason to doubt that America was always right and would always win. And suddenly we couldn't seem to win, and it wasn't very clear that we were right, either. It was very hard to feel enthusiastic for the war; on the other hand, the opposition to it seemed kind of alarming to me. There was a violence in both the rhetoric and the deeds of the anti-war forces. A kind of American self-hatred emerged in a way that I still can't quite approve of. I felt conflicted, as they say, and rather more conservative than most of my literary friends, which was really my problem. The Shillington boy in me was at war with the Harvard graduate and the eastern liberal, I suppose.[41]

This internal war between the rural Shillington boy and the urbane and modern eastern liberal—between what America once was and what it had become—is in some ways emblematic of the broader conflict between modernity and tradition that has shaped postwar politics and culture. Still overshadowing our contemporary society, it represents a new color line that continues to divide "red" and "blue" America. That Updike was able to sustain the tension as a novelist and a political thinker between these two forces and the competing sets of values and ideals that they embody is a testament to the resilience and profundity of his moderate imagination. In an age of polarization when dogmatism and ideological rigidity dominate political discourse and impede any fruitful debate, Updike's writings have much to teach us about transcending ideological conflict and securing compromise—when compromise is due. The liberal inclinations for ambiguity, nuance, irony, complexity, and especially pluralism that suffuse his writings are still potential tools for helping us bridge deep political divides. Reading Updike's fiction may not provide a solution to contemporary liberalism's problems, and it certainly does not offer a panacea for fixing America's broken political system. But it is a reminder that the literary and political imaginations occupy the same domain. And, that if we want to better understand and improve one of them, we must not shy away from exploring the other.

Notes

Introduction

1. President Donald Trump, Inaugural Address, January 20, 2017, https://www.whitehouse.gov/briefings-statements/the-inaugural-address/.
2. For examples see Robert Wuthnow, *Left Behind: Decline and Rage in Rural America* (Princeton, NJ: Princeton University Press, 2018); Ben Bradlee Jr., *The Forgotten: How the People of One Pennsylvania County Elected Donald Trump and Changed America* (New York: Little, Brown & Co., 2018); Isabel Sawhill, "What the Forgotten Americans Really Want—and How to Give It to Them," Brookings Institute, October, 2018, https://www.brookings.edu/longform/what-the-forgotten-americans-really-want-and-how-to-give-it-to-them/; "Trump Voters Were Motivated by Fear of Losing Their Status," *Economist*, April 26, 2018, https://www.economist.com/democracy-in-america/2018/04/26/trump-voters-were-motivated-by-fear-of-losing-their-status; Ta-Nehisi Coates, *We Were Eight Years in Power: An American Tragedy* (New York: One World, 2017); and Ronald Brownstein, "How the Rustbelt Paved Trump's Road to Victory," *Atlantic Monthly*, November 10, 2016, https://www.theatlantic.com/politics/archive/2016/11/trumps-road-to-victory/507203/.
3. Mark Lilla, *The Once and Future Liberal: After Identity Politics* (New York: Harper, 2017), 7–10.
4. Helena Rosenblatt, *The Lost History of Liberalism: From Ancient Rome to the Twenty-First Century* (Princeton, NJ: Princeton University Press, 2018), 1; George Klosko, *The Transformation of American Liberalism* (New York: Oxford University Press, 2017), 17, 248.
5. Patrick J. Deneen, *Why Liberalism Failed* (New Haven, CT: Yale University Press, 2018), xiv, 3, 6, 20.
6. "John Updike: An American Subversive," *Economist*, January 29, 2009, https://www.economist.com/books-and-arts/2009/01/29/an-american-subversive.
7. For more on the genealogy, meanings, origins, and evolution of liberalism see Rosenblatt, *Lost History of Liberalism*; Dan Edelstein, *On the Spirit of Rights* (Chicago: University of Chicago Press, 2018); James Miller, *Can Democracy Work? A Short History of a Radical Idea, from Ancient Athens to Our World* (New York: Farrar, Straus & Giroux, 2018); Edmund Fawcett, *Liberalism: The Life of an Idea* (Princeton, NJ: Princeton University Press, 2014); and Michael Sandel, ed., *Liberalism and Its Critics* (New York: NYU Press, 1984).
8. On the meanings of liberalism in America, see Fawcett, *Liberalism*, 214–

319; Jonathan Bell and Timothy Stanley, eds., *Making Sense of American Liberalism* (Urbana: University of Illinois Press, 2012); Eric Alterman and Kevin Mattson, *The Cause: The Fight for American Liberalism from Franklin Roosevelt to Barack Obama* (New York: Viking, 2012); and Alan Brinkley, *Liberalism and Its Discontents* (Cambridge, MA: Harvard University Press, 1998). On progressive liberals see John Dewey, *Liberalism and Social Action* (New York: Capricorn Books, 1935); Herbert Croly, *The Promise of American Life* (Princeton, NJ: Princeton University Press, 2014). On neoliberalism see Friedrich Hayek, *The Constitution of Liberty* (Chicago: University of Chicago Press, 1960); Milton Friedman, *Capitalism and Freedom* (Chicago: University of Chicago Press, 1962). On republicanism see Gordon Wood, *The Creation of the American Republic* (Chapel Hill: University of North Carolina Press, 1969); Daniel T. Rodgers, "Republicanism: The Career of a Concept," *Journal of American History* (June 1992): 11–38. On racial liberalism see Eric Schickler, *Racial Realignment: The Transformation of American Liberalism, 1932–1965* (Princeton, NJ: Princeton University Press, 2016); Karen Ferguson, *Top Down: The Ford Foundation, Black Power, and the Reinvention of Racial Liberalism* (Philadelphia: University of Pennsylvania Press, 2013). On rights-based liberalism see Jeffery Bloodworth, *Losing the Center: The Decline of American Liberalism 1968–1992* (Louisville: University of Kentucky Press, 2013); Bruce Miroff, *The Liberal's Moment: The McGovern Insurgency and the Identity Crisis of the Democratic Party* (Lawrence: University Press of Kansas, 2007).

    9. Lionel Trilling, *The Liberal Imagination* (New York: Anchor Books, 1953), vii.

    10. Richard Hofstadter, *Age of Reform* (New York: Knopf, 1955), 307.

    11. Wendy L. Wall, *Inventing the "American Way": The Politics of Consensus from the New Deal to the Civil Rights Movement* (New York: Oxford University Press, 2008), 8.

    12. For more on the origins and effects of the New Deal, see Ira Katznelson, *Fear Itself: The New Deal and the Origins of Our Time* (New York: Liveright, 2014); Lizabeth Cohen, *Making a New Deal: Industrial Workers in Chicago 1919–1939* (New York: Cambridge University Press, 2008); David Plotke, *Building A Democratic Political Order: Reshaping American Liberalism in the 1930s and 1940s* (New York: Cambridge University Press, 1996); Alan Brinkley, *The End of Reform: New Deal Liberalism in Recession and War* (New York: Knopf, 1995); Steve Fraser and Gary Gerstle, eds., *The Rise and Fall of the New Deal Order 1930–1980* (Princeton, NJ: Princeton University Press, 1990); William E. Leuchtenburg, *Franklin D. Roosevelt and the New Deal 1932–1940* (New York: Harper & Row, 1963); and Arthur M. Schlesinger Jr., *The Age of Roosevelt: The Coming of the New Deal* (Boston: Houghton Mifflin, 1959).

    13. Lizabeth Cohen, *A Consumer's Republic* (New York: Vintage, 2003); Robert N. Bellah, "Civil Religion in America," *Daedalus* 96, no. 1 (Winter 1967): 1–21.

    14. Wall, *Inventing the "American Way,"* 149–150; Ira Katznelson, *When Affirmative Action Was White* (New York: W. W. Norton, 2005).

    15. See Elaine Tyler May, *Homeward Bound: American Families in the Cold War Era* (New York: Basic Books, 1988); Odd Arne Westad, *The Cold War: A World*

History (New York: Basic Books, 2017); Robert Kagan, *The World America Made* (New York: Vintage, 2013); G. John Ikenberry, *Liberal Leviathan* (Princeton, NJ: Princeton University Press, 2011); David Kay Johnson, *The Lavender Scare: The Cold War Persecution of Gays and Lesbians in the Federal Government* (Chicago: University of Chicago Press, 2006); Thomas Doherty, *Cold War, Cool Medium: Television, McCarthyism, and American Culture* (New York: Columbia University Press, 2005); Steven J. Whitfield, *The Culture of the Cold War* (Baltimore: Johns Hopkins University Press, 1996); and David Halberstam, *The Fifties* (New York: Ballantine Books, 1994).

16. John Updike, "On Not Being a Dove," in *Self-Consciousness* (New York: Knopf, 1989), 126.

17. Jan Zielonka, *Counter-Revolution: Liberal Europe in Retreat* (New York: Oxford University Press, 2018), x.

18. James A. Schiff, "Updike and the American Presidency," in *Updike and Politics: Due Considerations*, ed. Matthew Shipe and Scott Dill (Lanham, MD: Lexington Books, 2019), 11–26; Frederic Svoboda, *Understanding John Updike* (Charleston: University of South Carolina Press, 2018); Michial Farmer, *Imagination and Idealism in John Updike's Fiction* (Rochester, NY: Camden House, 2017); Adam Begley, *Updike* (New York: Harper, 2014); Bob Batchelor, *Updike: A Critical Biography* (New York: Praeger, 2013); Jack De Bellis, *John Updike's Early Years* (Bethlehem, PA: Lehigh University Press, 2013); and Michael Szalay, *Hip Figures: A Literary History of the Democratic Party* (Stanford, CA: Stanford University Press, 2012).

19. For notable criticism over the years, see James Wood, "John Updike's Complacent God," in *The Broken Estate: Essays on Literature and Belief* (New York: Picador, 2010), 208–212; Morris Dickstein, *Leopards in the Temple: The Transformation of American Fiction 1945–1970* (Cambridge, MA: Harvard University Press, 2002), 18, 84; David Foster Wallace, "John Updike, Champion Literary Phallocrat, Drops One; Is This Finally the End for Magnificent Narcissists?" *New York Observer,* October 13, 1997, https://observer.com/1997/10/john-updike-champion-literary-phallocrat-drops-one-is-this-finally-the-end-for-magnificent-narcissists/; Gore Vidal, "Rabbit's Own Burrow," *Times Literary Supplement,* April 26, 1996; Harold Bloom, *John Updike: Modern Critical Views* (New York: Chelsea House, 1988); John W. Aldridge, *Time to Murder and Create* (New York: David McKay, 1966), 164–171; Norman Mailer, "Norman Mailer vs. Nine Writers," *Esquire,* July 1963, 63–69. For a survey of critical reception over the years, see Laurence W. Mazzeno, *Becoming John Updike: Critical Receptions, 1958–2010* (Rochester, NY: Camden House, 2013); Robert Gingher, "Has John Updike Anything to Say?" *Modern Fiction Studies* 20, no. 1 (Spring 1974): 97–105.

20. James Campbell, "Updike at Large," *Times Literary Supplement,* June 16, 2014, https://www.the-tls.co.uk/articles/public/updike-at-large/; David Baddiel and Jeffrey Meyers, "Judging John Updike," *New Statesman,* May 2, 2014, https://www.newstatesman.com/2014/04/judging-john-updike; James Dellingpole, "Whisper It: You Don't Need to Have Read John Updike," *Telegraph,* January 30, 2009, https://www.telegraph.co.uk/comment/4401990/Whisper-it-you-dont-need-to-have-read-John-Updike.html; Sarah Crown, "Have We Fallen Out

of Love with John Updike," *Guardian*, May 15, 2012, https://www.theguardian.com/books/booksblog/2012/may/15/have-we-fallen-out-of-love-with-john-updike.

21. The only scholarly attempts to search Updike's fiction for political insight have focused on particular themes or the Rabbit novels. No scholarship exists that reassesses his large body of fiction as an exploration into postwar liberal political thought and culture. See Shipe and Dill, eds., *Updike and Politics: Due Considerations*; Szalay, *Hip Figures*, 137–144; Marshall Boswell, *Mastered Irony in Motion: John Updike's Rabbit Tetralogy* (Columbia: University of Missouri Press, 2001); D. Quentin Miller, *John Updike and the Cold War* (Columbia: University of Missouri Press, 2001); Lawrence R. Broer, ed., *Rabbit Tales: Poetry and Politics in John Updike's Rabbit Novels* (Tuscaloosa: University of Alabama Press, 1998); Ethan Fishman, *Likely Stories: Essays on Political Philosophy and Contemporary American Literature* (Gainesville: University of Florida Press, 1989); and Dilvo I. Ristoff, *Updike's America: Presence of Contemporary American History in John Updike's Rabbit Trilogy* (New York: Peter Lang, 1989).

22. On the various narratives of liberal decline, see Jefferson Cowie, *The Great Exception: The New Deal and the Limits of American Politics* (Princeton, NJ: Princeton University Press, 2016); Michael W. Flamm, *Law and Order: Street Crime, Civil Unrest, and the Crisis of Liberalism in the 1960s* (New York: Columbia University Press, 2007); Judith Stein, *Running Steel, Running America: Race, Economic Policy and the Decline of Liberalism* (Chapel Hill: University of North Carolina Press, 1998); David Steigerwald, *The Sixties and the End of Modern America* (New York: St. Martin's Press, 1995); Fraser and Gerstle, eds., *The Rise and Fall of the New Deal Order 1930–1980*; Jonathan Rieder, *Canarsie: The Jews and Italians of Brooklyn against Liberalism* (Cambridge, MA: Harvard University Press, 1987); and Allen J. Matusow, *The Unraveling of America: A History of Liberalism in the 1960s* (New York: Harper & Row, 1984). On the rise of conservatism, see David Farber, *The Rise and Fall of Modern American Conservatism* (Princeton, NJ: Princeton University Press, 2010); Julian E. Zelizer, "Rethinking the History of American Conservatism," *Reviews in American History* 38, no. 2 (June 2010), 367–392; Donald T. Critchlow, *The Conservative Ascendancy: How the GOP Right Made Political History* (Cambridge, MA: Harvard University Press, 2007); and Bruce J. Schulman and Julian E. Zelizer, eds., *Rightward Bound: Making America Conservative in the 1970s* (Cambridge, MA: Harvard University Press, 2008). For particular case studies, see Sandra Scanlon, *The Pro-War Movement: Domestic Support for the Vietnam War and the Making of Modern American Conservatism* (Amherst: University of Massachusetts Press, 2013); Darren Dochuk, *From Bible Belt to Sunbelt: Plain-Folk Religion, Grassroots Politics, and the Rise of Evangelical Conservatism* (New York: W. W. Norton, 2012); Daniel K. Williams, *God's Own Party: The Making of the Christian Right* (New York: Oxford University Press, 2012); Michael Kimmage, *The Conservative Turn: Lionel Trilling, Whittaker Chambers and the Lessons of Anti-Communism* (Cambridge, MA: Harvard University Press, 2009); Kim Phillips-Fein, *Invisible Hands: The Businessmen's Crusade against the New Deal* (New York: W. W. Norton, 2010); Kevin M. Kruse, *White Flight: Atlanta and the Making of Modern Conservatism* (Princeton, NJ: Princeton University Press, 2007); Ronee

Scheiber, *Righting Feminism: Conservative Women and American Politics* (New York: Oxford University Press, 2008); Lisa McGirr, *Suburban Warriors: The Origins of the New American Right* (Princeton, NJ: Princeton University Press, 2002); and Thomas Edsall and Mary Edsall, *Chain Reaction: The Impact of Race, Rights and Taxes on American Politics* (New York: W. W. Norton, 1992).

23. John Updike, *Rabbit, Run, Rabbit Redux, Rabbit Is Rich* (New York: Quality Paperback Book Club, 1990), 7.

24. Catherine H. Zuckert, "Why Political Scientists Want to Study Literature," *PS: Political Science and Politics* 28, no. 2 (June 1995): 189–190.

25. For recent trends among political scientists, see Erin L. Dolgoy, ed., *Short Stories and Political Philosophies: Power, Prose and Persuasion* (Lanham, MD: Lexington Books, 2018); Gloria L. Cronin and Lee Trepanier, eds., *A Political Companion to Saul Bellow* (Louisville: University of Kentucky Press, 2013); Simon Stow, *Republic of Readers: The Literary Turn in Political Thought and Analysis* (Albany: SUNY Press, 2008); George Shulman, *American Prophesy: Race and Redemption in American Political Culture* (Minneapolis: University of Minnesota Press, 2008); Patrick J. Deneen and Joseph Romance, eds., *Democracy's Literature: Politics and Fiction in America* (Lanham, MD: Rowman & Littlefield, 2005); Catherine H. Zuckert, *Natural Right and the American Imagination: Political Philosophy in Novel Form* (Lanham, MD: Rowman & Littlefield, 1990). On this trend within historical scholarship, see Andrew Connolly, *Philip Roth and the American Liberal Tradition* (Lanham, MD: Lexington Books, 2017); Michael Kimmage, *In History's Grip: Philip Roth's Newark Trilogy* (Stanford, CA: Stanford University Press, 2012); Stephen Schryer, *Fantasies of the New Class: Ideologies of Professionalism in Post–World War II American Fiction* (New York: Columbia University Press, 2011); Sean McCann, *A Pinnacle of Feeling: American Literature and Presidential Government* (Princeton, NJ: Princeton University Press, 2008) and Sean McCann, *Gumshoe America: Hard-Boiled Crime Fiction and the Rise and Fall of New Deal Liberalism* (Raleigh-Durham: Duke University Press, 2000); and Michael Szalay, *New Deal Modernism* (Raleigh-Durham: Duke University Press, 2000).

26. James Plath, ed., *Conversations with John Updike* (Jackson: University Press of Mississippi, 1994), 36.

27. John Updike, *Picked-Up Pieces* (Greenwich, CT: Fawcett Books, 1975), 14–15.

28. Updike, "On Not Being a Dove," in *Self-Consciousness,* 125.

29. Arthur M. Schlesinger Jr., "The Historical Mind and the Literary Imagination," *Atlantic Monthly,* June 1974, 54–59 at 59.

1. The Man in the Middle

1. John Updike, "One Writer's Testimony," *National Review,* May 26, 1978, 641.

2. William F. Buckley Jr. to John Updike, March 15, 1978. William F. Buckley Jr. Papers, MS 576 S01, Yale University Library, Manuscripts and Archives Division, box 262, folder 2258. On Buckley's and the *National Review*'s influence,

see John Judis, *William F. Buckley Jr.: Patron Saint of the Conservatives* (New York: Simon & Schuster, 2001); Jeffrey Hart, *The Making of the American Conservative Mind: National Review and Its Times* (Wilmington, DE: Intercollegiate Studies Institute, 2005).

3. Buckley to Updike, September 12 and September 25, 1978, Buckley Papers, box 262, folder 2258.

4. Updike to Buckley, September 15, 1978, Buckley Papers, box 262, folder 2258.

5. For more on Chambers's legacy, see Michael Kimmage, *The Conservative Turn: Lionel Trilling, Whittaker Chambers and the Lessons of Anti-Communism* (Cambridge, MA: Harvard University Press, 2009); Sam Tanenhaus, *Whittaker Chambers: A Biography* (New York: Modern Library, 1998).

6. James E. Carter to John Updike, April 26, 1980, John Updike Papers (JUP), MS Am 1793, Houghton Library, Harvard University, folder 3396.

7. John H. Fenton, "Liberal Is Winner in Massachusetts," *New York Times*, October 1, 1969. Michael J. Harrington to John Updike, September 1, 1976 and Harrington to Updike, August 8, 1978, JUP, folder 4223.

8. John R. Everett to John Updike, January 28, 1972; Gerald A. Heeger to John Updike, August 14, 1990, JUP, folder 5368.

9. For more on this, see Alan I. Abramowitz, *The Polarized Public: Why American Government Is So Dysfunctional* (New York: Pearson, 2012); Morris P. Fiorina and Samuel J. Abrams, *Culture Wars? The Myth of a Polarized America* (New York: Longman, 2010).

10. On postwar liberal thought, see George M. Marsden, *The Twilight of the American Enlightenment: The 1950s and the Crisis of Liberal Belief* (New York: Basic Books, 2014); Eric Alterman and Kevin Mattson, *The Cause: The Fight for American Liberalism from Franklin Roosevelt to Barack Obama* (New York: Viking, 2012); Kevin Mattson, *When America Was Great: The Fighting Faith of Postwar Liberalism* (London: Routledge, 2004); Alan Brinkley, *The End of Reform: New Deal Liberalism in Recession and War* (New York: Knopf, 1995); Richard H. Pells, *The Liberal Mind in a Conservative Age* (Middletown, CT: Wesleyan University Press, 1989); and Robert Booth Fowler, *Believing Skeptics: American Political Intellectuals, 1945–1967* (Westport, CT: Westwood Press, 1978).

11. Fowler, *Believing Skeptics*, 16.

12. Howard Brick, *Transcending Capitalism: Visions of a New Society in Modern American Thought* (Ithaca: Cornell University Press, 2006), 4, 22.

13. Fowler, *Believing Skeptics*, 217. For more on the pluralist model, see Robert A. Dahl, *Who Governs? Democracy and Power in an American City* (New Haven, CT: Yale University Press, 1961).

14. Daniel Bell, *The End of Ideology* (New York: Free Press, 1962), 402.

15. Arthur M. Schlesinger Jr., *The Vital Center* (Boston: Houghton Mifflin, 1949), 255.

16. Schlesinger, 245.

17. James Neuchterlein, "Arthur Schlesinger Jr. and the Discontents of Postwar American Liberalism," *Review of Politics* 39, no. 1 (January 1977): 3–40 at 7. On Schlesinger's ideas, see Richard Aldous, *Schlesinger: The Imperial Historian*

(New York: W. W. Norton, 2017); John Patrick Diggins, ed., *The Liberal Persuasion: Arthur Schlesinger Jr. and the Challenge of the American Past* (Princeton, NJ: Princeton University Press, 1997).

18. Robert Nisbet, *The Quest for Community* (New York: Oxford University Press, 1953), 215.

19. Mark Greif, *The Age of the Crisis of Man: Thought and Fiction in America, 1933–1973* (Princeton, NJ: Princeton University Press, 2015), 23–24.

20. Eyal Naveh, *Reinhold Niebuhr and Non Utopian Liberalism: Beyond Illusion and Despair* (Brighton, UK: Sussex Academic Press, 2002). See also Richard Crouter, *Reinhold Niebuhr: On Politics, Religion and Christian Faith* (New York: Oxford University Press, 2010).

21. Naveh, *Reinhold Niebuhr and Non Utopian Liberalism*, 8.

22. For examples of this liberal optimism, see John Dewey, *The Public and Its Problems* (New York: Henry Holt, 1927). On pre–New Deal left-wing thought, see Michael Kazin, *American Dreamers: How the Left Changed a Nation* (New York: Vintage, 2012), chapters 4–5, and Michael Kazin, *The Populist Persuasion: An American History* (New York: Basic Books, 1995), chapter 4–6; Doug Rossinow, *Visions of Progress: The Left-Liberal Tradition in America* (Philadelphia: University of Pennsylvania Press, 2009); Edward A. Stettner, *Shaping Modern Liberalism: Herbert Croly and Progressive Thought* (Lawrence: University Press of Kansas, 1993); and Richard Hofstadter, *Age of Reform* (New York: Knopf, 1955).

23. Reinhold Niebuhr, *Moral Man and Immoral Society* (New York: Charles Scribner's Sons, 1932), 4; Alterman and Mattson, *The Cause*, 47.

24. John Kenneth Galbraith, *The Affluent Society* (Boston: Houghton Mifflin Harcourt, 1958), chapter 17. Daniel Bell, *The Cultural Contradictions of Capitalism* (New York: Basic Books, 1976).

25. Mattson, *When America Was Great*, 96.

26. James Plath, ed., *Conversations with John Updike* (Jackson: University Press of Mississippi, 1994), 16, 20, 34, 50.

27. On the theme of "middleness" in Updike's fiction, see D. Quentin Miller, "Updike, Middles, and the Spell of 'Subjective Geography,'" in *The Cambridge Companion to John Updike*, ed. Stacey Olster (New York: Cambridge University Press, 2006), 15–28; Jack De Bellis, *The John Updike Encyclopedia* (Westport, CT: Greenwood Press, 2000), 272; Alfred Kazin, "The Middle Way," *New York Review of Books*, December 17, 1992; Margaret M. Gullette, *Safe At Last in the Middle Years: The Invention of the Midlife Progress Novel* (Berkeley: University of California Press, 1988), 59–84; and Robert Alton Regan, "Updike's Symbol of the Center," *Modern Fiction Studies* 20, no. 1 (Spring 1974): 77–96.

28. Plath, *Conversations*, 11, 45. In his memoirs, he associated the "duplicity that generates plots and surprises and symbolism and layers of meaning" to the "dualism" caused by the struggle between "my skin and myself" due to his lifelong psoriasis. See John Updike, *Self-Consciousness* (New York: Knopf, 1989), 75.

29. John Updike, *Midpoint and Other Poems* (Knopf: New York, 1969), 42, 72.

30. Marshall Boswell has associated Updike's ambiguity with Soren Kierkegaard's propensity for "mastered irony," which presents two sides of an issue but leaves the paradox unresolved, with the intention that the readers "contend

privately and personally with the text's unresolved tensions" in search of their own answers. See Marshall Boswell, *Mastered Irony in Motion: John Updike's Rabbit Tetralogy* (Columbia: University of Missouri Press, 2001), 4–5. For more discussion of this, see De Bellis, *Updike Encyclopedia,* 495; Sue Mitchell Crowley, "John Updike and Kierkegaard's Negative Way: Irony and Indirect Communication in *A Month of Sundays*," *Soundings* 68, no. 2 (Summer 1985): 212–228.

31. Lionel Trilling, *The Liberal Imagination* (New York: Anchor Books, 1953), 289–290. For an analysis of "negative capability," see Robert Boyers, *Lionel Trilling* (Columbia: University of Missouri Press, 1977), 50.

32. Richard Sennett, "On Lionel Trilling," *New Yorker,* November 5, 1979, 204–217.

33. John Updike, "One Big Interview," in *Picked-Up Pieces* (Greenwich, CT: Fawcett Books, 1975), 407; Plath, *Conversations,* 37, 177. On Updike's historical realism, see Edward Vargo, "Updike, American History, and Historical Methodology," in *Cambridge Companion to Updike,* ed. Olster, 111–121.

34. Plath, *Conversations,* 31, 247; John Updike et al., "An Evening with John Updike," *Salmagundi* 57 (Summer 1982): 42–56 at 49.

35. See Kevin Mattson, *Upton Sinclair and the Other American Century* (Hoboken: Wiley & Sons, 2008); Cyrus Ernesto-Zirakzadeh and Simon Stow, eds., *A Political Companion to John Steinbeck* (Louisville: University of Kentucky Press, 2013); Michael Szalay, *New Deal Modernism* (Raleigh-Durham: Duke University Press, 2000); Michael Denning, *The Cultural Front* (New York: Verso, 1997); and Alan Filreis, *Modernism from Right to Left* (New York: Cambridge University Press, 1994).

36. Jennifer Burns, *Goddess of the Market: Ayn Rand and the American Right* (New York: Oxford University Press, 2009); Edward S. Shapiro, *We Are Many: Reflections on American Jewish History and Identity* (Syracuse: Syracuse University Press, 2005), chapter 4; John H. Wrenn, *John Dos Passos* (New York: Twayne, 1961).

37. Plath, *Conversations,* 60-61.

38. Updike, "Why Write?" and "From One Big Interview," in *Picked Up Pieces,* 47, 483.

39. John Updike to Plowville (i.e., Updike's parents), November 5, 1952, JUP, folder 6887; Plath, *Conversations,* 173.

40. John Updike, "The Dogwood Tree: A Boyhood," in *Assorted Prose* (New York: Knopf, 1965), 163; Sam Tanenhaus, "Man in the Middle," *New York Times Book Review,* November 18, 2012.

41. Alexander Bloom, *Prodigal Sons: The New York Intellectuals and Their World* (New York: Oxford University Press, 1986), 5.

42. George J. Searles, ed., *Conversations with Philip Roth* (Jackson: University Press of Mississippi, 1992), 151. On Roth and politics, see Andrew Connolly, *Philip Roth and the American Liberal Tradition* (Lanham, MD: Lexington Books, 2017).

43. On Updike's literary cohorts and the so-called inward turn of postwar fiction, see Morris Dickstein, *Leopards in the Temple: The Transformation of American Fiction 1945–1970* (Cambridge, MA: Harvard University Press, 2002).

44. On Updike and the *New Yorker* see Plath, *Conversations,* 12–13; Adam Beg-

ley, *Updike* (New York: Harper, 2014), 119–158; and Ben Yagoda, *About Town: The* New Yorker *and the World It Made* (New York: Scribner, 2000), 303–306.

45. Bloom, *Prodigal Sons,* 310–311; Mary F. Corey, *The World through a Monocle: The* New Yorker *at Midcentury* (Cambridge, MA: Harvard University Press, 1999), 41, 45.

46. William Phillips to John Updike, November 1972, JUP, folder 5529; Melvin J. Lasky to John Updike, June 8, 1964, JUP, folder 4770. On *Encounter,* see Frances S. Saunders, *Cultural Cold War: The CIA and the World of Arts and Letters* (New York: New Press, 2001).

47. Plath, *Conversations,* 65. Late in his career, Updike would eventually write for the *New York Review of Books* art reviews. See John Updike, "A Wee Irish Suit," *New York Review of Books,* October 23, 2008, and "Gold and Geld," *New York Review of Books,* December 20, 2007, https://www.nybooks.com/contributors/john-updike/. On the *New York Review of Books,* see Bloom, *Prodigal Sons,* 129–135.

48. John Updike, "On Not Being a Dove," *Commentary,* March 1989, https://www.commentarymagazine.com/articles/on-not-being-a-dove/. This piece also appeared in *Self-Consciousness.* On the magazine, see Benjamin Balint, *Running* Commentary*: The Contentious Magazine That Transformed the Jewish Left into the Neoconservative Right* (New York: Public Affairs, 2010).

49. On the New York intellectuals, see Alan M. Wald, *New York Intellectuals: The Rise and Decline of the Anti-Stalinist Left from the '30s to the '80s* (Chapel Hill: University of North Carolina Press, 1987); Bloom, *Prodigal Sons.* On Updike's relationship to them, see Yoav Fromer, "The Inside-Outsider: John Updike as a New York Intellectual—from Shillington, Pennsylvania," *John Updike Review* 4, no. 2 (Spring 2016): 29–55.

50. John Updike, *The Complete Henry Bech* (New York: Everyman's Library, 2001), 5. Adam Kirsch, "The Imaginary Jew," *New Republic,* July 9, 2012, https://newrepublic.com/article/104621/the-imaginary-jew; Cynthia Ozick, "Bech Passing," in *Art and Ardor* (New York: Knopf, 1983), 115–125. On Updike's fascination with Jewish culture, see Sanford Pinsker, "Updike, Ethnicity, and Jewish-American Drag," in *Cambridge Companion to Updike,* ed. Olster, 91–106. Interestingly, Stephan Shepard had added the Bech series to his list of canonical Jewish-American works, claiming that there is a "Jewish John Updike." See Stephan Shepard, *A Literary Journey to Jewish Identity* (New York: Bayberry Books, 2018), 136–147.

51. Plath, *Conversations,* 6–7. For more on his time in New York and his decision to move to Ipswich, see Adam Begley, *Updike* (New York: Harper, 2014), chapter 3.

52. Daniel Patrick Moynihan to John Updike, August 31 1992, JUP, folder 5250; Arthur M. Schlesinger Jr. to John Updike, June 21, 1994, Arthur M. Schlesinger Jr. Papers, New York Public Library, Manuscripts and Archives Division, box 137.2. For *Partisan Review* and *Commentary* reviews, see John Thompson, "Other People's Affairs," rev. of *Rabbit, Run,* by John Updike, and two other books, *Partisan Review* 28 (January–February 1961): 117–24; Morris Dickstein, "Black Humor and History: Fiction in the Sixties," *Partisan Review* 43 (Spring 1976): 185–211; David Fitelson, "Conflict Unresolved," rev. of *The Poorhouse*

Fair, by John Updike, *Commentary* (March 1959): 275–76; and Alfred Chester, "Twitches and Embarrassments," rev. of *Pigeon Feathers and Other Stories,* by John Updike, *Commentary* (July 1962): 77–79; for Lasch, see Jeffrey Ludwig, "Roommates and Rivals: John Updike, Christopher Lasch, and a Harvard University Friendship," *John Updike Review* 2, no. 2 (Spring 2013): 3–25.

53. Mary McCarthy, "The Art of Fiction," interview by Elisabeth Sifton, *Paris Review* 27 (Winter–Spring 1962), http://www.theparisreview.org/interviews/4618/the-art-of-fiction-no-27-mary-mccarthy.

54. Updike, *Assorted Prose,* 242, 255.

55. Dwight Macdonald to John Updike, May 20, 1968, JUP, folder 4920. John Updike to Mary McCarthy, 1979 and McCarthy to Updike, 1989, JUP, folder 5052. Macdonald to Updike, September 25, 1961; Updike to Macdonald, September 29, 1961; Macdonald to Updike, October 6, 1961, Dwight Macdonald Papers, Yale University Library, Archives and Manuscripts Division, MS 730, box 54, folder 1309.

56. Casey Blake and Christopher Phelps, "History as Social Criticism: Conversations with Christopher Lasch," *Journal of American History* 80, no. 4 (March 1994): 1310–1332; Jeffrey Ludwig, "Roommates and Rivals."

57. Arthur M. Schlesinger Jr., "The Historical Mind and the Literary Imagination," *Atlantic Monthly,* June 1974, 54–59.

58. Arthur M. Schlesinger Jr., "1928–1937," in *A Century of Arts & Letters,* ed. John Updike (New York: Columbia University Press, 1998), 102. Updike, "1938–1947," in *A Century of Arts & Letters,* 133.

59. Arthur M. Schlesinger Jr. to John Updike, June 21, 1994; Updike to Schlesinger, May 20, 1993; Updike to Schlesinger, February 3, 2002, Schlesinger Papers, box 137.2.

60. Arthur M. Schlesinger Jr., *Journals, 1952–2000* (New York: Penguin, 2007), 318.

61. See *Amesbury Daily News* July 15, 1958; July 18, 1958; July 22, 1958; August 15, 1958; September 22, 1958; February 26, 1959; November 12, 1959; and August 23, 1960. This information was generously provided to the author by Bill Wasserman, a friend of Updike and the former publisher of the *Amesbury Daily News.*

62. Neil Jumonville, ed., *The New York Intellectuals Reader* (London: Routledge, 2007), 7.

63. William H. Pritchard, *Updike: America's Man of Letters* (Amherst: University of Massachusetts Press, 2005), 230, 233.

64. John Updike, *Hugging the Shore: Essays and Criticism* (New York: Vintage, 1984), xv, xx.

65. Updike, xvii–xix.

66. Updike, "A Raw Something," in *Picked-Up Pieces,* 135.

67. For examples see Christopher Lasch, *The Culture of Narcissism: American Life in an Age of Diminishing Expectations* (New York: W. W. Norton, 1978); Robert Bellah, *Habits of the Heart: Individualism and Commitment in American Life* (Berkeley: University of California Press, 1985); and Philip Rieff, *The Triumph of the Therapeutic: Uses of Faith after Freud* (New York: Harper, 1966).

68. Plath, *Conversations*, 161.

69. Updike, "Young Americans: If At First You Do Succeed, Try, Try Again," in *Picked-Up Pieces*, 386.

70. Updike, 384.

71. On the New Left, see Kazin, *American Dreamers*, chapter 6; Jeremy Varon, *Bringing the War Home* (Berkeley: University of California Press, 2004); Kevin Mattson, *Intellectuals in Action: The Origins of the New Left and Radical Liberalism 1945–1970* (University Park: Penn State University Press, 2002); Morris Dickstein, *Gates of Eden: American Culture in the Sixties* (Cambridge, MA: Harvard University Press, 1997); and James Miller, *Democracy Is in the Streets: From Port Huron to the Siege of Chicago* (Cambridge, MA: Harvard University Press, 1994).

72. Updike, *Picked-Up Pieces*, 385–386.

73. John Updike, *Rabbit at Rest* (New York: Knopf, 1990), 367, 371. On how the Cold War shaped his fiction, see D. Quentin Miller, *John Updike and the Cold War* (Columbia: University of Missouri Press, 2001).

74. On ADA, see Lorna N. Kaufman to John Updike, November 5, 1973, JUP, folder 2921. On Sakharov see Adrian Karatnycky to John Updike, August 7 and December 16, 1980, JUP, folder 5891. On the committee see Midge Decter to John Updike, November 12, 1980, JUP, folder 3517. For more on these organizations see John Ehrman, *The Rise of Neoconservatism: Intellectuals and Foreign Affairs, 1945–1994* (New Haven, CT: Yale University Press, 1996), 139–141; Clifton Brock, *Americans for Democratic Action: It's Role in National Politics* (New York: Praeger, 1985).

75. For more on this, see Donald J. Greiner, "Updike, Rabbit, and the Myth of American Exceptionalism," in *Cambridge Companion to Updike*, ed. Olster, 149–161. For examples of the discourse of American exceptionalism, see Ernest Lee Tuveson, *Redeemer Nation: The Idea of America's Millennial Role* (Chicago: University of Chicago Press, 1968); Daniel J. Boorstin, *The Genius of American Politics* (Chicago: University of Chicago Press, 1953); and Clinton Rossiter, *Seedtime of the Republic* (New York: Harcourt, Brace & World, 1953). For a critical perspective see Godfrey Hodgson, *The Myth of American Exceptionalism* (New Haven: Yale University Press, 2009); Mary L. Dudziak, *Cold War Civil Rights: Race and the Image of American Democracy* (Princeton, NJ: Princeton University Press, 2008); and Seymour Martin Lipset, *American Exceptionalism: A Double-Edged Sword* (New York: W. W. Norton, 1997).

76. Updike, "On Not Being a Dove," in *Self-Consciousness*, 137–140; Plath, *Conversations*, 192, 206.

77. Updike, "Bech Meets Me," in *Picked-Up Pieces*, 29.

78. Plath, *Conversations*, 227.

79. Irving Howe, "This Age of Conformity," *Partisan Review* 21, no. 1 (January–February 1954): 7–33 at 12. For more examples, see the symposium "Our Country and Our Culture," *Partisan Review* 19 (May–June 1952). On the controversy, see Pells, *Liberal Mind*, 183–262.

80. R. E. Oldenburg, "America and the Intellectuals," *Harvard Crimson*, February 13, 1953, https://www.thecrimson.com/article/1953/2/14/america-and-the-intellectuals-pas-the/. On Oldenburg see Ann Lee Morgan, ed.,

The American Dictionary of Art and Artists (New York: Oxford University Press, 2007), 351.

81. Bloom, *Prodigal Sons*, 4.

82. Updike, "On Not Being a Dove," in *Self-Consciousness*, 122. For similar experiences compare with Irving Kristol, *Neoconservatism: The Autobiography of an Idea* (New York: Free Press, 1995), 92–103,179–184; Sidney Hook, *Out of Step: An Unquiet Life in the Twentieth Century* (New York: HarperCollins, 1987), 11–52; Norman Podhoretz, *Making It* (New York: HarperCollins, 1980); and William Phillips and Philip Rahv, "Our Country and Our Culture," *Partisan Review* 19 (May–June 1952): 282–322.

83. Updike, *Self-Consciousness*, 137.

2. The Liberal Education of John Updike

1. Jack De Bellis, *The John Updike Encyclopedia* (Westport, CT: Greenwood Press, 2000), 196.

2. De Bellis, 197.

3. John Updike, "Literarily Personal," *Harvard Gazette*, repr. in *Odd Jobs: Essays and Criticism* (New York: Knopf, 1991), 839.

4. James Plath, ed., *Conversations with John Updike* (Jackson: University Press of Mississippi, 1994), 23.

5. This sense of destiny and greater purpose is captured in his early autobiographical short story "Flight," published in John Updike, *Pigeon Feathers and Other Stories* (Greenwich, CT: Crest, 1963), 41–56.

6. Updike, "Literarily Personal," in *Odd Jobs*, 841.

7. Jack De Bellis, *John Updike's Early Years* (Bethlehem, PA: Lehigh University Press, 2013), xix; Jeffrey Ludwig, "Roommates and Rivals: John Updike, Christopher Lasch, and a Harvard University Friendship," *John Updike Review* 2, no. 2 (Spring 2013): 3–25; and Adam Begley, *Updike* (New York: Harper, 2014), chapter 2. On his relationship with Lasch, see Sam Tanenhaus, "The Roommates: Updike and Christopher Lasch," *New York Times*, June 20, 2010, http://www.nytimes.com/2010/06/21/books/21roommates.html?_r=0.

8. Robert K. Silverman, "Vets Flooded Campus under GI Bill," *Harvard Crimson*, June 7, 1999, http://www.thecrimson.com/article/1999/6/7/vets-flooded-campus-under-gi-bill/#.

9. Arthur M. Schlesinger Jr., *A Life in the Twentieth Century* (Boston: Houghton Mifflin, 2000), 120. For more on the meritocratic reforms, see Morton Keller and Phyllis Keller, *Making Harvard Modern: The Rise of America's University* (New York: Oxford University Press, 2001), 22–46; Richard Norton Smith, *The Harvard Century* (New York: Simon & Schuster, 1986), chapters 3–4. Matthew F. Quirk, "The Class of 1950," *Harvard Crimson*, June 5, 2000, http://www.thecrimson.com/article/2000/6/5/the-class-of-1950-pin-a/.

10. Seymour Martin Lipset and David Riesman, *Education and Politics at Harvard* (New York: McGraw Hill, 1971), 188–192.

11. Lipset and Riesman, 203, 199.

12. Keller, *Making Harvard Modern*, 43. On the *Redbook Report* and its legacy, see Smith, *Harvard Century*, chapter 5, 357–358; *The Report of the Harvard Committee on General Education in a Free Society* (Cambridge, MA: Harvard University Press, 1945); Jacques Barzun, "Harvard Takes Stock," *Atlantic Monthly*, October 1945, 52–55; and Charles W. Bevard Jr., "General Education: The Forgotten Goals," *Harvard Crimson*, March 4, 1964, http://www.thecrimson.com/article/1964/3/4/general-education-the-forgotten-goals-pat/.

13. Kenneth S. Lynn, "Son of 'Gen-Ed,'" *Commentary* 66, no. 3 (September 1978): 59–66 at 62.

14. Eric Miller, *Hope in a Scattering Time: A Life of Christopher Lasch* (Grand Rapids, MI: Eerdmans, 2010), 25–27.

15. Lynn, "Son of 'Gen-Ed,'" 59–66. Henry Adams's Pulitzer Prize–winning magnum opus voiced his frustrations at the inadequate education he had received at Harvard (nearly a century before Updike attended), which, in his mind, failed to prepare him for the scientific challenges of industrialization and modernity. See Henry Adams, *The Education of Henry Adams* (Boston: Houghton Mifflin, 1918). On Adams's contribution to American conservatism, see Russell Kirk, *The Conservative Mind* (Chicago: Regnery, 1953), 310–319.

16. Smith, *Harvard Century*, 163.

17. Smith, 163.

18. Isaiah Berlin, "Democracy, Communism and the Individual," lecture delivered at Mt. Holyoke College in 1949, http://berlin.wolf.ox.ac.uk/lists/nachlass/demcomind.pdf. Berlin developed and refined his pluralist vision in a more coherent manner years later in *The Crooked Timber of Humanity* (London: John Murray, 1990).

19. "Studies in the Freshman Year Including an Announcement of Courses in General Education," in *Official Register of Harvard University*, vol. 47, no. 16, July 1950, 13–14, 44–47, appendix 42, Harvard University Archives, Pusey Library, Harvard University, HU 75.25, box 85.

20. Alston Chase, "The Roots of the Unabomber," *Atlantic Monthly*, June 2000, https://www.theatlantic.com/magazine/archive/2000/06/harvard-and-the-making-of-the-unabomber/378239/.

21. Chase.

22. Miller, *Hope*, 28.

23. John Updike to Plowville (i.e., his parents), October 16, 1950, JUP, folder 6887.

24. Plath, *Conversations*, 23.

25. John Updike, "The Christian Roommates," in *The Music School* (New York: Knopf, 1966), 124–164 at 153. The only other works of fiction or poetry in which Updike refers to his college experiences are "Homage to Paul Klee; or, a Game of Botticelli," *Liberal Context* (1964): 8–12; "Humanities Course" in *The Carpeted Hen and Other Tame Creatures* (New York: Harper & Brothers, 1958), 28; and "Apologies to Harvard" in *Tossing and Turning* (New York: Knopf, 1977), 29–34.

26. Updike, "Christian Roommates," 128.

27. Updike, 133.

28. Updike, 135.
29. Updike, 149.
30. Updike, 134, 163.
31. Begley, *Updike*, 39; Updike to Plowville, April 13, 1951; October 20, 1952; November 5, 1952, JUP, folder 6887. On Updike's ingrained religious values and the import of faith to his fiction, see Begley, *Updike*, 38–40; James Yerkes, ed., *John Updike and Religion* (Grand Rapids, MI: Eerdmans, 1999); and George W. Hunt, *John Updike and the Three Great Secret Things: Sex, Religion and Art* (Grand Rapids, MI: Eerdmans, 1980).
32. Miller, *Hope*, 38–39. The beginning of his alienation from postwar liberalism and the gravitational pull further left is already evident in Lasch's early works, *The American Liberals and the Russian Revolution* (New York: Columbia University Press, 1962) and *The Agony of the American Left* (New York: Knopf, 1969).
33. Louis Hartz, *The Liberal Tradition in America* (Boston: Harcourt, Brace & World, 1955), 66. For more on Hartz's work and legacy, see James T. Kloppenberg, "In Retrospect: Louis Hartz's the Liberal Tradition in America," *Reviews in American History* 29, no. 3 (September 2001): 460–478; Rogers Smith, "Beyond Tocqueville, Myrdal and Hartz: The Multiple Traditions in America," *American Political Science Review* 87, no. 3 (September 1993): 549–566.
34. See Isaiah Berlin, *Enlightening: Letters 1946–1960* (London: Chatto & Windus, 2009), 244–412. For a detailed faculty guide for the relevant years, see "General Catalogue Issue," in *Official Register of Harvard University* published annually for the years 1950–1954, Harvard University Archives, Pusey Library, Harvard University, HU 75.25, boxes 85–90.
35. For more on this, see De Bellis, *Updike Encyclopedia*, 196, and Scott Donaldson, *Archibald MacLeish: An American Life* (Boston: Houghton Mifflin, 1992), 413–414. On their post-college friendship, see John Updike to Archibald MacLeish, undated, JUP, folder 4937. John Bethell, who was the general secretary of the Harvard Class of 1954 and Updike's classmate, recalls he took MacLeish's poetry class with Updike. Email with the author. The original email is in the possession of the author.
36. For more on his career, see Donaldson, *Archibald MacLeish*.
37. Bernard A. Drabeck and Helen E. Ellis, eds., *Archibald MacLeish, Reflections* (Amherst: University of Massachusetts Press, 1986), 84; Robert Vanderlan, *Intellectuals Incorporated: Politics, Art, and Ideas Inside Henry Luce's Media Empire* (Philadelphia: University of Pennsylvania Press, 2010), 9, 305.
38. David Bulwer Luytens, *The Creative Encounter* (London: Secker & Warburg, 1960), 76.
39. Henry R. Luce, "The American Century," *Life*, February 17, 1941, 61–65.
40. Archibald MacLeish, "The Unimagined America," in *Freedom Is the Right to Choose* (Boston: Beacon, 1951), 18–25.
41. Archibald MacLeish, "The Revulsion of Decency," in *Freedom Is the Right to Choose*, (Boston: Beacon, 1951), 103.
42. MacLeish, "The Revulsion of Decency," 103–111.
43. Lionel Trilling, *Matthew Arnold* (New York: W. W. Norton, 1939), 231.
44. Archibald MacLeish, "'Dover Beach'—a Note to That Poem," in *Collected*

Poems: 1917–1982 (Boston: Houghton Mifflin, 1985), 313. For more on his connection to Arnold, see R. H. Winnick, ed., *Letters of Archibald MacLeish 1907 to 1982* (Boston: Houghton Mifflin, 1983), 28, 61.

45. On Updike's admiration for him, see Updike to Plowville, January 8, 1952; February 23, 1953, JUP, folder 6887.

46. Although Morrison titled his essay a "fable" and used pseudonyms, it is quite apparent that there was substantial truth behind the experiment he parodies. Theodore Morrison, "'Dover Beach' Revisited: A New Fable for Critics," *Harper's*, December 1939–May 1940, 235–244.

47. Updike to Plowville, March 2, 1952, JUP, folder 6887.

48. Updike, "English 99 Paper," 10, JUP, folder 418.

49. Michael Kimmage, *The Conservative Turn: Lionel Trilling, Whittaker Chambers and the Lessons of Anti-Communism* (Cambridge, MA: Harvard University Press, 2009), 99, 17.

50. Trilling, *Matthew Arnold*, 127, 137. For more on the impact of Trilling's book and Arnold's reception in America, see Laurence W. Mazzeno, *Matthew Arnold: The Critical Legacy* (Rochester, NY: Camden House, 1999), 21–52.

51. Matthew Arnold, *Culture and Anarchy* (New York: Cambridge University Press, 1971), 63–71.

52. Updike often discussed this "existential desperation" of modern man and admitted that it inspired his fiction. See Plath, *Conversations*, 22–54, 159–163. This angst attracted him to the philosophies of Karl Barth and Soren Kierkegaard. For more on this, see De Bellis, *Updike Encyclopedia*, 47–49, 238; Marshall Boswell, *Mastered Irony in Motion: John Updike's Rabbit Tetralogy* (Columbia: University of Missouri Press, 2001); Victor Strandberg, "John Updike and the Changing of the Gods," in *Mosaic-a Journal for the Interdisciplinary Study of Literature* 12, no. 1 (1978): 157–175.

53. Trilling, *Matthew Arnold*, 79–80.

54. Kimmage, *The Conservative Turn*, 101.

55. Trilling, *Matthew Arnold*, 189, 194, 206.

56. Updike to Plowville, September 30, 1951, JUP, folder 6887; Levin to Updike, April 11, 1980 and July 16, 1981, JUP, folder 4808; and Updike, *Odd Jobs*, 840.

57. John Rodden, ed., *Lionel Trilling and the Critics: Opposing Selves* (Lincoln: University of Nebraska Press, 1999), 199–201.

58. Harry Levin, *Grounds for Comparison* (Cambridge, MA: Harvard University Press, 1972), 15.

59. Harry Levin, "An Urgent Awareness," in *Lionel Trilling* ed. Rodden, 200.

60. Updike, "Literarily Personal," in *Odd Jobs*, 840.

61. Levin, *Grounds for Comparison*, 4. For a comparison of their similar critical styles, see Lionel Trilling, *The Liberal Imagination* (New York: Anchor, 1953), 272–292.

62. Burton Pike, "Harry Levin: An Appreciation," *Comparative Literature* 40, no. 1 (Winter 1988): 29–43.

63. Updike to Plowville, April 29, 1953, JUP, folder 6887; Updike, "Criticism and Inspiration," 7, JUP, folder 395; Trilling, *Liberal Imagination*, 289–293.

64. Updike, "Criticism and Inspiration," 7–10, JUP, folder 395.
65. See Updike to Plowville, September 27, 1953; October 4, 1953; and November 2, 1953.
66. On Karpovich see Philip E. Mosely, "Michael Karpovich, 1888–1959," *Russian Review* 19, no. 1 (January 1960): 56–60.
67. Martin E. Malia, "Michael Karpovich, 1888–1959," *Russian Review*, 19, no. 1 (January 1960): 60–71.
68. Malia, 67–70.
69. Updike to Plowville, Thursday night, 1950 (the first letter after September 26, 1950), JUP, folder 6887; Updike to Plowville, October 16, 1950, JUP, folder 6887. In Updike's retrospective poem about Harvard, Havelock was tellingly one of the only faculty members he mentioned. See Updike, "Apologies to Harvard," 31.
70. Eric A. Havelock, *The Liberal Temper in Greek Politics* (New Haven: Yale University Press, 1964), 18–20.
71. Havelock, 383–386.
72. Havelock, 390–391.
73. On the appeal of Brinton's course, see Updike to Plowville, January 29, 1951, JUP, folder 6887. For a description of the course, see Philip M. Boffey, "Best in the System," *Harvard Crimson*, November 8, 1956, http://www.thecrimson.com/article/1956/11/8/best-in-the-system-pa-house/#.
74. Updike to Plowville, November, 9 1950; January 12, 1951; January 22, 1951; and February 6, 1951, JUP, folder 6887.
75. John Updike, "Marx: Man of Mission," 23–26, JUP, folder 416.
76. Updike, "Marx: Man of Mission," 9.
77. Updike, 20–21.
78. It's worth remembering that Updike was writing this at the height of McCarthyism and around the time the Supreme Court validated the controversial Smith Act and upheld the convictions of American Communist Party members for merely discussing Karl Marx's writings. See *Dennis v. US* (341 US 494). For a historical overview of the trial and period, see Scott Martelle, *The Fear Within: Spies, Commies and American Democracy on Trial* (New Brunswick, NJ: Rutgers University Press, 2011); Ellen Schrecker, *Many Are the Crimes: McCarthyism in America* (Boston: Little Brown & Co., 1998).
79. James Bryant Conant, *Education in a Divided World* (Cambridge, MA: Harvard University Press, 1948), 173.
80. Updike, "Marx: Man of Mission," 13.
81. Updike, 15, 22.
82. John Updike, "An Exposition of the Morality in the Communist Manifesto," 1, JUP, folder 431.
83. Updike, 7.
84. Martin Jay, "The Frankfurt School's Critique of Marxist Humanism," *Social Research* 39, no. 2 (Summer 1972): 285–305.
85. For some examples see Erich Fromm, *Marx's Concept of Man* (New York: Frederick Ungar Publishing, 1961); Raya Dunayevskaya, *Marxism and Freedom: From 1776 until Today* (New York: Bookman Associates, 1958).

86. John Updike, "An Exposition on the Morality in the Communist Manifesto," 8, JUP, folder 431.

87. John Updike, "Just Ruler, Pious Saint, Chivalrous Knight," 4, JUP, folder 414.

88. Updike, 5–6.

89. Updike, 10.

90. Updike, "The Tragedy of Peter Abelard," 14–16, JUP, folder 445. Updike had been enamored with medieval Christianity and scholasticism and would come to admire Aquinas and Dante—whose works, respectively, he considered as the two greatest books of the last millennia—and was influenced by the neo-Thomist philosopher Jacque Maritain. He even admitted that his first novel, *The Poorhouse Fair*, was "sketched along Thomist lines." On his medieval inspirations, see Updike to Plowville, October 4, 1951, JUP, folder 6887; John Updike, *More Matter: Essays and Criticism* (New York: Knopf, 1999), 846–850; Updike, *Self-Consciousness*, 98; and John Updike, *The Poorhouse Fair* (New York: Knopf, 1977), xvii. For influences on his fiction, see his "The Invention of the Horse Collar," in *Museums and Women*, 207–212 and see De Bellis, *Updike Encyclopedia*, 131–132, 434–435.

91. John Updike, "The Decline of Moral Stability since the *Divine Comedy*," 19–20, JUP, folder 397.

92. Updike, 20–21.

93. Crane Brinton, *The Anatomy of Revolution* (New York: Vintage, 1965), chapter 2.

94. David D. Bien, "Crane Brinton," *French Historical Studies*, 6, no. 1 (Spring 1969): 113–119.

95. For more on this see Richard H. Pells, *The Liberal Mind in a Conservative Age* (Middletown, CT: Wesleyan University Press, 1989), 183–292.

96. Crane Brinton, "Reflections on the Desertion of the Intellectuals," *Proceedings of the American Philosophical Society* (August 30, 1955): 219–223.

97. For his eloquent defense of "happiness," see Updike, *Self-Consciousness*, 253–257.

98. Updike, "Apologies to Harvard," 34. De Bellis, *Updike Encyclopedia*, 198. Alongside Harvard, the *New Yorker* and the American Academy and Institute of Arts & Letters both retained substantial roles in Updike's life.

99. Both excerpts from Updike's entry to the class of 1954 *Reunion Reports* (in 2004 and 2009) were provided to me via email (November 15, 2012) by John Bethell, the class secretary for the Harvard class of 1954. He moderated the panel at the fiftieth anniversary reunion, during which Updike made some of these remarks. The original email is in the possession of the author.

3. The Poorhouse Fair

1. John Updike, *The Poorhouse Fair* (New York: Knopf, 1977), ix–x.

2. James A. Schiff, *John Updike Revisited* (New York: Twayne, 1998), 11–20; Judie Newman, *John Updike* (London: Macmillan, 1988), 8–12; Donald J. Greiner,

John Updike's Novels (Athens: Ohio University Press, 1984), 3–27; George J. Searles, "TPF: Updike's Thesis Statement," in *Critical Essays on John Updike*, ed. William R. Macnaughton (Boston: G. K. Hall and Co., 1982), 231–236. On the novel's critical reception, see Laurence W. Mazzeno, *Becoming John Updike: Critical Reception, 1958–2010* (Rochester, NY: Camden House, 2013), chapter 1.

3. John Updike, *More Matter: Essays and Criticism* (New York: Knopf, 1999), 10.

4. John Updike, *The Poorhouse Fair* (New York: Knopf, 1963), 47. All subsequent citations in this chapter's notes are from the 1963 edition, unless otherwise noted.

5. Updike, 14, 17–18.

6. Max Weber, *The Protestant Ethic and the Spirit of Capitalism* (New York: Scribner's, 1958), 182.

7. Updike, *Poorhouse Fair*, 13–14, 155.

8. For more on his gratitude to Kafka, see John Updike, foreword to *Franz Kafka: The Complete Stories*, ed. Nahum N. Glatzer (New York: Schocken, 1995).

9. John Updike, "Environs: Fictional Houses," in *Odd Jobs: Essays and Criticism* (New York: Knopf, 1991), 48.

10. Updike, *Odd Jobs*, 120–122.

11. James C. Scott, *Seeing Like a State: How Certain Schemes to Improve the Human Condition Have Failed* (New Haven, CT: Yale University Press, 1998), 6.

12. Scott, *Seeing Like a State*, 4.

13. Scott, 4.

14. Updike, *Poorhouse Fair*, 16, 49, 114.

15. Scott, *Seeing Like a State*, 5.

16. Scott, 5.

17. Updike, *Poorhouse Fair*, 19, 43.

18. Updike, *Poorhouse Fair* (1977), x.

19. Ira Katznelson, *Fear Itself: The New Deal and the Origins of Our Time* (New York: Liveright, 2014), 7.

20. For more on this, see William E. Leuchtenburg, *Franklin D. Roosevelt and the New Deal 1932–1940* (New York: Harper & Row, 1963); Arthur M. Schlesinger Jr., *The Age of Roosevelt: The Coming of the New Deal* (Boston: Houghton Mifflin, 1959); and Richard Hofstadter, *Age of Reform* (New York: Knopf, 1955), chapter 7.

21. Leuchtenburg, *Roosevelt and the New Deal*, 331.

22. By the term "statism," I am referring to the process of increased public reliance upon the state and its institutions at the expense of nonpolitical forces within civil society or the free market for social goods, material prosperity, and cultural expression. See David Plotke, *Building a Democratic Political Order: Reshaping American Liberalism in the 1930s and 1940s* (New York: Cambridge University Press, 1996).

23. For more on this shift, see Lizabeth Cohen, *Making a New Deal: Industrial Workers in Chicago 1919–1939* (New York: Cambridge University Press, 2008).

24. Leuchtenburg, *Roosevelt and the New Deal*, 338, 342. For more on New Deal bureaucrats, see Jordan A. Schwarz, *The New Dealers: Power and Politics in the Age of Roosevelt* (New York: Knopf, 1993).

25. Updike, *Poorhouse Fair*, 78, 108, 124.

26. Isaiah Berlin, "Two Concepts of Liberty," in *Liberalism and Its Critics*, ed. Michael J. Sandel (New York: NYU Press, 1984), 15.

27. Berlin, "Two Concepts of Liberty," 24. For more on Berlin's concepts of liberty, see Joshua L. Cherniss, *A Mind and Its Time: The Development of Isaiah Berlin's Political Thought* (New York: Oxford University Press, 2013), chapters 7–8.

28. John Updike, "Marx: Man of Mission," 25, JUP, folder 416. John Updike, *Hugging the Shore: Essays and Criticism* (New York: Vintage, 1984), 583–590.

29. Updike, *Poorhouse Fair*, 65, 106–107, 119.

30. See Updike, "Marx: Man of Mission," 23–25. Edmund Wilson, *To the Finland Station: A Study in the Acting and Writing of History* (New York: Farrar, Straus & Giroux, 1972).

31. Updike, *Poorhouse Fair*, 19.

32. Updike, 43–45.

33. Updike, *Poorhouse Fair* (1977), xv–xvi.

34. Updike, *Poorhouse Fair*, 41, 137.

35. James Plath, ed., *Conversations with John Updike* (Jackson: University Press of Mississippi, 1994), 3.

36. Searles, "TPF: Updike's Thesis Statement," 235.

37. Updike, *Poorhouse Fair* (1977), xvi–xvii.

38. Updike, *Poorhouse Fair*, 113–114.

39. Updike, *Poorhouse Fair* (1977), xvii; On Aquinas see Updike, *More Matter*, 846; on scholasticism see John Updike, "The Tragedy of Peter Abelard," JUP, folder 445.

40. For more on this, see Plath, *Conversations*, 129, 174.

41. Updike, *Poorhouse Fair*, 108, 160.

42. On the republican tradition in America, see Sean Wilentz, *Chant's Democratic: New York City and the Rise of the American Working Class, 1788–1850* (New York: Oxford University Press, 2004); Gordon S. Wood, *The Radicalism of the American Revolution* (New York: Vintage, 1993); and J. G. A Pocock, *The Machiavellian Moment: Florentine Political Thought and the Atlantic Republican Tradition* (Princeton, NJ: Princeton University Press, 1975). For a survey of American republicanism, see Daniel T. Rodgers, "Republicanism: The Career of a Concept," *Journal of American History* 79, no. 1 (June 1992): 11–38.

43. Rodgers, "Republicanism: The Career of a Concept," 34.

44. Marshall Boswell, "Updike, Religion, and the Novel of Moral Debate," in *Cambridge Companion to Updike*, ed. Stacey Olster (New York: Cambridge University Press, 2006), 43–60 at 47.

45. Updike, *Poorhouse Fair*, 111, 160; James T. Kloppenberg, *The Virtues of Liberalism* (New York: Oxford University Press, 2001). On the liberal-Republican synthesis, see Peter Berkowitz, *Virtue and the Making of Modern Liberalism* (Princeton, NJ: Princeton University Press, 2000).

46. Charles Beard and Mary Beard, *The Rise of American Civilization*, vol. 2 (New York: Macmillan, 1934).

47. Updike, *Poorhouse Fair*, 29, 43.

48. John Updike to Plowville (i.e., his parents), January 8, 1961, JUP, folder 6887.

49. Michael Kazin, *A Godly Hero: The Life of William Jennings Bryan* (New York: Knopf, 2006), xiii.

50. Kazin, *A Godly Hero*, 45; William Jennings Bryan, *William Jennings Bryan: Selections* (Indianapolis: Bobbs Merrill Co., 1967), 88.

51. See Kazin, *A Godly Hero*; Jeff Taylor, *Where Did the Party Go? William Jennings Bryan, Hubert Humphrey and the Jeffersonian Tradition* (Columbia: University of Missouri Press, 2006); LeRoy Ashby, *William Jennings Bryan: Champion of Democracy* (New York: Twayne, 1987), 184; and Louis W. Koenig, *Bryan: A Political Biography of William Jennings Bryan* (New York: Putnam, 1971), 38. The progressive movement contained both the statist ambitions of Theodore Roosevelt's New Nationalism and the decentralized grassroots views of Woodrow Wilson's New Freedom. On these competing visions of democratic government, see Michael McGerr, *A Fierce Discontent: The Rise and Fall of the Progressive Movement in America, 1870–1920* (New York: Oxford University Press, 2005).

52. Walter Lippmann, *Drift and Mastery: An Attempt to Diagnose the Current Unrest* (Madison: University of Wisconsin Press, 1985), 81.

53. Ashby, *William Jennings Bryan*, 127.

54. Ashby, 185.

55. Alan Brinkley, *Voices of Protest: Huey Long, Father Coughlin and the Great Depression* (New York: Knopf, 1982), xi.

56. Berlin, "Two Concepts of Liberty," 15.

57. Berlin, 17.

58. Updike, *Poorhouse Fair*, 16, 127, 178.

59. Updike, 5, 46.

60. Updike, 46.

61. Updike, 68.

62. For examples see Kim Phillips-Fein, *Invisible Hands: The Businessmen's Crusade against the New Deal* (New York: W. W. Norton, 2010); Friedrich Hayek, *The Road to Serfdom* (Chicago: University of Chicago Press, 1944); and Jennifer Burns, "The Three Furies of Libertarianism: Rose Wilder Lane, Isabel Paterson and Ayn Rand," *Journal of American History* 102, no. 3 (December 2015): 746–774. For an overview of these various forces, see George H. Nash, *The Conservative Intellectual Movement in America Since 1945* (New York: Basic Books, 1976), chapter 1.

63. Theodore J. Lowi, *The End of Liberalism* (New York: W. W. Norton, 1969), 297; Arthur A. Ekirch, *The Decline of American Liberalism* (New York: Longmans & Green, 1955). On Lowi see Sam Roberts, "Theodore Lowi: Zealous Scholar of Presidents and Liberalism, Dies at 85," *New York Times*, February 24, 2017, https://www.nytimes.com/2017/02/24/us/theodore-lowi-dead.html.

64. Lowi, *End of Liberalism*, xi, 86, 292–293.

65. Updike, *Poorhouse Fair*, 3, 51, 66, 104.

66. Updike, 132–134.

67. Updike, 185.

68. Plath, *Conversations*, 33, 48. For examples of early criticism of the novel centering on the plot's inability to resolve itself, see David Fitelson, "Conflict

Unresolved," *Commentary* (March 1959): 275–276; Norman Podhoretz, "Novels: Style and Substance," *Reporter*, January 22, 1959, 42–43.

69. Updike, *Poorhouse Fair*, 87, 115.
70. Updike, 17.
71. Kloppenberg, *The Virtues of Liberalism*, 7–8.
72. Hofstadter, *Age of Reform*, 303.
73. Hofstadter, 11–12, 320.
74. Hofstadter, 12. On Lasch's relationship with Hofstadter in the late 1950s, just as *The Poorhouse Fair* was being written, see Eric Miller, *Hope in a Scattering Time: A Life of Christopher Lasch* (Grand Rapids, MI: Eerdmans, 2010), chapters 3–4. On Hofstadter and his ideas, see David S. Brown, *Richard Hofstadter: An Intellectual Biography* (Chicago: University of Chicago Press, 2007).
75. Plath, *Conversations*, 85; Updike, *Poorhouse Fair* (1977), xi.
76. For more on this, see Donald T. Critchlow, *The Conservative Ascendancy: How the GOP Right Made Political History* (Cambridge, MA: Harvard University Press, 2007); Bruce J. Schulman and Julian E. Zelizer, eds., *Rightward Bound: Making America Conservative in the 1970s* (Cambridge, MA: Harvard University Press, 2008); and Kim Phillips-Fein, "Conservatism: A State of the Field," *Journal of American History* 98, no. 3 (December 2001): 723–743.
77. Lisa McGirr, *Suburban Warriors: The Origins of the New American Right* (Princeton, NJ: Princeton University Press, 2002); Joseph E. Lowndes, *From the New Deal to the New Right* (New Haven: Yale University Press, 2008); Kevin M. Kruse, *White Flight: Atlanta and the Making of Modern Conservatism* (Princeton, NJ: Princeton University Press, 2007); Dan T. Carter, *The Politics of Rage: The Origins of the New Conservatism, and the Transformation of American Politics* (Baton Rouge: Louisiana State University Press, 2000); Daniel K. Williams, *God's Own Party: The Making of the Christian Right* (New York: Oxford University Press, 2012); and Donald T. Critchlow, *Phyllis Schlafly and Grassroots Conservatism: A Women's Crusade* (Princeton, NJ: Princeton University Press, 2008).
78. Nash, *Conservative Intellectual Movement*.
79. Franklin D. Roosevelt, Speech before a Joint Session of Congress, January 6, 1941, http://www.fdrlibrary.marist.edu/fourfreedoms.
80. Updike, "Matters of State," in *More Matter*, 3–15.
81. Searles, "TPF: Updike's Thesis Statement," 231.
82. Fitelson, "Conflict Unresolved," and Podhoretz, "Novels: Style and Substance." Judie Newman has pointed toward Amy Mortis's revered quilts as a potential "feminine resolution" to the irrepressible conflicts between the chief male protagonists: by incorporating both individual and communal aspects into her "social fabric," Amy is the only one who has actually provided the plot with an opportunity for harmony. See Newman, *John Updike*, 11.
83. Plath, *Conversations*, 45.

4. Family Matters

1. James A. Schiff, *John Updike Revisited* (New York: Twayne, 1998), 28–33.
2. On the initial reception, see Laurence W. Mazzeno, *Becoming John Updike:*

Critical Reception, 1958–2010 (Rochester, NY: Camden House, 2013), 6–26. On its success and legacy, see Schiff, *John Updike Revisited*, 28–41.

3. Updike himself conceded this point often and admitted that he and Rabbit were "rather similar." See John Updike, *Picked-Up Pieces* (Greenwich, CT: Fawcett Books, 1975), 489.

4. James Plath, ed., *Conversations with John Updike* (Jackson: University Press of Mississippi, 1994), 11. On the autobiographical themes in the Rabbit novels, see John Updike, *More Matter: Essays and Criticism* (New York: Knopf, 1999), 816–820.

5. John Updike, *Rabbit Angstrom: A Tetralogy* (New York: Everyman's Library, 1995), ix. For more on the novel's historical appeal, see Schiff, *John Updike Revisited*, 29; Dilvo I. Ristoff, *Updike's America: Presence of Contemporary American History in John Updike's Rabbit Trilogy* (New York: Peter Lang, 1989), 1–2.

6. Updike, "Personal Matters," in *More Matter*, 820.

7. Plath, *Conversations*, 184, 224.

8. Updike, *Rabbit Angstrom: A Tetralogy*, xii.

9. Morris Dickstein, *Leopards in the Temple: The Transformation of American Fiction 1945–1970* (Cambridge, MA: Harvard University Press, 2002), 104–106. For discussion on the role of the family in *Rabbit, Run*, see Jeff H. Campbell, "Middling, Hidden, Troubled America," in *Rabbit Tales: Poetry and Politics in John Updike's Rabbit Novels*, ed. Lawrence R. Broer, (Tuscaloosa: University of Alabama Press, 1998), 34–49; Judie Newman, *John Updike* (London: Macmillan, 1988), chapter 3; Kerry Ahearn, "Family and Adultery: Images and Ideas in Updike's Rabbit Novels," *Twentieth Century Literature* 34, no. 1 (Spring 1988): 62–83; and Clinton S. Burhans, Jr., "Things Fall Apart: Structure and Theme in *Rabbit, Run*," in *Critical Essays on John Updike*, ed. William R. Macnaughton (Boston: G. K. Hall and Co., 1982), 148–162.

10. Updike, *More Matter*, 10. Abby Ellin, "Norman Rockwell's Vision of FDR's Four Freedoms," *New York Times*, March 8, 2018, https://www.nytimes.com/2018/03/08/arts/new-york-historical-society-norman-rockwell-four-freedoms.html.

11. Robert O. Self, *All in the Family: The Realignment of American Democracy since the 1960s* (New York: Hill & Wang, 2012), 8, 10, 17–18.

12. Self, 8.

13. Matthew D. Lassiter, "Inventing Family Values," in *Rightward Bound: Making America Conservative in the 1970s*, ed. Bruce J. Schulman and Julian E. Zelizer (Cambridge, MA: Harvard University Press, 2008), 13–28 at 16, 28.

14. Elaine Tyler May, *Homeward Bound: American Families in the Cold War Era* (New York: Basic Books, 1988), 9, 14, 17.

15. John Updike, *Rabbit, Run, Rabbit Redux, Rabbit Is Rich* (New York: Quality Paperback Book Club, 1990), 93–94, 157, 219.

16. Matthew Wilson, "The Rabbit Tetralogy: From Solitude to Society to Solitude Again," in *Rabbit Tales*, ed. Broer, 89–110 at 89; Sanford Pinsker, "Restlessness in the Fifties: What Made Rabbit Run?" in *New Essays on Rabbit, Run*, ed. Stanley Trachtenberg (New York: Cambridge University Press, 1993), 53–76 at 67. On "the psychological society" of postwar America, see Jonathan Engel,

American Therapy: The Rise of Psychotherapy in the United States (New York: Gotham, 2008), 132–218.

17. Dickstein, *Leopards*, 18, 84.

18. The term "therapeutic liberalism" has been loosely used to describe a variety of liberal policies ranging from education and crime to the economy. It was often used pejoratively by critics on the communitarian left and conservatives on the right. See Martin Halliwell, *Therapeutic Revolutions: Medicine, Psychiatry and American Culture, 1945–1970* (New Brunswick, NJ: Rutgers University Press, 2014); Jonathan B. Imber, ed., *Therapeutic Culture: Triumph and Defeat* (Livingston, NJ: Transaction Publishers, 2004); Kevin Mattson, "Christopher Lasch and the Possibilities of a Chastened Liberalism," *Polity* 36, no. 3 (April 2004): 411–445; Paul E. Gottfried, *After Liberalism: Mass Democracy in the Managerial State* (Princeton, NJ: Princeton University Press, 2001); Louis Menand, "Christopher Lasch's Quarrel with Liberalism," in *The Liberal Persuasion: Arthur Schlesinger Jr., and the Challenge of The American Past*, ed. John Patrick Diggins (Princeton, NJ: Princeton University Press, 1997), chapter 16; and Philip Rieff and Jonathan B. Imber, *The Feeling Intellect: Selected Writings* (Chicago: University of Chicago Press, 1991).

19. Michael J. Sandel, *Democracy's Discontent* (Cambridge, MA: Belknap Press, 1996), 3–24.

20. Philip Rieff, *Triumph of the Therapeutic: Uses of Faith after Freud* (New York: Harper & Row, 1966), 10–23.

21. John Updike, "English 99 Paper," 10, JUP, folder 418.

22. Updike, "Personal Matters," in *More Matter*, 852; Plath, *Conversations*, 253. For more on the novel's religious motifs, see Alice Hamilton and Kenneth Hamilton, *The Elements of John Updike* (Grand Rapids, MI: Eerdmans Publishing, 1970).

23. John Updike, *Self-Consciousness* (New York: Knopf, 1989), 98; Plath, *Conversations*, 14, 96–97, 101–104. On Barth's influence in *Rabbit, Run*, see John McTavish, *Myth and Gospel in the Fiction of John Updike* (Eugene, OR: Cascade Books, 2016), 25–29; George W. Hunt, *John Updike and The Three Great Secret Things: Sex, Religion and Art* (Grand Rapids, MI: Eerdmans, 1980), 13–48.

24. Rieff, *Triumph*, 19.

25. Updike, *Rabbit, Run*, 308.

26. Burhans, "Things Fall Apart," 161.

27. Rieff, *Triumph*, 5.

28. Rieff, *Triumph*, 11.

29. Updike, *Rabbit, Run*, 15, 26, 36, 38, 216. For more on the motif of entrapment, see Gary Brenner, "*Rabbit, Run*: John Updike's Criticism of the 'Return to Nature,'" in *Critical Essays on John Updike*, ed. William R. Macnaughton (Boston: G. K. Hall and Co., 1982), 91–104.

30. Rieff, *Triumph*, 25.

31. Updike, *Rabbit, Run*, 6, 66, 106–107.

32. Updike, 127, 169, 306.

33. Updike, 249, 270.

34. Updike, 118, 127–128, 207, 241.

35. Updike, 169–170.
36. On the distinctions between them, see Dickstein, *Leopards*, 108. On Barth's influence on Kruppenbach, see McTavish, *Myth and Gospel*, 27–28. On the broader struggles they symbolize within American Christianity, see Garry Wills, *Head and Heart: American Christianities* (New York: Penguin, 2017), 397–495; Thomas E. McCollough, "Reinhold Niebuhr and Karl Barth on the Relevance of Theology," *Journal of Religion* 43. no. 1 (January 1963): 49–55.
37. Updike, *Rabbit, Run*, 267–268.
38. Plath, *Conversations*, 175, 264.
39. Newman, *John Updike*, 30–32.
40. Updike, *Rabbit, Run*, 149.
41. Plath, *Conversations*, 33; John Updike, "Speeches: Emersonianism," in *Odd Jobs: Essays and Criticism* (New York: Knopf, 1991), 160.
42. John Kenneth Galbraith, *The Affluent Society* (Boston: Houghton Mifflin Harcourt, 1958), 120, 150. Updike read Galbraith and was familiar with the book. See Updike, *More Matter*, 26–27.
43. Alan Brinkley, *The End of Reform: New Deal Liberalism in Recession and War* (New York: Knopf, 1995), 4, 10; Lizabeth Cohen, *A Consumer's Republic* (New York: Vintage, 2003), 7–11. For more on postwar consumer culture, see Louis Hyman, *Debtor Nation: The History of America in Red Ink* (Princeton, NJ: Princeton University Press, 2012); Daniel Horowitz, *The Anxieties of Affluence* (Amherst: University of Massachusetts Press, 2005).
44. The problem of declining work and of excessive consumption was often on Updike's mind. He further explored it in *Rabbit Is Rich* (1980) as well as in several of his early short stories and prose such as "A&P," "Farewell to the Middle Class," "Domestic Life in America," and "The Bankrupt Man."
45. John Updike, *Midpoint and Other Poems* (Knopf: New York, 1969), 40.
46. Plath, *Conversations*, 16. Updike's critique of the automated workplace and the Fordist economy echoes some of the more salient social commentaries of his time. For some examples, see Daniel Bell, *Work and Its Discontent: The Cult of Efficiency in America* (Boston: Beacon Press, 1956); William H. Whyte and Joseph Nocera, *The Organization Man* (New York: Simon & Schuster, 1956); and C. Wright Mills, *White Collar: The American Middle Classes* (New York: Oxford University Press, 1951).
47. For some examples, see Michael Szalay, *Hip Figures: A Literary History of the Democratic Party* (Stanford, CA: Stanford University Press, 2012), 137–144; Newman, *John Updike*, chapter 3; and Ristoff, *Updike's America*, chapter 2.
48. Daniel Bell, *The Cultural Contradictions of Capitalism* (New York: Basic Books, 1976), 21, 70. On reactions and legacy of his book, see Malcolm Waters, *Daniel Bell* (London: Routledge, 1996), 124–147; Howard Brick, *Daniel Bell and the Decline of Intellectual Radicalism* (Madison: University of Wisconsin Press, 1986).
49. Bell, *Cultural Contradictions*, 14, 75.
50. Updike discussed Weber in his later novel *Trust Me* and occasionally incorporated the Protestant work ethic into his nonfiction prose. For an example, see John Updike, *Hugging the Shore* (New York: Vintage, 1984), 76.

51. Updike, "On Not Being a Dove," in *Self-Consciousness,* 129; Max Weber, *The Protestant Ethic and the Spirit of Capitalism* (New York: Scribner's, 1958), chapters 2–3.

52. Updike, "A Letter to My Grandsons," in *Self-Consciousness,* 183; Plath, *Conversations,* 53, 79.

53. Ristoff, *Updike's America,* 69. For more on the influence of television on Americans, see Karal Ann Marling, *As Seen on TV: The Visual Culture of Everyday Life in the 1950s* (Cambridge, MA: Harvard University Press, 1996).

54. Updike, *Rabbit, Run,* 4, 10.

55. For more on the idea of sports as a calling, see Jack B. More, "Sports, Basketball and Fortunate Failure in the Rabbit Tetralogy," in *Rabbit Tales,* ed. Broer, 170–189.

56. Updike, *Rabbit, Run,* 51, 62, 72.

57. Updike, *Rabbit, Run,* 136, 163, 223.

58. On the etymology of his name, see Jack De Bellis, *John Updike Encyclopedia* (Westport, CT: Greenwood Press, 2000), 19.

59. For an analysis of the radio ads in the scene and their significance, see Szalay, *Hip Figures,* 137–144.

60. Updike, *Rabbit, Run,* 34, 37, 74.

61. Updike, 9–10.

62. Updike, 10, 15, 105.

63. Updike, 13, 25, 47.

64. For more on this, see Stacey Olster, "'Unadorned Woman, Beauty's Home Image': Updike's *Rabbit, Run,*" in *New Essays on Rabbit, Run,* ed. Trachtenberg, 95–117; Mary O'Connell, *The Patriarchal Dilemma: Masculinity in the Rabbit Novels* (Carbondale: Southern Illinois University Press, 1996); and Josephine Hendin, *Vulnerable People: A View of American Fiction since 1945* (New York: Oxford University Press, 1978), 88–99.

65. Newman, *John Updike,* 35.

66. Updike, *Rabbit, Run,* 148, 217.

67. Updike, 258–261.

68. Updike, 269–274.

69. On Moynihan's liberalism, see Eric Alterman and Kevin Mattson, *The Fight for American Liberalism from Franklin Roosevelt to Barack Obama* (New York: Viking, 2012), 263–284; Godfrey Hodgson, *The Gentleman from New York: Daniel Patrick Moynihan: A Biography* (Boston: Houghton Mifflin Harcourt, 2000). On Lasch see Eric Miller, *Hope in a Scattering Time: A Life of Christopher Lasch* (Grand Rapids, MI: Eerdmans, 2010); and Mattson, "Christopher Lasch and the Possibilities of a Chastened Liberalism."

70. On the reports impact and controversies, see Daniel Geary, *Beyond Civil Rights: The* Moynihan Report *and Its Legacy* (Philadelphia: University of Pennsylvania Press 2015); James T. Patterson, *Freedom Is Not Enough: The* Moynihan Report *and America's Struggle over Black Family Life—from LBJ to Obama* (New York: Basic Books, 2010).

71. Daniel P. Moynihan, "The *Moynihan Report,*" in *The* Moynihan Report *and the Politics of Controversy,* ed. Lee Rainwater and William L. Yancey (Cam-

bridge, MA: MIT Press, 1966), 21, 47. On this new economy, see Judith Stein, *Pivotal Decade: How the United States Traded Factories for Finance in the Seventies* (New Haven, CT: Yale University Press, 2011); Daniel Bell, *The Coming of Postindustrial Society: A Venture in Social Forecasting* (New York: Basic Books, 1976).

72. Thomas Meehan, "The Moynihan of the *Moynihan Report*," *New York Times Book Review*, July 31, 1966, http://movies2.nytimes.com/books/98/10/04/spe cials/moynihan-report.html.

For examples of his later advocacy on behalf of families, see Daniel P. Moynihan, *Miles to Go: A Personal History of Social Policy* (Cambridge, MA: Harvard University Press, 1997); Daniel P. Moynihan, *Family and Nation* (New York: Harcourt Brace Jovanovich, 1986); and Daniel P. Moynihan, *The Politics of a Guaranteed Income* (New York: Random House, 1973).

73. This was revealed by his widow, Mrs. Elizabeth B. Moynihan. Email with the author. The original email is in the author's possession.

74. Daniel P. Moynihan to John Updike, July 16, 1970, and Moynihan to Updike, May 22, 1993, JUP, folder 5250.

75. Daniel P. Moynihan, "Grey Truth," the Blashfield Address, the American Academy and Institute of Arts and Letters in New York City, May 20, 1992. The text is located in the JUP, folder 5250.

76. Updike to Moynihan, June 1, 1992, Daniel P. Moynihan Papers, Manuscript Division, Library of Congress, part II, box 32, folder 6.

77. Moynihan to Updike, August 31, 1992, Daniel P. Moynihan Papers, part II, box 32, folder 6.

78. On the role of family decline in mobilizing disenchanted liberals toward neoconservatism, see Peter Steinfels, *The Neoconservatives: The Origins of a Movement* (New York: Simon & Schuster, 1979), chapter 6.

79. For more on Lasch's intellectual influences and strange political evolution, see Miller, *Hope*; Norman Birnbaum, "Gratitude and Forbearance: On Christopher Lasch," *Nation*, September 14, 2011, https://www.thenation.com /article/gratitude-and-forbearance-christopher-lasch/.

80. Miller, *Hope*, 193, 197.

81. Christopher Lasch, *Haven in a Heartless World: The Family Besieged* (New York: W. W. Norton, 1995), xiii–xiv, xxii.

82. Lasch, *Haven*, xvi–xvii, xxiii–xxiv.

83. Christopher Lasch, "The Family as a Haven in a Heartless World," *Salmagundi* 35 (Fall 1976): 42–55 at 49.

84. Lasch, *Haven*, 183. For a critical view of Lasch's work, see Fred Siegel, "The Agony of Christopher Lasch," *Reviews in American History* 8, no. 3 (September 1980): 285–295.

85. Lasch was also influenced by the works of Philip Rieff and Daniel Bell. See Miller, *Hope*, 193–194, 237, 240–244, 248, 263–264.

86. Miller, *Hope*, 202.

87. Jeffrey Ludwig, "Roommates and Rivals: John Updike, Christopher Lasch, and a Harvard University Friendship," *John Updike Review* 2, no. 2 (Spring 2013): 3–25 at 16. Lasch to Updike, November 6, 1972, and January 7, 1982, JUP, folder 4768.

88. Ludwig, "Roommates," 2.

89. Lassiter, "Inventing Family Values," 14. On the discourse of family decline, see Daniel K. Williams, *God's Own Party: The Making of the Christian Right* (New York: Oxford University Press, 2012), chapter 6; Self, *All in the Family*; Lassiter, "Inventing Family Values"; Natasha Zaretsky, *No Direction Home: The American Family and the Fear of National Decline, 1968–1980* (Chapel Hill: University of North Carolina Press, 2007); and Stephanie Coontz, *The Way We Really Are: Coming to Terms with America's Changing Families* (New York: Basic Books, 1998).

90. In this sense, the novel reflects growing historical scholarship that locates continuity between the 1950s and 1960s. For examples see Kevin Mattson, *Intellectuals in Action: The Origins of the New Left and Radical Liberalism 1945–1970* (University Park: Penn State University Press, 2002); Richard H. Pells, *The Liberal Mind in a Conservative Age* (Middletown, CT: Wesleyan University Press, 1989), 401–409; Daniel Geary, "Children of *The Lonely Crowd*: David Riesman, the Young Radicals, and the Splitting of Liberalism in the 1960s," *Modern Intellectual History* 10, no. 3 (November 2013): 603–633.

5. *Sleeping Together, Bowling Alone*

1. John Updike, "London Life," in *Picked-Up Pieces* (Greenwich, CT: Fawcett Books, 1975), 55–56; John Updike, *Rabbit Angstrom: A Tetralogy* (New York: Everyman's Library, 1995), xiv. On Updike's time in London, see Adam Begley, *Updike* (New York: Harper, 2014), 295–307.

2. "View from the Catacombs," *Time*, April 26, 1968, 76–84.

3. On the novel's mixed reception, see Laurence W. Mazzeno, *Becoming John Updike: Critical Receptions, 1958–2010* (Rochester, NY: Camden House, 2013), 28–31; Begley, *Updike*, 294.

4. For more on the etymological wordplay in the novel, see Jack De Bellis, *John Updike Encyclopedia* (Westport, CT: Greenwood Press, 2000), 121.

5. Alexis de Tocqueville, *Democracy in America* (New York: Harper Perennial, 2000), 243.

6. See John Updike, *More Matter: Essays and Criticism* (New York: Knopf, 1999), 3–15.

7. James A. Schiff, *John Updike Revisited* (New York: Twayne, 1998), 68; Judie Newman, *John Updike* (London: Macmillan, 1988), 12–15. On this theme, see also Begley, *Updike*, chapter 6; John Neary, *Something and Nothingness: The Fiction of John Updike and John Fowles* (Carbondale: Southern Illinois University Press, 1992), 153–154.

8. On the Tocqueville revival, see Donald E. Pease, "After the Tocqueville Revival; or, the Return of the Political," *Boundary 2* 26, no. 3 (1999), 87–114.

9. He was not the only one to raise the alarm. For more studies on the decline of civic engagement, see Theda Skocpol, *Diminished Democracy: From Membership to Management in American Civic Life* (Norman: University of Oklahoma Press, 2004); Theda Skocpol and Morris P. Fiorina, *Civic Engagement in American Democracy* (Washington, DC: Brookings Institute Press, 1999); Michael J. San-

del, *Democracy's Discontent* (Cambridge, MA: Belknap Press, 1996); and Robert Nisbet, *Twilight of Authority* (New York: Oxford University Press, 1975). On the decline of voting, see Thomas E. Patterson, *The Vanishing Voter: Public Involvement in an Age of Uncertainty* (New York: Vintage, 2003); Martin P. Wattenberg, *Where Have All the Voters Gone?* (Cambridge, MA: Harvard University Press, 2002).

10. Robert D. Putnam, *Bowling Alone: The Collapse and Revival of American Community* (New York: Touchstone, 2000), 16–18, 27, 283–284.

11. For counter narratives, see Russell J. Dalton, *The Good Citizen: How a Younger Generation Is Reshaping American Politics* (Washington, DC: CQ Press, 2009), chapter 4; Scott L. McLean, David A. Schultz, and Manfred B. Steger, eds., *Social Capital: Critical Perspectives on Community and "Bowling Alone"* (New York: NYU Press, 2002); and Michael Schudson, *The Good Citizen: A History of American Civic Life* (New York: Free Press, 1998), 294–314.

12. Hannah Arendt, *The Human Condition* (Chicago: University of Chicago Press, 1958), 3–4.

13. Arendt, 49.

14. For example see the February 23, 1963, issue of the *New Yorker*.

15. On Arendt's debt to Aristotle, see Albrecht Wellmer, "Hannah Arendt on Judgment: The Unwritten Doctrine of Reason," in *Hannah Arendt: Twenty Years Later*, ed. Larry May and Jerome Kohn (Cambridge, MA: MIT Press, 1996), chapter 2; Lewis Hinchman and Sandra Hinchman, eds., *Hannah Arendt: Critical Essays* (Albany: SUNY Press, 1994).

16. John Updike, "Fish Story," in *Hugging the Shore: Essays and Criticism* (New York: Vintage, 1984), 479; John Updike, *Self-Consciousness* (New York: Knopf, 1989), 211. For more examples of Updike's use of Aristotle's ideas, see Updike, *Picked-Up Pieces*, 348. On his academic studies of Aristotle, see John Updike, "Apply Aristotle's Theory of Tragedy to King Lear," JUP, folder 433.

17. Arendt, *The Human Condition*, 36.

18. James Plath, ed., *Conversations with John Updike* (Jackson: University Press of Mississippi, 1994), 53.

19. John Updike, *Couples* (New York: Knopf, 1968). All subsequent quotes in parentheses are from this edition.

20. Updike, 93.

21. For an example of Updike's conflation of spiritual and civic religion, see George S. Diamond, "Chaos and Society: Religion and the Idea of Civil Order in Updike's *Memoirs of the Ford Administration*," in *John Updike and Religion*, ed. James Yerkes (Grand Rapids, MI: Eerdmans, 1999), 242–257.

22. Updike, *Couples*, 145, 148.

23. Updike, *Couples*, 106.

24. On the multiple forms of virtue and a discussion of their decline in the modern era, see Alasdair MacIntyre, *After Virtue: A Study in Moral Theory* (South Bend, IN: University of Notre Dame Press, 2007). On the decline of virtue in *Couples*, see Neary, *Something and Nothingness*, 154.

25. Updike, *Couples*, 31.

26. Updike, 170, 177.

27. Updike, 74, 178.

28. Updike, 158, 161, 279.
29. Updike, 96, 169. This may be a reference to Robert Rauschenberg's collage art, which Updike appreciated. See De Bellis, *Updike Encyclopedia*, 343.
30. Updike, 132, 135,
31. Updike, 229, 234, 247–249.
32. Updike, 125, 132, 317. In several of his earlier short stories, Updike satirized liberal smugness. See John Updike, "The Doctor's Wife" and "Marching through Boston" in *John Updike: The Early Stories 1953–1975* (New York: Ballantine Books, 2003), 261–269, 380–389. For more on his critique of liberal sententiousness, see Updike, *Self-Consciousness*, chapter 4.
33. Updike, *Couples*, 145, 161, 214.
34. Updike, 294–295.
35. Updike, 296, 301, 306.
36. Updike, 300, 316.
37. For Updike's response to the traumatic event, see John Updike, *Assorted Prose* (New York: Knopf, 1965), 118; Begley, *Updike*, 256.
38. Updike, *Couples*, 306.
39. Updike, 308, 310.
40. Updike, 320.
41. Tocqueville, *Democracy in America*, 249.
42. Updike, *Couples*, 27, 386.
43. Updike, 386–387.
44. Updike, 387–388.
45. Hannah Arendt, *On Revolution* (New York: Penguin, 1963), 253–254.
46. For more on this, see Vidya Ravi, "'Outdoors to Indoors, Detail to Detail': The Domestic Topography of John Updike's *Couples*," *John Updike Review* 1, no. 2 (Spring 2013): 27–41; D. Quentin Miller, "Updike, Middles, and the Spell of 'Subjective Geography,'" in *The Cambridge Companion to John Updike*, ed. Stacey Olster (New York: Cambridge University Press, 2006), 15–29; De Bellis, *Updike Encyclopedia*, 415.
47. Arendt, *On Revolution*, 269.
48. On his animosity for the New Left, see Updike, *Self-Consciousness*, chapter 4.
49. Updike, *Couples*, 444.
50. Plath, *Conversations*, 251, 255.
51. Updike, *Hugging*, 64.
52. Updike, *Picked-Up Pieces*, 486.
53. Updike, "On One's Own Oeuvre," in *Hugging*, 856; Begley, *Updike*, 249.
54. Aristotle, *Nicomachean Ethics* (Mineola, NY: Dover, 1998), 138, 150.
55. Aristotle, 141–142.
56. For more on the importance of friendship to Aristotle's vision of democracy, see Lorraine Smith Pangle, *Aristotle and the Philosophy of Friendship* (New York: Cambridge University Press, 2008), chapter 4; Jason A. Scorza, "Liberal Citizenship and Civic Friendship," *Political Theory* 32, no. 1 (February 2004): 85–108.
57. Updike, *Couples*, 112, 142, 165, 449.

58. Updike, *Couples*, 387, 419, 429.
59. Mark Vernon, *The Meaning of Friendship* (New York: Palgrave Macmillan, 2010), 6.
60. Updike, *Couples*, 357, 398.
61. Vance Packard, *A Nation of Strangers* (New York: Pocket Books, 1972); Troy D. Glover, "All the Lonely People: Social Isolation and the Promises and Pitfall of Leisure," *Leisure Sciences* 40, no. 1 (January 2018): 25–35; Hua Wang and Barry Hellman, "Social Connectivity in America: Changes in Adult Friendship Network Size from 2002 to 2007," *American Behavioral Scientist* 53, no. 8 (April 2010): 1148–1169; Miller McPherson, Lynn Smith-Lovin, and Matthew E. Brashears, "Social Isolation in America: Changes in Core Discussion Network over Two Decades," *American Sociological Review* 71, no. 3 (June 2006): 353–375; and Putnam, *Bowling Alone*, chapter 6. For a counter narrative that rejects the decline of friendship, see Claude S. Fischer, *Still Connected: Family and Friends in America since the 1970s* (New York: Russell Sage Foundation, 2011).
62. "View from the Catacombs," 83.
63. Begley, *Updike*, chapters 4–6.
64. Updike, "At War with My Skin," in *Self-Consciousness*, 52–55. For more on his communal life, see Begley, *Updike*, chapter 4.
65. Plath, *Conversations*, 14.
66. Updike, "London Life," in *Picked-Up Pieces*, 55–56.
67. Updike, "Non-Fiction," in *Picked-Up Pieces*, 471–472; Narayan quoted from R. K. Narayan, *My Days* (New York: Viking, 1974).
68. Updike, "Common Land," in *Hugging*, 63–64.
69. Plath, *Conversations*, 79, 108, 161, 163.
70. Robert A. Dahl, *Who Governs? Democracy and Power in an American City* (New Haven, CT: Yale University Press, 1961), 8, 279. On the book's legacy and criticism, see Terry N. Clark, "Power and Community Structure: Who Governs, Where and When?" *Sociological Quarterly* 8, no. 3 (Summer 1967): 291–316.
71. Schudson, *Good Citizen*, 290–306.
72. Updike, *Couples*, 449.
73. Robert Detweiler, "Updike's *Couples*: Eros Demythologized," in *Critical Essays on John Updike*, ed. William R. Macnaughton (Boston: G. K. Hall and Co., 1982), 128–139 at 129.

6. Things Don't Mix

1. John Updike, *Rabbit Angstrom: A Tetralogy* (New York: Everyman's Library, 1995), xiv; John Updike, *Self-Consciousness* (New York: Knopf, 1989), 146.
2. On the teach-in movement, see Todd Gitlin, *The Sixties: Years of Hope, Days of Rage* (New York: Bantam, 1987), 187–188.
3. For more on its reception, see Laurence W. Mazzeno, *Becoming John Updike: Critical Reception, 1958–2010* (Rochester, NY: Camden House, 2013), 37–39. On the novel's political implications, see Marshall Boswell, *Mastered Irony in Motion: John Updike's Rabbit Tetralogy* (Columbia: University of Missouri Press,

2001), chapter 2; Lawrence R. Broer, ed., *Rabbit Tales: Poetry and Politics in John Updike's Rabbit Novels* (Tuscaloosa: University of Alabama Press, 1998), chapters 3 and 6; James A. Schiff, *John Updike Revisited* (New York: Twayne, 1998), 41–47; Dilvo I. Ristoff, *Updike's America: Presence of Contemporary American History in John Updike's Rabbit Trilogy* (New York: Peter Lang, 1989), chapter 3; and Gordon E. Slethaug, "*Rabbit Redux*: Freedom Is Made of Brambles," in *Critical Essays on John Updike*, ed. William R. Macnaughton (Boston: G. K. Hall and Co., 1982), 237–253.

4. Marshall Boswell, "The Black Jesus: Racism and Redemption in John Updike's *Rabbit Redux*," *Contemporary Literature* 39. no. 1 (Spring 1998): 99–132 at 99.

5. Updike, *Rabbit Angstrom: A Tetralogy*, xvii; James Plath, ed., *Conversations with John Updike* (Jackson: University Press of Mississippi, 1994), 133.

6. Allen J. Matusow, *The Unraveling of America: A History of Liberalism in the 1960s* (New York: Harper & Row, 1984), 395.

7. On the various narratives of liberal decline, see Jefferson Cowie, *The Great Exception: The New Deal and the Limits of American Politics* (Princeton, NJ: Princeton University Press, 2016); Michael W. Flamm, *Law and Order: Street Crime, Civil Unrest, and the Crisis of Liberalism in the 1960s* (New York: Columbia University Press, 2007); Judith Stein, *Running Steel, Running America: Race, Economic Policy and the Decline of Liberalism* (Chapel Hill: University of North Carolina Press, 1998); David Steigerwald, *The Sixties and the End of Modern America* (New York: St. Martin's Press, 1995); Steve Fraser and Gary Gerstle, eds., *The Rise and Fall of the New Deal Order 1930–1980* (Princeton, NJ: Princeton University Press, 1990); and Jonathan Rieder, *Canarsie: The Jews and Italians of Brooklyn against Liberalism* (Cambridge, MA: Harvard University Press, 1987).

8. John Updike, *Rabbit, Run, Rabbit Redux, Rabbit Is Rich* (New York: Quality Paperback Book Club, 1990), 7.

9. Updike, *Rabbit, Redux*, 26.

10. See Michelle Foucault's *Madness and Civilization: A History of Insanity in the Age of Reason* (New York: Vintage, 1988). On Updike's reading of Foucault, see John Updike, *Odd Jobs: Essays and Criticism* (New York: Knopf, 1991), 432, 749–755, 795.

11. William Butler Yeats, "The Second Coming," in *The Collected Poems of W. B. Yeats* (New York, Scribner, 1996), 187. On Yeats's influence on postwar liberals, see Arthur M. Schlesinger Jr., *The Vital Center* (Boston: Houghton Mifflin, 1949), viii; Daniel P. Moynihan, "The End of Innocence," Address at Franklin and Marshall College, December 1967, Daniel P. Moynihan Papers, Manuscript Division, Library of Congress, part 1, box 207, folder 8.

12. Updike, *Rabbit Redux*, 330, 396.

13. Luc Boltanski and Eve Chiapello, *The New Spirit of Capitalism* (New York: Verso, 2007), chapters 1–5.

14. Updike, *Rabbit Redux*, 3–4.

15. Karl Polanyi, *The Great Transformation: Political and Economic Origins of Our Time* (Boston: Beacon, 2001).

16. Updike, *Rabbit Redux*, 29–30.

17. Judie Newman made this point by arguing that Rabbit has transformed into a "Gutenberg man, sensually deprived and passively dependent upon the machine." See Judie Newman, *John Updike* (London: Macmillan, 1988), 41–43.

18. See Students for a Democratic Society, "The Port Huron Statement," in *Democracy Is in the Streets: From Port Huron to the Siege of Chicago* by James Miller (Cambridge, MA: Harvard University Press, 1994), 330–338.

19. Updike, *Rabbit Redux*, 158–161.

20. Updike, 341–342.

21. Charlie Reilly, "An Interview with John Updike," *Contemporary Literature* 43, no. 2 (Summer 2002): 217–248 at 234.

22. Daniel Bell, *The Coming of Postindustrial Society: A Venture in Social Forecasting* (New York: Basic Books, 1976).

23. This is consistent with what actually happened to Reading, Pennsylvania, on which the fictional city of Brewer is based. See Sabrina Tavernise, "Reading, Pa., Knew It was Poor. Now It Knows Just How Poor," *New York Times*, September 26, 2011, https://www.nytimes.com/2011/09/27/us/reading-pa-tops-list-poverty-list-census-shows.html. On urban decline, see Kim Phillips-Fein, *Fear City: New York's Fiscal Crisis and the Rise of Austerity Politics* (New York: Metropolitan Books, 2017); Thomas Sugrue, *The Origins of the Urban Crisis: Race and Inequality in Postwar Detroit* (Princeton, NJ: Princeton University Press, 1996).

24. Updike, *Rabbit Redux*, 13–14, 139.

25. Updike, 184–191.

26. Jefferson R. Cowie, *Stayin Alive: The 1970s and the Last Days of the Working Class* (New York: New Press, 2010), 7.

27. Updike, *Rabbit Redux*, 306.

28. Updike, 343, 372, 397; John Updike, *Picked-Up Pieces* (Greenwich, CT: Fawcett Crest, 1975), 490.

29. Judith Stein, *Pivotal Decade: How the United States Traded Factories for Finance in the Seventies* (New Haven: Yale University Press, 2011).

30. Cowie, *Stayin Alive*, 11, 16, 18–19.

31. On Updike's attitude on race, see Jay Prosser, "Updike, Race, and the Postcolonial Project," in *Cambridge Companion to John Updike*, ed. Stacey Olster (New York: Cambridge University Press, 2006), 76–91, and "Under the Skin of John Updike: Self-Consciousness and the Racial Unconscious," *PMLA* 116, no. 3 (May 2001): 579–593; Boswell, "The Black Jesus"; and Edward M. Jackson, "Rabbit Is Racist," *College Language Association Journal* 28 (1985): 445–451.

32. For more on this, see Joshua Bloom and Waldo E. Martin, *Black against Empire: The History and Politics of the Black Panther Party* (Berkeley: University of California Press, 2014); Manning Marable, *Malcolm X: A Life of Reinvention* (New York: Viking, 2011).

33. On Skeeter's economic critique, see Ristoff, *Updike's America*, chapter 3. For more on the historical connection between economic and racial injustice in America, see Heather Cox Richardson, *The Death of Reconstruction: Race, Labor, and Politics in the Post–Civil War North 1861–1901* (Cambridge, MA: Harvard University Press, 2004); Grace E. Hale, *Making Whiteness: The Culture of Segrega-*

tion in the South 1890–1940 (New York: Vintage, 1999); and Leon F. Litwack, *Been in the Storm So Long: Aftermath of Slavery* (New York: Vintage, 1979).

34. Updike, *Rabbit Redux*, 233–235.

35. For more on this, see Daniel Geary, *Beyond Civil Rights: The* Moynihan Report *and Its Legacy* (Philadelphia: University of Pennsylvania Press 2015); Gordon K. Mantler, *Power to the Poor: Black-Brown Coalition and the Fight for Economic Justice* (Chapel Hill: University of North Carolina Press, 2013); Nancy MacLean, *Freedom Is Not Enough: The Opening of the American Workplace* (Cambridge, MA: Harvard University Press, 2008); and Fred R. Harris and Lynn Curtis, eds., *Locked in the Poorhouse: Cities, Race and Poverty in the United States* (Lanham, MD: Rowman & Littlefield, 1998).

36. Updike, *Rabbit Redux*, 288–290.

37. Matthew D. Lassiter, *The Silent Majority: Suburban Politics in the Sunbelt South* (Princeton, NJ: Princeton University Press, 2006), 1. On the colorblind rhetoric of property rights prevalent in the 1960s, see Kevin M. Kruse, *White Flight: Atlanta and the Making of Modern Conservatism* (Princeton, NJ: Princeton University Press, 2007); and Max Felker-Kantor, "Fighting the Segregation Amendment," in *Black and Brown in Los Angeles*, ed. Josh Kun and Laura Pulido (Berkeley: University of California Press, 2014), 143–175.

38. On the New Deal's structural racism, see Ira Katznelson, *When Affirmative Action Was White* (New York: W. W. Norton, 2005); Arnold R. Hirsch, *Making the Second Ghetto: Race and Housing in Chicago 1940–1960* (Chicago: University of Chicago Press, 1998); and Kenneth T. Jackson, *Crabgrass Frontier: The Suburbanization of the United States* (New York: Oxford University Press, 1987), 219–230.

39. John Updike, "Matters of State," in *More Matter: Essays and Criticism* (New York: Knopf, 1999), 15.

40. Updike, *Rabbit Redux*, 12, 138, 218.

41. Updike, 296.

42. Updike, 405.

43. George Yancy, *Black Bodies, White Gazes* (Lanham, MD: Rowman & Littlefield, 2008), xvi. That Skeeter reads Frantz Fanon further invites considerations of white fantasies and black bodies. See Frantz Fanon, *Black Skin, White Masks* (New York: Grove Press, 2008).

44. For more on this, see Wayne M. Mellinger and Rodney Beaulieu, "White Fantasies, Black Bodies: Racial Power, Disgust and Desire in American Popular Culture," *Visual Anthropology* 9, no. 2 (1997): 117–147; Robert J. C. Young, *Colonial Desire: Hybridity in Theory, Culture and Race* (London: Routledge, 1995).

45. Plath, *Conversations*, 88.

46. John F. Kennedy, Acceptance Speech at the Democratic National Convention in Los Angeles, July 15, 1960, https://www.jfklibrary.org/learn/about-jfk/historic-speeches/acceptance-of-democratic-nomination-for-president; John F. Kennedy, Speech at Rice University, September 12, 1962, https://er.jsc.nasa.gov/seh/ricetalk.htm. On the New Frontier, see Mark J. White, *Kennedy: The New Frontier Revisited* (New York: NYU Press, 1998).

47. For examples see Jacques Ellul, *The Technological Society* (New York: Vin-

tage, 1964); George H. Nash, *The Conservative Intellectual Movement in America since 1945* (New York: Basic Books, 1976), chapter 3.

48. On the role of technology in the novel, see Newman, *John Updike*, chapter 2; and Boswell, *Mastered Irony*, chapter 2. On public attitudes toward science and the fascination with space and technology during this period, see Ken Hollings, *Welcome to Mars: Politics, Pop Culture and Weird Science in 1950s America* (Berkeley: North Atlantic Press, 2014); David Meerman Scott and Richard Jurek, *Marketing the Moon: The Selling of the Apollo Lunar Program* (Cambridge, MA: MIT Press, 2014); and Walter A. McDougall, *The Heavens and the Earth: A Political History of the Space Age* (Baltimore: Johns Hopkins University Press, 1997).

49. Updike, *Rabbit Redux*, 15, 72.

50. Updike, 55, 99–100.

51. Updike, 8, 11.

52. Updike, 90, 193, 196.

53. Since Updike had closely read Pascal's *Pensees,* this may be a reference to "Pascal's Wager," a philosophical attempt to engage the dilemmas of reason and faith. Plath, *Conversations*, 85. See also Margaret Hallissy, "Updike's *Rabbit, Run* and Pascal's *Pensees*," *Christianity and Literature* 30, no. 2 (March 1981): 25–32.

54. Updike, *Rabbit Redux*, 95, 120–122.

55. Updike, 12, 114, 146–148, 163–168, 276.

56. Plath, *Conversations*, 181.

57. Updike, 284. For alternative readings of religion in *Rabbit Redux*, see Boswell, *Mastered Irony*, chapter 2; Wayne Falk, "*Rabbit Redux*: Time/Order/God," *Modern Fiction Studies* 20 (Spring 1974): 59–75.

58. Robert D. Putnam and David E. Campbell, *American Grace: How Religion Divides and Unites Us* (New York: Simon & Schuster, 2010), 3. John T. Elson, "Towards a Hidden God," *Time*, April 8, 1966.

59. Garry Wills, *Head and Heart: A History of Christianity in America* (New York: Penguin, 2007), 465–488. On the competing trends within American Christianity, see Mark A. Knoll, *The Old Religion in a New World: The History of North American Christianity* (Grand Rapids, MI: Eerdmans, 2002), chapter 7; Christian Smith, ed., *The Secular Revolution: Power, Interests, and Conflict in the Secularization of American Public Life* (Berkeley: University of California Press, 2003).

60. On this "spiritual consensus" and the impact of the Cold War on religion in America, see Jonathan P. Herzog, *The Spiritual-Industrial Complex: America's Religious Battle against Communism in the Early Cold War* (New York: Oxford University Press, 2011); and Jeremy T. Gunn, *Spiritual Weapons: The Cold War and the Forging of an American National Religion* (New York: Praeger, 2008).

61. Antony Alumkal, *Paranoid Science: The Christian Right's War on Reality* (New York: NYU Press, 2017); Jonathan Dudley, *Broken Words: The Abuse of Science and Faith in American Politics* (New York: Crown, 2011); Chris Mooney, *The Republican War on Science* (New York: Basic Books, 2006); and Edward J. Larson, *Summer for the Gods: The Scopes Trial and America's Continuing Debate over Science and Religion* (New York: Basic Books, 2007), chapters 8–10.

62. George M. Marsden, *The Twilight of the American Enlightenment: The 1950s and the Crisis of Liberal Belief* (New York: Basic Books, 2014), 156.

63. On Updike's personal struggle with such competing forms of Christianity, see Updike, *Self-Consciousness*, 129–130; John Updike, *Hugging the Shore* (New York: Vintage, 1984), 825–836.

64. Robert Booth Fowler, *Believing Skeptics: American Political Intellectuals, 1945–1967* (Westport, CT: Westwood Press, 1978), 215.

65. Robert A. Dahl, *A Preface to Democratic Theory* (Chicago: University of Chicago Press, 1956), chapter 5.

66. Updike, *Rabbit Redux*, 83–84.

67. Updike, *Picked-Up Pieces*, 490.

68. Updike, *Rabbit, Redux*, 11.

69. On the role of law and order in the collapse of liberalism, see Flamm, *Law and Order*; Rieder, *Canarsie*; and Rick Perlstein, *Nixonland* (New York: Scribner, 2008), chapters 10–17.

70. Updike, *Rabbit Redux*, 79–80, 166. Richard Hofstadter, "The Pseudo-Conservative Revolt," in *The Radical Right*, ed. Daniel Bell (Livingston, NJ: Transaction, 2002), chapter 2.

71. Updike, *Rabbit Redux*, 44–45.

72. Updike, 46. On this criticism against bureaucratic elites, see David Halberstam, *The Best and the Brightest* (New York: Ballantine Books, 1993).

73. Updike, *Rabbit Redux*, 47–50.

74. Updike, 44–47.

75. Updike, 228.

76. Matthew Wilson, "From Solitude to Society to Solitude Again," in *Rabbit Tales: Poetry and Politics in John Updike's Rabbit Novels*, ed. Lawrence R. Broer (Tuscaloosa: University of Alabama Press, 1998), 89–110 at 96.

77. Updike, *Rabbit Redux*, 82, 131.

78. One wonders if his admiration for Voltaire's *Candide* may have led to this recurring fascination with the garden metaphor. See Updike, *More Matter*, 847.

79. Updike, *Rabbit Redux*, 88.

80. Wilson, "From Solitude," 93–96.

81. SDS, "Port Huron Statement," in *Democracy Is in the Streets*, by Miller, 333.

82. Updike, *Rabbit Redux*, 242, 342, 348, 370.

83. Updike, "On Not Being a Dove," in *Self-Consciousness*, 117–120, 129.

84. Plath, *Conversations*, 119; Updike, "On Not Being a Dove," in *Self-Consciousness*, 143–144.

85. Updike, *Rabbit Redux*, 245, 322.

Conclusion

1. Sam Tanenhaus, "Man in the Middle," *New York Times Book Review*, November 18, 2012.

2. On Trump's support in Pennsylvania, see Ben Bradlee Jr., *The Forgotten: How the People of One Pennsylvania County Elected Trump and Changed America* (New York: Little, Brown & Co., 2018); Matt Flegenheimer and Thomas Kaplan, "Trump Won Pennsylvania, Democrats Want the State (and His Voters) Back,"

New York Times, August 19, 2018, https://www.nytimes.com/2018/08/19/us/politics/pennsylvania-democrats-trump.html; and Maria Panaritis et al., "How Trump Took Pennsylvania: Wins Everywhere (Almost) but the Southeast," *Philadelphia Enquirer,* November 9, 2016, https://www.philly.com/philly/news/politics/presidential/20161110_How_Trump_took_Pennsylvania_Wins_almost_everywhere_but_the_southeast.html.

3. Lane Windham, *Knocking on Labor's Door: Union Organizing in the 1970s and the Roots of a New Economic Divide* (Chapel Hill: University of North Carolina Press, 2017); Robert J. Gordon, *The Rise and Fall of American Growth* (Princeton, NJ: Princeton University Press, 2017); Alan Abramowitz and Ruy Teixeira, "The Decline of the White Working Class and the Rise of a Mass Upper-Middle Class," *Political Science Quarterly* 124, no. 3 (Fall 2009): 391–422.

4. On the changing nature of racism, see Justin Gest, *The New Minority: White Working Class Politics in an Age of Immigration and Inequality* (New York: Oxford University Press, 2016); Marisa Abrajano and Zoltan L. Hajnal, *White Backlash: Immigration, Race, and American Politics* (Princeton, NJ: Princeton University Press, 2015); F. Michael Higginbotham, *Ghosts of Jim Crow: Ending Racism in Post Racial America* (New York: NYU Press, 2013); and Michelle Alexander, *The New Jim Crow: Mass Incarceration in the Age of Colorblindness* (New York: New Press, 2012).

5. See Morris P. Fiorina, *Unstable Majorities: Polarization, Party Sorting and Political Stalemate* (Stanford: Hoover Institution Press, 2017). Geoffrey Kabaservice, *Rule and Ruin: The Downfall of Moderation and the Destruction of the Republican Party from Eisenhower to the Tea Party* (New Haven, CT: Yale University Press, 2013); Eric Alterman and Kevin Mattson, *The Cause: The Fight for American Liberalism from Franklin Roosevelt to Barack Obama* (New York: Viking, 2012); Bill Bishop, *The Big Sort: Why the Clustering of Like-Minded America Is Tearing Us Apart* (New York: Mariner Books, 2009).

6. Robert Wuthnow, *Left Behind: Decline and Rage in Rural America* (Princeton, NJ: Princeton University Press, 2018), 6, 9, 11. For similar narratives see Bradlee Jr., *The Forgotten*; J. D. Vance, *Hillbilly Elegy: A Memoir of a Family and Culture in Crisis* (New York: Harper, 2018); Arlie Russell Hochschild, *Strangers in Their Own Land: Anger and Mourning on the American Right* (New York: New Press, 2016); George Packer, *The Unwinding: An Inner History of a New America* (New York: Farrar, Straus & Giroux, 2014).

7. Tanenhaus, "Man in the Middle."

8. Flegenheimer and Kaplan, "Trump Won Pennsylvania."

9. Todd Gitlin, *The Sixties: Years of Hope, Days of Rage* (New York: Bantam, 1993), xiv.

10. Robert Kagan, *The World America Made* (New York: Knopf, 2012); G. John Ikenberry, *Liberal Leviathan: The Origins, Crisis and Transformation of the American World Order* (Princeton, NJ: Princeton University Press, 2011).

11. See Kim Phillips-Fein, *Fear City: New York's Fiscal Crisis and the Rise of Austerity Politics* (New York: Metropolitan Books, 2017); Nancy Fraser, "From Progressive Neoliberalism to Trump—and Beyond," *American Affairs* 1, no. 4 (Winter 2017), 46–64; Shane Hamilton, *Trucking Country: The Road to America's*

Wal-Mart Economy (Princeton, NJ: Princeton University Press, 2014), chapter 7; and Judith Stein, *Pivotal Decade: How the United States Traded Factories for Finance in the Seventies* (New Haven, CT: Yale University Press, 2010).

12. Kerner Commission, *Report of the National Advisory Commission on Civil Disorder* (New York: Bantam Books, 1968), 9. On its legacy, see Steven M. Gillon, *Separate and Unequal: The Kerner Commission and the Unraveling of American Liberalism* (New York: Basic Books, 2018), 5. On the failures of racial liberalism and the Great Society, see Daniel Geary, *Beyond Civil Rights: The Moynihan Report and Its Legacy* (Philadelphia: University of Pennsylvania Press, 2015); Nancy MacLean, *Freedom Is Not Enough: The Opening of the American Workplace* (Cambridge, MA: Harvard University Press, 2008); Elizabeth Hinton, *From the War on Poverty to the War on Crime: The Making of Mass Incarceration in America* (Cambridge, MA: Harvard University Press, 2017); and Julian E. Zelizer, *The Fierce Urgency of Now: Lyndon Johnson, Congress, and the Battle for the Great Society* (New York: Penguin, 2015), chapter 8.

13. On civil religion, see Kevin M. Kruse, *One Nation under God: How Corporate America Invented Christian America* (New York: Basic Books, 2015), chapters 3–6.

14. Michael McGerr, *A Fierce Discontent: The Rise and Fall of the Progressive Movement in America, 1870–1920* (New York: Oxford University Press, 2005); Michael Kazin, *A Godly Hero: The Life of William Jennings Bryan* (New York: Knopf, 2006); Christopher H. Evans, *The Social Gospel in American Religion: A History* (New York: NYU Press, 2017); Leigh E. Schmidt and Sally M. Promey, eds., *American Religious Liberalism* (Bloomington: Indiana University Press, 2012).

15. For examples see Jeff Taylor, *Where Did the Party Go? William Jennings Bryan, Hubert Humphrey and the Jeffersonian Tradition* (Columbia: University of Missouri Press, 2006); Kazin, *A Godly Hero*; Richard Hofstadter, *The Age of Reform* (New York: Knopf, 1955); Woodrow Wilson, *The New Freedom: A Call for Emancipation of the Generous Energies of A People* (New York: Doubleday, 1913).

16. John F. Kennedy, Acceptance speech at the Democratic National Convention, July 15, 1960, https://www.jfklibrary.org/learn/about-jfk/historic-speeches/acceptance-of-democratic-nomination-for-president.

17. John Updike, "Africa: Out of the Glum Continent," in *Picked-Up Pieces* (Greenwich, CT: Fawcett, 1975), 319.

18. John Updike, *Hugging the Shore: Essays and Criticism* (New York: Vintage, 1984), xix.

19. John Updike to Plowville (i.e., his parents), November 3, 1951, JUP, folder 6887.

20. On the criticism, see John Updike, *Self-Consciousness* (New York: Knopf, 1989), chapter 4; David Denby, "A Life of Sundays," *New Republic*, May 22, 1989, 29–33; and Elizabeth Hardwick, "Citizen Updike," *New York Review of Books*, May 18, 1989, https://www.nybooks.com/articles/1989/05/18/citizen-updike/.

21. Jim Plath, ed., *Conversations with John Updike* (Jackson: University Press of Mississippi, 1994), 50, 61.

22. Plath, *Conversations*, 78.

23. William Deresiewicz, "Controlled Rapture," *New Republic,* September 14, 2014, https://newrepublic.com/article/119200/updike-reviewed-william-deresiewicz; Michael Potemra, "Looking for Updike, Again," *National Review Online,* September 10, 2010, http://www.nationalreview.com/corner/387549/looking-updike-again-michael-potemra.

24. The impact of the Cold War on Updike's work is dealt with at length in D. Quentin Miller, *John Updike and the Cold War* (Columbia: University of Missouri Press, 2001).

25. See Jeffery Bloodworth, *Losing the Center: The Decline of American Liberalism 1968–1992* (Louisville: University of Kentucky Press, 2013); Bruce Miroff, *The Liberal's Moment: The McGovern Insurgency and the Identity Crisis of the Democratic Party* (Lawrence: University Press of Kansas, 2007); Timothy Stanley, *Kennedy vs. Carter: The 1980 Battle for the Democratic Party's Soul* (Lawrence: University Press of Kansas, 2010); and Steven M. Gillon, *The Democrats' Dilemma: Walter Mondale and the Liberal Legacy* (New York: Columbia University Press, 1992). The pendulum swung back toward the center with the establishment of the Democratic Leadership Council and the reestablishment of more centrist candidates in the party leadership. See Al From and Bill Clinton, *The New Democrats and the Return to Power* (New York: Palgrave Macmillan 2013); Kenneth S. Baer, *Reinventing Democrats* (Lawrence: University Press of Kansas, 2000).

26. Doug Rossinow, "Partners for Progress? Liberals and Radicals in the Long Twentieth Century," in *Making Sense of American Liberalism,* ed. Jonathan Bell and Timothy Stanley (Urbana: University of Illinois Press, 2012), 17–33 at 32.

27. Updike, "On Not Being a Dove," in *Self-Consciousness,* 112–114; Cecil Woolf and John Bagguley, eds., *Authors Take Sides on Vietnam* (New York: Simon & Schuster, 1967).

28. Updike, "On Not Being a Dove," in *Self-Consciousness,* 127–28; John Updike, *Rabbit Angstrom: A Tetralogy* (New York: Everyman's Library, 1995), xiii–xiv.

29. Yoav Fromer, "Democrats Shouldn't Fear Sanders Talk of Revolution. Their Party Was Built on It," *Washington Post,* February 14, 2016; Michael Kazin, *American Dreamers: How the Left Changed a Nation* (New York: Vintage, 2012); Doug Rossinow, *Visions of Progress: The Left-Liberal Tradition in America* (Philadelphia: University of Pennsylvania Press, 2009); Kevin Mattson, *Intellectuals in Action: The Origins of the New Left and Radical Liberalism 1945–1970* (University Park: Penn State University Press, 2002).

30. Students for a Democratic Society, "The Port Huron Statement," in *Democracy Is in the Streets: From Port Huron to the Siege of Chicago* by James Miller (Cambridge, MA: Harvard University Press, 1994), 331–333.

31. Updike, "A Soft Spring Night in Shillington," and "At War with My Skin," in *Self-Consciousness,* 30, 55.

32. Christopher Lasch, *The True and Only Heaven: Progress and Its Critics* (New York: W. W. Norton, 1991), 17.

33. Richard Chase, *The Democratic Vista* (New York: Doubleday, 1958), 145.

34. John Updike, *Buchanan Dying: A Play* (New York: Random House, 2013),

x–xi. On Updike's political inspirations for writing the play, see Plath, *Conversations*, 140–143.

35. Updike, *Picked-Up Pieces*, 491.

36. Martin Luther King Jr., "Letter from Birmingham City Jail," April 16, 1963, http://www.africa.upenn.edu/Articles_Gen/Letter_Birmingham.html.

37. Alexis de Tocqueville, *Democracy in America* (New York: Harper Perennial, 2006), 638.

38. For examples see Louis Hartz, *The Liberal Tradition in America* (New York: Harcourt, Brace & World, 1955); and Richard Hofstadter, *The American Political Tradition and the Men Who Made It* (New York: Knopf, 1948).

39. Updike, *Rabbit Angstrom*, xv–xvi.

40. John Updike, *Rabbit, Run, Rabbit Redux, Rabbit Is Rich* (New York: Quality Paperback Book Club, 1990), 263–264, 349. On Rabbit's reeducation, see Adam Begley, *Updike* (New York: Harper, 2014), 334–336.

41. Plath, *Conversations*, 224; Charlie Reilly, "An Interview with John Updike," *Contemporary Literature* 43, no. 2 (Summer 2002): 217–248 at 239.

Bibliography

Books

Abrajano, Marisa, and Zoltan L. Hajnal. *White Backlash: Immigration, Race, and American Politics.* Princeton, NJ: Princeton University Press, 2015.
Abramowitz, Alan I. *The Polarized Public: Why American Government Is So Dysfunctional.* New York: Pearson, 2012.
Adams, Henry. *The Education of Henry Adams.* Boston: Houghton Mifflin, 1918.
Aldridge, John W. *Time to Murder and Create.* New York: David McKay, 1966.
Alexander, Michelle. *The New Jim Crow: Mass Incarceration in the Age of Colorblindness.* New York: New Press, 2012.
Alterman, Eric, and Kevin Mattson. *The Cause: The Fight for American Liberalism from Franklin Roosevelt to Barack Obama.* New York: Viking, 2012.
Alumkal, Antony. *Paranoid Science: The Christian Right's War on Reality.* New York: NYU Press, 2017.
Arendt, Hannah. *The Human Condition.* Chicago: University of Chicago Press, 1958.
———. *On Revolution.* New York: Penguin, 1963.
———. *The Origins of Totalitarianism.* New York: Harcourt Brace Jovanovich, 1973.
———. *The Portable Hannah Arendt.* New York: Penguin, 2000.
Aristotle. *Nicomachean Ethics.* Mineola, NY: Dover, 1998.
———. *The Poetics.* London: Macmillan and Co., 1917.
Arnold, Matthew. *Culture and Anarchy.* New York: Cambridge University Press, 1971.
Ashby, LeRoy. *William Jennings Bryan: Champion of Democracy.* New York: Twayne, 1987.
Baer, Kenneth S. *Reinventing Democrats.* Lawrence: University Press of Kansas, 2000.
Balint, Benjamin. *Running Commentary: The Contentious Magazine That Transformed the Jewish Left into the Neoconservative Right.* New York: Public Affairs, 2010.
Batchelor, Bob. *Updike: A Critical Biography.* New York: Praeger, 2013.
Beard, Charles, and Mary Beard. *The Rise of American Civilization.* Vol. 2. New York: Macmillan, 1934.
Begley, Adam. *Updike.* New York: Harper, 2014.
Bell, Daniel, ed. *The Coming of Postindustrial Society: A Venture in Social Forecasting.* New York: Basic Books, 1976.

———. *The Cultural Contradictions of Capitalism*. New York: Basic Books, 1976.
———. *The End of Ideology*. New York: Free Press, 1962.
———, ed. *The Radical Right*. Livingston, NJ: Transaction, 2002.
———. *Work and Its Discontent: The Cult of Efficiency in America*. Boston: Beacon Press, 1956.
Bell, Jonathan, and Timothy Stanley, eds. *Making Sense of American Liberalism*. Urbana: University of Illinois Press, 2012.
Bellah, Robert N. *Habits of the Heart: Individualism and Commitment in American Life*. Berkeley: University of California Press, 1985.
Berkowitz, Peter. *Virtue and the Making of Modern Liberalism*. Princeton, NJ: Princeton University Press, 1999.
Berlin, Isaiah. *The Crooked Timber of Humanity*. London: John Murray, 1990.
———. *Enlightening: Letters 1946–1960*. London: Chatto & Windus, 2009.
Bishop, Bill. *The Big Sort: Why the Clustering of Like-Minded America Is Tearing Us Apart*. New York: Mariner Books, 2009.
Bloodworth, Jeffery. *Losing the Center: The Decline of American Liberalism 1968–1992*. Louisville: University of Kentucky Press, 2013.
Bloom, Alexander. *Prodigal Sons: The New York Intellectuals and Their World*. New York: Oxford University Press, 1986.
Bloom, Harold. *John Updike: Modern Critical Views*. New York: Chelsea House, 1988.
Bloom, Joshua, and Waldo E. Martin. *Black against Empire: The History and Politics of the Black Panther Party*. Berkeley: University of California Press, 2014.
Boltanski, Luc, and Eve Chiapello. *The New Spirit of Capitalism*. New York: Verso, 2007.
Boorstin, Daniel J. *The Genius of American Politics*. Chicago: University of Chicago Press, 1953.
Boswell, Marshall. *Mastered Irony in Motion: John Updike's Rabbit Tetralogy*. Columbia: University of Missouri Press, 2001.
Boyers, Robert. *The Dictator's Dictation: The Politics of Novels and Novelists*. New York: Columbia University Press, 2005.
———. *Lionel Trilling*. Columbia: University of Missouri Press, 1977.
Bradlee, Ben, Jr. *The Forgotten: How the People of One Pennsylvania County Elected Donald Trump and Changed America*. New York: Little, Brown and Co., 2018.
Brick, Howard. *Daniel Bell and the Decline of Intellectual Radicalism*. Madison: University of Wisconsin Press, 1986.
———. *Transcending Capitalism: Visions of a New Society in Modern American Thought*. Ithaca: Cornell University Press, 2006.
Brinkley, Alan. *The End of Reform*. New York: Knopf, 1995.
———. *Liberalism and Its Discontents*. Cambridge, MA: Harvard University Press, 1998.
———. *Voices of Protest: Huey Long, Father Coughlin and the Great Depression*. New York: Knopf, 1982.
Brinton, Crane. *The Anatomy of Revolution*. New York: Vintage, 1965.
Brock, Clifton. *Americans for Democratic Action: Its Role in National Politics*. New York: Praeger, 1985.

Broer, Lawrence R., ed. *Rabbit Tales: Poetry and Politics in John Updike's Rabbit Novels*. Tuscaloosa: University of Alabama Press, 1998.
Brown, David S. *Richard Hofstadter: An Intellectual Biography*. Chicago: University of Chicago Press, 2007.
Bryan, William Jennings. *William Jennings Bryan: Selections*. Indianapolis: Bobbs Merrill, 1967.
Burns, Jennifer. *Goddess of the Market: Ayn Rand and the American Right*. New York: Oxford University Press, 2009.
Campbell, Angus. *The American Voter*. New York: John Wiley & Sons, 1960.
Campbell, Jeff H. *Updike's Novels: Thorns Spell a Word*. Wichita Falls, TX: Midwestern State University Press, 1988.
Chase, Richard. *The Democratic Vista*. New York: Doubleday, 1958.
Coates, Ta-Nehisi. *Between the World and Me*. New York: Spiegel & Grau, 2015.
———. *We Were Eight Years in Power: An American Tragedy*. New York: One World, 2017.
Cohen, Lizabeth. *A Consumer's Republic*. New York: Vintage, 2003.
———. *Making a New Deal: Industrial Workers in Chicago 1919–1939*. New York: Cambridge University Press, 2008.
Conant, James Bryant. *Education in a Divided World*. Cambridge, MA: Harvard University Press, 1948.
Connolly, Andrew. *Philip Roth and the American Liberal Tradition*. Lanham, MD: Lexington Books, 2017.
Cowie, Jefferson R. *The Great Exception: The New Deal and the Limits of American Politics*. Princeton, NJ: Princeton University Press, 2016.
———. *Stayin Alive: The 1970s and the Last Days of the Working Class*. New York: New Press, 2010.
Critchlow, Donald T. *The Conservative Ascendancy: How the GOP Right Made Political History*. Cambridge, MA: Harvard University Press, 2007.
———. *Phyllis Schlafly and Grassroots Conservatism: A Women's Crusade*. Princeton, NJ: Princeton University Press, 2008.
Croly, Herbert. *The Promise of American Life*. Princeton, NJ: Princeton University Press, 2014.
Cronin, Gloria L., and Lee Trepanier, eds. *A Political Companion to Saul Bellow*. Louisville: University of Kentucky Press, 2013.
Crouter, Richard. *Reinhold Niebuhr: On Politics, Religion and Christian Faith*. New York: Oxford University Press, 2010.
Dahl, Robert A. *Polyarchy: Participation and Opposition*. New Haven, CT: Yale University Press, 1972.
———. *A Preface to Democratic Theory*. Chicago: University of Chicago Press, 1956.
———. *Who Governs? Democracy and Power in an American City*. New Haven, CT Yale University Press, 1966.
Dalton, Russell J. *The Good Citizen*. Washington, DC: CQ Press, 2009.
De Bellis, Jack. *The John Updike Encyclopedia*. Westport, CT: Greenwood Press, 2000.
———. *John Updike's Early Years*. Bethlehem, PA: Lehigh University Press, 2013.
Deneen, Patrick J. *Why Liberalism Failed*. New Haven, CT: Yale University Press, 2018.

Deneen, Patrick J., and Joseph Romance, eds. *Democracy's Literature: Politics and Fiction in America.* Lanham, MD: Rowman & Littlefield, 2005.
Denning, Michael. *The Cultural Front.* New York: Verso, 1997.
Dewey, John. *Liberalism and Social Action.* New York: Capricorn Books, 1935.
———. *The Public and Its Problems.* New York: Henry Holt, 1927.
Dickstein, Morris. *Gates of Eden: American Culture in the Sixties.* Cambridge, MA: Harvard University Press, 1997.
———. *Leopards in the Temple.* Cambridge, MA: Harvard University Press, 2002.
Diggins, John Patrick, ed. *The Liberal Persuasion: Arthur Schlesinger Jr. and the Challenge of the American Past.* Princeton, NJ: Princeton University Press, 1997.
Dill, Scott, and Matthew Shipe, eds., *Updike and Politics: Due Considerations.* Lanham, MD: Lexington Books, 2019.
Dochuk, Darren. *From Bible Belt to Sunbelt: Plain-Folk Religion, Grassroots Politics, and the Rise of Evangelical Conservatism.* New York: W. W. Norton, 2012.
Doherty, Thomas. *Cold War, Cool Medium: Television, McCarthyism, and American Culture.* New York: Columbia University Press, 2005.
Dolgoy, Erin L., ed. *Short Stories and Political Philosophies: Power, Prose and Persuasion.* Lanham, MD: Lexington Books, 2018.
Donaldson, Scott. *Archibald MacLeish: An American Life.* Boston: Houghton Mifflin, 1992.
Drabeck, Bernard A., and Helen E. Ellis, eds. *Archibald MacLeish, Reflections.* Amherst: University of Massachusetts Press, 1986.
Dudley, Jonathan. *Broken Words: The Abuse of Science and Faith in American Politics.* New York: Crown, 2011.
Dudziak, Mary L. *Cold War Civil Rights: Race and the Image of American Democracy.* Princeton, NJ: Princeton University Press, 2008.
Dunayevskaya, Raya. *Marxism and Freedom . . . from 1776 until Today.* New York: Bookman Associates, 1958.
Eagleton, Terry. *Literary Criticism: An Introduction.* Minneapolis: University of Minnesota Press, 2008.
Edelstein, Dan. *On the Spirit of Rights.* Chicago: University of Chicago Press, 2018.
Edsall, Thomas, and Mary Edsall. *Chain Reaction: The Impact of Race, Rights and Taxes on American Politics.* New York: W. W. Norton & Co., 1992.
Ehrman, John. *The Rise of Neoconservatism: Intellectuals and Foreign Affairs, 1945–1994.* New Haven, CT: Yale University Press, 1996.
Ekirch, Arthur A. *The Decline of American Liberalism.* New York: Longmans & Green, 1955.
Ellul, Jacques. *The Technological Society.* New York: Vintage, 1964.
Engel, Jonathan. *American Therapy: The Rise of Psychotherapy in the United States.* New York: Gotham, 2008.
Ernesto-Zirakzadeh, Cyrus, and Simon Stow, eds. *A Political Companion to John Steinbeck.* Louisville: University of Kentucky Press, 2013.
Fanon, Frantz. *Black Skin, White Masks.* New York: Grove Press, 2008.
Farber, David. *The Age of Great Dreams.* New York: Hill & Wang, 1994.
———. *The Rise and Fall of Modern American Conservatism.* Princeton, NJ: Princeton University Press, 2008.

Farmer, Michial. *Imagination and Idealism in John Updike's Fiction*. Rochester, NY: Camden House, 2017.
Fawcett, Edmund. *Liberalism: The Life of an Idea*. Princeton, NJ: Princeton University Press, 2014.
Ferguson, Karen. *Top Down: The Ford Foundation, Black Power, and the Reinvention of Racial Liberalism*. Philadelphia: University of Pennsylvania Press, 2013.
Filreis, Alan. *Modernism from Right to Left*. New York: Cambridge University Press, 1994.
Fiorina, Morris P. *Unstable Majorities: Polarization, Party Sorting and Political Stalemate*. Stanford, CA: Hoover Institution Press, 2017.
Fiorina, Morris P., and Samuel Abrams. *Culture Wars? The Myth of a Polarized America*. New York: Longman, 2010.
Fischer, Claude S. *Still Connected: Family and Friends in America since the 1970s*. New York: Russell Sage Foundation, 2011.
Fishman, Ethan. *Likely Stories: Essays on Political Philosophy and Contemporary American Literature*. Gainesville: University of Florida Press, 1989.
Flamm, Michael W. *Law and Order: Street Crime, Civil Unrest, and the Crisis of Liberalism in the 1960s*. New York: Columbia University Press, 2007.
Foucault, Michel. *Madness and Civilization: A History of Insanity in the Age of Reason*. New York: Vintage, 1988.
Fowler, Robert B. *Believing Skeptics: American Political Intellectuals, 1945–1967*. Westport, CT: Greenwood Press, 1978.
Fraser, Steve, and Gary Gerstle, eds. *The Rise and Fall of the New Deal Order 1930–1980*. Princeton, NJ: Princeton University Press, 1990.
Freidman, Milton. *Capitalism and Freedom*. Chicago: University of Chicago Press: 1962.
From, Al, and Bill Clinton. *The New Democrats and the Return to Power*. New York: Palgrave Macmillan, 2013.
Fromm, Erich. *Marx's Concept of Man*. New York: Frederick Ungar Publishing, 1961.
Galbraith, John Kenneth. *The Affluent Society*. London: Hamish Hamilton, 1958.
Gest, Justin. *The New Minority: White Working Class Politics in an Age of Immigration and Inequality*. New York: Oxford University Press, 2016.
Gillon, Steven M. *The Democrats' Dilemma: Walter Mondale and the Liberal Legacy*. New York: Columbia University Press, 1992.
———. *Separate and Unequal: The Kerner Commission and the Unraveling of American Liberalism*. New York: Basic Books, 2018.
Gitlin, Todd. *The Sixties: Years of Hope, Days of Rage*. New York: Bantam, 1993.
Goodman, Paul. *Growing Up Absurd*. New York: Vintage, 1962.
Gottfried, Paul E. *After Liberalism: Mass Democracy in the Managerial State*. Princeton, NJ: Princeton University Press, 2001.
Greiner, Donald J. *John Updike's Novels*. Athens: Ohio University Press, 1984.
Gullette, Margaret M. *Safe at Last in the Middle Years: The Invention of the Midlife Progress Novel*. Berkeley: University of California Press, 1988.
Gunn, Jeremy T. *Spiritual Weapons: The Cold War and the Forging of an American National Religion*. New York: Praeger, 2008.
Halberstam, David. *The Best and the Brightest*. New York: Ballantine Book, 1993.

———. *The Fifties*. New York: Ballantine Books, 1994.
Hale, Grace E. *Making Whiteness: The Culture of Segregation in the South 1890–1940*. New York: Vintage, 1999.
Halliwell, Martin. *Therapeutic Revolutions: Medicine, Psychiatry and American Culture, 1945–1970*. New Brunswick, NJ: Rutgers University Press, 2014.
Hamilton, Shane. *Trucking Country: The Road to America's Wal-Mart Economy*. Princeton, NJ: Princeton University Press, 2008.
Harris, Fred R., and Lynn Curtis, eds. *Locked in the Poorhouse: Cities, Race and Poverty in the United States*. Lanham, MD: Rowman & Littlefield, 1998.
Hartz, Louis. *The Liberal Tradition in America*. Boston: Harcourt, Brace & World, 1955.
Havelock, Eric A. *The Liberal Temper in Greek Politics*. New Haven, CT: Yale University Press, 1964.
Hayek, Friedrich. *The Constitution of Liberty*. Chicago: University of Chicago Press, 1960.
———. *The Road to Serfdom*. Chicago: University of Chicago Press, 1944.
Hendin, Josephine. *Vulnerable People: A View of American Fiction since 1945*. New York: Oxford University Press, 1978.
Herzog, Jonathan P. *The Spiritual-Industrial Complex: America's Religious Battle against Communism in the Early Cold War*. New York: Oxford University Press, 2011.
Higginbotham, F. Michael. *Ghosts of Jim Crow: Ending Racism in Post Racial America*. New York: NYU Press, 2013.
Hinchman, Lewis, and Sandra Hinchman, eds. *Hannah Arendt: Critical Essays*. Albany: SUNY Press, 1994.
Hirsch, Arnold R. *Making the Second Ghetto: Race and Housing in Chicago 1940–1960*. Chicago: University of Chicago Press, 1998.
Hoberek, Andrew. *The Twilight of the Middle Class: Post–World War II Fiction and White Collar Work*. Princeton, NJ: Princeton University Press, 2005.
Hochschild, Arlie Russell. *Strangers in their Own Land: Anger and Mourning on the American Right*. New York: New Press, 2016.
Hodgson, Godfrey. *The Gentleman from New York: Daniel Patrick Moynihan: A Biography*. Boston: Houghton Mifflin Harcourt, 2000.
———. *The Myth of American Exceptionalism*. New Haven, CT: Yale University Press, 2009.
Hofstadter, Richard. *The Age of Reform*. New York: Knopf, 1955.
———. *The American Political Tradition and the Men Who Made It*. New York: Knopf, 1948.
Hollinger, David A. *In the American Province*. Baltimore: Johns Hopkins University Press, 1985.
Hollings, Ken. *Welcome to Mars: Politics, Pop Culture and Weird Science in 1950s America*. Berkley: North Atlantic Press, 2014.
Hook, Sidney. *Out of Step: An Unquiet Life in the Twentieth Century*. New York: HarperCollins, 1987.
Horowitz, Daniel. *The Anxieties of Affluence*. Amherst: University of Massachusetts Press, 2005.

Hunt, George W. *John Updike and the Three Great Secret Things: Sex, Religion and Art.* Grand Rapids, MI: Eerdmans, 1980.
Hutchinson, William R. *The Modernist Impulse in American Protestantism.* Raleigh-Durham: Duke University Press, 1992.
Hyman, Louis. *Debtor Nation: The History of America in Red Ink.* Princeton, NJ: Princeton University Press, 2012.
Ikenberry, John G. *Liberal Leviathan.* Princeton, NJ: Princeton University Press, 2011.
Imber, Jonathan B., ed. *Therapeutic Culture: Triumph and Defeat.* Livingston, NJ: Transaction Publishers, 2004.
Jackson, Kenneth T. *Crabgrass Frontier: The Suburbanization of the United States.* New York: Oxford University Press, 1987.
Jenkins, Philip. *Decades of Nightmares: The End of the Sixties and the Making of the Eighties.* New York: Oxford University Press, 2008.
Johnson, David Kay. *The Lavender Scare: The Cold War Persecution of Gays and Lesbians in the Federal Government.* Chicago: University of Chicago Press, 2006.
Jumonville, Neil, ed. *The New York Intellectuals Reader.* London: Routledge, 2007.
Kabaservice, Geoffrey. *Rule and Ruin: The Downfall of Moderation and the Destruction of the Republican Party from Eisenhower to the Tea Party.* New Haven, CT: Yale University Press, 2013.
Kagan, Robert. *The World America Made.* New York: Knopf, 2012.
Katznelson, Ira. *Fear Itself: The New Deal and the Origins of Our Time.* New York: Liveright Publishing, 2014.
———. *When Affirmative Action Was White.* New York: W. W. Norton, 2005.
Kazin, Michael. *American Dreamers: How the Left Changed a Nation.* New York: Vintage, 2012.
———. *A Godly Hero: The Life of William Jennings Bryan.* New York: Knopf, 2006.
———. *The Populist Persuasion: An American History.* New York: Basic Books, 1995.
Keller, Morton, and Phyllis Keller. *Making Harvard Modern: The Rise of America's University.* New York: Oxford University Press, 2001.
Kierkegaard, Soren. *Fear and Trembling.* New York: Penguin, 1986.
Kimmage, Michael. *The Conservative Turn: Lionel Trilling, Whittaker Chambers, and the Lessons of Anti-Communism.* Cambridge, MA: Harvard University Press, 2009.
———. *In History's Grip: Philip Roth's Newark Trilogy.* Stanford, CA: Stanford University Press, 2012.
Kirk, Russell. *The Conservative Mind.* Chicago: Regnery, 1953.
Kirsch, Adam. *Why Trilling Matters.* New Haven, CT: Yale University Press, 2011.
Kloppenberg, James T. *The Virtues of Liberalism.* New York: Oxford University Press, 1998.
Klosko, George. *The Transformation of American Liberalism.* New York: Oxford University Press, 2017.
Knoll, Mark A. *The Old Religion in a New World: The History of North American Christianity.* Grand Rapids, MI: Eerdmans, 2002.

Koenig, Louis W. *Bryan: A Political Biography of William Jennings Bryan.* New York: Putnam, 1971.
Kristol, Irving. *Neoconservatism: The Autobiography of an Idea.* New York: Free Press, 1995.
Krupnik, Mark. *Lionel Trilling and the Fate of Cultural Criticism.* Evanston, IL: Northwestern University Press, 1986.
Kruse, Kevin M. *White Flight: Atlanta and the Making of Modern Conservatism.* Princeton, NJ: Princeton University Press, 2007.
Kun, Josh, and Laura Pulido, eds. *Black and Brown in Los Angeles.* Berkeley: University of California Press, 2014.
Larson, Edward J. *Summer for the Gods: The Scopes Trial and America's Continuing Debate over Science and Religion.* New York: Basic Books, 2006.
Lasch, Christopher. *The Agony of the American Left.* New York: Knopf, 1969.
———. *The American Liberals and the Russian Revolution.* New York: Columbia University Press, 1962.
———. *The Culture of Narcissism: American Life in an Age of Diminishing Expectations.* New York: W. W. Norton, 1991.
———. *Haven in a Heartless World: The Family Besieged.* New York: W. W. Norton, 1978.
———. *The New Radicalism in America 1889–1963: The Intellectual as a Social Type.* New York: W. W. Norton, 1965.
———. *The True and Only Heaven: Progress and Its Critics.* New York: W. W. Norton, 1991.
Lassiter, Matthew D. *The Silent Majority: Suburban Politics in the Sunbelt South.* Princeton, NJ: Princeton University Press, 2007.
Leuchtenburg, William E. *Franklin D. Roosevelt and the New Deal 1932–1940.* New York: Harpers & Row, 1963.
Levin, Harry. *Grounds for Comparison.* Cambridge, MA: Harvard University Press, 1972.
Lilla, Mark. *The Once and Future Liberal: After Identity Politics.* New York: Harper, 2017.
Lippmann, Walter. *Drift and Mastery.* New York: Henry Holt & Co., 1917.
Lipset, Seymour Martin. *American Exceptionalism: A Double-Edged Sword.* New York: W. W. Norton, 1997.
Lipset, S. M., and David Riesman. *Education and Politics at Harvard.* New York: McGraw Hill, 1971.
Litwack, Leon F. *Been in the Storm So Long: Aftermath of Slavery.* New York: Vintage, 1979.
Lowi, Theodore J. *The End of Liberalism.* New York: W. W. Norton, 1969.
Luytens, David Bulwer. *The Creative Encounter.* London: Secker & Warburg, 1960.
MacIntyre, Alasdair. *After Virtue: A Study in Moral Theory.* Notre Dame: University of Notre Dame Press, 2007.
Mackenzie, G. Calvin, and Robert Weisbrot. *The Liberal Hour: Washington and the Politics of Change in the 1960s.* New York: Penguin, 2009.
MacLean, Nancy. *Freedom Is Not Enough: The Opening of the American Workplace.* Cambridge, MA: Harvard University Press, 2008.

MacLeish, Archibald. *Collected Poems: 1917–1982*. New York: Mariner, 1985.
———. *Freedom Is the Right to Choose*. Boston: Beacon, 1951.
Macnaughton, William R., ed. *Critical Essays on John Updike*. Boston: G. K. Hall and Co., 1982.
Mantler, Gordon K. *Power to the Poor: Black-Brown Coalition and the Fight for Economic Justice*. Chapel Hill: University of North Carolina Press, 2013.
Marable, Manning. *Malcolm X: A Life of Reinvention*. New York: Viking, 2011.
Marling, Karal Ann. *As Seen on TV: The Visual Culture of Everyday Life in the 1950s*. Cambridge, MA: Harvard University Press, 1996.
Marsden, George M. *Fundamentalism in American Culture*. New York: Oxford University Press, 2006.
———. *The Twilight of the American Enlightenment: The 1950s and the Crisis of Liberal Belief*. New York: Basic Books, 2014.
Martelle, Scott. *The Fear Within: Spies, Commies and American Democracy on Trial*. New Brunswick, NJ: Rutgers University Press, 2011.
Mattson, Kevin. *Intellectuals in Action: The Origins of the New Left and Radical Liberalism 1945–1970*. University Park: Pennsylvania State University Press, 2002.
———. *When America Was Great: The Fighting Faith of Postwar Liberalism*. London: Routledge, 2004.
Matusow, Allen. *The Unraveling of America: A History of Liberalism in the 1960s*. New York: Harper & Row, 1984.
May, Elaine Tyler. *Homeward Bound: American Families in the Cold War Era*. New York: Basic Books, 1988.
May, Larry and Jerome Kohn, eds. *Hannah Arendt: Twenty Years Later*. Cambridge, MA: MIT Press, 1996.
Mazzeno, Laurence W. *Becoming John Updike: Critical Receptions, 1958–2010*. Rochester, NY: Camden House, 2013.
———. *Matthew Arnold: The Critical Legacy*. Rochester, NY: Camden House, 1999.
McCann, Sean. *Gumshoe America: Hard-Boiled Crime Fiction and the Rise and Fall of New Deal Liberalism*. Raleigh-Durham: Duke University Press, 2000.
———. *A Pinnacle of Feeling: American Literature and Presidential Government*. Princeton, NJ: Princeton University Press, 2008.
McGirr, Lisa. *Suburban Warriors: The Origins of the New American Right*. Princeton, NJ: Princeton University Press, 2002.
McInerny, Ralph. *Thomas Aquinas: Selected Writings*. London: Penguin, 1998.
McLean, Scott L., David A. Schultz, and Manfred B. Steger, eds. *Social Capital: Critical Perspectives on Community and "Bowling Alone."* New York: NYU Press, 2002.
McTavish, John. *Myth and Gospel in the Fiction of John Updike*. Eugene, OR: Cascade Books, 2016.
Mencken, H.L. *The Vintage Mencken*. New York: Knopf, 1955.
Miller, D. Quentin. *John Updike and the Cold War*. Columbia: University of Missouri Press, 2001.
Miller, Eric. *Hope in a Scattering Time: A Life of Christopher Lasch*. Grand Rapids, MI: Eerdmans, 2010.

Miller, James. *Can Democracy Work? A Short History of a Radical Idea, from Ancient Athens to Our World.* New York: Farrar, Straus & Giroux, 2018.

———. *Democracy Is in the Streets: From Port Huron to the Siege of Chicago.* Cambridge, MA: Harvard University Press, 1994.

Miller, Steven P. *Billy Graham and the Rise of the Republican South.* Philadelphia: University of Pennsylvania Press, 2011.

Mills, C. Wright. *White Collar.* New York: Oxford University Press, 1956.

Miroff, Bruce. *The Liberal's Moment: The McGovern Insurgency and the Identity Crisis of the Democratic Party.* Lawrence: University Press of Kansas, 2007.

Mooney, Chris. *The Republican War on Science.* New York: Basic Books, 2006.

Moreton, Bethany. *To Serve God and Walmart: The Making of Christian Free Enterprise.* Cambridge, MA: Harvard University Press, 2010.

Moynihan, Daniel P. *Family and Nation.* New York: Harcourt Brace Jovanovich, 1986.

———. *Miles to Go: A Personal History of Social Policy.* Cambridge, MA: Harvard University Press, 1997.

———. *The Politics of a Guaranteed Income.* New York: Random House, 1973.

———. *The Report of the National Advisory Commission on Civil Disorders.* Washington, DC: United States Department of Labor, 1965.

Moynihan, Daniel P., Timothy M. Smeeding, and Lee Rainwater, eds. *The Future of the Family.* New York: Russell Sage Foundation, 2006.

Nash, George H. *The Conservative Intellectual Movement in America since 1945.* New York: Basic Books, 1976.

Naveh, Eyal. *Reinhold Niebuhr and Non Utopian Liberalism: Beyond Illusion and Despair.* Brighton, UK: Sussex Academic Press, 2002.

Neary, John. *Something and Nothingness: The Fiction of John Updike and John Fowles.* Carbondale: Southern Illinois University Press, 1992.

Newman, Judie. *John Updike.* London: Macmillan Publishers, 1988.

Niebuhr, Reinhold. *The Irony of American History.* Chicago: University of Chicago Press, 2008.

———. *Moral Man, Immoral Society.* New York: Charles Scribner's Sons, 1932.

Nisbet, Robert. *The Quest for Community.* New York: Oxford University Press, 1953.

O'Connell, Mary. *The Patriarchal Dilemma: Masculinity in the Rabbit Novels.* Carbondale: Southern Illinois University Press, 1996.

Olster, Stacey, ed. *Cambridge Companion to John Updike.* New York: Cambridge University Press, 2006.

Ozick, Cynthia. *Art and Ardor.* New York: Knopf, 1983.

Packard, Vance. *A Nation of Strangers.* New York: Pocket Books, 1972.

Packer, George. *The Unwinding: An Inner History of a New America.* New York: Farrar, Straus & Giroux, 2014.

Pangle, Lorraine Smith. *Aristotle and the Philosophy of Friendship.* Cambridge, MA: Cambridge University Press, 2008.

Patterson, James T. *Freedom Is Not Enough: The Moynihan Report and America's Struggle over Black Family Life—from LBJ to Obama.* New York: Basic Books, 2010.

Patterson, Thomas E. *The Vanishing Voter: Public Involvement in an Age of Uncertainty.* New York: Vintage, 2003.
Pells, Richard H. *The Liberal Mind in a Conservative Age.* Middletown, CT: Wesleyan University Press, 1989.
Perlstein, Rick. *Nixonland: The Rise of a President and the Fracturing of America.* New York: Scribner, 2009.
Phillips-Fein, Kim. *Fear City: New York's Fiscal Crisis and the Rise of Austerity Politics.* New York: Metropolitan Books, 2017.
———. *Invisible Hands: The Businessmen's Crusade against the New Deal.* New York: W. W. Norton, 2010.
Plath, James, ed. *Conversations with John Updike.* Jackson: University Press of Mississippi, 1994.
Plotke, David. *Building a Democratic Political Order: Reshaping American Liberalism in the 1930s and 1940s.* New York: Cambridge University Press, 1996.
Pocock, J. G. A. *The Machiavellian Moment: Florentine Political Thought and the Atlantic Republican Tradition.* Princeton, NJ: Princeton: Princeton University Press, 1975.
Podhoretz, Norman. *Doings and Undoings.* New York: Farrar, Straus & Co., 1964.
———. *Making It.* New York: HarperCollins, 1980.
Polanyi, Karl. *The Great Transformation: Political and Economic Origins of Our Time.* Boston: Beacon, 2001.
Pritchard, William H. *Updike: America's Man of Letters.* Amherst: University of Massachusetts Press, 2005.
Putnam, Robert D. *Bowling Alone: The Collapse and Revival of American Community.* New York: Touchstone, 2000.
Putnam, Robert D., and David E. Campbell. *American Grace: How Religion Divides and Unites Us.* New York: Simon & Schuster, 2010.
Rainwater, Lee, and William L. Yancey, eds. *The* Moynihan Report *and the Politics of Controversy.* Cambridge, MA: MIT Press, 1967.
Rawls, John. *Political Liberalism.* New York: Columbia University Press, 1993.
The Report of the Harvard Committee on General Education in a Free Society. Cambridge, MA: Harvard University Press, 1945.
Rice, Daniel F. *Reinhold Niebuhr and John Dewey: An American Odyssey.* Albany: SUNY Press, 1993.
Richardson, Heather Cox. *The Death of Reconstruction: Race, Labor, and Politics in the Post–Civil War North 1861–1901.* Cambridge, MA: Harvard University Press, 2004.
Rieder, Jonathan. *Canarsie: The Jews and Italians of Brooklyn against Liberalism.* Cambridge, MA: Harvard University Press, 1987.
Rieff, Philip. *The Triumph of the Therapeutic: Uses of Faith after Freud.* New York: Harper & Row, 1966.
Rieff, Philip, and Jonathan B. Imber. *The Feeling Intellect: Selected Writings.* Chicago: University of Chicago Press, 1991.
Riesman, David. *The Lonely Crowd.* New York: Doubleday-Anchor, 1953.
Ristoff, Dilvo I. *Updike's America: Presence of Contemporary American History in John Updike's Rabbit Trilogy.* New York: Peter Lang, 1989.

Rorty, Richard. *Contingency, Irony and Solidarity.* Cambridge: Cambridge University Press, 1989.
Rosenblatt, Helena. *The Lost History of Liberalism: From Ancient Rome to the Twenty-First Century.* Princeton, NJ: Princeton University Press, 2018.
Rossinow, Doug. *Visions of Progress: The Left-Liberal Tradition in America.* Philadelphia: University of Pennsylvania Press, 2009.
Rossiter, Clinton. *Seedtime of the Republic.* New York: Harcourt, Brace & World, 1953.
Sandel, Michael D., *Democracy's Discontent.* Cambridge, MA: Belknap Press, 1996.
———, ed. *Liberalism and Its Critics.* New York: NYU Press, 1984.
Saunders, Frances S. *Cultural Cold War: The CIA and the World of Arts and Letters.* New York: New Press, 2001.
Scanlon, Sandra. *The Pro-War Movement: Domestic Support for the Vietnam War and the Making of Modern American Conservatism.* Amherst: University of Massachusetts Press, 2013.
Schickler, Eric. *Racial Realignment: The Transformation of American Liberalism, 1932–1965.* Princeton, NJ: Princeton University Press, 2016.
Schiff, James A. *John Updike Revisited.* New York: Twayne Publishers, 1998.
Schlesinger, Arthur M., Jr. *The Age of Jackson.* Boston: Little Brown & Co., 1945.
———. *The Age of Roosevelt: The Coming of the New Deal.* Boston: Houghton Mifflin, 1959.
———. *Journals, 1952–2000.* New York: Penguin, 2007.
———. *A Life in the Twentieth Century.* Boston: Houghton Mifflin, 2000.
———. *The Vital Center.* Boston: Houghton Mifflin, 1949.
Schreiber, Ronee. *Righting Feminism: Conservative Women and American Politics.* New York: Oxford University Press, 2008.
Schryer, Stephen. *Fantasies of the New Class: Ideologies of Professionalism in Post–World War II American Fiction.* New York: Columbia University Press, 2011.
Schudson, Michael. *The Good Citizen: A History of American Civic Life.* New York: Free Press, 1998.
Schulman, Bruce J., and Julian E. Zelizer, eds. *Rightward Bound: Making America Conservative in the 1970s.* Cambridge, MA: Harvard University Press, 2008.
Schulman, George. *American Prophesy: Race and Redemption in American Political Culture.* Minneapolis: University of Minnesota Press, 2008.
Schwartz, David R. *Moral Minority: The Evangelical Left in an Age of Conservatism.* Philadelphia: University of Pennsylvania Press, 2012.
Scott, David Meerman, and Richard Jurek. *Marketing the Moon: The Selling of the Apollo Lunar Program.* Cambridge, MA: MIT Press, 2014.
Scott, James C. *Seeing Like a State: How Certain Schemes to Improve the Human Condition Have Failed.* New Haven, CT: Yale University Press, 1998.
Searles, George J., ed. *Conversations with Philip Roth.* Jackson: University Press of Mississippi, 1992.
Self, Robert O. *All in the Family: The Realignment of American Democracy since the 1960s.* New York: Hill & Wang, 2012.
Shapiro, Edward S. *We Are Many: Reflections on American Jewish History and Identity.* Syracuse: Syracuse University Press, 2005.

Shepard, Stephan. *A Literary Journey to Jewish Identity*. New York: Bayberry Books, 2018.
Skocpol, Theda. *Diminished Democracy: From Membership to Management in American Civic Life*. Norman: University of Oklahoma Press, 2004.
Skocpol, Theda, and Morris P. Fiorina. *Civic Engagement in American Democracy*. Washington, DC: Brookings Institute Press, 1999.
Smith, Christian, ed. *The Secular Revolution: Power, Interests, and Conflict in the Secularization of American Public Life*. Berkeley: University of California Press, 2003.
Smith, Richard Norton. *The Harvard Century*. New York: Simon & Schuster, 1986.
Stanley, Timothy. *Kennedy vs. Carter: The 1980 Battle for the Democratic Party's Soul*. Lawrence: University Press of Kansas, 2010.
Steigerwald, David. *The Sixties and the End of Modern America*. New York: St. Martin's Press, 1995.
Stein, Judith. *Pivotal Decade: How the United States Traded Factories for Finance in the Seventies*. New Haven, CT: Yale University Press, 2011.
———. *Running Steel, Running America: Race, Economic Policy and the Decline of Liberalism*. Chapel Hill: University of North Carolina Press, 1998.
Steinfels, Peter. *The Neoconservatives: The Origins of a Movement*. New York: Simon & Schuster, 1979.
Stettner, Edward A. *Shaping Modern Liberalism: Herbert Croly and Progressive Thought*. Lawrence: University Press of Kansas, 1993.
Stow, Simon. *Republic of Readers: Literary Turn in Political Thought and Analysis*. Albany: SUNY Press, 2008.
Sugrue, Thomas J. *The Origins of the Urban Crisis*. Princeton, NJ: Princeton University Press, 2005.
Svoboda, Frederic. *Understanding John Updike*. Charleston: University of South Carolina Press, 2018.
Szalay, Michael. *Hip Figures: A Literary History of the Democratic Party*. Stanford, CA: Stanford University Press, 2012.
———. *New Deal Modernism*. Raleigh-Durham: Duke University Press, 2000.
Tanenhaus, Sam. *Whittaker Chambers: A Biography*. New York: Modern Library, 1998.
Taylor, Jeff. *Where Did the Party Go? William Jennings Bryan, Hubert Humphrey and the Jeffersonian Tradition*. Columbia: University of Missouri Press, 2006.
Tocqueville, Alexis de, *Democracy in America*. New York: Harper Perennial, 2006.
Trachtenberg, Stanley, ed. *New Essays on* Rabbit, Run. New York: Cambridge University Press, 1993.
Trilling, Lionel. *The Liberal Imagination*. New York: Anchor Books, 1953.
———. *Matthew Arnold*. New York: W. W. Norton, 1949.
Truman, David B. *The Governmental Process*. New York: Knopf, 1951.
Tuveson, Ernest Lee. *Redeemer Nation: The Idea of America's Millennial Role*. Chicago: University of Chicago Press, 1968.
Updike, John. *Assorted Prose*. New York: Knopf, 1965.
———. *Buchanan Dying: A Play*. New York: Random House, 2013.

———. *The Carpeted Hen and Other Tame Creatures*. New York: Harper & Brothers, 1958.
———, ed. *A Century of Arts & Letters*. New York: Columbia University Press, 1998.
———. *The Complete Henry Bech*. New York: Everyman's Library, 2001.
———. *Couples*. New York: Knopf, 1968.
———. *Hugging the Shore*. New York: Vintage, 1984.
———. *John Updike: The Early Stories 1953–1975*. New York: Ballantine Books, 2003.
———. *Midpoint and Other Poems*. New York: Knopf, 1969.
———. *More Matter: Essays and Criticism*. New York: Knopf, 1999.
———. *Museums and Women*. New York: Knopf, 1972.
———. *The Music School*. New York: Knopf, 1966.
———. *Odd Jobs: Essays and Criticism*. New York: Knopf, 1991.
———. *Picked-Up Pieces*. Greenwich, CT: Fawcett Crest, 1975.
———. *Pigeon Feathers and Other Stories*. Greenwich, CT: Crest, 1963.
———. *The Poorhouse Fair*. New York: Knopf, 1963.
———. *The Poorhouse Fair*. New York: Knopf, 1977.
———. *Rabbit Angstrom: A Tetralogy*. New York: Everyman's Library, 1995.
———. *Rabbit, Run, Rabbit Redux, Rabbit Is Rich*. New York: Quality Paperback Book Club, 1990.
———. *Rabbit at Rest*. New York: Knopf, 1990.
———. *Self-Consciousness*. New York: Knopf, 1989.
———. *Tossing and Turning*. New York: Knopf, 1977.
Vance, J. D. *Hillbilly Elegy: A Memoir of a Family and Culture in Crisis*. New York: Harper, 2018.
Vanderlan, Robert. *Intellectuals Incorporated: Politics, Art, and Ideas inside Henry Luce's Media Empire*. Philadelphia: University of Pennsylvania Press, 2010.
Vernon, Mark. *The Meaning of Friendship*. New York: Palgrave Macmillan, 2010.
Wald, Alan M. *New York Intellectuals: The Rise and Decline of the Anti-Stalinist Left from the '30s to the '80s*. Chapel Hill: University of North Carolina Press, 1987.
Wall, Wendy L. *Inventing the "American Way": The Politics of Consensus from the New Deal to the Civil Rights Movement*. New York: Oxford University Press, 2008.
Waters, Malcolm. *Daniel Bell*. London: Routledge, 1996.
Wattenberg, Martin P. *Where Have All the Voters Gone?* Cambridge, MA: Harvard University Press, 2002.
Wayne, Stephen J. *Is This Any Way to Run a Democratic Election?* Washington, DC: CQ Press, 2011.
Weber, Max. *The Protestant Work Ethic and the Spirit of Capitalism*. New Yorker: Scribner's, 1958.
Westad, Odd Arne. *The Cold War: A World History*. New York: Basic Books, 2017.
White, Mark J. *Kennedy: The New Frontier Revisited*. New York: NYU Press, 1998.
Whyte, William H. *The Organization Man*. New York: Doubleday-Anchor, 1957.
Wilentz, Sean. *Chant's Democratic: New York City and the Rise of the American Working Class, 1788–1850*. New York: Oxford University Press, 2004.

Williams, Daniel K. *God's Own Party: The Making of the Christian Right.* New York: Oxford University Press, 2012.
Wills, Garry. *Head and Heart: A History of Christianity in America.* New York: Penguin, 2007.
Wilson, Edmund. *To the Finland Station: A Study in the Acting and Writing of History.* New York: Farrar, Straus & Giroux, 1972.
Windham, Lane. *Knocking on Labor's Door: Union Organizing in the 1970s and the Roots of a New Economic Divide.* Chapel Hill: University of North Carolina Press, 2017.
Winnick, R. H., ed. *Letters of Archibald MacLeish 1907 to 1982.* Boston: Houghton Mifflin, 1983.
Wood, Gordon S. *The Radicalism of the American Revolution.* New York: Vintage, 1993.
Wood, James. *The Broken Estate: Essays on Literature and Belief.* New York: Picador, 2010.
Woolf, Cecil, and John Bagguley, eds. *Authors Take Sides on Vietnam.* New York: Simon & Schuster, 1967.
Wrenn, John H. *John Dos Passos.* New York: Twayne, 1961.
Wuthnow, Robert. *Left Behind: Decline and Rage in Rural America.* Princeton, NJ: Princeton University Press, 2018.
Yagoda, Ben. *About Town: The New Yorker and the World It Made.* New York: Scribner, 2000.
Yancy, George. *Black Bodies, White Gazes.* Lanham, MD: Rowman & Littlefield, 2008.
Yeats, William Butler. *The Collected Poems of W. B. Yeats.* New York, Scribner, 1996.
Yerkes, James, ed. *John Updike and Religion.* Grand Rapids, MI: Eerdmans, 1999.
Young, Robert J. C. *Colonial Desire: Hybridity in Theory, Culture and Race.* London: Routledge, 1995.
Zaretsky, Natasha. *No Direction Home: The American Family and the Fear of National Decline, 1968–1980.* Chapel Hill: University of North Carolina Press, 2007.
Zielonka, Jan. *Counter-Revolution: Liberal Europe in Retreat.* New York: Oxford University Press, 2018.
Zuckert, Catherine H. *Natural Right and the American Imagination: Political Philosophy in Novel Form.* Lanham, MD: Rowman & Littlefield, 1990.

Articles, Book Chapters, Interviews, and Speeches

Abramowitz, Alan, and Ruy Teixeira. "The Decline of the White Working Class and the Rise of a Mass Upper-Middle Class." *Political Science Quarterly* 124, no. 3 (Fall 2009): 391–422.
Ahearn, Kerry. "Family and Adultery: Images and Ideas in Updike's Rabbit Novels." *Twentieth Century Literature* 34, no. 1 (Spring 1988): 62–83.
Arendt, Hannah. "Reflections on Little Rock." In *The Portable Hannah Arendt*, 231–245. New York: Penguin, 2000.

Fraser, Nancy. "From Progressive Neoliberalism to Trump—and Beyond." *American Affairs* 1, no. 4 (Winter 2017): 46–64.
Fromer, Yoav. "Democrats Shouldn't Fear Sanders's Talk of Revolution. Their Party Was Built on It." *Washington Post*, February 14, 2016.
———. "The Inside-Outsider: John Updike as a New York Intellectual—from Shillington, Pennsylvania." *John Updike Review* 4, no. 2 (Spring 2016): 29–55.
Geary, Daniel. "Children of the Lonely Crowd: David Riesman, the Young Radicals, and the Splitting of Liberalism in the 1960s." *Modern Intellectual History* 10, no. 3 (November, 2013): 603–633.
Gerstle, Gary. "Race and the Myth of the Liberal Consensus." *Journal of American History* 82, no. 2 (September 1995): 579–586.
Gingher, Robert. "Has John Updike Anything to Say?" *Modern Fiction Studies* 20, no. 1 (Spring 1974): 97–105.
Glover, Troy D. "All the Lonely People: Social Isolation and the Promises and Pitfall of Leisure." *Leisure Sciences* 40, no. 1 (January 2018): 25–35.
Greiner, Donald J. "Updike, Rabbit, and the Myth of American Exceptionalism." In *Cambridge Companion to John Updike*, edited by Stacey Olster, 149–161. New York: Cambridge University Press, 2006.
Hallissy, Margaret. "Updike's *Rabbit, Run* and Pascal's *Pensees*." *Christianity and Literature* 30, no. 2 (March 1981): 25–32.
Hardwick, Elizabeth. "Citizen Updike." *New York Review of Books*, May 18, 1989. https://www.nybooks.com/articles/1989/05/18/citizen-updike/.
Hofstadter, Richard. "The Pseudo-Conservative Revolt." In *The Radical Right*, edited by Daniel Bell, 63–81. Livingston, NJ: Transaction, 2001.
Howard, Jane. "Can a Nice Novelist Finish First?" *Life*, November 4, 1966, 74, 76, 79–82.
Howe, Irving. "This Age of Conformity." *Partisan Review* 21, no. 1 (January–February 1954): 7–33.
Iwamato, Iwao. "A Visit to Mr. Updike." In *Conversations with John Updike*, edited by James Plath, 115–123. Jackson: University Press of Mississippi, 1994.
Jackson, Edward M. "Rabbit Is Racist." *College Language Association Journal* 28 (1985): 445–451.
Jay, Martin. "The Frankfurt School's Critique of Marxist Humanism." *Social Research* 39, no. 3 (Summer 1972): 285–305.
Kazin, Alfred. "The Middle Way." *New York Review of Books*, December 17, 1992. https://www.nybooks.com/articles/1992/12/17/the-middle-way-2/.
Kennedy, John F. Acceptance Speech at the Democratic National Convention in Los Angeles, July 15, 1960. https://www.jfklibrary.org/learn/about-jfk/historic-speeches/acceptance-of-democratic-nomination-for-president.
———. Speech at Rice University, September 12, 1962. https://er.jsc.nasa.gov/seh/ricetalk.htm.
King, Martin Luther, Jr. "Letter from Birmingham City Jail." April 16, 1963. http://www.africa.upenn.edu/Articles_Gen/Letter_Birmingham.html.
Kirsch, Adam. "The Imaginary Jew." *New Republic*, July 9, 2012. http://www.newrepublic.com/book/review/the-imaginary-jew.
Kloppenberg, James T. "In Retrospect: Louis Hartz's the Liberal Tradition

in America." *Reviews in American History* 29, no. 3 (September 2001): 460–478.
Lasch, Christopher. "The Family as a Haven in a Heartless World." *Salmagundi* (Fall 1976): 42–55.
Lassiter, Matthew D. "Inventing Family Values." In *Rightward Bound: Making America Conservative in the 1970s*, edited by Bruce J. Schulman and Julian E. Zelizer, 13–28. Cambridge, MA: Harvard University Press, 2008.
Luce, Henry R. "The American Century." *Life*. February 17, 1941: 61–65.
Ludwig, Jeffrey. "Roommates and Rivals: John Updike, Christopher Lasch, and a Harvard University Friendship." *John Updike Review* (Spring 2013): 3–25.
Lynn, Kenneth S. "Son of 'Gen-Ed.'" *Commentary* 66, no. 3 (September 1978): 59–66.
Mailer, Norman. "Norman Mailer vs. Nine Writers." *Esquire* (July 1963): 63–69.
———. "The White Negro: Superficial Reflections on the Hipster." *Dissent* (Fall 1957): 276–296.
Malia, Martin E. "Michael Karpovich, 1888–1959." *Russian Review* 19, no. 1 (January 1960): 60–71.
Mattson, Kevin. "Christopher Lasch and the Possibilities of a Chastened Liberalism." *Polity* 36, no. 3 (April 2004): 411–445.
McCollough, Thomas E. "Reinhold Niebuhr and Karl Barth on the Relevance of Theology." *Journal of Religion* 43, no. 1 (January 1963): 49–55.
McPherson, Miller, Lynn Smith-Lovin, and Matthew E. Brashears. "Social Isolation in America: Changes in Core Discussion Network over Two Decades." *American Sociological Review* 71, no. 3 (June 2006): 353–375.
McWilliams, Susan. "Ahab, American." *Review of Politics* 74, no. 2 (2012): 233–260.
Meehan, Thomas. "The Moynihan of the *Moynihan Report*." *New York Times Book Review*, July 31, 1966. http://www.nytimes.com/books/98/10/04/specials/moynihan-report.html.
Mellinger, Wayne M., and Rodney Beaulieu. "White Fantasies, Black Bodies: Racial Power, Disgust and Desire in American Popular Culture." *Visual Anthropology* 9, no. 2 (1997): 117–147.
Menand, Louis. "Christopher Lasch's Quarrel with Liberalism." In *The Liberal Persuasion: Arthur Schlesinger Jr. and the Challenge of the American Past*, edited by John Patrick Diggins, 233–250. Princeton, NJ: Princeton University Press, 1997.
Miller, Quentin D. "Updike, Middles, and the Spell of 'Subjective Geography.'" In *Cambridge Companion to John Updike*, edited by Stacey Olster, 15–28. New York: Cambridge University Press, 2006.
More, Jack B. "Sports, Basketball and Fortunate Failure in the Rabbit Tetralogy." In *Rabbit Tales: Poetry and Politics in John Updike's Rabbit Novels*, edited by Lawrence R. Broer, 170–189. Tuscaloosa: University of Alabama Press, 1998.
Morrison, Theodore. "Dover Beach Revisited: A New Fable for Critics." *Harper's* (December 1939-May 1940): 235–244.
Mosely, Philip E. "Michael Karpovich, 1888–1959." *Russian Review* 19, no. 1 (January 1960): 56–60.

Neuchterlein, James. "Arthur Schlesinger Jr. and the Discontents of Postwar American Liberalism." *Review of Politics* 39, no. 1 (January 1977): 3–40.

Niebuhr, Reinhold. "Impotent Liberalism." *Christian Century*, February 11, 1926.

———. "Liberalism, Illusions and Realities." *New Republic*, July 4, 1955, 11–12.

Oldenburg, R. E. "America and the Intellectuals." *Harvard Crimson*, February 13, 1953. https://www.thecrimson.com/article/1953/2/14/america-and-the-intellectuals-pas-the/.

Olster, Stacey. "'Unadorned Woman, Beauty's Home Image': Updike's *Rabbit Run*." In *New Essays on* Rabbit Run, edited by Stanley Trachtenberg, 95–117. New York: Cambridge University Press, 1993.

Orr, John. "Interview with John Updike." In *Conversations with John Updike*, edited by James Plath, 159–163. Jackson: University Press of Mississippi, 1994.

Pease, Donald E. "After the Tocqueville Revival; or, the Return of the Political." *Boundary* 2 26, no. 3 (1999): 87–114.

Phillips, William, and Philip Rahv. "Our Country and Our Culture." *Partisan Review* 19 (May–June 1952): 282–322.

Phillips-Fein, Kim. "Conservatism: A State of the Field." *Journal of American History* 98, no. 3 (December 2001): 723–743.

Pike, Burton. "Harry Levin: An Appreciation." *Comparative Literature* 40, no. 1 (Winter 1988): 29–43.

Pinsker, Sanford. "Restlessness in the Fifties: What Made Rabbit Run?" In *New Essays on* Rabbit, Run, edited by Stanley Trachtenberg, 53–76. New York: Cambridge University Press, 1993.

———. "Updike, Ethnicity, and Jewish-American Drag." In *Cambridge Companion to John Updike*, edited by Stacey Olster, 91–106. New York: Cambridge University Press, 2006.

Podhoretz, Norman. "Novels: Style and Substance." *Reporter*, January 22, 1959: 42–43.

Potemra, Michael. "Looking for Updike, Again." *National Review Online*, September 10, 2010. http://www.nationalreview.com/corner/387549/looking-updike-again-michael-potemra.

Prosser, Jay. "Under the Skin of John Updike: Self-Consciousness and the Racial Unconscious." *PMLA* 116, no. 3 (May 2001): 579–593.

———. "Updike, Race, and the Postcolonial Project." In *Cambridge Companion to John Updike*, edited by Stacey Olster, 76–91. New York: Cambridge University Press, 2006.

Quirk, Matthew F. "The Class of 1950." *Harvard Crimson*, June 5, 2000. http://www.thecrimson.com/article/2000/6/5/the-class-of-1950-pin-a/.

Ravi, Vidya. "'Outdoors to Indoors, Detail to Detail': The Domestic Topography of John Updike's *Couples*." *John Updike Review* 1, no. 2 (Spring 2013): 27–41.

Regan, Robert Alton. "Updike's Symbol of the Center." *Modern Fiction Studies* 20, no. 1 (Spring 1974): 77–96.

Reilly, Charlie. "A Conversation with John Updike." In *Conversations with John Updike*, edited by James Plath, 124–150. Jackson: University Press of Mississippi, 1994.

———. "An Interview with John Updike." *Contemporary Literature* 43, no. 2 (Summer 2002): 217–248.
Rhode, Eric. "John Updike Talks about the Shapes and Subjects of His Fiction." In *Conversations with John Updike*, edited by James Plath, 46–54. Jackson: University Press of Mississippi, 1994.
Roberts, Sam. "Theodore Lowi: Zealous Scholar of Presidents and Liberalism, Dies at 85." *New York Times*, February 24, 2017. https://www.nytimes.com/2017/02/24/us/theodore-lowi-dead.html.
Rodgers, Daniel T. "Republicanism: The Career of a Concept." *Journal of American History* 79, no. 1 (June 1992): 11–38.
Roosevelt, Franklin D. Speech before a Joint Session of Congress, January 6, 1941. http://www.fdrlibrary.marist.edu/fourfreedoms.
Rosenberg, Harold. "Twilight of the Intellectuals." *Dissent* (Summer 1958): 228.
Rossinow, Doug. "Partners for Progress? Liberals and Radicals in the Long Twentieth Century." In *Making Sense of American Liberalism*, edited by Jonathan Bell and Timothy Stanley, 17–33. Urbana: University of Illinois Press, 2012.
Samuels, Charles Thomas. "The Art of Fiction XLIII: John Updike." In *Conversations with John Updike*, edited by James Plath, 22–45. Jackson: University Press of Mississippi, 1994.
Sawhill, Isabel. "What the Forgotten Americans Really Want—and How to Give It to Them." Brookings Institute, October 2018. https://www.brookings.edu/longform/what-the-forgotten-americans-really-want-and-how-to-give-it-to-them/.
Schiff, James A. "Updike and the American Presidency." In *Updike and Politics: Due Considerations*, edited by Scott Dill and Matthew Shipe, 11–25. Lanham, MD: Lexington Books, 2019.
Schlesinger, Arthur M., Jr. "1928–1937." In *A Century of Arts & Letters*, edited by John Updike, 86–102. New York: Columbia University Press, 1998.
———. "The Historical Mind and the Literary Imagination." *Atlantic Monthly*, June 1974, 54–59.
Scorza, Jason A. "Liberal Citizenship and Civic Friendship." *Political Theory* 32, no. 1 (February 2004): 85–108.
Searles, George J. "TPF: Updike's Thesis Statement." In *Critical Essays on John Updike*, edited by William R. Macnaughton, 231–236. Boston: G. K. Hall and Co., 1982.
Sennett, Richard. "On Lionel Trilling." *New Yorker*, November 5, 1979, 204–217.
Siegel, Fred. "The Agony of Christopher Lasch." *Reviews in American History* 8, no. 3 (September 1980): 285–295.
Silverman, Robert K. "Vets Flooded Campus under GI Bill." *Harvard Crimson*, June 7, 1999. http://www.thecrimson.com/article/1999/6/7/vets-flooded-campus-under-gi-bill/#.
Slethaug, Gordon E. "*Rabbit Redux*: Freedom Is Made of Brambles." In *Critical Essays on John Updike*, edited by William R. Macnaughton, 237–253. Boston: G. K. Hall & Co., 1982.
Smith, Rogers. "Beyond Tocqueville, Myrdal and Hartz: The Multiple Traditions

in America." *American Political Science Review* 87, no. 3 (September 1993): 549–566.

Sragow, Michael. "Updike Redux." In *Conversations with John Updike*, edited by James Plath, 59–66. Jackson: University Press of Mississippi, 1994.

Stout, Elinor. "Interview with John Updike." In *Conversations with John Updike*, edited by James Plath, 74–84. Jackson: University Press of Mississippi, 1994.

Strandberg, Victor. "John Updike and the Changing of the Gods." *Mosaic-a Journal for the Interdisciplinary Study of Literature* 12, no. 1 (1978): 157–175.

Tanenhaus, Sam. "Man in the Middle." *New York Times Books Review*, November 18, 2012.

———. "The Roommates: Updike and Christopher Lasch." *New York Times*, June 20, 2010. http://www.nytimes.com/2010/06/21/books/21roommates.html?_r=0.

Tavernise, Sabrina. "Reading, Pa., Knew It was Poor. Now It Knows Just How Poor." *New York Times*, September 26, 2011. https://www.nytimes.com/2011/09/27/us/reading-pa-tops-list-poverty-list-census-shows.html.

"Trump Voters Were Motivated by Fear of Losing Their Status." *Economist*, April 26, 2018. https://www.economist.com/democracy-in-america/2018/04/26/trump-voters-were-motivated-by-fear-of-losing-their-status.

Updike, John. Foreword to *Franz Kafka: The Complete Stories*, edited by Nahum N. Glatzer. New York: Schocken Books, 1995.

———. "Homage to Paul Klee; or, a Game of Botticelli." *Liberal Context* (1964): 8–12.

———. "One Writer's Testimony," *National Review*, May 26, 1978, 641.

———. "On Not Being a Dove," *Commentary*, March 1989. http://www.commentarymagazine.com/article/on-not-being-a-dove/.

———. "Party Knee." *New Yorker*, December 13, 1958, 46.

———. "A Wee Irish Suit." *New York Review of Books*, October 23, 2008. https://www.nybooks.com/contributors/john-updike/.

Updike, John, Robert Boyers, Bharti Mukherjee, and Robert Foulke. "An Evening with John Updike." *Salmagundi* 57 (Summer 1982): 42–56.

Vargo, Edward. "Updike, American History, and Historical Methodology." In *Cambridge Companion to Updike*, edited by Stacey Olster, 107–121. New York: Cambridge University Press, 2006.

Vidal, Gore. "Rabbit's Own Burrow." *Times Literary Supplement*, April 26, 1996. https://www.the-tls.co.uk/articles/public/gore-vidal-john-updike-rabbits-own-burrow/.

"View from the Catacombs." *Time*, April 26, 1968, 76–84.

Wallace, David Foster. "John Updike, Champion Literary Phallocrat, Drops One; Is This Finally the End for Magnificent Narcissists?" *New York Observer*, October 13, 1997. http://observer.com/1997/10/john-updike-champion-literary-phallocrat-drops-one-is-this-finally-the-end-for-magnificent-narcissists/.

Wang, Hua, and Barry Hellman. "Social Connectivity in America: Changes in Adult Friendship Network Size from 2002 to 2007." *American Behavioral Scientist* 53, no. 8 (April 2010): 1148–1169.

Wellmer, Albrecht. "Hannah Arendt on Judgment: The Unwritten Doctrine of Reason." In *Hannah Arendt: Twenty Years Later*, 33–52. Cambridge, MA: MIT Press, 1996.
Wilson, Matthew. "The Rabbit Tetralogy: From Solitude to Society to Solitude Again." In *Rabbit Tales: Poetry and Politics in John Updike's Rabbit Novels*, edited by Lawrence R. Broer, 89–110. Tuscaloosa: University of Alabama Press, 1998.
Wood, Ralph. "Karl Barth, John Updike and the Cheerful God." *Books and Religion* 16 (Winter 1989): 26–31.
Zelizer, Julian E. "Rethinking the History of American Conservatism." *Reviews in American History* 38, no. 2 (June 2010): 367–392.
Zuckert, Catherine H. "Why Political Scientists Want to Study Literature." *PS: Political Science and Politics* 28, no. 2 (June 1995): 189–190.

Archival Material

Buckley, William F. Jr. Papers. Manuscripts and Archives Division. Yale University Library.
Harvard University Archives. Pusey Library. Harvard University.
Lasch, Christopher. Papers. Department of Rare Books, Special Collections and Preservations. University of Rochester Libraries.
Macdonald, Dwight. Papers. Archives and Manuscripts Division. Yale University Library.
Moynihan, Daniel P. Papers. Manuscript Division. Library of Congress.
Schlesinger, Arthur M. Jr. Papers. Manuscripts and Archives Division, New York Public Library.
Updike, John. Papers. Houghton Library. Harvard University.
Updike, John. Political cartoons published in *Amesbury Daily News*, 1958–1960. Microfilm. Boston Public Library.

Index

1930s, 7, 30, 44, 85, 168
1950s, 10, 28, 65
    Harvard in, 15, 32, 42, 44, 46–47
    and liberalism, 3, 39, 67, 201
    and *The Poorhouse Fair*, 70, 94
    and *Rabbit, Run*, 98, 100, 102–103, 124–125
    and therapeutic liberalism, 102–103, 112, 125
1960s
    1968, 158, 188, 198
    civic life in, 129, 131, 149, 145
    family in, 95, 101, 124
    as golden age, 16, 129, 196
    and liberalism, 11–12, 71, 158, 161–162, 182, 187–188, 193
    polarization in, 20, 199
    and race, 169–170, 179
    and religion, 177–178
    Updike on, 15–16, 30, 33, 35, 40–41, 203
1970s
    family in, 95
    liberalism in, 12, 195, 197
    political climate of, 30, 35, 168, 170, 178, 193
    in *The Poorhouse Fair*, 69
2016 presidential election, 1–2, 190–192, 198

Abelard, Peter, 63–64
Adams, Henry, 33, 45, 54, 219n15
adultery, 110, 126–127, 142–143, 149
affluence, 99, 103, 129, 132, 160
African Americans, 127, 191
    and liberalism, 6, 8, 194
    and Moynihan, 119–120
    in *Rabbit Redux*, 39, 157–158, 169–172, 181–182, 204
Aldridge, John, 10
alienation
    of capitalism, 62
    of community, 146, 148, 153
    of postwar liberalism, 12–13, 16, 158, 192–193
    of revolutionary behavior, 62
ambiguity, 23–25, 27, 43, 91, 202–203
ambivalence, 20, 50–51, 54–55, 172, 203
America. *See* United States
American Academy, the, 31–32
American Dream, 157, 175, 192
American exceptionalism, 9, 38
Americans for Democratic Action, 38
anarchy, 39, 55, 143, 199
Andrei Sakharov Defense Campaign, 38
Angstrom, Harry "Rabbit" (character), 10, 190–191, 196, 200–204
    in *Rabbit, Run*, 15, 97–99, 101–109, 113–119, 123
    in *Rabbit at Rest*, 38
    in *Rabbit Redux*, 12–13, 39, 157–160, 162–189
anticommunism, 9, 37–38, 63, 194
antistatism, 6, 94–95, 201
antiwar movement, 41, 184, 193, 199, 204–205
apathy, 12, 44, 136, 141, 152–153, 185–186
Apollo 11, 13, 77
Aquinas, Thomas, 60, 81, 223n90
architecture, 73, 145, 151

Arendt, Hannah, 29, 131–134, 144–145
The Human Condition, 131
Aristotle, 59, 132, 146–147
art, 13, 18, 32–33, 57–58
Ashby, LeRoy, 85
atheism, 74, 76, 81, 92, 176
authoritarianism, 71, 73, 75, 79, 85, 90
autobiographical writing, 10, 24, 57, 99, 149–150
automation, 101, 125, 166, 230n46
autonomy, 12, 46, 58, 85, 162–164, 194

Baldwin, James, 121
Barth, Karl, 26, 104–105, 109
baseball, 179–180
Begley, Adam, 10, 43, 49
behavior, 65–66, 136, 142, 172, 178
Bell, Daniel, 21, 23, 37, 97, 111–113, 165
Bellah, Robert, 8
Bellow, Saul, 26, 30, 38, 156
Berlin, Isaiah, 15, 46, 50, 77–79, 85–87
Berman, Ronald, 121
Bible, 60, 175
black people, 127, 191
  and liberalism, 6, 8, 194
  and Moynihan, 119–120
  in *Rabbit Redux*, 39, 157–158, 169–172, 181–182, 204
Black Power, 157–158, 181, 204
Bloom, Harold, 10
blue-collar workers, 76, 165, 168
Boltanski, Luc, 162
book reviews, 34–35
Boswell, Marshall, 158, 213n30
Bowling Alone: The Collapse and Revival of American Community, 165, 129
Bragg, Melvyn, 39, 204
Brick, Howard, 21
Brinkley, Alan, 85, 111
Brinton, Crane, 50, 59–60, 65–66
Bryan, William Jennings, 6, 83–85

Buchanan, James, 32, 202
Buchanan Dying, 32, 202
Buckley, William, Jr., 14, 18–19
bureaucracy
  and the family, 122
  of liberalism, 3, 5, 15, 179
  of the New Deal, 12, 21, 70–73, 94
  of politics, 144, 161, 178, 195
Burhans, Clinton, 105
Byron, Lord, 53

Calvinism, 30, 112
Campbell, David, 177
capitalism
  consumer, 12, 16, 102, 122–123, 161, 188
  contradictions of, 110–119, 162, 164–165, 167, 169, 195
  critiques of, 20–21, 27
  and Marx, 61
  and New Deal, 8, 21, 101
  postindustrial, 157
  and postwar liberalism, 20, 113
Carter, Jimmy, 19, 197
cartoons, political, 29, 33–34, 42
centralization, state, 74, 144, 185, 193, 195
centrism, 21, 25, 177, 244n25
Chambers, Whittaker, 19
characters
  in "The Christian Roommates," 48
  in *Couples*, 127–128, 132–133, 136–137, 151–154
  in *The Poorhouse Fair*, 70–71, 73, 87, 91–92
  in *Rabbit, Run*, 98, 102–103, 110–111
  in *Rabbit Redux*, 161–162, 169, 180, 184, 189
  radical, 37, 39
  and self-consciousness, 200
Chase, Alston, 47
Chase, Richard, 202
Chiapello, Eve, 162
children
  and capitalism, 122

childhood, 65
  in *Couples*, 139, 141
  poorhouse residents as, 76
  and psychology, 108
  in *Rabbit Redux*, 157, 160, 175
Christianity
  in "The Christian Roommates," 47–48
  in *Couples*, 130, 145
  Episcopal Church, 98, 108
  Evangelical, 130, 177
  at Harvard, 47, 60, 62–63, 65, 104, 176
  Judeo-Christian tradition, 8, 47
  Lutheran, 81, 109, 199
  medieval, 59–60, 63–64, 161, 176, 223n90
  and the New Deal, 8
  in *The Poorhouse Fair*, 91
  and postwar liberalism, 23, 62–63
  Puritanism, 87, 111, 113, 132, 164
  and *Rabbit Redux*, 176–178
  in *Rabbit, Run*, 104, 108–109
  and Updike's upbringing, 4
  See also Protestantism
church
  and *Couples*, 128–129, 133, 145–146, 150
  and *The Poorhouse Fair*, 94
  and *Rabbit, Run*, 105–106, 108
  and *Rabbit Redux*, 175–177
citizenship, 3, 8, 14, 195
  and civic engagement, 132, 144–145, 147, 154
  and education, 45–46
  and New Deal, 100, 103
  and state power, 79
  Updike's attitudes about, 149–151
  and Vietnam War, 187
civic engagement, 16
  and American democracy, 128–130
  civic organizations, 129
  and *Couples*, 129–131, 137–139, 146, 150–151, 153–154
  decline of, 12, 130, 142, 153, 158, 192

  in London, 126, 156
  and speech, 131–132
civilization, 10, 58, 72, 100, 103, 105
  Western, 47, 59, 65, 122, 193
civil rights
  and liberalism, 6
  movement, 128, 137–138, 170, 193–194, 203
civil society, 7, 12, 75, 129–130, 153
Civil War, US, 32–33, 83, 169, 202
class
  competition, 10, 21
  at Harvard, 44
  and Marx, 60, 62
  middle, 4, 22, 36, 99, 190
  and New Deal, 7
  and race, 171
  Updike's, 4, 151
  working, 168, 181, 190, 192
Clinton, Bill, 197
Clinton, Hillary, 1, 198
Cohen, Lizabeth, 111
Cold War
  and civic engagement, 129
  and Harvard, 45
  and postwar liberalism, 5, 20–21, 52, 191
  and Rabbit series, 38, 182, 197
  and religion, 177, 194
  and therapeutic liberalism, 103, 125
  Updike's views on, 37–38, 197
college experience, Updike's, 15, 42–43, 46, 48, 66–67
Committee for the Free World, 38
communal life
  in *Couples*, 127, 134, 145, 150–151
  in *The Poorhouse Fair*, 75, 82–83
  and therapeutic liberalism, 103–104, 125
  Updike's views on, 125, 150–151, 196
communism
  anticommunism, 9, 37–38, 63, 194
  The Communist Manifesto, 60, 62
  contrast with liberalism, 46
  and New Deal liberalism, 7–8

communism, *continued*
  and Schlesinger, 21
  and Updike, 37–38
community
  after 2016 election, 192
  and capitalism, 111–112
  and civic engagement, 126, 129–131, 133–134, 145–147, 150–153
  and liberalism, 3–4, 12
  and *The Poorhouse Fair*, 89, 94–95
  and *Rabbit Redux*, 185, 188
  in Updike's novels, 200–201
competition, 8, 21–22, 152
compromise, 18
  and liberalism, 22–23
  limits of, 198, 202–203
  and Matthew Arnold, 54
  and polarization, 49
  in *Rabbit Redux*, 178–187
  Updike's views on, 54–65, 67, 160–161, 202–203, 205
Conant, James Bryant, 45, 61–62
conflict
  and economic development, 162
  ideological, 89, 92, 161, 176, 205
  and liberalism, 22, 49, 64
conformity, 39–40, 125, 139, 173
  intellectual, 26, 40, 66
Congress, United States, 18–19, 191–192
Conner, Stephen (character), 69–94, 173, 176, 192
consensus, 7, 21–22, 50, 59, 88–89, 203
conservatism
  and civic engagement, 134
  in the Democratic Party, 12
  and the family, 100–101, 119, 121
  and Harvard, 44–45
  and Henry Bech, 39
  and liberalism, 89, 95, 198, 201–202
  and Matthew Arnold, 55
  neoconservatives, 29, 38, 121, 124
  in *Rabbit Redux*, 158, 181, 188, 203
  and Updike, 18–19, 26–27, 29, 196, 205
Constitution, US, 21, 63, 138, 194, 203
consumer capitalism, 102, 111, 122–123, 128, 161, 188
consumer culture, 12, 111, 118, 194
  and the family, 16
  and New Deal liberalism, 8, 12
consumption, 5, 8, 23, 52, 100
  in *Rabbit, Run*, 100, 110–112, 115–118, 122, 125
Corey, Mary F., 29
corporate capitalism, 40, 104, 201–202
Coughlin, Charles, 85
counterculture, 11, 71, 156–157, 181
Coup, The, 38, 197
Couples
  and civil society, 128–131, 145, 152–155
  and friendship, 146–149
  inspiration for, 35–36
  plot of, 127–128
  and private/public, 131–145, 192
  and *Rabbit Redux*, 161–162, 176
  reception of, 38, 126–127, 155
  and religion, 145
  speech and, 131–132
  Tarbox, Massachusetts in, 127–129, 131, 141–143, 146–148, 143, 192
  town meetings in, 131, 142–143, 153
  and Updike's personal life, 149–152
Cowie, Jefferson, 167–168
criticism
  cultural, 16, 34
  of liberalism, 26
  literary, 14, 28, 56–57, 132
  social, 31, 55, 199
  Updike's, 14, 33–37
culture
  and the Cold War, 37–38
  consumer, 12, 111, 118, 194
  counterculture, 11, 71, 156–157, 181

in *Couples*, 16, 127, 129–130, 139, 153–154
cultural criticism, 16, 34
cultural values, 44, 70
Culture Wars, 16, 101, 193
and Harvard, 45, 49
and New York intellectuals, 28
political, 3–4, 20, 49, 88, 103, 129–130
in *The Poorhouse Fair*, 70–71, 88, 94
and postwar liberalism, 5–8, 20, 23, 54–55, 197, 201
in *Rabbit, Run*, 16, 99–106, 110–113, 115, 122–125
in *Rabbit Redux*, 16, 156–157, 178–179, 181
Updike's influence on, 10–11
Updike's views on, 18, 33–34, 63–64, 193–194

Dahl, Robert, 152–153, 179
Daiches, David, 28
Dante, 58, 64, 223n90
Day, Doris, 141
death
in *Couples*, 128, 140–141
in *The Poorhouse Fair*, 77
in *Rabbit, Run*, 99, 105–109, 118
in *Rabbit Redux*, 163, 167–168, 174–175
De Bellis, Jack, 10, 42–43, 67
Decter, Midge, 29, 38
Dellingpole, James, 11
democracy
and *Couples*, 16, 128–130, 133, 141–145, 152–154
democratic theory, 16, 179
democratization, 33, 55
demos, 130, 179
direct, 84, 103
and Harvard, 11, 45–46
Jacksonian, 22
and liberalism, 4, 6, 20, 55, 59, 200
and literature, 14
and New Deal, 12, 75

participatory, 12, 94, 130, 153, 185, 195
and *The Poorhouse Fair*, 69, 70, 84, 89, 94–95
and *Rabbit, Run*, 103
and *Rabbit Redux*, 16, 161, 169, 178–179, 185, 187
Democratic Party
and liberalism, 2, 46, 191, 195, 197–198
and Moynihan, 119
and New Deal, 4, 7
and Updike, 26–28
and Updike novels, 10, 12, 181, 188
Deneen, Patrick, 3
Depression, Great, 7, 20, 28, 76, 85, 88
Deresiewicz, William, 197
Detweiler, Robert, 154
Dickstein, Morris, 10, 100, 103
Diem, Ngo Dinh, 128, 134, 136–137
discipline, 86, 88, 105, 122, 163
diversity
ethnic, 1, 5–7, 44, 200
racial, 1–2, 5–8, 16, 169–170, 194, 203
social, 18, 22–23, 58, 179
dogmatism, 36–37, 109, 176, 205
Dohrn, Bernardine, 37
domesticity, 100, 102, 144–145, 160, 163
Dostoevsky, Fyodor, 22, 35, 58
Douglass, Frederick, 157, 204
"Dover Beach" (poem), 53–54, 104
dystopian novels, 69–70, 75, 173

economic issues
and *Couples*, 134, 153
and Fordism, 112, 122, 163–164, 230n46
and New Deal, 7–9
and *The Poorhouse Fair*, 78, 94, 96
and post-Trump United States, 1–3, 191
and postwar liberalism, 12–13, 20–23, 40, 52, 193–194, 202

economic issues, *continued*
 and *Rabbit, Run*, 100–103, 110–113, 115, 119–120, 124–125
 and *Rabbit Redux*, 16, 158–159, 161–168, 170–171, 179
 and race, 120, 170–171
 service economy, 165, 191
 and Updike's education, 60–62
Eisenhower, Dwight, 8, 34, 94
elections, US presidential
 1968, 188
 2016, 1–2, 190–192, 198
 of Barack Obama, 190–191
 and liberalism, 152
 of Ronald Reagan, 158–159
 Updike on, 27
elites, 1, 5, 85, 152, 179
Ellison, Ralph, 121
Emerson, Ralph Waldo, 76, 97, 103, 110
employment, 120, 162, 165
Encounter (journal), 29
Enlightenment
 and liberalism, 6, 193, 198
 re-Enlightenment, 22
 and religion, 58, 177
 and therapeutic liberalism, 104
 and Updike's education, 58, 64, 77, 161
equality
 and Christianity, 63
 gender, 16
 inequality, 1, 8, 95, 191, 194
 and liberalism, 46, 187, 203
 and *The Poorhouse Fair*, 91, 93–96
 and *Rabbit Redux*, 170–171, 199
 and race, 95, 169–170, 191, 194
 social, 6, 8, 84, 93
ethnic diversity, 1, 5–7, 44, 200
Europe, 27–28, 54, 64
evil, 22, 24, 77, 82, 87
existentialism, 54, 98, 105, 160, 195

fair housing, 127, 131, 137–138
faith
 in "The Christian Roommates," 48–49
 and civil religion, 194–195
 in *Couples*, 152
 democratic, 18, 22
 in *The Poorhouse Fair*, 74, 81–82, 92–93
 in *Rabbit, Run*, 104–105, 108–110
 in *Rabbit Redux*, 175–178
 and Updike's education, 53, 55, 58, 64, 66, 104
family
 and Christopher Lasch, 121–124, 202
 and consumer culture, 16, 195
 and Daniel Patrick Moynihan, 119–121, 202
 decline of, 12, 100, 119, 122–123
 and the liberal state, 89, 95
 nuclear, 99–102, 122, 124–125
 in *Rabbit, Run*, 99–100, 102, 105–107, 113, 115, 117–119
 in *Rabbit Redux*, 161, 178, 188
 and therapeutic liberalism, 101–102, 124–125
 values, 16, 95, 101, 119, 202
Fanon, Frantz, 157, 239n43
federal government, US, 5, 8, 70–71, 75, 84–85, 158
fiction
 and *Couples*, 130, 149, 153
 and *The Poorhouse Fair*, 71, 73, 91–92, 94, 96
 and *Rabbit, Run*, 99, 109–110, 113, 120, 123–124
 and *Rabbit Redux*, 16, 39, 156, 161, 188, 202
 and Updike at Harvard, 15, 42, 50, 57, 66–67
 Updike on, 14, 23–24, 26, 34–35
 Updike's, 4–5, 9–12, 17, 28, 191–193, 200
Fordism, 112, 122, 163–164, 230n46
foreign policy, 137, 186, 197–198
formalism, 14, 57
Fowler, Robert B., 20–21, 179
Franklin, Benjamin, 112
freedom, 52, 95–96, 97
 and capitalism, 97, 112

in *Couples*, 144
free enterprise, 12, 16
free markets, 6, 27, 84, 171, 224n22
free will, 62, 79
  individual, 62, 88, 188, 201
  and Karl Marx, 62
  and liberalism, 22, 95–96, 144, 171
  in *The Poorhouse Fair*, 77, 81, 88, 93, 95–95
  in *Rabbit Redux*, 169, 171, 183, 188
French Revolution, 6, 55, 59–61
Freud, Sigmund
  Freudianism, 98, 103–104, 108, 110, 123
friendship
  in *Couples*, 146–152
  Updike's, 32, 43, 49, 67, 94, 119–123

Galbraith, John Kenneth, 23, 38, 50, 110–111
  The Affluent Society, 50, 110
garden motif, 99, 114–115, 167, 185–186
Garrison, William Lloyd, 157, 189
gay rights, 101, 130
gender, 117, 119, 120
  rights, 6, 16, 41
  See also women
Gitlin, Todd, 193
globalization, 1, 3, 9
God, 47–48, 52, 63–64
  in *The Poorhouse Fair*, 72, 76, 81–82, 92
  in *Rabbit, Run*, 104, 108, 113–114
  in *Rabbit Redux*, 175–177, 183–184
Goldwater, Barry, 95
goodness, 24, 76, 78, 104, 146–147
  common good, 103–104
  good life, 132, 193
government
  and the Cold War, 52
  contemporary, 191–193
  in *Couples*, 138, 143–144, 152–153
  and family, 122
  federal, 5, 8, 70–71, 75, 84–85, 158

governmental activism, 15
  and liberalism, 3, 7–8, 23, 80, 194
  New Deal, 21, 70, 89, 194
  in *The Poorhouse Fair*, 71, 73, 75, 80, 84–85, 89
  in *Rabbit Redux*, 158, 175, 179, 187
  self-government, 6, 52, 89, 188
  Updike's views on, 18, 40, 58, 69
  and William Jennings Bryan, 84
Great Depression, 7, 20, 28, 76, 85, 88
Great Society, 100, 194
Greece, ancient, 6, 59, 132
Greif, Mark, 22

Harrington, Michael J., 19
Hartz, Louis, 7, 50, 67, 171
Harvard Crimson, 27, 30, 40, 180
Harvard University
  Arthur Schlesinger Jr. at, 32
  curriculum at, 45, 47
  effect on Updike's fiction, 132, 161, 176, 178, 205
  English Department, 42–43, 50, 53, 56–57
  faculty at, 47, 49–50, 58, 67
  general education at, 44–47, 59–60
  Harvard Lampoon, 42
  John Updike papers at, 9
  New Criticism at, 14
  Updike at, 15, 42–50, 58–61, 67–68, 132
Havelock, Eric, 50, 58–59, 67, 222n69
heartland, American, 190, 192–193
heaven, 24, 72, 78, 114, 173, 201
hedonism, 112, 127, 134, 148
heteronormativity, 9, 124
Hiss, Alger, 19
history
  and capitalism, 62, 104
  at Harvard, 58
  historiography, 5, 14
  limits of, 13
  in *The Poorhouse Fair*, 71, 82–83, 96

history, *continued*
  of race in the United States, 92, 119, 170, 172–173
  and Updike's fiction, 11, 14–15, 26, 28, 119, 196–197
  Updike's study of, 33, 59–60, 95, 193
Hitler, Adolph, 24, 174
Hofstadter, Richard, 7, 26, 88, 93–94, 181
home, the
  in *Couples*, 134
  homeownership, 101
  in *Rabbit, Run*, 102, 113, 118, 122, 125, 192
  in *Rabbit Redux*, 156, 160, 164
Hook (character), 69–70, 77, 80–93, 175–176, 192
Howe, Irving, 40
Hoyer, Artie, 15, 186
Hugging the Shore, 34, 196
humanism, 45, 47, 56, 109
  Marxist, 62
  secular, 46, 70, 76, 81
humanities, 15, 18–19, 62, 65, 95
humanity, 72, 78–79, 151, 163, 174
human nature, 23, 27, 62, 74, 87, 198
humor, 31–32
Humphrey, Hubert, 181–182, 198

idealism, 59, 61
identity, 104, 106, 129, 180
  identity politics, 2–3, 6, 200
ideology
  and consensus, 15, 50, 89
  of liberalism, 2, 5, 20–21, 23, 80, 92
  and the New Deal, 7
  in *The Poorhouse Fair*, 71, 80, 92, 96, 119, 176
  in *Rabbit Redux*, 188
  and Updike, 17, 29, 35–37, 46, 197, 205
immigrants, 38, 40, 169, 191
independence, 85, 200
  economic, 120, 167

individualism, 6, 83, 123, 171, 179, 188
  and decline of civic engagement, 134, 138, 148, 154
  and decline of liberalism, 162, 171, 178–179, 188
individual freedom, 62, 88, 188
individual liberty, 7, 84–85, 87, 89
individual rights, 6, 103, 138
  and liberalism, 12, 16, 23, 46, 58, 200
  and Marxism, 62
  and McCarthyism, 52
  in *The Poorhouse Fair*, 77, 83–85, 87–89, 93
  and therapeutic liberalism, 103–106, 110, 122–123
industrial society, 61, 80, 191, 194
  and the Cold War, 52
  industrialization, 5, 55
  industrial revolution, 61, 120
  industrial state, 86
  postindustrial society, 16, 71, 120, 157, 165, 193–194
  and race, 8
inequality
  and 2016 election, 1
  racial, 8, 95, 189, 191, 194
Institute of Arts and Letters, 31, 33, 120–121
institutions
  and civic engagement, 126, 143, 150–151
  and decline of liberalism, 171, 181, 183
  and liberalism, 2–4, 12, 59, 193
  and the New Deal, 75–76, 85, 201
  and therapeutic liberalism, 103–105, 110
  Updike's views on, 12, 27, 40–41, 63
intellectuals
  and Harvard, 65–67
  liberal, 16, 23, 37–40
  and the New Deal, 7, 51

New York, 28–30, 34–35
and the postwar liberal mindset, 20–23
public, 7, 14, 26, 51, 119
interest groups, 16, 22, 103, 130, 153, 161
introspection, 36, 43, 48, 203
Ipswich, Massachusetts, 127, 145, 149–150
irony, 20, 23, 80, 193, 205
and *Couples*, 128, 133, 145, 147–148
and *The Poorhouse Fair*, 77, 80, 95
and *Rabbit, Run*, 99, 102, 206, 109, 113
and *Rabbit Redux*, 161–162, 166, 174

Jefferson, Thomas, 12, 51, 54, 94, 161, 195
Jewish people, 28, 30, 40, 56
Judeo-Christian tradition, 8, 47
Johnson, Lyndon Baines, 25, 34, 135, 198, 202
in *Rabbit* novels, 157, 174, 178, 181–182, 187
Jumonville, Neil, 34
justice, 146, 189
economic, 16
injustice, 170, 191, 203
social, 187

Kafka, Franz, 73, 132
Kant, Immanuel, 6, 58, 60–61, 200
Karpovich, Michael, 58, 67
Katznelson, Ira, 75
Kazin, Michael, 84
Keats, John, 25, 57
Kennedy, John F., 190–195
appeal of, 173
in *Couples*, 128, 131, 136–137, 140–141, 152, 154
and space exploration, 13
Updike's cartoon of, 34
Kerouac, Jack, 99–100
Keynesianism, 8, 100
Kierkegaard, Soren, 83

Kimmage, Michael, 54–55
King, Martin Luther King, Jr., 203
Kloppenberg, James, 83, 92–93
Klosko, George, 3
Kristol, Irving, 29, 38

labor
and the family, 122
and Karl Marx, 61, 164
and liberalism's decline, 165, 167, 169, 191
manual, 12, 165
and the New Deal, 7–8, 101
and public/private spheres, 132
and race, 120
unions, 100, 165
Langmuir, Gavin, 50, 59–60
Lasch, Christopher, 32, 43, 45, 94, 119, 201
and family values, 16, 121–124
and religion, 47, 49
Lassiter, Matthew, 101, 124, 170
law and order, 11, 158, 181
Left, the, 196
and Christopher Lasch, 121, 124
competing view in, 6
critiques of liberalism, 39, 184
critiques of Updike, 196
decline of, 29
and the family, 101
and "the middle," 26–27
in *The Poorhouse Fair*, 83
and postwar liberalism, 20–22
See also New Left
leisure, 74, 78, 129, 132
lesbian rights, 101, 130
Leuchtenburg, William, 75–76
Levin, Harry, 56–57, 67
liberal arts, 11, 42, 45, 66
liberalism, 2–5, 19–20, 192–195, 197–205
and analysis of Updike, 9–13, 15–17
and the Cold War, 37–40
and *Couples*, 130, 139, 151–152, 155

liberalism, *continued*
  decline of, 2, 9, 159, 161
  definitions of, 5–9
  and Harvard, 42–46, 49–55, 58–61, 63–67
  liberal activists, 76, 134, 139
  liberal imagination, 25–26, 54, 60
  liberal-republican ideology, 83–84
  and literary criticism, 36–37
  literature of, 23–27
  New York, 30, 33
  and *The Poorhouse Fair*, 70–71, 75–77, 80, 83–86, 88–89, 91–96
  and *Rabbit, Run*, 99–104, 110, 119–121, 123–125
  and *Rabbit Redux*, 158–162, 169–172, 173, 178–183, 186–189
  racial, 169–172, 194
  therapeutic, 16, 102–104, 106–110, 122–123, 161
  See also New Deal liberalism; postwar liberalism
liberty, 15–16, 70, 85–89, 94–95, 194–195
  individual, 16, 78, 84–85, 87, 89
  negative, 15, 86, 88
  positive, 15, 77, 79, 85
Lilla, Mark, 2
Lippmann, Walter, 84
literary criticism, 14, 26, 33–37, 56–57, 132
  New Criticism, 14, 57
literature
  of liberalism, 23–28
  literary criticism, 14, 26, 33–37, 56–57, 132
  Updike's, 4, 9–15, 97, 121, 123–124, 198
  and Updike's education, 31–32, 42–43, 56, 65–67
Locke, John, 3, 6, 50, 60, 84, 171
London, England, 126–127, 150, 156
Long, Huey, 85
Louis IX, King, 63–64
love, 78, 117, 122, 196, 200

Lowi, Theodore, 89
Ludwig, Jeffrey, 43, 123
Lynn, Kenneth S., 45

Macdonald, Dwight, 29, 31–32
MacLeish, Archibald, 50–53, 56, 67
Mailer, Norman, 10, 26–27, 30, 156, 199
Malia, Martin, 58
man
  and the Cold War, 52
  crisis of, 22–23
  and Marxism, 62
  modern, 54–55
  perfectibility of, 20
  in *The Poorhouse Fair*, 76–78, 80
  in *Rabbit, Run*, 104, 106–107, 111, 113
  in *Rabbit Redux*, 164, 170, 174, 181
management, 76, 94, 122, 165–167, 188
  scientific, 76, 188
Maritain, Jacques, 64, 223n90
markets, 8, 21, 122–123, 134, 170–171
  free markets, 6, 27, 84, 171, 224n22
  market forces, 6, 84, 122
Marsden, George, 178
Marx, Karl, 157, 164
  Marxism, 22, 103, 119, 121, 124
  neo-Marxism, 119, 121
  Updike's views on, 60–64
Massachusetts, 30, 34, 127
material concerns, 23, 82, 194
  and the New Deal, 52
  and postwar liberalism, 70
  in *Rabbit, Run*, 100, 102, 115–117
  in *Rabbit Redux*, 160, 162–164, 173
Matusow, Allen, 158
May, Elaine Tyler, 102
McCarthy, Eugene, 187–188, 198
  McCarthyism, 52, 61
McCarthy, Mary, 29, 31
McGovern, George, 188, 197–198
Medicare, 174, 181

medicine, 73–74, 92, 174
medieval Christianity, 59–60, 63–64, 161, 176, 223n90
Melville, Herman, 22, 26, 121
memoirs, John Updike's, 200–201, 213n28
  and 1960s, 15, 188, 198–199
  and communism, 38
  and Franz Kafka, 132
  and social mobility, 40–41
  and the Vietnam War, 186–187
meritocracy, 44, 171
metaphor, 14, 57
  in *The Poorhouse Fair*, 87–88, 92, 94
  in *Rabbit, Run*, 106
  in *Rabbit Redux*, 156, 159–161, 163, 180, 241n78
Meyers, Jeffrey, 10–11
"middle," the
  Updike's preference for, 24, 26, 57–58, 67, 160–161, 202–203
middle America, 98, 166, 201
middle class
  and liberalism, 22, 54
  Updike as, 4
  in Updike's novels, 12, 24, 36, 99, 127, 190
"Midpoint" (poem), 18, 24
Midwest, 49, 121, 151, 165
military intervention
  Updike's support for, 135, 191, 198
Mill, John Stuart, 6, 55, 60, 86
Miller, Eric, 45, 121
Minh, Ho Chi, 25, 135
moderates, 202–203
  moderate imagination, 27, 43, 203, 205
  moderate liberalism, 44
  moderate religion, 177–178
  moderation, 20, 58, 65, 202–203
modernity
  and *Couples*, 129, 131, 133, 143
  and liberalism, 12–13, 193, 195–196, 201, 205
  modern culture, 97, 104, 112
  modern family, 122

modernism, 33, 56, 73–74, 112, 166, 195
modern states, 73–74
  and *The Poorhouse Fair*, 15, 71, 73–74, 80, 84–85
  and *Rabbit, Run*, 16, 97, 100, 104–106, 112, 122
  and *Rabbit Redux*, 157, 159–160, 170, 172, 177–180, 186–188
  and religion, 109, 178
  and Updike's education, 47–48, 54–57, 60, 63–64
Mondale, Walter, 197–198
moon landing, 13, 156, 159, 173
morals
  and contemporary liberalism, 190–191, 201, 203
  in *Couples*, 124, 127
  of McCarthyism, 52
  of politics, 23
  in *The Poorhouse Fair*, 70, 83, 90, 93–94
  of postwar liberalism, 49, 55
  in *Rabbit, Run*, 101, 104–105, 124
  in *Rabbit Redux*, 158, 169, 171, 178
  and Updike's education, 56–57, 60, 62, 65
  in Updike's novels, 27
Morrison, Theodore, 50, 53, 56, 221n46
Moynihan, Daniel P., 14, 16, 31, 119–121, 123–124
  Moynihan Report, 119, 121, 124
mysteriousness, 13, 24–25, 57, 96

Narayan, R. K., 150–151
narcissism, 10, 123, 201
Nash, George, 95
National Review, 18–20, 30
natural rights, 59, 84
nature, 74, 80–81, 87, 93, 160, 173
neoconservatism, 29, 38, 121, 124
neoliberalism, 6, 101, 124, 194
Neuchterlein, James, 22
neutrality, 57, 76, 134, 139
New Criticism, 14, 57

New Deal, 12, 73, 75–76, 181, 194
  and Harvard, 50–52
  and labor, 167–168
  and *The Poorhouse Fair*, 70, 73, 75–76, 85, 93–96
  and postwar liberal mindset, 20–21
  and therapeutic liberalism, 102–103, 111
  See also New Deal liberalism
New Deal liberalism, 4–5, 7–9, 11–12, 17
  contemporary effects of, 193–195, 197–203
  and *Couples*, 130, 151–152
  and *The Poorhouse Fair*, 80, 83, 93
  and *Rabbit, Run*, 99–100, 102, 125
  and *Rabbit Redux*, 158–159, 161–162, 170–171, 183, 187
  and Updike's education, 42
  and Updike's middle orientation, 37, 41
New England, 127, 129, 145, 151–152
New Left
  and Christopher Lasch, 124
  in *Rabbit Redux*, 156, 157, 184–186, 188
  and Updike's views on, 30, 36–37, 145, 198–201
Newman, Judie, 70, 110, 117, 129, 227n82
New Right, 11, 19, 94–95, 201
New School for Social Research, 19–20
New York City, New York
  intellectuals in, 30, 34–35, 40
  Updike and, 19, 28, 30
New Yorker, 11, 28–29, 30–32, 132
New York Review of Books (*NYRB*), 30, 56
Niebuhr, Chris, 44–45
Niebuhr, Reinhold, 7, 23, 26, 37–38
Nineteen Eighty-Four, 69, 75, 87
nineteenth century, 35, 53, 56, 82
Nisbet, Robert, 22, 89
Nixon, Richard, 8, 34, 157, 181, 191

nonfiction
  John Updike's, 14, 34, 203, 230n50
norms, 3, 20, 154, 161, 179
  heteronormativity, 9, 100, 124
  normative institutions, 105, 138, 178
novels, 25–27
  novelists, 4, 10, 27, 66, 94, 121
  Updike's, 4, 10, 14–16, 38, 203–205
  Updike's early, 12
  Updike's later, 197
  and Updike's literary criticism, 35–37
  See also *Couples*; *Poorhouse Fair, The*; *Rabbit* novels; *Rabbit, Run*; *Rabbit Redux*

Obama, Barack, 28, 190, 192, 197
Oedipal struggles, 10, 103, 108
"On Not Being a Dove," 30, 37
On the Road, 99–100
optimism, 22–23, 120, 196, 203
Orwell, George, 69, 75, 87
outdoors, 163, 167–168
Oxford, University of, 41–42

Packard, Vance, 149
participatory democracy, 12, 94, 130, 153, 185, 195
Partisan Review, 29, 30, 57
past, the
  in *Couples*, 143
  nostalgia for, 56
  in *The Poorhouse Fair*, 77, 80, 82, 94
  in *Rabbit Redux*, 164, 172, 189
  Updike's usage of, 63–64, 160, 193, 195–196
patriotism, 37–39, 45, 93–94, 184, 199, 202
Pennsylvania
  in *Rabbit* novels, 12, 98–99, 157, 204
  Updike in, 4, 28, 99, 127, 150, 200
pessimism, 81, 120

INDEX | 283

philosophy
  of Updike, 24, 132
  and Updike's education, 58–61
  Updike's usage of, 11, 81–82, 109, 151
Picked-Up Pieces, 14, 34–35
Piercy, Marge, 36–37
Pinsker, Sanford, 103
Plato, 48, 59–60, 133
pleasure, 112–113, 142, 146
Plotke, David, 76
pluralism, 16, 20–21, 25, 43, 46–47
  and contemporary liberalism, 198, 203, 205
  and *Couples*, 152, 154
  and Harvard, 50, 53, 57–58, 61, 63, 66–67
  and *The Poorhouse Fair*, 92
  and *Rabbit Redux*, 150, 178–180, 183–185
Podhoretz, Norman, 31, 38
poetry, 51, 53, 57–58, 104, 121
  Updike's, 4, 10, 24–25, 67
Polanyi, Karl, 163
polarization, 20, 49, 92, 177, 205
political cartoons, 33–34, 42
political climate, 29, 44, 99, 198
  political culture, 3–4, 20, 49, 88, 103, 129–130
  political economy, 8, 40, 100
  political imagination, 11, 27, 42, 50, 58, 71
  political science, 13, 89, 152–153
  political system, 1, 26, 50, 103, 187, 205
  political theory, 3, 11, 13–15, 95, 103, 179
  political thought, 28, 60, 71, 111, 193
politicians, 2, 66, 83, 91, 121
Poorhouse Fair, The, 15, 69–71, 93–96, 176, 223n90
  inmates in, 69, 75–76, 78–79, 86–92
  and liberal consensus, 88–93
  Mary McCarthy on, 31

  and *Rabbit, Run*, 100
  and *Rabbit Redux*, 161–162, 173
  sheepherding in, 87, 90
  standardization in, 73–74
  statism and, 71–79
  and virtues of liberalism, 80–88
Pope, Alexander, 57
Popular Front, 23, 199
populism
  and anti-Semitism, 85
  and Christopher Lasch, 119, 121
  left-wing, 6, 23–27, 85, 93, 199
  right-wing, 2
  rise of, 9
Port Huron Statement, 185, 199
postindustrial society, 16, 71, 120, 157, 165, 193–194
postwar liberalism, 3–5, 4–7, 9
  contemporary effects of, 196–199, 201–205
  and *Couples*, 129–130, 143, 154
  and Harvard, 44–45, 49, 52, 54–55, 66
  and literature, 23, 27, 36
  mindset of, 20–22, 41, 42–43, 92
  and *The Poorhouse Fair*, 70–71, 85, 92, 96
  and *Rabbit, Run*, 99–100, 102–103, 111, 124–125
  and *Rabbit Redux*, 157–161, 172–173, 178–180, 183–184, 187–188
  and Updike, 9–13, 15–16
  and William Buckley Jr., 19
poverty, 78, 101, 119–120, 194
power, 23, 27, 39
  Black Power, 157–158, 181, 204
  and *Couples*, 144, 151, 152
  decentralized, 21
  and modern democracy, 59
  and the New Deal, 7, 51, 195
  and *The Poorhouse Fair*, 70–75, 78–79, 89, 95
  powerlessness, 5, 75, 89, 193
  and *Rabbit, Run*, 103, 120
  and *Rabbit Redux*, 161, 183
pragmatism, 8, 20–21, 59, 94, 184, 196

Pritchard, William H., 34
private
   and *Couples*, 126, 130–132, 134, 136–145, 152, 154
   and family, 99, 102, 110
   goods, 23, 110
   and liberty, 86
   lives, 35–37, 126, 139, 142–143, 152
   privatization of publics, 16, 131–146, 154, 188
   and *Rabbit Redux*, 178, 180, 186
   sphere, 79, 84, 99, 110, 130, 132
production, 5, 8, 100, 110–112, 125
progress, 22–23, 77, 120, 173–176, 201
   scientific, 65, 74, 159–160, 173–174
progressivism, 22–23, 194–196, 199
   of Christopher Lasch, 49, 119
   of Matthew Arnold, 55
   in *The Poorhouse Fair*, 83–84, 93–94
proletariat, 61–62
property rights, 170–171
Protestantism, 99, 177–178
   Protestant Anglo-Saxon morality, 93
   Protestant work ethic, 111–112, 125, 161–162
psychoanalysis, 98, 102, 133
psychology
   in *Couples*, 133, 161
   in *The Poorhouse Fair*, 74
   in *Rabbit, Run*, 100, 102–103, 106–109, 125
public, 5, 23, 192–193
   in *Couples*, 130–138, 140–147, 152, 154
   health, 74
   intellectuals, 7, 26, 29, 51, 119
   privatization of, 16, 131–146, 154, 188
   in *Rabbit, Run*, 101, 103, 110
   in *Rabbit Redux*, 178, 180, 185, 188
   sphere, 16, 35, 131–132, 147, 180, 188
   virtue, 129, 134
   welfare, 75, 77, 85
Pulitzer Prize, 4, 51, 97, 219n15

Rabbit, Run, 15, 31–32, 97–102, 124–125
   contradictions of capitalism in, 110–119
   gratification in, 103, 105–106, 112–113, 122
   and Moynihan and Lasch, 119–124
   and *Rabbit Redux*, 161–163, 167, 175, 178, 185
   therapeutic culture in, 102–110
Rabbit at Rest, 38, 197
Rabbit Is Rich, 168, 197
Rabbit novels, 10, 38, 97, 123, 204, 210n21
   and contemporary liberalism, 191–192, 196–197, 199–204
   stereotypes in, 169–171, 204
   See also Angstrom, Harry "Rabbit" (character)
Rabbit Redux, 1, 12, 16, 156–161, 188–189
   and contemporary liberalism, 190, 196, 199, 202–204
   democracy in, 178–188
   economic unraveling in, 161–168
   homoeroticism in, 172
   racial liberalism in, 169–172
   space in, 172–178
   teach-ins in, 157, 169, 186
race, 1–2, 5–8, 13–14, 95
   contemporary, 191, 193–194, 199–200, 203–204
   and Daniel P. Moynihan, 119
   in *Rabbit Redux*, 16, 138, 157–159, 169–172, 179
   racial liberalism, 169–172, 194
racism, 8, 39, 119, 170–171, 191, 204
radicalism
   Leftist, 145, 198–199
   and postwar liberal mindset, 21–22
   in *Rabbit Redux*, 158
   radical Right, 181
   and Updike's characters, 37
rationalism, 55, 57–58, 61, 64, 91, 161

in *The Poorhouse Fair*, 70–72, 74, 79, 81
Reagan, Ronald, 2, 124, 158
realism, 4, 11, 20, 201
reason, 6, 57–58, 64
  in *The Poorhouse Fair*, 81, 91
  in *Rabbit Redux*, 175–177
reconciliation, 46, 55, 81, 91–92, 161
Redbook Report, 45–46
reforms
  at Harvard, 44–47
  liberal, 191, 194, 198
  and the New Deal, 7, 76, 93
  reform politics, 21
religion
  and *Couples*, 128, 133–134, 145–146, 152
  and liberalism, 3, 7, 11–12, 16, 194, 197
  and *The Poorhouse Fair*, 70, 74, 81–84, 90, 95–96
  and *Rabbit, Run*, 104, 107–110
  and *Rabbit Redux*, 161, 175–178, 188
  and Updike's education, 45, 47–49, 53–55, 58, 63–64
  See also Christianity
repression, 110, 123, 172
republicanism, 6, 82–84, 133, 143–145, 178, 186
Republican Party, 8, 15, 119, 181, 191, 201
resources, 38, 44, 77, 122, 171
revolutionaries
  French Revolution, 6, 55, 60–61
  revolutionary ideas, 27, 35–47, 65–66, 154
  in Russia, 35, 58
  sexual revolution, 5, 124
  Updike's attitude toward 35–37, 41, 65–66, 202
  in Updike's novels, 39, 144, 170, 181–182, 184, 189
Rhode, Eric, 196
Rieff, Philip, 15, 103–107, 112

Riesman, David, 44
Right, the
  and the family, 101
  and liberalism, 2, 6–7, 26
  New Right, 11, 19, 94–95, 201
  and *Rabbit* novels, 188
  and Updike, 30
  See also conservativism
rights
  in *Couples*, 137–138, 154
  gay rights, 101, 130
  gender, 6, 16, 41
  human, 9, 38, 63
  individual, 6, 103, 138
  lesbian, 101, 130
  and liberalism, 6, 84–86, 103, 194
  natural, 59, 84
  in *The Poorhouse Fair*, 84–86
  property, 170–171
  in *Rabbit Redux*, 170–171, 183
  See also civil rights
riots, 13, 157, 174, 194
Ristoff, Dilvo, 113
Rockwell, Norman, 100
Rodden, John, 56
Rodgers, Daniel T., 82
Roman Empire, 6, 82, 133
romanticism, 53, 55, 57, 62
Roosevelt, Franklin Delano, 2, 95, 100, 158, 199
  and Updike, 4, 27–29
Rosenblatt, Helena, 3
Rossinow, Doug, 198
Roth, Philip, 28, 30
Rousseau, Jean-Jacques, 59–60, 76
rural United States, 5, 191–192
  and *The Poorhouse Fair*, 70, 82
  and Rabbit series, 167
  and Updike, 28, 43, 127, 205
Russia, 2, 34–35, 58, 61

Sandel, Michael, 103
Sanders, Bernie, 198
Schiff, James, 10, 70, 97, 129
Schlesinger, Arthur, Jr., 7, 14, 17
  and Harvard, 44, 49–51, 67

Schlesinger, Arthur, Jr., *continued*
   and Updike's centrism, 21–23, 26, 31–33, 38, 40, 160
   The Vital Center by, 21, 24, 49, 160
scholarship
   about *Couples*, 129, 144
   about the family, 124
   at Harvard, 47, 50, 56–67, 67, 70–71
   about liberalism, 4–6, 13–14
   and New York intellectuals, 30
   about *Rabbit, Run*, 102, 111
   about *Rabbit Redux*, 158
   about Updike, 10, 43, 100, 197, 210n21
Schudson, Michael, 154
science
   and liberalism, 5, 20, 194
   limits of, 22
   and modernity, 47
   and the New Deal, 8
   in *The Poorhouse Fair*, 72–74, 78, 82, 84–85
   in *Rabbit Redux*, 16, 161, 172, 175–178, 188
   and religion, 48–49, 65, 161, 175–178
   scientific management, 76, 188
   social sciences, 53, 73, 119, 129, 153–154
Scott, James C., 73–74
Searles, George, 70, 80, 96
secularism
   and contemporary liberalism, 2, 5, 193
   in *Couples*, 145, 176
   at Harvard, 45, 63
   and the New Deal, 8, 12
   in *The Poorhouse Fair*, 70, 76, 78, 81–82, 90
   in *Rabbit Redux*, 16, 176–177
   secular humanism, 49, 70, 76, 81
security
   economic, 12, 16, 103, 161–162, 167, 194
   and liberalism, 93, 194
   and the New Deal, 9, 101, 194
   in *Rabbit, Run*, 101–103, 103
   in *Rabbit Redux*, 161–162, 164, 167–168
segregation, racial, 8, 95, 171
self, 97
   self-consciousness, 12, 152, 200
   self-fulfillment, 35, 62, 112, 125, 162, 176
   self-interest, 104, 147
   selfishness, 35, 93, 103, 110, 180
   self-mastery, 77–78, 85
   self-realization, 97, 106, 112, 163, 178, 195
   self-reliance, 12, 52, 83, 94, 170
   self-restraint, 113, 116
   self-righteousness, 139, 144
   and therapeutic liberalism, 103–104
   in Updike's fiction, 10–11, 200
Self, Robert O., 100
Self-Consciousness, 15
Sennett, Richard, 25–26
sex
   in *Couples*, 16, 133, 135–138, 140–143, 145–147
   and the culture wars, 101
   and the New Left, 199–200
   in *Rabbit, Run*, 106–108, 114, 116–117, 123–124
   in *Rabbit Redux*, 157–158, 172
   sexual revolution, 5, 124
   and therapeutic liberalism, 123–124
Shelley, Percy, 57
Shillington, Pennsylvania, 28, 41, 98, 200, 205
silent majority, 12, 157, 171, 183
Sinclair, Upton, 27, 33
slavery, 32, 119, 186, 189, 204
Smith, Richard, 46
social factors
   and contemporary liberalism, 191–192, 194–195, 199–201
   and *Couples*, 126–129, 131–133, 145–146, 148–149, 153–154

and Harvard, 44, 55
and liberalism, 8–9, 21–23
and *The Poorhouse Fair*, 70–71, 84, 95–96
and *Rabbit, Run*, 99–100, 103–104, 106, 109–111, 119–123
and *Rabbit Redux*, 168–169, 178–179, 185, 188
social capital, 129, 131
social criticism, 31, 199
social engineering, 20, 71, 121
social equality, 6, 8, 84, 93
social fabric, 97, 110, 126, 149, 227n82
social mobility, 55, 168, 194
social solidarity, 35, 52
Updike's commentary on, 14–15, 34–35, 39, 192
socialism, 60–61, 95
social sciences, 5, 15, 63, 73, 119, 153
society
civil, 7, 12, 75, 129–130, 153
in *Couples*, 126, 129–130, 133, 142, 149
and liberalism, 2, 5–7, 21–22, 195, 201, 205
in *The Poorhouse Fair*, 75–76, 78, 80, 82, 85
in *Rabbit, Run*, 102–103, 110, 122
in *Rabbit Redux*, 156, 165, 173, 178–180, 185
Updike's commentary on, 17, 26, 31
and Updike's education, 44–46, 54, 59, 64, 66
sociology, 22, 25–26, 36, 40–41, 103–104, 191
Socrates, 59–60, 133, 182
solipsism, 103, 123, 128, 172, 200
South
Civil War in, 32
and race, 8, 95, 170, 191, 194
sovereignty, democratic, 12, 85, 94
Soviets, 34, 38, 61
space, geographical, 144–145, 166
space, outer, 13, 145, 172–174, 194

spirituality
in *Couples*, 145, 160
in *The Poorhouse Fair*, 70, 72, 77, 82–84, 91
in *Rabbit, Run*, 100, 105–106
in *Rabbit Redux*, 163, 168, 175–178
state
administrative state,
antistatism, 6, 94–95, 201
and centralization, 74, 144, 185, 193, 195
and Harvard curriculum, 46
liberal state, 73–74, 77–79, 84–85, 95
and the New Deal, 11–12, 70, 75–77, 89, 170
in *The Poorhouse Fair*, 73, 75–79, 84–85, 89, 95
in *Rabbit Redux*, 171, 179, 181, 189
state power, 71, 73
statism, 71–79, 224n22
See also welfare state
stereotypes, in *Rabbit* novels, 169–171, 204
Stevenson, Adlai, 49
structural forces, 5, 100, 131, 144, 153, 168
structural racism, 8, 119, 170–171, 193
Students for a Democratic Society, 185
Port Huron Statement, 185, 199
suburbs
in *Couples*, 16, 127, 129–130, 151
and liberalism, 95, 102
in *Rabbit, Run*, 102, 124
in *Rabbit Redux*, 166, 171, 173
Supreme Court, United States, 177, 222n78
symbolism
in *Couples*, 135, 137, 141, 152–153
in *The Poorhouse Fair*, 75–76, 82–84, 87
in *Rabbit, Run*, 103, 108
in *Rabbit Redux*, 156, 172
Szalay, Michael, 10

Tanenhaus, Sam, 190
technocrats, 12, 69, 80, 130, 179–180, 195
technology
    and civil religion, 194
    and *Couples*, 130, 149, 153
    and Harvard, 47
    and liberalism, 3–4, 12–13, 52
    and *The Poorhouse Fair*, 85
    in *Rabbit Redux*, 160–161, 165, 175
television
    in *Couples*, 139, 141, 157
    in *Rabbit, Run*, 113, 116–117
    in *Rabbit Redux*, 13, 174–175, 182, 185
Tennyson, Alfred, 53
theology, 26, 98, 104–105, 133, 178
theory
    and *Couples*, 132
    at Harvard, 60–61
    of liberalism, 6
    and *The Poorhouse Fair*, 83, 86, 95
    and *Rabbit, Run*, 103, 123
    and *Rabbit Redux*, 162, 179
    and Updike, 11, 13–16
therapeutic liberalism, 16, 102–104, 106–110, 125
    and Moynihan, Lasch, and Updike, 122–123
    and *Rabbit Redux*, 161, 164
Thomism, 81, 223n90
Tocqueville, Alexis de, 95, 126, 128–129, 142, 203
tolerance, 6, 22, 58, 63, 179
    intolerance, 63, 83, 199
totalitarianism, 20–21, 46, 51, 69, 199
tradition
    and Harvard education, 47–49, 64
    liberal, 6–7, 15–16, 80, 89, 194–195, 205
    and New Deal liberalism, 12
    and *The Poorhouse Fair*, 80, 82, 89, 91–93
    and *Rabbit, Run*, 104, 106, 125
    and *Rabbit Redux*, 160–161, 171, 176–178, 187–188

Trilling, Lionel, 7, 25–26, 40, 54–57, 88, 197
    The Liberal Imagination by, 25–26, 54
Truman, Harry S., 7, 27, 49, 63
Trump, Donald, 1–2, 190–192
truth
    and *Couples*, 136, 149
    and fiction, 24–26, 57, 136
    in *Rabbit Redux*, 178
    and racial liberalism, 194
twentieth century
    and capitalism, 162
    and civic engagement, 130
    and liberalism, 6
    and Lionel Trilling, 56
    and *The Poorhouse Fair*, 70
    and Updike, 4, 17, 196

United States
    and the 2016 election, 1–3
    and the Cold War, 38–40, 45, 191, 194
    and contemporary liberalism, 3–4, 190–194, 196–205
    and *Couples*, 126–132, 134–135, 142–146, 149–155
    and Harvard education, 45–46, 51–52, 62–66
    and liberalism, 5–9
    and literary criticism, 35
    and *The Poorhouse Fair*, 69–71, 75–76, 80, 82–83, 89, 93–96
    and postwar liberal mindset, 20–21, 23
    and *Rabbit, Run*, 97, 99–101, 103, 111–115, 120–125
    and *Rabbit Redux*, 156–159, 168–169, 173, 177–179, 183–184, 188
    and Updike, 4–5, 10–17, 18–20, 26, 28–33, 40–41
Updike, John, 4–5
    centrism of, 18–20, 40–41
    and the Cold War, 37–40
    and contemporary liberalism, 190–192, 195–205

and *Couples*, 126–127, 129–134, 136, 139, 145–146, 149–154
and Harvard education, 41–44, 46–54, 57–68
John Updike Papers, 9, 14
and literary criticism, 33–37
and literature of liberalism, 23–28
and New Deal liberalism, 9–13, 14–17
and New York intellectualism, 28–38
and *The Poorhouse Fair*, 69, 71–73, 75–78, 80–83, 86–88, 91–96
and postwar liberal mindset, 20
and *Rabbit, Run*, 97–99, 104–105, 107, 109–112, 117–124
and *Rabbit Redux*, 156, 158–162, 165–169, 171, 175–180, 182–189
youth of, 27, 43, 112, 127
urban areas
in *The Poorhouse Fair*, 80, 82
in *Rabbit Redux*, 157–158, 165
and race, 8, 119–120
riots in, 157, 174, 194
urban decay, 158, 165, 192
utilitarianism, 48, 54, 146–147, 164
utopian thought
and liberalism, 20–21, 23
in Updike's education, 60–61, 78
in Updike's fiction, 39, 131

values
and the Cold War, 38
of conservatism, 198
in *Couples*, 130, 134, 147
family, 16, 95, 119, 202
at Harvard, 43–47, 49, 70
of New Left, 199
in *The Poorhouse Fair*, 82–83, 85, 91–93, 96, 101
and postwar liberalism, 21, 29, 193, 201
in *Rabbit, Run*, 104, 115, 119, 125
in *Rabbit Redux*, 160–161, 175, 179, 185, 187–188
religious, 63, 82, 161

Vanderlan, Robert, 51
Vernon, Mark, 148
Vidal, Gore, 10, 27, 199
Vietnam War, 134, 157
in *Couples*, 128, 131, 135–136
and liberalism, 11, 13, 16, 203–204
in *Rabbit Redux*, 156–157, 179, 181–187
Updike's stance on, 30, 41, 46, 186, 198, 204
violence
in *Rabbit, Run*, 106
in *Rabbit Redux*, 158, 180–181, 185
virtue
civic, 16, 161, 188
and friendship, 146–147
and liberalism, 6, 92–93, 202
in *The Poorhouse Fair*, 70, 80–84, 92–93, 161
public, 129, 134
and religion, 63–64
of work, 112–113
Voltaire, 48, 56, 241n78

Wall, Wendy, 71
Wallace, David Foster, 10
war, 22, 34, 55. *See also* Civil War, US; Cold War; Vietnam War; World War II
"Washington" (poem), 25
Weather Underground, 37, 41
Weber, Max, 71, 74, 105, 112
welfare
in the New Deal, 3, 8
in *The Poorhouse Fair*, 79, 85, 87
in *Rabbit, Run*, 100
welfare state
in *Couples*, 138, 144
decline of, 11–12, 193–195
and the New Deal, 6, 11–12, 21
in *The Poorhouse Fair*, 15–16, 71, 75–76
in *Rabbit Redux*, 13, 156, 171, 179
Western Civilization education, 47, 59–60, 63–65, 122, 193

whiteness
   and Donald Trump, 1, 190
   of John Updike, 200
   in *Rabbit Redux*, 169, 172, 175
   white working class, 12, 158
Wills, Garry, 177–178
Wilson, Edmund, 29, 60
women
   in *Couples*, 127–128, 134
   and inequality, 38, 101, 193
   in *Rabbit, Run*, 117
   social gains by, 9
Wordsworth, William, 53
work
   in *Couples*, 132, 134
   nature of, 14
   in *Rabbit, Run*, 105, 111–115, 117–118, 122–123
   in *Rabbit Redux*, 161–164, 167–168
   work ethic, 112–114, 122, 125, 132, 161–162
World War II, 7, 20, 44–45, 47, 70, 177. *See also* postwar liberalism
Wuthnow, Robert, 191–192

Yancy, George, 172
Yeats, W. B., 51, 121, 156, 160

Zielonka, Jan, 9
Zuckert, Catherine, 13